MARXISM
AND THE CHINESE EXPERIENCE

THE POLITICAL ECONOMY OF SOCIALISM

Mark Selden, Series Editor

THE POLITICAL ECONOMY OF CHINESE SOCIALISM
Mark Selden

MARXISM AND THE CHINESE EXPERIENCE
Edited by Arif Dirlik and Maurice Meisner

★ *The Political Economy of Socialism* ★

MARXISM AND THE CHINESE EXPERIENCE

ISSUES IN CONTEMPORARY CHINESE SOCIALISM

ARIF DIRLIK
MAURICE MEISNER
ANN ANAGNOST
ROXANN PRAZNIAK
MARC BLECHER
PENELOPE B. PRIME
BILL BRUGGER
LISA ROFEL
EDWARD FRIEDMAN
PETER SCHRAN
TED HUTERS
MARK SELDEN
RICHARD C. KRAUS
GORDON WHITE
MARILYN YOUNG

Edited by

Arif Dirlik and Maurice Meisner

An East Gate Book

M. E. Sharpe, Inc.
Armonk, New York
London, England

An East Gate Book

Available in the United Kingdom and Europe from M. E. Sharpe, Publishers, 3 Henrietta Street, London WC2E 8LU.

Library of Congress Cataloging-in-Publication Data

Marxism and the Chinese experience : issues in contemporary Chinese socialism / by Arif Dirlik and Maurice Meisner, editors.
p. cm.—(The Political economy of socialism)
Includes bibliographies and index.
ISBN 0-87332-515-X—ISBN 0-87332-546-X (pbk.)
1. Communism—China. 2. China—Economic policy—1976–
3. China—Politics and government—1976– I. Dirlik, Arif.
II. Meisner, Maurice J., 1931– . III. Series.
HX418.5.M3495 1989 89-4251
335.43'45—dc19 CIP

Printed in the United States of America

EB 10 9 8 7 6 5 4 3 2 1

For Benjamin I. Schwartz

CONTENTS

Part III
Social Relations, Political Power, and Culture

Part IV
Conclusions

ACKNOWLEDGMENTS

A volume such as this one owes what merits it may claim to the contributors who made it possible. We have been fortunate in its compilation in dealing with colleagues who have demonstrated commitment to the highest standards of intellectual responsibility and scholarly cooperation, from their initial participation in the symposium, "From Mao to Deng: Marxism and the Chinese Experience" (held at Duke University, October 30–November 1, 1986), to the final preparation of the papers for publication. We are grateful for their contributions.

Professor Jing Wang of Duke University was co-organizer of the symposium with Arif Dirlik. Her contribution as organizer and participant was much appreciated. So were the contributions of participants in the symposium who are not represented in this volume: David Apter (Yale University), Ch'i Hsi-sheng (University of North Carolina-Chapel Hill), Bruce Cumings (University of Chicago), Fredric Jameson (Duke University), Ellen Laing (University of Oregon), Carl Riskin (Queens College), Benjamin Schwartz (Harvard University), Edward Tiryakian (Duke University), Wang Bingzhang (*China Spring*), and Robert Weller (Duke University).

We are also grateful to those nonparticipants who kindly agreed to submit papers that have enriched the volume significantly: Bill Brugger, Roxann Prazniak, Lisa Rofel, and Gordon White.

Finally, we would like to acknowledge the invaluable contributions of Mavis Mayer and Gail Woods of the Asian/Pacific Studies Institute at Duke University for their meticulous arrangements, which made the symposium a rewarding social experience, and of Thelma Kithcart of the Department of History at Duke University for her assistance in the preparation of the manuscript.

The symposium was made possible by funding from the Asian/Pacific Studies Institute and the Center for International Studies at Duke University (under its former director Charles Bergquist), and a grant from the Josiah Charles Trent Foundation. Some of these funds were also used in the preparation of the volume for publication.

We dedicate this book to Benjamin I. Schwartz, not only for his contributions to the study of Chinese Marxism, but for the example of scholarly integrity he has set over the years, and for his deep appreciation of the moral dilemmas presented by revolution.

CONTRIBUTORS

ANN ANAGNOST teaches anthropology and Asian studies at the University of Illinois, Urbana-Champaign. She is currently at work on a book tentatively entitled "Imagining the State: The Power of Representation and the Representation of Power in Post-Mao China."

MARC BLECHER is professor of government at Oberlin College. He is the author of *Micropolitics in Contemporary China* (with Gordon White), *China: Politics, Economics and Society—Iconoclasm and Innovation in a Revolutionary Socialist Country*, and general editor and coauthor of a forthcoming volume tentatively entitled "The Tethered Deer and the Hard-Work Market: The Political Economy of Shulu County."

BILL BRUGGER is professor of politics at Flinders University of South Australia. He is the author and editor of a number of books on China and on social and political theory.

ARIF DIRLIK teaches history at Duke University. He is the author of *Revolution and History: Origins of Marxist Historiography in China* (University of California Press, 1978) and *The Origins of Chinese Communism* (Oxford University Press, 1989).

EDWARD FRIEDMAN is a professor in the political science department at the University of Wisconsin, Madison, where he also chairs the Center for East Asian Studies. A Guggenheim Fellowship facilitated the research for the essay in this book. He is coauthor of *Chinese Village, Socialist State*, a forthcoming study based on ten years of work in the Chinese countryside.

TED HUTERS teaches in the department of East Asian languages and literatures at the University of Oregon. His book *Qian Zhongshu* and a number of articles concern themselves with the transformation of Chinese literary ideas in the posttraditional period.

RICHARD C. KRAUS teaches Chinese politics at the University of Oregon. He has written *Class Conflict in Chinese Socialism* and *Pianos and Politics in China: Middle-Class Ambitions and the Struggle over Western Music* and is now preparing a study of the politics of Chinese calligraphy.

MAURICE MEISNER teaches history at the University of Wisconsin at Madison. His major works include *Li Ta-chao and the Origins of Chinese Marxism* (Harvard University Press, 1967) and *Mao's China and After* (Free Press, 1986).

ROXANN PRAZNIAK teaches at Hampden-Sydney College in Virginia where she specializes in Asian history. She has published work on rural protest and women in China during the decade before the 1911 Revolution. Currently she is writing a comparative history text that stresses historical exchanges between East Asian and Western European civilizations.

PENELOPE B. PRIME is assistant professor of economics at Carleton College. Her research has focused on industrialization in China. She has worked in the China Division of the World Bank and as a consultant for a variety of projects concerning China's economy.

LISA ROFEL is an assistant professor with a joint position in the Massachusetts Institute of Technology's anthropology/archaeology and science, technology, and society programs. Her interests include the intersections of gender and class, and political economy in contemporary China.

PETER SCHRAN is professor of economics and Asian studies at the University of Illinois, Urbana-Champaign. He is the author of *The Development of Chinese Agriculture, 1950–1959* and *The Development of the Shensi-Kansu-Ninghsia Border Region, 1937–1945.*

MARK SELDEN's most recent book is *The Political Economy of Chinese Socialism* (M. E. Sharpe, 1988). He is professor of sociology and research associate of the Fernand Braudel Center at the State University of New York at Binghamton.

GORDON WHITE is a professorial fellow at the Institute of Development Studies, University of Sussex, specializing on patterns of socialist development with particular interest in China. His most recent book is *Developmental States in East Asia* (Macmillan, 1988).

MARILYN B. YOUNG teaches history at New York University. She is the author, with William Rosenberg, of *Transforming Russia and China: Revolutionary Struggle in the Twentieth Century.*

Part I
Introduction

1

POLITICS, SCHOLARSHIP, AND CHINESE SOCIALISM

Arif Dirlik and Maurice Meisner

In the years since the death of Mao Zedong and the ascendancy of Deng Xiaoping, China's modern social and economic development has undergone a dramatic transformation. The Mao era in the history of the People's Republic, however one wishes to assess its successes and failures, was distinguished by a historically unique attempt to bring about a socialist transformation of China's society and the consciousness of its people in ways that defied accepted political and ideological norms in capitalist and established socialist states alike, thereby earning the wrath of both the United States and the Soviet Union. China under Deng Xiaoping, by contrast, has pursued modernization through quasi-capitalist means while seeking to incorporate the People's Republic into the existing world order in a manner acceptable to both Russia and America. Both the internal and external policies of Mao's successors have been so accommodating of capitalism that they have raised questions not only about the future of socialism in China but also about the legitimacy of the revolution that brought the Chinese Communists to power in the first place, a revolution which the present regime continues to claim as its legacy.

No less striking than the changes that have taken place in post-Mao China has been the transformation of Western (and especially American) perceptions of the People's Republic. The country that not long ago was seen by some as a revolutionary model for the world, and condemned by others as a revolutionary menace to the world, is now almost universally praised for its "pragmatic" leadership and its reformist policies. While there may well be a great deal in the history of post-Mao China deserving of praise, one suspects that the current American celebration of China is dictated as much by immediate political, economic, and cultural interests as by actual developments in Chinese society. For this is not the first time that there has been a sudden wholesale turnabout in American attitudes toward China. It might be recalled that when Henry Kissinger and Richard Nixon visited Zhou Enlai and Mao Zedong in 1971–72, more than two decades of relentless American hostility to the Chinese revolution quickly turned into enthusiastic admiration as liberals and even some conservative observers, now finally able to visit China, joined radicals in praising the country's achievements under Mao Zedong's leadership.[1]

Following Mao's death in 1976, the subsequent ascendancy of Deng Xiaoping, and the Chinese repudiation of the Cultural Revolution, this enthusiasm evaporated as rapidly as it had materialized. American applause for China was now transferred to Mao's successors, while Mao Zedong and the Cultural Revolution once again became objects of ideological vilification, as had been the custom prior to 1971. Since 1978, many long-time celebrants of Mao and the Cultural Revolution have joined in the general indictment of "Maoist totalitarianism" and political "madness." If Mao's successors come under criticism nowadays, it is usually for not abandoning their revolutionary legacy with sufficient rapidity.

One of the casualties of these fluctuations in perception and opinion has been our ability to discuss intelligently the more critical issues posed by the history of the People's Republic, especially the issue of socialism. That history, complex enough in itself, has been rendered opaque to understanding by interpretations that are molded more by the political events of the day than by any critical historical consciousness. Stanley Karnow, discussing media reports on China, has attributed this fickleness to the media's characteristically "short span of attention."[2] That may be only part of the problem, however. With its recent "reopening" to the world, China has once again become an object of consumption for a public with an apparently voracious appetite for things Chinese, and a stage for the enactment of age-old American fantasies. Ironically, a decade-long effort by the radical Cultural Revolution regime to close out the world seems to have whetted the American appetite for possessing China.[3] It is disturbingly uncertain, however, that this appetite testifies either to a lasting concern or to a patience for understanding China beyond its own consumptive interests; indeed, more often than not, many Americans evaluate developments in Chinese socialism for their implications for the United States rather than for China. Businessmen who seek trade or investments in China, aficionados of Chinese culture seeking to recreate a romanticized past that exists only in their imaginations, and even the casual tourist in search of new frontiers all present us with evaluations and interpretations that are bound not merely by a "short span of attention" but by a brief and ideologically limited interest in China.

Not surprisingly, with Chinese society itself in a confusing state of ideological flux, each group readily finds Chinese witnesses to testify to the particular interests and prejudices it brings to its own testimonial on China. And for a curious but historically naive public, increasing numbers of Chinese visitors to the United States (self- or officially selected, if not directly selected by American recruiters) serve as authoritative judges on the past, present, and future of China, their particular desires taken as the Chinese national will. We are, it seems, in the midst of a late twentieth century Chinoiserie!

We will shortly discuss the ideological problems that are implicit in this desire to appropriate China. We may note here that the problem of ideology is complicated by the intellectual and emotional pitfalls to understanding presented by the sudden intensification of direct contact between Americans and Chinese after three decades of mutual isolation. While access to China has created fresh opportunities for understanding Chinese society in ways possible only through direct involvement in its everyday life, face-to-face contact is not as unproblematic as it may seem where broader issues of Chinese socialism are concerned. To the extent that the immediate experience of China is informed by a grasp of the historical and social context of which contemporary China is a product, as well as critical self-reflection on the ideological roots and implications of interpretation, its consequences are salutary for it enables us to reformulate the issues of Chinese socialism with a concreteness that was not possible earlier.

It is another matter, however, when the immediate experience of Chinese society becomes the basis for interpreting long-term issues that are beyond its compass; so that rather than add to a historical perspective, the problematic of personal encounters is substituted for a historical problematic. The result is to subject our understanding of Chinese socialism as a historical problem to spatially and temporally (not to say ideologically) limited interpretive tropisms—which nevertheless carry immense emotive power because of the immediacy of the experiences that invoke them. Rather than broaden understanding, these tropisms reduce the historical to the personal, and dissemble in a nonproblematic simplicity issues in which are embedded complex problems of a century of revolution.[4] In a cultural environment that privileges immediate experience over reflective memory, this is a problem in any case. Where China is concerned, it may be the very sense of the remoteness of Chinese society, mystifying in its alienness, that ironically bestows upon the direct experience of things Chinese an epistemological status that such experience does not command in more familiar contexts, where we have a keener sense of what we know and do not know, and a framework within which to judge the general relevance of personal experience. To be fair, revolution and mutual isolation have reinforced this

China. We seek to consider the implications for Chinese socialism of the repudiation of the Cultural Revolution and the legacy of Mao Zedong, and the meaning of the new definition and direction Mao's successors have given to socialism. The concern is with issues of broad historical and theoretical import rather than a specific time period or a detailed examination of the political and economic changes that have brought these issues to our attention. Similarly, the themes that are pursued have been selected not because they are topical or of practical utility but rather out of consideration for conceptual coherence within a socialist problematic. We have sought to direct the various inquiries in a twofold direction: the meaning of socialism for China, and the meaning of Chinese socialism for socialism as a global phenomenon—"meaning" not in some abstract sense but rather as it is constituted in the process of political and ideological activity that expresses and defines social relationships within China as well as China's relationship to the world.

This common goal presupposes the shared premise that we need to take socialism seriously, both as an attribute of Chinese politics and in our conceptualization of politics globally. The authors of the essays in this volume bring quite different political and interpretive orientations to the problems of Chinese socialism, but they all recognize the important role socialism has played in the making of modern Chinese history and the shaping of contemporary Chinese society. They view socialism as a crucial component of present-day Chinese social and intellectual life, and they are aware of the possibly adverse consequences that would follow a total Chinese abandonment of socialist values and goals.

This by no means implies that the Chinese Communists, either in the Maoist or post-Mao era, have been successful in achieving the socialist goals they have professed, or that socialism as China's leaders have conceived and practiced it (now or earlier) has been an unmixed blessing for the Chinese people. On the contrary, the discussions that follow, while appreciating the contributions socialism has made to China's development, are critical of the forms that Chinese socialism has taken and recognize that these distorted forms have contributed to the increasing elusiveness of socialism as a political concept, thereby rendering the future of socialism more uncertain than ever, not only in China but in the world as a whole. But this, rather than serving as a reason to dismiss socialism, provides an occasion for reconsidering its premises and aspirations. Arbitrary interpretations of socialism designed to suit changing political needs have long contributed to undermining it as a viable political theory. But a serious confrontation with socialism's problems and distortions may serve to recall its genuine historical significance and recover the promise of its social vision, a vision that dynamized a century of revolution in China.

Certainly, one of the major obstacles to fulfilling that task is our image of the Cultural Revolution, an event that has dominated our consciousness of Chinese socialism (although in different ways) since the mid-1960s. This is obviously not the place to discuss the Cultural Revolution, whose history has yet to be written. And we have no desire to defend a movement that, whatever the original intentions of its authors, brought such enormous psychic and physical damage to society, imposed an arbitrary despotism on the Chinese people, victimizing friend and foe of the revolution alike, and served to discredit socialism in the process. But a few words need to be said about the role of politics and ideology in our changing perceptions of the Cultural Revolution, and the implications of those changes for our understanding of the history of socialism in China.

It is difficult to recall today that not so long ago the Cultural Revolution was widely praised as an innovative and revitalizing socialist solution for China's problems, that it rejuvenated socialist movements around the world, and that even many conservative and liberal Western commentators ranging from Joseph Alsop to John K. Galbraith expressed admiration for aspects of the upheaval. Since the official repudiation of the Cultural Revolution by the post-Mao regime, this praise has given way to wholesale condemnations. Revelations about the cruelties the Cultural Revolution inflicted on the Chinese people—"revelations" that should not have been so revealing since most of the evidence for these cruelties was available from the outset—have had a sobering effect on the world. The image of the Cultural Revolution that prevails today is that of an irrational and atavistic political movement presided over by an aging despot obsessed with recouping his waning authority, a movement whose lofty ideals served only to disguise conflicts for power at the top and petty factional struggles below. The Cultural Revolution is now held responsible for everything from retarding China's economic development to destroying public morality, making tolerable to decent and ordinary people the most intolerable acts of public and private vindictiveness. The aberrant behavior it encouraged brands the Cultural Revolution as a historical aberration. Deprived of its original aims and ideals, and torn from its historical context of half a century of revolution, the Cultural Revolution appears as an episode of political madness, a holocaust carried out merely to fulfill Mao Zedong's senile fantasies.

The Cultural Revolution did indeed give rise to most of the evils for which it is now condemned. A major problem emerges, however, if we recall and set beside this portrait the earlier, positive image of the Cultural Revolution that it suppresses. The problem cannot be ignored simply by declaring that the earlier image was the result of misinformation, erroneous evaluations, and self-delusion. While a confession of error may be laudable, it does not address of the question of why so many were able to delude themselves when there was more than sufficient evidence of irrationality and destructiveness from the outset of the upheaval. Dismissing the earlier image as erroneous ignores the need to deal with the reasons why so many were able to make so great an error, and thereby ignores the question of the role that ideology and politics play in our understanding of Chinese politics, then and now. Indeed, the extraordinary contrast between the two representations of the Cultural Revolution raises questions about both. If our current dominant image of the Cultural Revolution is valid, then what do we make of the earlier image, which in its day seemed equally true? Conversely, if there was any truth to this earlier image, what does it say about the image that prevails at present? And what meaning do we assign to this suppression of one representation by the other? Must the repudiation of the Cultural Revolution for its crimes and stupidities also necessitate the repudiation of the revolutionary motivations that once endowed it with such great historical significance?

Such questions suggest problems not merely of evidence but of interpretation—and how and why certain interpretations prevail over others at different times. To be sure, there is a question of evidence, not so much of its sufficiency or veracity but its sources. For many leftist scholars sympathetic to the People's Republic, the Cultural Revolution was judged earlier mainly on the testimony of its proponents and beneficiaries, which naturally yielded an adulatory picture of its achievements. Today, by contrast, the dominant image of the Cultural Revolution is based almost entirely on the evidence of its opponents and victims, which, needless to say, supports an irredeemably negative evaluation of the movement and its consequences. In both cases, dissident voices have been largely absent in providing the evidence on which our evaluations rest. That we have been willing to base our evaluations on these sources, however, indicates that what is at issue is more than evidence. Rather, in both cases, we have believed what we have heard or seen (or thought we had seen) because we were willing to do so—a willingness not just with respect to evidence but, more importantly, with respect to standards of evaluation upon which the status of evidence ultimately must depend.

What really has changed in recent years is not so much what we know about the Cultural Revolution as our evaluations of what we know. Earlier, sympathetic observers were willing to judge the Cultural Revolution by its own standards and claims, and to ignore or view as marginal what it suppressed. Hence it was possible, in the name of revolution, to overlook available evidence of the unjust and brutal treatment of individuals within and outside the party. The idolization of Mao Zedong seemed excessive but nonetheless was accepted as well-deserved homage to a great leader. And the restriction of cultural activity to what the Cultural Revolutionaries deemed fit for public consumption, while often deplored, was ultimately justified as necessary to imbue the masses with the proper revolutionary consciousness. The social and political values the Cultural Revolution propagated seemed to some precisely what the world needed to abolish the evils of capitalism and create a new socialist order.[8] Others, of more conservative political bent, were less sanguine about the desirability or universal applicability of these values but nevertheless perceived them to be quite in keeping with China's cultural traditions and political needs.[9]

With the political ascendancy of Deng Xiaoping and the official Chinese condemnation of "the ten lost years," almost overnight many came to see the Cultural Revolution in a new light—a light that was "new" only for its one-time celebrants, for there had been no shortage of conservative and other critics of the Cultural Revolution all along.[10] Prominent in the new critique is an almost voyeuristic preoccupation with the sufferings of individuals, especially intellectuals, who, once viewed by some as beneficiaries of revolutionary reeducation, now are seen as the principal victims of a holocaust. The cult of Mao Zedong now appears as proof of the persistence of the traditions of oriental despotism or a manifestation of feudal-fascism. Collectivistic and egalitarian values, which formerly were hailed as the source of Chinese success in development, thereby qualifying the People's Republic for worldwide socialist leadership, have become explanations for the almost hopeless backwardness of Chinese society. The most successful historical example of socialism in the world has suddenly turned into one of the greatest aberrations in modern history.

It may not be surprising that students and observers of a revolutionary society should, in their evaluations, be at the mercy of changes in the fortunes of revolution, for revolutions invoke in their witnesses both the greatest of hopes and the greatest of horrors. Awareness of this predicament, however, should serve as an occasion for greater circumspection, rather than a hasty exchange of one view for another, an importunate forgetting of the gullibility of yesterday which only may hasten escape into another gullibility. If we are so readily willing to renounce the credibility of our former convictions, how can we be sure that our present convictions are not equally at the mercy of newly acquired political and ideological prejudices?

One of the problems with contemporary criticism of the Cultural Revolution is not that it is unjustified or unduly harsh but rather that it ignores the critical political and historical issues the Cultural Revolution raised, and likewise ignores the real social problems that the history of the movement revealed. Implicitly or explicitly, the Cultural Revolution is now subjected to criticism from the very ideological perspectives that were once the object of its ideological critique. Fear of being tarred with a Maoist brush no doubt discourages some from reviving these issues for serious discussion, but much of contemporary criticism has its own ideological motivations. Indeed, it might be suggested that the Cultural Revolution is denounced today for precisely the same reasons it was so widely admired in earlier days. This creates the impression that there was no political or historical basis for the Cultural Revolution, that it was, in fact, a historical aberration. Dismissing the Cultural Revolution in this manner, as an event that requires no historical explanation, also serves to dismiss the problems of socialism that the Cultural Revolution attempted to address, problems and issues that stand condemned by their very association with the Cultural Revolution, as if they had no independent significance of their own.

While the original aims and goals of the Cultural Revolution were distorted and betrayed by its leaders, not excluding Mao Zedong, the abortive movement nonetheless raised issues that are crucial to any socialist undertaking. Among those issues were a host of problems associated with the bureaucratization of the postrevolutionary order and the forces fostering elitism and hierarchy; the sources of these phenomena in the social division of labor, especially the distinction between mental and manual labor; the fetishism of development, especially as manifested in ignoring the social consequences of economic and technological progress; and the threat of foreign material and ideological hegemony posed by the incorporation of an economically backward society into the world capitalist system. Mao, for one, saw these and other problems as structurally interrelated, so that one opened the way to others with a dialectical inevitability.[11] That these were legitimate issues of concern is suggested by the fact that the post-Mao regime, despite its wholesale renunciations of the Cultural Revolution, periodically revives these issues as problems confronting Chinese socialism. And yet, ironically, both for leaders in Beijing and for foreign critics of the Cultural Revolution, expressions of concern with these problems often provoke renewed condemnations of the Cultural Revolution. It is highly ironic that while both media and academics celebrate the imminent restoration of capitalism in China, they should condemn the Cultural Revolutionaries for their "paranoiac" fear of such an eventuality.

A further and more serious difficulty with contemporary criticism of the Cultural Revolution is that for many it provides an occasion for the wholesale repudiation of the history of the socialist revolution in China and, along with it, socialism in general. Although the Chinese revolution cannot be reduced to a mere prelude to the Cultural Revolution, as some were once inclined to do, it is nevertheless nearly impossible to dismiss the Cultural Revolution as an historical aberration without casting doubts about the validity and utility of China's socialist revolution as a whole. For the values that the Cultural Revolution proclaimed, and which it sought (albeit ultimately unsuccessfully) to instill in popular consciousness as a precondition for socialism, were values deeply rooted in the experience of the Chinese revolution, especially the protosocialist experiences of the celebrated Yan'an era.[12]

That what is really at issue today is not just the Cultural Revolution but Chinese socialism itself is reflected in Western evaluations of the so-called second revolution of Deng Xiaoping.[13] The widespread praise lavished on the post-Mao regime is based on much the same criteria that underlie the unconditional repudiation of the Cultural Revolution. Indeed, Westerners tend to admire contemporary China to the extent that it is perceived to have broken with the Cultural Revolution and its Maoist past, whereas suspicious eyebrows are raised when it appears that the break may not be as complete as Western minds desire. Certainly, the criteria by which Western observers judge the "second revolution" are derived not from the standards of socialism but from those of capitalism. What is regarded as praiseworthy about the post-Mao regime is clearly not progress in social welfare and justice, not greater popular participation in decision making, not greater equality in the distribution of goods and power, and certainly not any renewed commitment to a socialist vision of the future. Rather, what is celebrated is "progress" in privatizing a collectivized economy, the recognition of the assumed "imperatives" of hierarchical decision making and economic inequality, the subordination of all social (and certainly all socialist) considerations to rapid economic development by whatever means promise the greatest efficiency, the discovery of "the magic of the market," the supposed abandonment of "ideological thinking" in favor of "pragmatism," and a new Chinese receptivity to Western capitalist culture and commodities. All the economic successes of post-Mao China, perhaps prematurely celebrated, are attributed to the adoption of capitalist methods and techniques, while the economic accomplishments of the Mao period, without which the current successes might have been impossible, are ignored or denigrated. Similarly, all difficulties encountered by the Deng regime are attributed to the evil legacies of Maoism, whereas the possibility that they may be products of the new policies themselves is rarely entertained.

The new course pursued by Mao Zedong's successors is frequently depicted as a return to the true course of Chinese history, but those who do so ignore a century-long history of revolution and four generations of Chinese revolutionaries who believed that China's modern development and the welfare of its people could best be served by pursuing a socialist road that would guarantee national autonomy in a hostile world capitalist environment. Those who describe the post-Mao course as a "second revolution" debase the meaning of the term revolution, since they can only logically mean it to be a "revolution" of capitalism against earlier socialism that has restored China on its proper historical course, a course from which socialist endeavors deviated. It is hardly surprising that against this conception of history, which assumes capitalism to be history's final destination, the Cultural Revolution should appear as an aberration—not for what it did but for the very presumptuousness of its challenge to history.

For most Western observers, the Cultural Revolution serves today as the occasion for a binary opposition that sets the post-Mao order of things against the socialism of the Cultural Revolution, and Deng Xiaoping against Mao Zedong, as the organizing principle of the history of the People's Republic.[14] This dichotomy, purportedly based on the evidence of history, in fact provides an interpretive framework that disposes of historical evidence. Two sequential events in history are placed apart, as "history" is distinguished from "prehistory," with a nearly absolute ideological division between them, separating all that is desirable from all that is undesirable.

This dichotomy is sustained by a remarkable reversal of meaning in the vocabulary that is utilized to describe it. The key word, of course, is revolution. As noted earlier, the break with the Cultural Revolution is often called a second revolution that has restored Chinese history to its proper course. This use of the term "revolution" to denote restoration seems more than a little misplaced, unless it is seen in the context of the historical division it is intended to establish. The second revolution confirms the break with the Cultural Revolution—and it is ultimately desirable not only because of that but because it is actually "a revolution against the revolution," a revolution of order against a revolution that sought to subvert the course of history. One of the fundamental implications of the notion of a second revolution is to deny the revolutionariness of the revolution that it is intended to repudiate, the "first" revolution. The equation of the second revolution with the restoration of China to what is assumed to be its appropriate path of development deprives the first revolution of its historicity and presents it as an historical aberration.

It is thus not surprising that the repudiation of the Cultural Revolution has been followed by questions about whether China's socialist revolution was really necessary, or worth the price China had to pay for it. It is not a matter of whether such questions are legitimate. Nor is the Chinese revolution unique in having its legitimacy questioned. All great social revolutions have been followed by voices questioning their necessity; indeed, heated debates still rage today about the historical legitimacy of the English and French revolutions. The point to be made here is that there is an intimate connection between the legitimacy of the Cultural Revolution and the legitimacy of China's socialist revolution as a whole, and that what is at stake in the issue of the second revolution is not merely a repudiation of the Cultural Revolution but a break with China's socialist revolutionary tradition, perhaps the most heroic revolutionary heritage in our century. The binary opposition that lies at the heart of present-day Western images of

Chinese socialism is in essence an opposition not between contemporary socialism and the Cultural Revolution, but between contemporary socialism (or what now passes for socialism) and its revolutionary past. In condemning the socialist goals and values that the Cultural Revolution originally proclaimed, which in no sense is necessary for condemning the course the upheaval took and what it wrought, there is an implicit condemnation of the values that were fundamental to China's socialist revolution.

Illustrative of how criticism of the Cultural Revolution has been extended to the socialist revolution as a whole are a number of arguments prominent in recent years among Western scholars and journalists alike. We are told time and again, for example, that socialism, as a theory with its own philosophic and historical premises, has been ultimately irrelevant to China, serving simply as an ideological disguise for a nationalist quest for "wealth and power."[15] Another pervasive view is that socialism has been responsible for perpetuating China's backwardness, even exacerbating it.[16] Socialism is also accused of culpability in the general breakdown of public and private morality in China.[17]

The message conveyed by these arguments and themes (individually or as parts of a discourse) is predicated not on selective criticism of one aspect or another of Chinese socialism but upon a wholesale condemnation of socialism in Chinese history. It is a message that suggests that the Chinese revolution was a mistake to the extent that it was socialist, which diverted China from its proper course of historical development. The problem with Chinese socialists was not that they made errors but that they took socialism too seriously, in short, that they were socialists at all.[18]

Thus, within the space of a few years, widespread admiration for Mao Zedong's "road to socialism" has given way to praise for his successors, who are perceived as having abandoned not only Maoism but socialism in general. What accounts for this shift in views? What is really surprising is not currently dominant American attitudes toward Chinese socialism, but the earlier enthusiasm for it. Much of the radical enthusiasm for the Cultural Revolution in the 1960s and 1970s was not the product of any consistent Marxist analysis of socialism and capitalism but rather the product of the peculiarities of American politics, which led many radicals to look to China (and the Third World in general) for political inspiration. Stalinist-style socialism, after all, held little appeal for anyone, and Maoism seemed a hopeful alternative. Other celebrants of China in the 1970s based their admiration for Mao and the Cultural Revolution not on Chinese revolutionary achievements but on their "discovery" in China of the values they thought the United States had lost. But enthusiasm for China need not be based on anything very profound. Stanley Karnow has observed that fear of being denied access to China has discouraged reporters from asking hard questions.[19] The same might well be said about scholars. The simple fact of being allowed to visit China (not to mention access to Chinese officials and dignitaries) is often enough to turn the visitor into an ardent celebrant of what he or she might see there. The enthusiasm might be justified, but it is unstable.

Yet the negative attitudes toward Chinese socialism that now prevail are more in keeping with the traditional mainstream of American views about the Chinese Communist revolution, more logical in terms of the capitalist ideological context from which they spring, and easier to explain. That these negative assessments are reinforced by the current Chinese ambivalence about socialism endows them with an almost hegemonic power. They draw additional power and persuasiveness from the dominance of worldwide conservative tendencies since the mid-1970s, which, in turn, are themselves nourished by signs of deep problems afflicting socialist societies, and further reinforced by the growing difficulties confronting national liberation movements throughout the Third World.

For a quarter of a century the People's Republic of China posed a grave challenge both to the world capitalist order and to the status quo of Soviet-style socialism. Today the much celebrated "integration" of China into the world market breathes new life into the capitalist system—which, discussions of socialist economic failures rarely acknowledge, is itself in a chronic state of crisis—by providing new sources of cheap labor and new markets for capital and commodities. Perhaps more importantly, the virtually unqualified admiration Chinese leaders express for capitalist techniques and methods of development nourishes bourgeois ideological hegemony around the world by renewing faith in a capitalist system that has long been unsure of its own future. It is little wonder that the antisocialist press in the United States seizes the quasi-capitalist "reforms" of Deng Xiaoping's China as a harbinger of the demise of socialism in the world.[20]

It would be misleading, however, to focus too narrowly on the question of self-interest and ignore the more fundamental (and opaque) question of the utopianism that ultimately legitimizes this self-interest: a bourgeois or capitalist utopianism that portrays the present capitalist organization of the world as the best of all possible worlds, and projects this present world into the foreseeable future as the inevitable destiny of humankind, sustained by an immense faith in the ability of capital to resolve the problems afflicting the world, including those of its own making.[21] What makes an event such as the Cultural Revolution seem a so hopelessly mad adventure is its presumptuous challenge to this utopian vision which permits no alternative to its conception of the future. By the same token, contemporary Chinese socialism, in its return to the stream of history that is prescribed by this utopia, appears as a return to sanity.

This confrontation between socialist and capitalist visions of the world is complicated, however, by an orientation to the question of change in Chinese history that is embedded in the cultural confrontation between China and the West in modern history. Our perceptions of Chinese socialism have long been distorted by a profound inability to take history seriously where China is concerned, which manifests itself among students of China and the general public alike in denying the possibility of significant change in Chinese society despite a century of revolution. Chinese history appears to be so long, and the burden of the past so weighty, that the momentum of Chinese society seems to have carried it unscathed through the ages—and even a historical event of such magnitude as a revolution appears to have accomplished little more than scratch the surface of a society hardened into immutability under the weight of its past. This general cultural orientation finds expression in attenuated and more subtle but equally significant ways in scholarly studies of China as well.

The orientation is not reserved for China alone. As Johannes Fabian has argued in *Time and the Other*, the freezing of other (what today we would describe as Third World) societies in time has been a basic component of the Western consciousness of the world since Europe, ironically, embarked upon the revolutionization of the globe, creating the origins of the modern world.[22] Friedrich Hegel, who played a seminal role in articulating this aspect of modern historical consciousness, placed China in the "childhood" of history.[23] Karl Marx, Hegel's disciple, to whose ideas the Chinese revolution owes its inspiration, referred to China as a society "vegetating in the teeth of time" and discovered in the Great Wall of China a metaphor for the universal resistance of non-European societies to change.[24] The attitude was partly a product of the seeming immobility of other societies when contrasted to the daily revolutionization of European society under modern capitalist productive forces, partly a rationalization for establishing European hegemony over societies that, so Europeans thought, were incapable of change if left on their own. If there is any difference in this respect where China is concerned, it rests upon the unique ability of Chinese society to have escaped full-scale colonization and political disintegration under the European assault, accompanied by an apparent but not so unique conviction of some Chinese in the immutability of Chinese culture, which in turn has reinforced Western perceptions of Chinese history.

This orientation has resurfaced in recent years in the prevailing attitude toward China of what Raymond Schwab has termed "condescending veneration,"[25] a veneration of China for its mystifying antiquity combined with a condescending attitude toward Chinese resistance (or inability) to become more like ourselves.[26] What appears as Chinese resistance to change, however, may well be a reluctance on our part to recognize change unless it is the kind of change that follows in our historical footsteps. If China has yet to "enter the twentieth century," it is not because China has not changed, but because these changes have not brought China into *our* twentieth century. Denial to China of a place in the twentieth century may help cover up our complicity in Chinese history by distancing it from our own history, but in the process it also covers up the most important phenomena of Chinese history, including the socialist revolution that was the product not of historical absent-mindedness but of the deepest urges of a society to gain entry into the stream of history as its subject against forces that denied to it such entry! Do we celebrate China today because it has given up the socialist effort, and once again qualifies for our veneration—and patronage?

The unraveling of Chinese socialism in our day presents students of both China and socialism (as well as Chinese socialists themselves) with issues that profoundly challenge our sense of the past, the present, and the future. The sight of a dying revolution—witnessed for the first time in history on television screens around the world—lends a peculiar sense of urgency and immediacy to the question of whether the Chinese revolution has yielded anything more than another tragic betrayal that socialist regimes typically have visited on society in the name of revolutionary ideals. Deprived of its ability to inspire hope for the future, the revolution congeals into an image of "madness,"[27] which seemingly transforms it from a problem in history to an aberration outside of history. And socialism, its original ideological motive force, is similarly transformed into a pathological ideological escape from present reality.

Questions raised by revolution are not to be ignored, and revolutionaries inevitably betray their ideals, especially if they ignore the tragic element inherent in the revolutionary endeavor. The questions are endless. Do the accomplishments of the revolution justify its human and material costs? Could those accomplishments have been achieved at less cost? Or without revolutionary violence? Were there not better ways to seek the same ends? And what happens to revolutionaries (like all who commit themselves to what Weber called "the ethic of responsibility"[28]) who perforce must employ immoral means in their search for good ends? Such questions (and many others) have followed in the wake of all great revolutions, and no amount of historical research will yield fully satisfactory answers to the moral dilemmas posed. One can only recall Trevelyan's words, written in his famous defense of the accomplishments of the seventeenth-century English Revolution: "Men were what they were, uninfluenced by the belated wisdom of posterity, and thus they acted."[29] And one might also remember E. H. Carr's warning, issued upon completing his monumental history of Soviet Russia: "The danger is not that we shall draw a veil over the enormous blots on the record of the Revolution, over the cost in human suffering, over the crimes committed in its name. The danger is that we shall be tempted to forget altogether, and to pass over in silence, its immense achievements."[30]

If the moral questions raised by revolution are to serve a purpose other than as an excuse to reaffirm the social status quo, it is necessary to pursue those questions to their roots in the dilemmas with which revolutions, socialist or otherwise, present us—and this demands the recognition (without apologetics) of the necessity of revolution as the historical expression of the human aspiration for liberation, and the unavoidably tragic consequences which ensue when historical circumstances impose severe limitations on the fulfillment of those aspirations. In the words of Raymond Williams, "We have . . . to see the actual liberation as part of the same process as the terror; I mean only that they are connected, and that the connection is tragic."[31] If such be the tragic historical case, it is not ambivalence about revolution but the absolutist denial of ambiguity to its historical meaning (whether by revolutionaries or their opponents) that may be morally and intellectually irresponsible.

The socialist revolution in China, with all its moral and historical ambiguities, stands as one of the most crucial events in modern history, the product of the most massive and militantly heroic human struggle of the twentieth century. To dismiss it as a historical aberration is to dismiss the history of which it was a product and in which it played so central a role. Indeed, it is to ignore a history that is not just China's alone but part of the collective history of the contemporary world, for the fate of Chinese socialism is inexorably bound up with the fate of socialism in modern world history. Whatever position we may wish to take toward that revolution, it is impossible to pretend political or ideological innocence in our evaluations, which inevitably entail a statement on the historical significance of the foremost revolutionary ideology of our age. If there was indeed tragedy for the Chinese people in the consequences of China's socialist revolution, we must seek to understand that tragedy as one act in the broader tragedy of a history that called forth that revolution as historical necessity, rather than obscure the historical issues it raises by denying its historicity. "Forgetting" may ease the pain of the tragedy by the distance it affords us from its causes and consequences, but that is only a self-deception that conceals the larger tragedy, which we can ill-afford to ignore. The purpose of this volume is to remember and recall the issues posed by Chinese socialism, issues which should not and cannot be passed over in silence.

Notes

The essays in this volume share a common problematic but otherwise represent different appreciations of developments in Chinese socialism. The editors are solely responsible for the views expressed in this introduction. We are grateful to Mark

Selden for his conscientious and constructive criticism.

1. In addition to President Nixon himself, this included prominent liberal and conservative journalists such as James Reston and Joseph Alsop. Academics, too, were not unaffected.

2. Stanley Karnow, "Changing (Mis)Conceptions of China," in *The American Image of China*, ed. Benson L. Grayson (New York: Frederick Ungar, 1979), pp. 284–92, 290.

3. Some of this is so much a part of everyday life that it is barely noticeable. For an instance of "figurative possession," see the advertisement of a tourist agency for its tours to the "Orient," where inscribed on a map of the "Far East" with China at its center are the words "This Land is Our Land" (*New Yorker*, May 19, 1986, p. 58). China as a "stage" is the unspoken presumption of an advertisement in the *China Daily News* of "The Golden Flower Hotel announcing July 4 barbecue in the ancient capital of Xian, complete with 'Live Country Western Music.' " This time the ad tells us to "Saddle Up and Go West." For those who cannot afford the cost of the Golden Flower, there may be good news in a planned Chinese-American venture to establish a Chinese theme park near West Point, New York. These examples are also indicative of a Chinese culpability (or innocence?) in perpetuating the imagery of an exotic China.

The possession is not always figurative. While there is little reason here to single out any institution by name, over the last decade many an American college and university has been anxious to recruit its "own" Chinese or establish its own "educational" tours to China, which are then touted as significant accomplishments in promoting understanding, while ignoring serious investment in promoting Chinese studies. We are not against mutual understanding, and the hope for peace that it promises, but oppose unstable undertakings that contribute less to mutual understanding than to academic salesmanship that is at best patronizing, at worst hegemonic in its assumptions and motivations.

4. The placement of personal rather than long-term historical issues in the foreground is a problem both in the personalized interpretations of China by outsiders and in the interpretations of the Chinese revolutionary experience based on personal experiences of Chinese themselves. For an example of the former, see E. E. Bauer, *China Takes Off: Technology Transfer and Modernization* (Seattle: University of Washington Press, 1986). Examples of the latter are Nien Cheng, *Life and Death in Shanghai* (New York: Penguin Books, 1988); Yue Daiyun and Carolyn Wakeman, *To the Storm: The Odyssey of a Revolutionary Chinese Woman* (Berkeley: University of California Press, 1985); and the many cases included in Anne Thurston, *Enemies of the People* (New York: Knopf, 1987). These works are singled out here not to trivialize what they have to tell us about individual experiences of the Cultural Revolution, but because it is impossible to be callous about what they have to tell us, which dramatizes the moral difficulties posed for historical explanation and interpretation by individual experiences. The moral difficulties involved, however, are not even apparent unless we bring to the foreground the moral dilemmas presented by intellectual choice. Should we be so overwhelmed with the profound sufferings of the individuals chronicled in these works that we should sweep aside issues raised by the Chinese revolution? This may be no less irresponsible, both intellectually and morally, than "forgetting" that the Chinese revolution was a product of efforts by three or four generations of Chinese to resolve

the everyday tragedy of millions. We will speak to this issue further below. Suffice it to say that the plea here for the necessity of recognizing the moral ambiguities of intellectual choice, upon which a critical historical consciousness may be contingent, itself had to overcome an inclination on the part of the authors to exercise self-censorship in the face of overwhelming evidence of personal suffering. The personal element finds its way into interpretation in the interaction between Chinese witnesses and foreign observers. Even as we accord to Chinese testimonial on the Cultural Revolution the privilege it deserves, therefore, we must nevertheless question the tacit or explicit considerations that go into our choice of witnesses. Nien Cheng is the widow of an official of the Guomindang regime who was also an employee of a foreign oil company; in empathizing with her suffering, should we not also recall that the Chinese revolution was a socialist revolution, and one for which the issue of foreign economic control of China was a central issue? Thurston attributes the suffering she chronicles to the moral and psychological breakdown of Chinese society with the revolution (preceding 1949), which she believes has resulted in a profound confusion of victimizing and being victimized; should we not remember that the revolution was also a social and political revolution, and that a great deal of the confusion it created was a product of complex social interests positioning themselves vis-à-vis the revolution in order to appropriate it for themselves? How we respond to the revolution and its consequences is an individual moral choice. The covering up of the complex historical and ethical issues it presents by reducing them to personal experiences, or simplistic moral and psychologistic evaluations, is another matter. Is the preoccupation with the sufferings of individuals to whom we feel socially or personally close disinterested, finally, or easily distinguishable from our own attitudes toward a socialist revolution?

5. For an outstanding example among these works, see Harold R. Isaacs, *Scratches on Our Minds: American Views of China and India* (White Plains, N.Y.: M. E. Sharpe, 1980). For "Orientalism," see Edward W. Said, *Orientalism* (New York: Vintage, 1978).

6. Why there should be reluctance to discuss certain issues has been alluded to in note 4 for these authors. For examples of more explicit efforts to discourage the discussion of such issues, see note 14, and the criticism directed at Orville Schell for his reflections on his own ambivalent attitudes toward China in *Discos and Democracy* (New York: Pantheon, 1988) by the reviewer in the *New York Times Book Review* (June 19, 1988). This vacuous review charges Schell with being a "cultural Maoist," which, the reviewer explains, does not "mean to say he (Schell) is a hard-line Communist," but rather indicates a "zeal for native values that are too often used to justify authoritarian politics." Is Schell then a "soft-line" Communist? Is it because of his nostalgia for Maoist collectivism, a "romantic" attachment to native Chinese conceptions of moral order (comparable to eighteenth-century admirers), or simply because he wonders about the degenerative effects of some of the recent reforms? The confusion may not be surprising, since the chief qualification of the reviewer seems to be that he lives in Hong Kong, and the gratuitousness of much of the criticism may mean nothing more than petty journalistic envy. Nevertheless, the red-baiting tone of the review is instructive and needs to be taken seriously, if only because it is authorized by a newspaper that speaks for (and shapes) elite culture around the country.

7. Raymond Williams, *Marxism and Literature* (New York: Oxford University

Press, 1977). See chapter 9.

8. For examples of this observation, see the contributions by Richard Pfeffer and Andrew Walder, which initiated the symposium on Marx and Mao in *Modern China* 2, 4 (October 1976); 3, 1 (January 1977); and 3, 2 (April 1977). Walder has since reformed his views of the Cultural Revolution.

9. The relationship of the Cultural Revolution to China's past has been problematic, subject to the interpreter's political inclinations and the prevailing mood. Such a relationship is assumed today in the attribution of the Cultural Revolution by the Chinese themselves to persistent traces of "feudal" and "Asiatic" habits among Chinese leaders and the population at large. Similarly uncomplimentary associations were suggested earlier by American scholars who offered cultural and even psychological-determinist explanations of the Cultural Revolution (and of Chinese Communism in general). For examples, see Lucian W. Pye, *The Spirit of Chinese Politics* (Cambridge: MIT Press, 1968), and Richard H. Solomon, *Mao's Revolution and the Chinese Political Culture* (Berkeley: University of California Press, 1971).

10. See the various works by Simon Leys, starting with his *Chinese Shadows* (New York: Penguin, 1978). Leys presented his views with such eloquence that he possibly played an important part in shaping subsequent critiques of Chinese socialism. The politically conditioned changes of views discussed here are so pervasive in Western scholarship on China that it would be unfair to cite particular examples.

11. The most thorough exposition of Mao's views on these questions is in Mao Tse-tung, *A Critique of Soviet Economics* (New York: Monthly Review Press, 1977).

12. Mark Selden, "The Yenan Legacy: The Mass Line," in *Chinese Communist Politics in Action*, ed. A. Doak Barnett (Seattle: University of Washington Press, 1969), pp. 99–157.

13. Harry Harding, *China's Second Revolution* (Washington, D.C.: Brookings Institution, 1987), p. 1 for the origins of the term.

A brief comment is necessary here on the use of the term "revolution" to clarify the authors' position. As with kindred political terms such as reform and conservatism, revolution is used in current writing in a short-term, contextual sense to suppress its long-term implications. Hence questions of reform and conservatism are presented in the abstract, without any explication that they involve in the long term the confrontation between socialism and capitalism. Reform is desirable, but it needs to distinguish reforms that are informed by socialist considerations from reforms that simply imply transforming the existing system, regardless of social and political considerations. Current usage tacitly assumes reform to be the use of capitalist methods to change socialism and makes this distinction itself appear to be "conservative." Likewise, conservatism is divorced from any connection to a "conservative" philosophy and points to any hesitation over change. Hence anyone who is serious about socialism, or is hesitant about abandoning the legacy of the revolution, is immediately dubbed a conservative. As we will explain below, a similar distinction is necessary with regard to the term "revolution," which, in current usage, does not specify whether the reference is to further revolution within socialism or to a break with the revolutionary past. But it does imply the latter, with the consequence that the "second revolution" appears as a "revolution against the revolution" and is easily conflated with restoration: a return to a prerevolutionary path of development. Its meaning is comparable to the use of revolution in, for example, the "Reagan Revolution." Capitalism is the hidden agenda in the positive evaluations of reform and the "second revolution," which then imply an equivalence between socialism and conservatism of the "first revolution."

These distinctions are also necessary to problematize our understanding of developments in China, the complexities of which are lost when they are bundled together simplistically under these labels. Advocates of change do not all share a single vision of change; nor are people "conservative" opponents of change because they oppose *some* changes. We need to distinguish not only the different realms of society (politics, economics, culture), but different positions within each realm. It is well known, for example, that advocates of economic change do not necessarily desire political or cultural changes. Even in the same realm, there are important differences with regard to the past or socialism, or social relations in general. To take one realm where the need for change may hardly be disputed, the realm of literature, the participants in the current literary revolution are informed by radically different attitudes toward the society around them. We may observe that the literary revolution in China today (if that is indeed what it is) is a product not of the relaxation in cultural policy—which is merely its condition—but of experiences of Chinese intellectuals with the Cultural Revolution, which indeed radicalized them and turned them to radical opposition to the existing system and its cultural outlook. One of Mao's goals during the Cultural Revolution was to bring intellectuals and "people" together. It is possible that he succeeded all too well, but the results were not what he had anticipated. The discovery of the people's condition was an element in turning some intellectuals against the party, and the existing system. Such was the case with Wei Jingsheng and Liu Binyan. (For the case of Wei, see Roger Garside, *Coming Alive: China After Mao* [New York: McGraw-Hill, 1981], pp. 268–69. For Liu, see his "Listen Carefully to the Voice of the People" [speech at the 1981 Fourth Congress of Chinese Literature and Art Workers], in *People or Monsters?*, ed. P. Link [Bloomington: Indiana University Press, 1983].) For Liu, for example, the experience was to enhance his commitment to a socially oriented literature, to expose the ideological coverup of the condition of the people in "official" literature, and to give voice to the people themselves. Similar experiences turned other intellectuals to a subjective preoccupation with the self and have led to the renunciation not just of the party or communism but of social concerns as a proper concern for literature. Such is the case with the artists and poets of the so-called Mist school. (For statements on and a selection of works, see *Renditions* 19/20 [Spring/Autumn 1983]: 181–270.) We may find parallels to these divergences in the approach to literature in earlier periods of Chinese history, such as the post-May Fourth period or the period after the suppression of the revolutionary movement in 1927, in which perspective the current literary revolution appears as the most recent episode in the continuing struggle in literature for identity. What is most important, however, is that the revolution does not mean the same thing to everyone—even within the single realm of literature—but reflects different individual and social experiences. These complexities are lost in the crude bundling of different groups under a single label. That Chinese themselves may be doing the same thing does not justify the practice. On the contrary, the effort to contain reform or revolution in some mode of change or other (which also changes the meaning of "conservative") may represent efforts at ideological appropriation and needs to be analyzed to reveal the complexities of change in contemporary

China, and its relationship to the revolutionary past. Moreover, since much of the cultural activity in China consciously or unconsciously also plays to the world outside, the very definition of culture among Chinese intellectuals inevitably is implicated within a global politics of culture and ties in with the broader problem of the confrontation between socialism and capitalism.

14. Official historiography in China has sought since 1982 to repudiate the Cultural Revolution while salvaging the pre-1956 history of the revolution, although even the latter is in some minds open to question. For an unusual, and fascinating, account of how the party leadership evolved a negotiated history to suit contemporary political needs, see Deng Xiaoping, "Remarks on Successive Drafts of the 'Resolution on Certain Questions in the History of Our Party Since the Founding of the People's Republic of China,' " in *Selected Works, 1975–1982* (Beijing: Foreign Languages Press, 1984), pp. 276–96. The intimate connection between the Cultural Revolution and the legacy of the revolution, however, has made it difficult to repudiate the one without raising questions about the other. The "conservative" (i.e., old revolutionaries') use of the Yan'an period to criticize the contemporary decline of revolutionary values has proved to be an embarrassment to the "reform" leadership. The connection has also had an effect on historiography even outside of China. An anonymous reader for *Modern China* of a manuscript by one of the authors offering a Gramscian interpretation of Mao Zedong's Marxism during the Yan'an period, after admitting that he was a reformed supporter of the Cultural Revolution, recommended against publication, not on the grounds of documentation or argument, but because the article seemed to him to be favorable to the Cultural Revolution, which had little to do with the intentions of the article. It merely sought to offer a historical explanation of the peculiarities of Mao's Marxism based on the history of the revolution. In other words, even historical explanations that suggest a history to the Cultural Revolution need to be suppressed!

15. See Dirlik's essay, "Postsocialism," chapter 18 of this volume, for a discussion of this problem. It might be useful here to take note of a recent essay by Paul Cohen that not only illustrates this point but is exemplary as a text of much of the discussion. Cohen, "The Post-Mao Reforms in Historical Perspective," *Journal of Asian Studies* 47, 3 (August 1988): 518–40. Cohen draws a distinction between "systemic analysis" of China and a perspective that "lays a much greater stress on those characteristics of the Chinese situation that are peculiar to China" (p. 518). He then proceeds to place Deng Xiaoping and the current "reforms" in a "historical perspective," which renders Deng as the latest in a series of "authoritarian reformers" beginning with the Empress Dowager Ci Xi and continuing with Yuan Shikai and Jiang Jieshi (Chiang Kai-shek). Deng's reforms in this historical perspective are "guided by a very potent ideology—we may call it an ideology of 'authoritarian modernization'—and it is precisely this ideology that Deng shares with his non-Communist predecessors" (p. 535). We presume that the essay is meant to illustrate what Cohen calls a "China-specific perspective," an example of writing Chinese history "from within" of which he has been an advocate. The essay in fact illustrates how an abstract historicism may distance actual history in the very process of purportedly placing it within a "historical perspective." Aside from a reference to Mao's Cultural Revolution and passing references to Deng's "communism," which, as used, reduce communism to a mere label without content, the discussion makes no reference to socialism and no effort to place Deng within the

immediate perspective provided by the history of socialism in China; indeed, the revolution disappears from sight as Cohen establishes a lineage of reform that focuses on a series of "reformers" who, the author neglects to say, were not only informed by vastly different ideological perspectives on the question of reform, but whose reform efforts took place under radically different social, political, and global circumstances. As is typical of this kind of "historical perspective," history is reduced to the activities of individual leaders, and the social and political relations that the individuals articulate (or must respond to) form no part of the analysis. This kind of dehistoricizing and desocializing approach in the end uses history to disguise its basically culturalist assumptions about other societies.

16. See Fox Butterfield's report on a conference at Brown University in the fall of 1987 that undertook to evaluate Deng Xiaoping's reforms, "Mao and Deng: Competitors for History's Judgment," *New York Times*, November 15, 1987.

17. Thurston, *Enemies of the People*.

18. Mao Zedong's greatest mistake, one expert has concluded, was to remake revolution from a means to an end. Attributed to Prof. Roderick McFarquhar in Butterfield, "Mao and Deng." Revolutionary socialists in China throughout the twentieth century viewed "social revolution" as an end and opposed those who sought to reduce it to a "means" in a national struggle, which is what McFarquhar seems to have in mind.

19. Karnow, "Changing (Mis)Conceptions of China."

20. Deng was voted "Man of the Year" by *Time Magazine* in 1984 and 1985 and by *National Review* in 1985. This analysis of the elements that go into evaluations of China is not intended to imply that its conditions are the same as those that prevailed in the past. Nowhere is this more evident than in the use of the changes in China to prove the viability of capitalism. (At the Republican convention in 1988, Jack Kemp repeatedly used the example of China to demonstrate the superiority of capitalism. In the confident days of capitalism, its ideologues did not require the witness of "backward" societies to prove its viability.) We may simply point to other changes in society that may affect these evaluations and their presentation: changing attitudes toward the upheaval of the 1960s (in which the Cultural Revolution and the revolutions in the Third World played a major part), the changing role of the media in American society, and changes in publishing, which, in its search for best-sellers, encourages the publication of certain kinds of literature over others. With all these changes on the American scene, the evaluation of the changes in China returns in its articulation to an earlier discourse, and perhaps even magnifies it, since it now draws upon a much larger group of consumers. What the long-term implications of these changes may be, as well as of the global elite culture that they are in the process of creating, remains to be seen. For raising these questions, we are grateful to participants in a seminar sponsored jointly by the departments of History and East Asian Languages and Civilizations at the University of Chicago (October 28, 1988), in which one of the authors presented this introduction as a paper.

21. Vincent Geoghegan has described this as "utopianizing the present." See his *Utopianism and Marxism* (London: Methuen, 1987), especially the introduction.

22. J. Fabian, *Time and the Other: How Anthropology Makes Its Object* (New York: Columbia University Press, 1983).

23. G. W. Friedrich Hegel, *The Philosophy of History* (New York: Dover, 1956), part 1.

24. Karl Marx, "History of the Opium Trade," in *Collected Works*, vol. 16 (New York: International Publishers, 1981), p. 16; and K. Marx and G. Engels, *The Communist Manifesto*.

25. Raymond Schwab, *The Oriental Renaissance* (New York: Columbia University Press, 1986).

26. These are the implications when Tom Brokaw on NBC Nightly News broadcasts from China (against a background in which the NBC logo has been superimposed upon the Great Wall of China—and an anchorwoman of Chinese origin presides over the report) that China has yet to enter the twentieth century; as if all the historical events of the twentieth century have had nothing whatsoever to do with the state of Chinese society in our day, rhetorically denying any progressive significance to a history that the viewer knows full well to be the history of socialism in China, but, on the contrary, placing that history in the "prehistory" of modernity. The same implications are present when Barbara Walters "discovers" in a special edition of the ABC program "20/20" that American musicals and hard rock offer a liberating promise to a Chinese youth long stifled by socialism (underlying the authority of the report by references to three personal trips to China, an interview with Henry Kissinger who has traveled to China on more than ten occasions and has been involved in the most dramatic events in the new "opening" of China, and, once again, ironically, the personal involvement in the cultural liberation of China from socialism of the wife of the American ambassador to China, who also happens to be of Chinese origin). We single out these reports because of their immense potential for shaping general cultural orientations in the United States, which no learned treatise on Chinese socialism could ever hope to match. These were both broadcast during the week of September 25–October 2, 1987. The NBC broadcast was cleverly entitled "Changing China."

27. See Ronald Paulson's study of the French Revolution, *Representations of Revolution, 1789–1820* (New Haven: Yale University Press, 1983).

28. Max Weber, "Politics as a Vocation," in *From Max Weber: Essays in Sociology*, ed. H. H. Gerth and C. Wright Mills (New York: Oxford University Press, 1958), pp. 77–128.

29. G. M. Trevelyan, *A Shortened History of England*, book 4, chap. 2. Cited in Isaac Deutscher, *The Unfinished Revolution: Russia, 1917–1967* (London: Oxford University Press, 1967), p. 9.

30. Quoted in Tarik Ali, ed., *The Stalinist Legacy: Its Impact on Twentieth Century World Politics* (Harmondsworth, England: Penguin, 1984), p. 9.

31. Raymond Williams, *Modern Tragedy* (Stanford: Stanford University Press, 1967), pp. 81–82.

2

REVOLUTIONARY HEGEMONY AND THE LANGUAGE OF REVOLUTION: CHINESE SOCIALISM BETWEEN PRESENT AND FUTURE

Arif Dirlik

"A beginner who has learnt a new language," Karl Marx wrote in *The Eighteenth Brumaire of Louis Bonaparte*, "always translates it into his mother tongue, but he has assimilated the spirit of the new language and can freely express himself in it only when he finds his way in it without recalling the old and forgets his native tongue in the use of the new."[1] Revolution, the metaphor suggests, is learning. It is also forgetting; forgetting not in the sense of loss of memory, but in the sense of relegating to memory that which obstructs the assimilation of the new.

The metaphor of language offers an illuminating perspective on the tortuous course the Chinese Revolution has followed over the last three decades.[2] Learning a new language and forgetting the old has been a basic problem in Chinese politics, as is evident in the radical shifts in the language of socialist ideology. The problem does not lie in a choice between revolution and restoration; there is no dispute among China's socialists over the transformative role socialism must play in creating a new society. The dispute has been over the best way to reconcile the demands of the revolutionary vision that brought the Communists to power with the responsibilities placed upon a revolutionary party in control of state power. This has called forth a synthesis of two meanings of socialism, both of which have deep roots in the history of Chinese socialism: socialism as an ideology of revolution and socialism as an ideology of modernization. Revolution and development have long been associated in Chinese socialist thought as interdependent constituents of socialist ideology, and the historical experience of Chinese socialism shows that neglect of one almost inevitably undermines the other. There has also been a perennial contradiction, however, between an idea of socialism that derives its language from a universal ideal of an egalitarian and democratic society, and one that renders socialism into an instrument of parochial pragmatic goals of national development. These alternative conceptions of socialism also have different implications for China's relationship to its past, and to the historical context out of which Chinese socialism has grown.

The contradiction is a contradiction between the language of vision and the language of economism. Unable to integrate these two languages into a new language of socialist progress, socialist ideology in China has ended up for the most part speaking two languages at once, which has confounded the speakers no less than the listeners. But it is also true that one or the other has been spoken with the louder voice in different phases of the revolution. Ideological struggle in Chinese politics expresses a struggle to capture the ideology of socialism for the dominance of one or the other of these languages. So far, neither has achieved a clear-cut victory.

The difficulties the Chinese have encountered in discovering a new language of socialism disclose a fundamental problem that Marx's metaphor overlooks. The new language is new to the neophyte who encounters it for the first time, but the language already exists before the encounter as a completed design, which the neophyte needs only to assimilate in order to express himself freely. Not so with revolution. The new society that is the promise of revolution does not appear as a completed design, but as a project to be realized. The revolutionary neophyte must create the language in which he is to learn to express himself. This makes the task more, not less, difficult. For the new language, if it is to be intelligible, can only be generated out of the language of present reality. The revolutionary consciousness that bears the responsibility for creating the new language is itself the product of the history it seeks to transcend.

Herein lies the predicament of revolution, and of socialism. The problem of language for the revolutionary is not simply the problem of acquiring a new skill, but a problem of discovering new ways in which to think about the world, its constitution and purpose. It is, in a fundamental sense, a problem of what Antonio Gramsci described as "Hegemony." The struggle to create a new language of revolution is but a struggle to assert the hegemony of revolution over its historical inheritance.

A revolution, if it is authentic, must create a new language of its own. A revolution that employs the language of the society it has rejected in order to comprehend its own meaning is a revolution that has conceded defeat at the moment of its conception. To the extent that revolutionaries must translate their goals back into the language of prerevolutionary society in order to render them intelligible, they must perpetuate the hegemony of the past over the present and the future.

On the other hand, revolution is not the substitution of an arbitrary language for an existing one. The new society must transcend the old society, not merely negate it; and this it can achieve only by generating the new language out of the language it finds at hand. Even if it were possible for revolutionaries to sever their ties to the past, to start off with a blank sheet of paper as it were, a new language created out of thin air lacks the ability to articulate the social experiences upon which its vitality depends. A revolution that seeks to escape the past by refusing to speak its language is deprived of its own source of intelligibility and isolates itself from the reality it would transform. Revolution is of necessity a historical process where the revolutionary consciousness must be transformed in its own activity to revolutionize the world. The alternatives must be, on the one hand, fossilization under the pressure of the past or, on the other hand, loss of intelligibility in a present to which it is alien and, therefore, incomprehensible.

The progress of Chinese socialism over the last three decades illustrates this predicament of revolutionary socialism. The Cultural Revolution of the 1960s, in a fundamental sense, was an attempt to create a new language of revolution. Mao Zedong was preoccupied with the fossilization of the revolution under the new regime, not because Chinese society ceased to change after 1949, which it obviously did not, but because it was becoming increasingly clear that the revolutionary leadership had lost sight of its socialist vision once the revolution had accomplished its immediate goals. The Cultural Revolution expressed the conviction that without a renewed effort to create a new language, the past must inevitably reassert hegemony over the revolution and divert it from the path of socialist progress.

It has become fashionable in recent years to portray the Cultural Revolution as an aberration in the history of Chinese socialism. The Cultural Revolution was to end up as an aberration, a parody of its own aspirations; but that is no reason to deny the reality of the problems it sought to resolve or the seriousness of its intentions. Indeed, it is possible to see in the failure of the Cultural Revolution the intractability of the problems that the Chinese Revolution has had to confront.

The Cultural Revolution claim that without further revolution China would inevitably gravitate back toward capitalism was a misleading one. China had never been a capitalist society in a technical sense, nor was it likely to become one after the revolution. But neither can it be disputed that there were significant social groups in Chinese society, including some within the Communist Party, whose thinking was informed by a paradigm of development to which the social goals of socialism were marginal. These social groups were potential instruments for the perpetuation of the hegemony over revolution of this paradigm. If this paradigm were to take hold of Chinese thinking, the socialist vision would be relegated to a future so distant that it would cease to have any bearing on the present. With the creation of a socialist language—a socialist society—indefinitely postponed, it was inevitable that this paradigm would come to dominate Chinese thinking, and drive the revolution away from the socialist vision that informed it. The forces and attitudes that have resurfaced with the termination of the Cultural Revolution bear ample testimonial to the validity of these fears.

Rather than an effort to institute socialism immediately, the Cultural Revolution was an attempt to create a new language of revolution that would reshape Chinese thinking on socialist development and guarantee the hegemony of revolution. Briefly, the Cultural Revolution sought to restructure the language of development by politicizing it. Its basic premise was that it was not developmental needs that must determine the course of revolution but, on the contrary, revolutionary goals that must shape the course development would take. Contrary to current charges brought against it, the Cultural Revolution did not reject development, but only development based on economistic assumptions that reduced socialist progress to economic development: that economic, or even simply technological, progress is the ultimate meaning of socialism; that social inequality and authoritarian political relations are the price we must pay for the social order necessary for economic progress; that economic efficiency must take precedence over considerations of equality and democracy in the organization of work, and the structure of social relations in general.

The Cultural Revolution sought to make a break with these economistic premises. It held that social relations must be informed by revolutionary goals; that economic development must proceed in such a way as to reinforce these social relations; that self-reliance at the local and national level was essential to break down the hegemony over China of the capitalist world economy; that social commitment must take precedence over professional ideological commitments (red over expert). The grammar of this language was dialectical: revolutionaries must remake themselves through their activity of remaking the world. Crucial to the language of the Cultural Revolution was the premise that the social goals of the revolution must not await the development of its economic basis, but must be incorporated into the very process of development.

This idea of development has an internal coherence that is at odds with currently prevalent notions of the Cultural Revolution as a product of deranged minds. Moreover, the idea draws upon a vision of socialist society that was informed by the experiences of the Chinese Revolution. Self-reliance, commitment to revolutionary goals, transformation of social relations in order to promote socialist development, and even the idea that revolution must create its own language were ideas that went back to the pre-1949 phase of the revolution, in particular the war years (1937–1945) when the Communists had developed the strategy that carried the revolution to victory. It was not the language of revolution that had changed, but the circumstances of the revolution.

The Cultural Revolution failed to formulate a strategy of revolution that would correspond to its language of development in these new circumstances. The strategy of a revolutionary party in insurgency was not appropriate to a revolutionary party in power. The problem with the Cultural Revolution was that it not only took as a given the political structure that had emerged with the revolution, but tried to use that same political structure to achieve its own ends. This structure imposed upon Chinese society a form that was antithetical to the values the Cultural Revolution espoused in the abstract. The result was a confusion born of the disjuncture between the Cultural Revolutionary language and the language of its structural context, which confounded both the proponents and the subjects of the revolution.

This was a basic reason that the social policies of the Cultural Revolution almost uniformly contradicted its verbal aspirations. The politicization of the issue of development led not to a reconsideration of the meaning of economic development, but to the use of politics to mobilize society more effectively for economic development. The liberation of labor was to end up in the conversion of labor to forced labor. The substitution of moral for material incentives led not to the abolition of incentives, but to the addition of considerations of political gain to existing considerations of material gain.

Likewise, input from the masses into politics, intended to counteract party and government bureaucratization, was converted rapidly into the subjection of the people to mindless recitation of officially sanctioned slogans and "quotations" that could only dull their political senses. As the Cultural Revolution did not question the economic ends of socialism, neither did it consider restructuring politics to abolish hierarchy. "Dictatorship of the proletariat" and the rule of the party remained as matters of faith. The attack on bureaucracy did not eliminate bureaucracy but disoriented it, which only enhanced the possibility of arbitrary despotism.

And so with the other aspects of the Cultural Revolution. Self-reliance ended up as an atavistic assertion of a revolutionary brand of nationalistic chauvinism. The liberation of imagination in culture turned into the confinement of cultural imagination in the straitjacket of political clichés. The reassertion of political commitment over expertise degenerated rapidly from an attack on the elitism of professionals to a pervasive anti-intellectualism.

The denouement of the Cultural Revolution illustrates what I meant above by loss of intelligibility in a revolutionary attempt to impose upon society a language that is the product of revolutionary vision divorced from social reality. The Cultural Revolution suggested an almost magical notion that revolution could conjure a new society simply by invoking its language.

This language, coherent in the abstract, lost its coherence when applied through the realities of power in Chinese society. The intention underlying the Cultural Revolution was coherent; not so its practice of revolution. In the end, the contradiction between an ideology derived from revolutionary vision and a social reality to which to vision had little relevance was resolved by the subjection of the vision to social reality. Instead of abolishing economic and political hierarchy, as it professed, the Cultural Revolution assumed in exaggerated form the hierarchical disposition of its social and ideological context. The divorce of intention from result, theory from practice, rendered both the intention and the theory meaningless.

When in 1957 Mao Zedong described the Chinese people as "poor and blank," upon whom one could presumably write any script, he had forgotten the lessons of the revolutionary experience which he had done so much to articulate: that the intelligibility of the revolutionary message depended on its ability to speak the language of the people. The Cultural Revolution, unable to formulate an intelligible message, was to isolate itself from the people it hoped to lead. It could be sustained for as long as it was, not because it was able to establish the hegemony of revolution in Chinese thinking, but because of the threat of coercion it held against all who deviated from officially sanctioned norms. A revolutionary language, divorced from reality, and hence lacking concrete referents, could not but become a plaything at the hands of revolutionary whims. As the whims changes, so did the winds of revolution. The paradigm of revolution the Cultural Revolution offered is already overshadowed in historical memory by its betrayal of its own policies. In hindsight, it appears more an episode of terror born of power struggles among the Chinese elite than an authentic revolutionary effort.

In contrast, the post–Cultural Revolution leadership in China is convinced that the language of revolutionary society can only be generated out of the present language of socialism through an arduous historical process that builds upon the past. It has not only renounced the Cultural Revolution, but has proceeded to abolish revolution as a principle of Chinese politics.

As noted in the introduction, the changes since Mao's death in 1976 have been described by Chinese leaders as a "second revolution," which has been heartily echoed among sympathizers of the regime abroad. What the future of this "revolution" might be is impossible to say, but its meaning is clear: it expresses the victory of an uncompromising economism in the understanding of socialist development that matches in its obdurateness the Cultural Revolution will to put "politics in command." Its goal is not to create a revolutionary society, but to achieve a "pragmatic" adjustment of revolution to the demands of present reality.

The present regime promotes the definition of socialism as an ideology of modernization. The new attitude is cogently captured in the following lines written by a prominent economist in 1980: "The basic Marxist approach to socialist ownership is: anything that can best promote the development of the productive forces, yes, and it may count on the support of Marxists; anything that does not, no, and Marxists will not support it; anything that actually impedes the development of the productive forces will be firmly opposed."[3] Absent from this statement and, with a rare exception, from socialist ideology since 1978, is any suggestion that further change in social relations might be necessary in China's socialist progress. If there is to be further social change, it must follow the demands of economic development.

The underlying premise of this definition of socialism is that China had already become a socialist society in 1956, when the socialist transformation of production had been accomplished with the abolition of private ownership of the means of production. The basic contradiction in China since then has been the contradiction between a socialist economy and backward forces of production. The most urgent need for China, therefore, is economic development and the technological modernization that is essential to economic development. Under a socialist regime, economic development must ensure the eventual realization of socialist society.

In accordance with these premises, the regime proceeded to establish new policies designed to foster rapid economic development. These policies are well known by now: reprivatization of the economy, increased material incentives to encourage labor productivity, attack on egalitarian practices that interfered with economic efficiency, political relaxation to mobilize support for the regime, especially among the professional-managerial class, and a rapidly intensified program of technological, economic, and intellectual exchange with advanced countries of the capitalist world. The key to all these changes was the shift to a more individualized conception of economic organization and activity.

These policies do not represent a restoration of capitalism, but they do express acceptance of a paradigm of development that was the product of capitalism, and to which socialism as it exists today has become heir. Chinese leaders justify their policies through an empiricist pragmatic claim: that these policies best suit the realities of Chinese society. Poverty is not the only reality of Chinese society, however, for so are political and economic inequality. Resignation to a paradigm of development that does not address these other realities implies acceptance, even the reinforcement, of a social system that is antithetical in structure to the social goals of socialism.

This, of course, exposes the fallacy of "seeking truth from facts," as the new pragmatism is described. Pragmatism is a term without ideological content of its own, implying only the willingness to approach practically tasks defined outside of itself. It may be invoked in service of a given ideological and social system, or it may be invoked in service of a revolutionary ideology that challenges the system. To portray pragmatism as an alternative to ideology rather than as its servant serves only to universalize the ideological claims of the existing structure of power. To a socialist revolutionary, pragmatism within a hierarchical social and political structure may only mean legitimization of a structure that impedes socialist progress. A revolutionary pragmatism must seek practical ways of transcending the existing system, not a practical adjustment to it. Socialists have tried to escape the dilemmas created by their "pragmatism" by explaining such pragmatism as a necessity of a transitional period. The cliché of "transition" does not do away with the reality, as Rudolf Bahro has said of Eastern Europe in his *The Alternative in Eastern Europe*, that the very structures that are relied upon to guarantee socialist progress may themselves become the biggest obstacle to socialism.[4] Policies that reinforce these structures must of necessity undercut the very promise they hold forth.

The notion of pragmatism mystifies the ideological and social implications of the new policies in China. These policies clearly give priority to reasons of state over the call of revolution. The Chinese conception of socialism today is that of a bureaucratic-managerial society, where a bureaucracy of experts plans and administers social order and development. The Cultural Revolution had attacked this bureaucratic conception of socialism. Conflicts over bureaucracy since then have not involved the question of the political place of bureaucracy under socialism, but rather have revolved around the questions of bureaucratic efficiency and integrity. To this end, Chinese leaders seek to improve the quality of China's bureaucracy through better education of bureaucrats, transfer of power to experts, and better management techniques. This technical administrative conception of politics corresponds to their conception of economic problems essentially as problems of the technology of production and management.

If the regime takes the bureaucratic organization of society for granted in its conception of socialism, its economic policies promise to further reinforce existing hierarchies in Chinese society. The idea that as long as a socialist regime remains in power, economic development will automatically abolish inequality, is the product either of a premeditated myopia, or of an ideological blind spot where the regime's social basis is concerned. Present developmental policies are informed by the premise that economic inequality is the only means to achieve development: inequality here implies not simply inequality in income, but inequality in the management of production and social power. The regime believes that development is contingent upon the creation of an economic-political elite that will supervise the process of development. This elite has already come to identify the interests of society as a whole with its own interests as a social class. Economic development under the guidance of such an elite is not likely to create a democratic and egalitarian society, but to reinforce hierarchy. If current tendencies continue, moreover, this elite will increasingly share an ideological affinity with the global economic and technocratic elite, which will only enhance its distance from the population it "manages." Already, the language of this elite is the language of management: efficiency, productivity, labor discipline, expertise, administrative skills, etc. Chinese students today study administrative and policy-making skills in the United States and Japan, even as China imports capitalist technology and methods of organization that are designed to control labor, not to liberate it. What is good enough for capitalism, evidently, is good enough for socialism.

The forces unleashed by the new policies have created a predicament for China's socialist system. Economism, taken to its logical conclusions, is at odds not only with the socialist revolutionary vision, but with the existing socialist system as well. The regime's idealization of economic development has licensed opposition to party rule and its ideological basis, socialism, on the grounds that they interfere with efficient development. The uncompromising economism of the initial period of the new regime has been qualified by the revival of ideological issues, which seeks to restore the vocabulary of revolution to the language of socialism. Over the last five years, there has been an increasing concern with ideological education to create a "socialist spiritual civilization." These concerns were incorporated into official policy in the Twentieth Congress of the Communist Party in September 1982. In the words of then Party Secretary Hu Yaobang,

> Socialist spiritual civilization constitutes an important characteristic of the socialist system and a major aspect of its superiority. In the past, when referring to the characteristics of socialism, people laid stress on the elimination of the system of exploitation, public ownership of the means of production, distribution according to work, planned and proportionate development of the national economy, and political power of the working class and other working people. They also laid stress on another characteristic of socialism, the high development of the productive forces and a labor productivity higher than that under capitalism as both as a necessity and the end result of the development of socialism. All this is undoubtedly true, but it does not cover all the characteristics. Socialism must possess one more characteristic, that is, socialist spiritual civilization with communist ideology at its core. *Without this, the building of socialism would be out of the question.*[5]

Hu's speech did not call for a reevaluation of the regime's development policies, but simply added a "spiritual" to the "material" aspect of development. There is no true dialectic here, only the simultaneous pursuit of two formally distinguished aspects of socialist development. The language of spiritual mobilization is not the language of revolution but the language of social control. The so-called Five Stresses and Four Beauties, which have been enunciated as the behavioral norms that the spiritual mobilization campaign seeks to establish give a good idea of the order the regime seeks to achieve. The Five Stresses refer to stress on civil manners, propriety, cleanliness, order, and morality; the Four Beauties, to the beautification of spirit, language, behavior, and environment.[6]

There is no question that the new stress on ideology represents a shift in the regime's approach to socialism. The question is the meaning of this shift. Some of the themes of the campaign for spiritual mobilization are quite reminiscent of the themes promoted by the Cultural Revolution. But there is a crucial difference: the goal of the new campaign is not to create a new paradigm of socialist development, but to secure and consolidate the economistic paradigm that continues to shape the regime's thinking on development. In other words, it does not seek to supersede the economistic paradigm, but to guarantee its welfare by counteracting the adverse tendencies it has created. This is confirmed by the most recent manifestation of the regime's efforts to contain the contradictions created by its economic policies: the so-called new authoritarianism (*xin quanwei zhuyi*), which seeks to keep in check the social, political, and cultural consequences of economic individualism through an authoritarian political structure. The inspiration for "new authoritarianism" is rooted not in any socialism, but in the experience of right-wing dictatorships in East and Southeast Asia (Taiwan, South Korea, Singapore) that have achieved economic miracles without the benefit of democracy.[7]

Contrary to much wishful thinking, the discrepancy between revolutionary vision and social reality continues to haunt Chinese politics today, as it did under Mao Zedong. The difference is in the meaning of the vision in politics. The revolutionary vision no longer serves as a principle of politics, but only as ideological legitimacy for policies that are antithetical to the promise they hold forth. Unlike during the Cultural Revolution, when political incoherence arose out of the discrepancy between the language of revolution and the language of the existing political structure, today it is the discrepancy between the language of the existing political structure and that of economism that lies at the source of political incoherence. The Cultural Revolutionaries had accused the party of having become an obstacle to revolution; the basic charge brought against the party at present is that it obstructs economic development. While the regime has moved toward restructuring power to meet the demands of the economy, it has also chronically revived the language of revolution to keep these demands in check.

That the new regime has had to revive revolutionary idealism to defend its evidently antirevolutionary policies underlines the "pragmatic" significance of revolutionary idealism in Chinese politics. The revolutionary vision of socialism carries the weight it does in Chinese politics not because it offers a remote promise, but because the socialist revolution played a significant practical role in China's national integration and development, which all Chinese socialists recognize. The concrete contributions of the revolution to popular welfare and national autonomy make it a powerful symbol around which to unify a society where the bonds of "socialist unity" remain more apparent than real. Chinese leaders may abandon the vision at their own risk. It is also clear, however, that in this "pragmatic" role, the vision promises not liberation but consolidation of a hierarchical system that is fashioned by the economistic assumptions that dominate Chinese socialism today. The socialist vision, in other words, serves to guard politics that negate the meaning of socialism as social vision.

The problem of creating a language free from the hegemony of inherited paradigms of development, and yet adequate to reforming existing social reality, is a universal problem of socialism. This is not surprising. Socialism as a political idea seeks to transcend capitalism. But the idea is itself a product of capitalist society; not simply an outgrowth of capitalism but a dialectical product born of capitalism in opposition to it. Still, the language of capitalism infuses the consciousness of socialists who, though rebels against capitalism, share many of its premises with regard to the purpose and process of historical development.

This is as true of socialists in the capitalist periphery as it is in the core capitalist states of Western Europe, Northern America, and Japan, though it is not as evident in the case of the former. Socialists in advanced capitalist societies have willingly subordinated their socialist vision to the hegemony of capital. The language of socialism in these societies appears as a language of corporatism, which represents but the assimilation of the vocabulary of socialism into the language of capitalism. Socialists of the periphery have upheld the vision of a revolutionary socialism; but there, too, the hegemony of capital has persisted in the language of national development, although the use of a national idiom in these cases often disguises the continuing reality of this hegemony.

Indeed, socialists in these societies have often turned to the national idiom as a source from which to generate an autonomous language of socialism free from the cultural hegemony of capital. The danger here, of course, has been the risk of assimilating socialism to the national language in the very effort to assimilate the national idiom to the language of socialism. Such a nationalized socialism may serve to ward off control by global capital, but it no longer carries the meaning of socialism as a universal ideal of human liberation. On the contrary, it may assume the colorings of its precapitalist environment both socially and in its conception of politics. This is to some extent what happened in China during the Cultural Revolution.

Keeping global capital at a distance, moreover, does not mean abolition of the hegemony of capital. Too much emphasis on the burden of the precapitalist past in shaping socialism in these societies conceals the dynamic forces that shape socialism, and the role socialism plays as a transformative ideology. Socialism has been as much a product of capitalism in peripheral societies as it was in the capitalist core: a product, in the one case, of the autonomous development of capitalism, and, in the other, of its worldwide diffusion. It is ultimately from the intrusion of capital that socialism has derived its political relevance in peripheral societies.

In either case, the socialist goal has been to transcend capitalism, not to escape back from it into a precapitalist past. The effort to assimilate the national idiom into the language of socialism is itself motivated by the search for a locally acceptable language of socialism. Socialism is not a plaything at the hands of some unconscious traditionalism, therefore, but a transformative ideology that seeks to create a postcapitalist society out of the dialectical synthesis of the national idiom with the language of development. For the same reason, socialism appears in these societies not only as a vision of equality and democracy, but as an ideology of development. The burden of development, achieved in core societies by capitalism, falls here upon socialist shoulders.

It is this burden that ushers in the hegemony of capital over the socialism of peripheral societies which, in spite of its intended goal to ward off global capitalism, draws its inspiration from a paradigm of development that is the product of capitalism. This has meant the incorporation into socialist language of the grammar of capitalist development.

The fact that in these circumstances class struggle is placed in the context of a national struggle against global capital, moreover, creates the predicament that the nation may overshadow class as the locus of socialist activity. When this happens, socialism is reduced to an instrument in the cause of national development which, in a world under the material sway of capital, must result in a "pragmatic" adjustment of socialism to the hegemony of capital. This mode of development, Rudolf Bahro suggests, is better described as "noncapitalist development" than as socialist development. Some Chinese socialists used this term in the early part of the century to describe a nonrevolutionary socialism that would bypass capitalism to achieve more efficiently the goals of capitalist society. The language of noncapitalist development is not a socialist language but a dialect of capitalism. This is the language that dominates Chinese socialism today.

The Chinese experience with socialism is the most recent example of the difficulties that have confronted socialism historically. What is clear from accumulated experience is that if socialism is to retain its viability as an alternative to capitalism, it must create a language of its own. This requires, first and foremost, a reconsideration of the meaning of development that, at present, is fashioned by a paradigm of development rooted in capitalist assumptions on the ends and meanings of human progress. It also requires, therefore, that socialists abandon the illusion of present-day socialism as the end, rather than the beginning, of the history of socialism.

Such a language, to be intelligible, can only be created out of the language of the present. But to be authentically revolutionary, it must derive its grammar from the language of the future: a language that articulates the vision of a social existence free of exploitation and oppression. Without such a language, socialists must be deprived of an identity to call their own.

Notes

1. Karl Marx, *The Eighteenth Brumaire of Louis Bonaparte* (New York: International Publishers, 1967), pp. 15–16.

2. This essay deals with the general problem of interpreting socialism. As the other essays (especially in part 3) indicate, there is another, equally significant, aspect to the problem of language: its use in the articulation of social interest. Socialism in China provides the common language of politics but is subject to discursive appropriation by different groups in society, which interpret it in accordance with their own group interests and ideology. The different interpretations of socialism point, in other words, to contradictions in the social situation out of which they spring. There is no need to belabor this point, since the following essays illustrate these conflicts cogently. It may be worth pointing out, however, that the tendency of some groups in China today to derogate socialism may have less to do with the "failures" of socialism per se than the animosity to socialism of groups who, in order to realize their group interests and fulfill their ideological aspirations as a group, indiscriminately blame all of China's woes on socialism. The various conflicting discourses on socialism, in other words, point ultimately to social conflicts, including class conflict. The economistic interpretation of socialism discussed in this essay also coincides with the social interests and ideology of the professional-managerial groups in Chinese society who seek to render it into the "hegemonic" interpretation of socialism for the society as a whole. Other essays discuss the resistance to this hegemony of groups that stand to lose by it, or do not share its ideological assumptions for a variety of reasons.

3. Yu Guangyuan, "The Basic Approach to Socialist Ownership," *Beijing Review* 49 (December 8, 1980).

4. Rudolf Bahro, *The Alternative in Eastern Europe* (London: New Left Books, Verso edition, 1981) pp. 6–14 and chap. 2.

5. Hu Yaobang, "Create a New Situation in All Fields of Socialist Modernization," *Beijing Review* 25, 37 (September 13, 1987): 21.

6. For a further discussion of this campaign, see Arif Dirlik, "Spiritual Solutions to Material Problems: The 'Socialist Ethics and Courtesy Month' in China," *The South Atlantic Quarterly* 81, 4 (Autumn 1982): 359–75.

7. For a sketchy discussion of this current (and controversial) idea, see " 'New Authoritarianism' Seen in Chinese Actions," *New York Times*, February 28, 1989, p. A13.

Part II
Political Economy

3

MAO ZEDONG AND THE POLITICAL ECONOMY OF CHINESE DEVELOPMENT

Mark Selden

Recent scholarship and political commentary in China and abroad have not dealt kindly with the legacy of Mao Zedong. While the harshest criticisms have centered on Mao's leadership of the Great Proletarian Cultural Revolution and the Great Leap Forward, they have also extended to his entire stewardship. At the heart of this criticism is not only a political assessment but a cutting economic critique. In assessing this criticism it is worth recalling, therefore, the important achievements hitherto widely associated with Chinese and Maoist political economy. A poor agrarian nation in the decades of Mao's leadership was said to have achieved developmental and socialist goals that defied those for most postcolonial and developing nations. These included:

—A self-sufficient and self-reliant economy free from foreign capital and foreign control.

—The elimination of capitalist exploitation and the creation of a highly egalitarian and participatory society.

—The feeding of one billion people, that is, the solution to the problem of hunger, and the provision of basic welfare guarantees for all.

—Rapid industrialization including both heavy industry and small-scale decentralized rural industry.

—The solution to the peasant question: equity via land reform, cooperation, and communization for the peasant majority and avoidance of a host of problems from unemployment to marginality associated with the rush to cities elsewhere.

These claims, and Mao's personal contributions to Chinese development, are considered below. But in assessing Mao Zedong's contributions to the theory and practice of political economy it is essential to comprehend their origins. I begin, therefore, with the years in the maquis when Mao and his associates formulated and implemented the essential elements of the political economy of people's war. I then turn to the People's Republic, focusing on the years 1955–1960 when Mao advanced and implemented his most distinctive concepts associated with the political economy of uninterrupted revolution, notably collectivization, communization, and the Great Leap Forward. I conclude with a discussion of Mao's thought and practice in relationship to the political economy of guerrilla war, the Soviet model, and alternative Chinese formulations.

Mao and the Political Economy of People's War

Mao's most fruitful contributions to political economy took shape in the course of two decades in the countryside (1928–1949), a product of the attempt to forge mobilization strategies directed toward two complementary yet, in practice, sometimes contradictory goals: social transformation emphasizing the reduction of exploitation and gross inequality of wealth and power, on the one hand, and survival and economic advance, on the other. While substantial attention has been paid to Mao's role as a guerrilla and political leader, his innovations in the realm of political economy remain less well known.

My discussion of the political economy of people's war and Mao's contribution to it focuses on those ideas and institutions which, while forged under harsh conditions in China's guerrilla base areas, bear relevance to the problematic of development—including socialist development—in the People's Republic and in other contemporary poor agrarian nations.

Beginning from a single small poverty-stricken base in Northwest China in 1935, in the course of a decade the Communist Party and its army came to administer far-flung territories behind Japanese lines across North and Central China. By the time of Japan's surrender in 1945 the inhabitants of the Communist-led base areas numbered nearly 100 million people. Cut off from major cities and the international economy, and subject to repeated attack and blockade by Japanese (and in the late war years Guomindang) forces, each of the nineteen base areas perforce constructed an independent and self-sufficient economy with the capacity to sustain the war effort.

In the years 1928–1945 Mao Zedong emerged as the principal theoretician and architect of the political, military, and economic principles first of guerrilla warfare and land revolution and subsequently, in the course of the anti-Japanese resistance, of people's war. Six principles of the political economy of people's war implemented in the wartime base areas are at the heart of the synthesis Mao called the New Democracy. Operating in a milieu for which Marxism and Marxism-Leninism provided few guidelines, the theory and practice that emerged from the first great people's war, combining a national liberation struggle with what might be styled protosocialist reforms, constitute a richly creative contribution.[1]

Self-sufficiency and Self-reliance

The political economy of the base areas was a response to conditions of scarcity, deprivation, and instability. The development of an economy capable not only of assuring subsistence for peasant producers, but of providing a modest surplus to support the resistance military and government in the face of repeated attack and blockade was essential for the survival and growth of the movement. The responses of the party-army to these strictures included the formation of the institutional economy with military and governmental units made responsible for producing substantial portions of their own food and supplies. Modeled in part on frontier military colonies going back at least to the Han dynasty, the self-reliance strategy was extended from the populace to the military and government as all were enjoined to produce. From this experience derives the Maoist premise that untapped labor resources could be mobilized to good economic effect. While the focus of the self-reliant institutional economy was the production of food, military and governmental units also initiated small factories and workshops producing everything from clothing to weapons. Self-reliance was also predicated in part on the mobilization of such underutilized or untapped sources of labor as women and the elderly to boost the economy in diverse ways, from home cotton-spinning to making shoes to field work.

In contradistinction to its Guomindang rival, whose economy and government finance were deeply bound up with international markets, capital, and foreign aid, and which never developed an effective rural policy, the isolated base area governments, cut off from international and even Chinese markets and external resources, had no choice but to rely principally on their own resources and to place agrarian and handicraft concerns at the center of their agenda—no choice, that is, short of defeat.

Rent and Interest Reduction and Tax Reform as Gradual Land Reform

The focus of political mobilization and economic transformation in the Jiangxi Soviet period (1928–1934) was confiscatory land reform and antilandlord struggle. As early as 1926–1927 Mao was drawn to the explosive revolutionary power and potential of the poorest and most oppressed of the peasants, and in the base areas he vigorously promoted land reform. Nevertheless, what most clearly distinguished Mao's perspective from that of many of his comrades in the late 1920s and early 1930s was his sensitive handling of the problem of the middle peasants: the recognition that the battle for support of the large group of owner cultivators could determine the success or failure of the guerrilla movement. Mao therefore came to emphasize narrowing the target of attack in the land reform and reassuring owner cultivators that their property was safe from confiscation. The land laws of the Central Soviet that were most closely associated with Mao's authorship called for redistribution not of all land but only of the surplus land of landlords and rich peasants above a specified subsistence level.[2] This sensitivity to the possibilities of mobilizational politics in the service of redistributive justice for the poor, coupled with the necessity to assure justice for owner cultivators, was characteristic of Mao's leadership style of coalition building and the encouragement of economic equity and growth during this period. These policies were all the more critical to the success of the wartime base areas in North China where tenancy rates were low and where owner cultivators constituted the overwhelming majority of peasant households.

With the Guomindang-Communist united front providing the political framework for the anti-Japanese resistance, the Communists abandoned the confiscatory provisions of earlier land policy. The attempt to transform agrarian relations in the base areas continued, however. The double reduction policy (rent and interest reduction) and tax reform held the key to the party's reform policy implemented in the base areas in the early 1940s. The rent and interest reduction movement derived, in the spirit of the united front, from Guomindang legislation ratified but never implemented in the late 1920s. It illustrates the astute use of reformist policies to foster revolutionary goals. Landlords and rich peasants faced income reductions but their right to collect rent was assured, and many remained loyal to the anti-Japanese resistance. In tandem with the progressive tax policies of the 1940s, policies which shifted the tax burden from the poor to the more prosperous, rent and interest reduction inaugurated a quiet revolution.

Within the framework of sustaining the wartime united front with landlords and rich peasants and of promoting the self-sufficient economy, rent and tax reform provided the vehicles for gradually but decisively reducing the wealth and power of traditional powerholders and building an economy of more or less homogeneous owner cultivators. The task was facilitated by two facts. First, in North China, where the base areas were centered, landlords were far weaker than those in wealthier and more productive central and southern areas. Second, landlord and other elite families rallied to the patriotic resistance and smoothed the path for reform. With nationalist unity legitimating the reform process, the wartime communist movement generally succeeded both in preserving the multiclass united front in the base areas and in assisting the poor to rise through restrained and gradual redistributive policies. Rent reduction did not formally challenge the landlord-tenant relationship, but in conjunction with tax reform it undermined the power of the landlord class. Rent reduction and anticorruption campaigns frequently involved struggle meetings to attack and humiliate recalcitrant landlords and arouse tenant and poor-peasant activism, a process symbolic of the transfer of power from the old elite to the party of the poor.

Mutual Aid and Cooperation

As the base areas contracted under the brunt of the Japanese offensive in the years 1942–1943, Mao and other party leaders called for mutual aid and cooperation as a supplement to the dominant household economy and a means to overcome the economic crisis. The basic strategy was the pooling of resources and labor among small groups of households (frequently with state financial and organizational support) in an effort to rationalize labor and promote both agriculture and sideline enterprise. By 1943 Mao saw in these modest cooperative experiments not only a way out of the wartime economic and financial crisis but the seeds of the great transformation which revolution would eventually bring to China's countryside:

> Among the peasant masses for several thousand years the individual economy has prevailed with one family, one household, as the economic unit. This kind of dispersed individual economy is the basis for feudal control and causes the peasants themselves to succumb to permanent impoverishment. The only method to overcome such a situation is to gradually collectivize [*jitihua*], and the only road to achieve collectivization, as Lenin said, is through cooperatives [*hezuoshe*].[3]

Mao's evocation of Lenin underlined the long-range significance he attributed to the small-scale cooperatives. In portraying cooperatives as a bridge to a socialist future, however, Mao emphasized that the party's wartime cooperative program was far different from the collective farming of Stalin's Soviet Union. "Our economy is a new democratic one, and our cooperatives [*hezuoshe*], built using collective labor, rest on the foundation of the individual economy (on the foundation of private property)."

Mao's discussion of the fledgling cooperatives of the war period suggests three conclusions: first, a clear conceptualization of a theory of stages in which the individual peasant economy supplemented by rudimentary but growing cooperative institutions constituted the heart of the New Democratic economy. The party would not raise peasant anxieties by taking measures that challenged the primacy of the household economy; but it would gradually encourage and support a kernel of semisocialist cooperatives within the predominant household economy. Second, no later than 1943, Mao had reached a conclusion that he would never alter: Collectivization of the Soviet type—that is large-scale, mechanized collective agriculture—was the essence of the socialist transition in the countryside, the road that China would ultimately travel in building a modern socialist economy. Finally, Mao's wartime discussion of cooperation is the clearest available indication that he was already struggling with the theoretical and practical issues of the socialist transition in China, a technologically backward agrarian nation. Just as the late Marx was intrigued with the possibility of building socialism in agrarian Russia on the cooperative foundations of the mir, Mao pondered the possibility that protosocialist cooperative institutions, based on and further developing traditional Chinese forms of mutual aid, could provide a bridge to socialism.[4]

Mixed Economy: State, Cooperative, and Household Sectors

The principal axis of the wartime base area economy was private ownership and cultivation of the land and household sidelines. In the late war years, however, with the growth of cooperatives and of the institutional economy, under the direction of the party, army, and government, cooperatives gave rise to a mixed economy with the private sector predominant. Already during the wartime period conflicts periodically erupted among the sectors, and official power at times formalistically favored the state and the coops at the expense of the household sector, frequently with negative effects on the economy. Nevertheless, in the face of foreign invasion and civil war, the household, cooperative, and state sectors for the most part coexisted and, within the limits of severe financial constraints, served the needs both of government and of popular welfare.

The Market: Stimulus and Control

One area of tension was the market. Throughout the war years, with the base areas subject to repeated blockade and scorched earth tactics, the struggle for the market was crucial: not only were the contestants the Japanese, the Guomindang, and the Communists, but within the base areas, the emerging party-state sometimes clashed with private peddlers. When Japanese and puppet forces imposed a tight blockade on the exposed Central Hebei region, for example, villagers were deprived of salt and other prime necessities. In North China plain localities where the soil was saline, base area governments encouraged such traditional solutions as running water through soil placed in a sieve and then boiling the resulting sediment. In this way households not only alleviated the impact of the blockade by producing a form of slightly bitter salt, but also reaped as a byproduct saltpeter, which the resistance forces used for land mines. Japanese efforts to crack down on this native industry were hampered by the fact that both salt and explosives could be produced by individual households. At the same time the area governments encouraged and protected local merchants in efforts to run the blockade, not only to assure supplies of salt but to trade in grain, cloth, and other commodities traditionally available in periodic markets.

The trade policies of the base areas promoted self-sufficiency and exchange, not autarky. Traders were particularly encouraged to import necessities to solve problems of military supply and livelihood. To be sure, the state sometimes cracked down on the import of luxury of goods and items deemed of a feudal or superstitious character. On balance, however, Mao and his associates recognized the economic contribution of commerce to the economy of the base areas and the livelihood of the people and sought to protect it.

Frugality and Improving the Livelihood of the People

A similar tension existed around this pair of principles. On the one hand Mao and base area administrators attempted with considerable success to encourage frugality through an egalitarian system of subsistence rations in the ranks of the army and administration and by curbing luxury consumption. On the other hand, the resistance government, within the constraints of the war milieu and the poverty characteristic of the base areas, encouraged individuals and groups to improve their livelihood, using both the cooperative movement and the production campaign to praise and reward individual as well as cooperative prosperity. The party's promise and premise were that it would help to improve people's livelihood, and within the limits of wartime austerity it made vigorous efforts to do so. As Mao put it, characteristically linking the economic and the political, "The primary aspect of our work is not to ask things of the people but to give things to the people. What can we give the people? Under present conditions in the Shen-Gan-Ning Border Region, we can organize, lead and help the people to develop production and increase their material wealth. And on this basis we can step-by-step raise their political awareness and their cultural level."[5] The central principle that Mao advanced in the war years and after was that of mutual prosperity (*gongtong fuyu*), building on foundations of both cooperation and the household economy to raise rural incomes and solidify the bonds between party and people.

By 1942 Mao had asserted that the political economy of the resistance bases, far from representing mere ad hoc survival measures, constituted a new and important economic model: "The reason that this is a new model is that it is neither the old Bismarckian model of the national economy nor the new Soviet model of the national economy but it is the national economy of the New Democracy or the Three People's Principles."[6] The claim that a distinctive political economy of self-reliant, cooperative and egalitarian development had emerged in the base areas is valid, and its relevance is certainly not limited to China. The political economy of people's war embodied Mao's most important theoretical and practical contributions to political economy.

Mao and the Political Economy of the Transition to Socialism

Mao had charted the winning strategy of the countryside surrounding the city, and his career as a leader rested on his ability to build political coalitions that would effectively tap the revolutionary potential of broad strata of the peasantry. Yet as the Communist Party moved toward the assumption of national power, Mao signaled the start of a new era and new priorities: After two decades in the countryside, he said, the period "of the city leading the village has now begun. The center of gravity of the party's work has shifted from the village to the city."[7] Indeed, as the party leadership shifted its base from the countryside to the city, and as China's top political and military leaders took up residence in the Forbidden City, once home to the emperors, the tension between city and countryside and between officials and people would constitute central axes of conflict around which China's distinctive political economy would unfold. Mao's personal preoccupation would remain the countryside, particularly the creation of viable forms of cooperation, collectivization, and communization. Yet his views of the full range of socioeconomic issues, particularly the development of nationalized heavy industry, while less fully articulated and less distinctive, nevertheless also decisively shaped the contours of China's socialist development trajectory.

With these issues at the center of the discussion, as they were at the center of Mao's own preoccupations, I turn to the political economy of the transition to socialism in the early People's Republic.

A striking feature of the early 1950s is the new socialist party-state's fidelity to core principles of the political economy of people's war in the evolution of rural policy. The national slogan of the era urged Chinese to model themselves on their big brothers, the Soviet Union, but in agriculture, where China's leaders had abundant experience, there was much continuity with principles of the guerrilla economy. In contrast to the early years of Soviet socialism in which the Bolshevik Party remained institutionally and politically aloof from, and largely indifferent to, the countryside, except as a critical source of state revenue and supplies, the Chinese Communist Party, with deep roots in the countryside, continued its efforts to uplift and transform rural economy and society. Following the redistributive land reform, the core of this strategy, one with no significant Soviet precedent, but with rich experience in China's rural base areas, was the commitment to gradual voluntary cooperation as the bridge to socialism and development in the countryside.

Building on the Chinese Communist Party's long and fruitful rural experience, and aware of the heavy price the Soviet people had paid for Stalinist forced collectivization, Mao and his fellow leaders initiated a socialist development path that wedded the permanent elimination of landlord exploitation and popular forms of cooperation with efforts to promote the prosperity of the peasantry.[8] Even as it moved to channel a substantial part of the rural surplus into productive investment in the years immediately following land reform, the party permitted a portion of the fruits of redistribution and rising productivity to be consumed by peasant producers enjoying the bounty of land and peace.

If Mao and China had embarked on a distinctive road to building a socialist agriculture, in the early years of the People's Republic their approach to industry was orthodox, borrowing heavily, perhaps even slavishly, from Soviet experience and priorities. Mao shared the leadership consensus that placed the highest priority on the development of nationalized heavy industry. Chinese industrialization closely followed Soviet precedent in essentials ranging from the emphasis on capital-intensive, centralized heavy industry with steel at its core to one-man management of nationalized factories. Moreover, virtually cut off from trade, aid, or investment with its traditional trading partners, as a result of the U.S. blockade beginning in the Korean War, China's First Five-Year Plan was heavily dependent on Soviet and East European technical assistance, blueprints, trade, oil and modest amounts of financial aid. The 156 core industrial projects, with their enormous Soviet component, were the heart of the plan.

In the years 1955–1960, spanning the "high tide" of collectivization in agriculture and the Great Leap Forward, the combination of the crisis of the First Five-Year Plan (1953–1957) and Mao's discontent with both industrial and agricultural progress and priorities gave rise to a second Maoist economic vision and model for China's socialist (and communist) development and led the nation to embark on a frenzy of socioeconomic transformation and economic activity. If the political economy of people's war constituted Mao's first important synthesis, the political economy of the Great Leap Forward represents a second attempt to define an independent Chinese road.[9]

Just as the economic and military crisis of the years 1942–1944 contributed to the crystallization of the people's war model, the crisis of the First Five-Year Plan in the summer of 1955 gave rise to the train of thought and activity that culminated in collectivization and the Great Leap.[10] The essential problems of development in the poor agrarian Chinese nation as Mao then perceived them were three: First, by the summer of 1955 it became clear that the ambitious industrialization targets of the plan were jeopardized by the lagging productivity of agriculture. Second, despite rapid industrialization, China faced mounting problems of urban unemployment and rural underemployment, a phenomenon aggravated by the capital-intensive industrial priorities of the plan and substantial urban migration. Finally, Mao became convinced that class polarization was once again becoming acute in the countryside, and that this and other rural and developmental problems required the abandonment of the strategy of gradual, voluntary cooperation in favor of sharply accelerated collectivization.

Out of these concerns Mao initiated a mobilization strategy designed to cut the Gordian knot: The problems of economic and technical development and social transformation could be simultaneously solved by a strategy of permanent revolution that began with instant universal collectivization. But village-level collectives had barely been formed before Mao insisted that a Chinese nation which he termed "poor and blank" could march forward to communism with its promise of abundance and the elimination of the "three great differences" between industry and agriculture, worker and peasant, and mental and manual labor.

Drawing in part on inspiration from the earlier successful national mobilization which had permitted the defeat of Japan and the U.S.-backed Guomindang, Mao stressed the power of ideological and institutional transformation to resolve the economic problems confronting the People's Republic.

The discussion seeks to extract the central principles of Mao's synthesis of the collectivization–Great Leap years to differentiate it both from the people's war and the Soviet models, and to assess its significance.[11]

In the summer and fall of 1955 the process of gradual voluntary socialist transition, that is, the building of a cooperative framework for the rural economy—projected to take place over a fifteen-year period—was abruptly terminated when Mao overrode the Central Committee consensus and pressed for universal collectivization. In less than one year, virtually the entire countryside, including large areas of Central and South China that had little or no experience with mutual aid or elementary forms of cooperation, was organized in large, state-imposed collectives coinciding with the natural village. In the same stroke China abandoned the premise that cooperation would advance in step with the technical transformation of agriculture so that by the time of collectivization industry would provide the tractors, diesel engines, fertilizer, and other modern inputs to facilitate the transition, thereby demonstrating the superiority of large-scale, mechanized collective agriculture. The same processes would permit the training of a corps of skilled cooperative leaders and permit resolution of some of the complex problems associated with a shift from individual and household to group farming.[12] It was not to be.

"The cooperative," model regulations explained, "must not violate the interests of any poor peasant, or any middle peasant."[13] Yet beginning with the collectivization of 1955–1956 and reaching a peak in the Great Leap Forward of 1958–1960 one discerns a profound disjuncture between official claims and experienced reality. The claim was that China's peasantry, above all the rural poor, were the beneficiaries of policies bringing mutual prosperity, equality, participation and liberation from the travails of the market, gains which, in varying degrees, were won through the party's wartime reforms, land reform, and early phases of mutual aid and cooperation. The realities confronting the peasantry in the years after 1955 were the imposition of large collectives and communes and a constellation of anti-market and grain-first mobilizing policies. These undermined the rural incentive structure, deprived peasant households of autonomy, and created a structure of dependence on collective leaders and the state. Rural producers were deprived of traditional sources of income in sideline and market activities which were eliminated or monopolized by the state. The result of this constellation of policies, intensified by bad weather, was the famine disaster of the great leap whose principal victims were the collectivized and communized peasantry.[14]

Collectivization was the center of a constellation of policies that promised everything to the peasantry—abundance, industrialization, education, and welfare—but in practice brought to an end many of the most innovative and certainly the most hopeful elements of the political economy of people's war, land reform and the early transition. The two central points are these: First, the collective replaced the household economy not with the cooperative economy of the associated producers but, as in the Soviet-type collectives on which they were modeled, with centralized statist institutions. In the name of socialism, collectives and communes sapped popular initiative and enforced high accumulation and low consumption on rural producers. Second, collectives and communes provided a convenient vehicle for transferring a significant portion of the rural surplus to China's costly heavy industry program. Collective self-reliance meant not only the budgetary priority of heavy industry (state investment would focus on heavy industry, the countryside would make do with collective investment), but also that in the course of the Mao era heavy industry never structured its output in the service of agriculture.[15] Quite the contrary, the subsidy of the countryside to the city and to industry, predominantly in the form of high compulsory agricultural sales to the state at low fixed prices, continued unabated during Mao's lifetime. The unstated premise accompanying Mao's emphasis on large collectives and self-reliance was the extraction of rural resources to fuel heavy industry. Agriculture was left to develop through a combination of institutional restructuring, labor mobilization, and the use of traditional inputs.[16] Carried to disastrous extremes during the Great Leap, the insistence on ever larger collective forms (the communes) and unremitting pressures to raise accumulation, eliminate sideline enterprise, household production, and private markets, and achieve instant advance to communism led to nationwide famine.

Following the sobering lessons of the Leap, Mao and other leaders never again implemented such extreme economic measures. And, with the important exception of the economic disasters of the Leap and the downturn at the height of the Cultural Revolution, the Chinese economy not only achieved rapid industrialization, particularly the growth of heavy industry, but succeeded in feeding (if at low levels) a population of one billion people, and assuring large gains in life expectancy, nutrition, and health services for the general population. By contrast with India and a number of other large agrarian states, China's economic performance—with the single disastrous exception of the Great Leap famine—appears impressive. The point, however, is that inherent features of the antimarket collectivism carried to fundamentalist limits in the years 1955–1960 continued in essentials (in less extreme form) during the remaining years of the Mao period. The collective system pitted the interests of substantial portions of the peasantry, including the rural poor, against the guardians of the state and left unrealized both the political and the economic promise inherent in the goals of achieving common prosperity. Two decades of Maoist collectivism left per capita incomes of China's eight hundred million peasants at levels comparable to those of the early 1950s, and the countryside facing problems of mounting population pressure on the land and labor surplus.

Conclusion

How is one to explain the disjuncture in the political economy of Mao Zedong, the break in the party's performance, and the yawning gap between theory and practice with particular reference to the welfare of the peasantry? It should be noted at the outset that important continuities in Mao's thought and practice run through both periods: These include the fierce commitment to eliminate exploitation and property-based inequality; the emphasis on political mobilization, class struggle, and political and ideological transformation and their relationship to economic development; the proclivity to replace the market and the household economy by large cooperative, collective, and state institutions; and the emphasis on self-reliance and the suspicion of intellectuals and technical personnel. All these themes are traceable to earlier periods of Mao's leadership, and several are consistent with Marxist and/or Stalinist thought.

The principal reasons for the disjuncture are these: First, the difference between the imperatives of survival and growth in the guerrilla milieu of people's war and those of sustaining power after 1949 help one to understand the party's emphasis in the early period on solving concrete problems of peasant livelihood and pressing for reforms if and only if a substantial popular base existed for their implementation. To be sure, destructive fundamentalist tendencies surfaced repeatedly in earlier periods, for example, in the 1942 party rectification movement and the terrorist extremes of the Jiangxi period and 1947 land reforms. The point, however, is that survival imperatives contributed to the party's willingness to back away quickly from costly alienating and unproductive policies that threatened the broad base of its support and to respond to popular ideas and demands. These pressures were greatly reduced after the establishment of the People's Republic, the elimination of major class antagonists, and the organization of the party-state throughout city and countryside and in collective and state institutions.

Second, one notes the increasing rigidity of Mao's leadership and his growing distance from actual conditions in the countryside in the years following collectivization, the failure of the Leap, and the plunge into famine. The problem lay less in the fact that China committed major errors in collectivization and the Great Leap and more in the inability of the system to respond creatively to the signals of distress and resistance. Beginning with Mao's angry and defensive reaction to the muted criticism of his policies in the Great Leap by Marshall Peng Dehuai (Mao had Peng purged of his positions), and continuing with the hardening of Mao's critique of the Soviet Union and of capitalist roaders within the Communist Party, the opportunity for flexible responses to disastrous policies was sharply reduced. Calls for change subsequently risked being branded as examples of lèse majesté or the machinations of capitalist roaders as China moved toward the fundamentalist politics and personality cult of the Cultural Revolution. The result was a hardening of policy options as China turned away from many of the most hopeful and fruitful developmental and protosocialist policies of an earlier era. In the process, the peasantry bore the major brunt of extremist policies: As rural incomes stagnated, the gap between city and countryside increased and the oppressive character of collective institutions and bondage to the land grew. Pressures for rural change mounted but found no outlet during Mao's lifetime.

This analysis suggests that the golden age of Maoist political economy spanned the years of the Anti-Japanese Resistance and continued into the early 1950s. The lessons from that period, particularly the possibilities of creating a mixed economy involving the interaction of state, cooperative, and private sectors and of market and plan, the encouragement of individual and cooperative prosperity, the integration of intellectuals and peasants in a common effort, merits further study as China's leaders in the 1980s again grapple with rethinking the parameters of the socialist economy and society.

Notes

1. Mao's most comprehensive economic statement is his 1942 book-length manuscript, "Economic and Financial Problems," in Andrew Watson, *Mao Zedong and the Political Economy of the Border Region: A Translation of Mao's Economic and Financial Problems* (London: Cambridge University Press, 1980). I first explored issues of the wartime economy in *The Yenan Way in Revolutionary China* (Cambridge: Harvard University Press, 1971). This chapter draws on subsequent collaborative research with Edward Friedman, Kay Johnson, and Paul Pickowicz. See our forthcoming *Chinese Village, Socialist State*. See also Peter Schran's *Guerrilla Economy: The Development of the Shensi-Kansu-Ninghsia Border Region, 1937–1945* (Albany: State University of New York, 1976); Pauline Keating, "Beyond Land Revolution: The Rent Reduction Campaigns in the Shaanganning Border Region, 1937–1946," Australian National University, *Papers in Far Eastern History* 36 (September 1987): 1–52; and Yung-fa Chen, *Making Revolution: The Communist Movement in East and Central China, 1937–1945* (Berkeley: University of California Press, 1986), particularly chapters 6 and 7.

2. John Rue, *Mao Tse-tung in Opposition, 1927–1935* (Stanford: Stanford University Press, 1966), pp. 189–203.

3. This and the following quotation are from Mao's 1943 talk "Zuzhichilai" (Get organized), in *Mao Zedong ji* (Collected works of Mao Zedong), ed. Takeuchi Minoru, 9:88–89. As early as 1926 Mao had written appreciatively and in some detail about cooperatives in "Nongcun hezuoshe wenti jueyian" (Draft resolution on the problems of village cooperatives), ibid., pp. 227–28. I would like to thank Cheng Tiejun for calling this document to my attention, and for his discussion of the issues posed in this chapter.

4. Teodor Shanin, *Late Marx and the Russian Road: Marx and the Peripheries of Capitalism* (New York: Monthly Review Press, 1983), particularly the pioneering scholarship of Wada Haruki on "Marx and Revolutionary Russia," pp. 40–76.

5. Watson, *Mao Zedong*, pp. 23–24.

6. Ibid., p. 25. When *The Selected Works of Mao Tse-tung* were published in 1953, the claim of model was sharply reduced with the insertion of this passage in the text: "This self-supporting economy, which has been developed by the troops and the various organizations and schools, is a special product of the special conditions of today. It would be unreasonable and incomprehensible in other historical conditions, but it is perfectly reasonable and necessary at present" (3:112).

7. "Report to the Second Plenary Session of the Seventh Central Committee" (1949), *Selected Works of Mao Tse-tung* (Beijing: Foreign Languages Press, 1965), 4:363.

8. Mark Selden, *The People's Republic of China: A Documentary History of Revolutionary Change* (New York: Monthly Review Press, 1978), pp. 234–40. In 1950 Mao, no less than Liu Shaoqi and other central leaders, pressed the "rich peasant line" emphasizing the right and wisdom of encouraging individual households, as well as cooperative units, to prosper.

9. The fullest statement of Mao's political economy in these years is his "Reading Notes on the Soviet Text Political Economy," in *A Critique of Soviet Economics* (New York: Monthly Review Press, 1977).

10. The crisis of the plan is perceptively analyzed in Kenneth Walker, "Collectivism in Retrospect: The 'Socialist High Tide' of Autumn 1955–Spring 1956," *China Quarterly* 26 (April–June 1966): 1–43; Nicholas Lardy, "Economic Recovery and the 1st Five-Year Plan," in *The People's Republic of China*, part 1: *The Emergence of Revolutionary China 1949–1965*, ed. Roderick MacFarquhar and John K. Fairbank, vol. 14 of the *Cambridge History of China* (Cambridge: Cambridge University Press, 1987), pp. 144–84. See also Mark Selden, "Cooperation and Conflict: Cooperative and Collective Formation in China's Countryside" in *The Transition to Socialism in China*, ed. Mark Selden and Victor Lippit (Armonk, N.Y.: M. E. Sharpe, 1982).

11. Two discussions surveying the principles of Mao's economics centered on the synthesis of the collectivization-Leap period are Christopher Howe and Kenneth Walker, "The Economist," in *Mao in the Scales of History*, ed. Dick Wilson (Cambridge: Cambridge University Press, 1977), pp. 174–222, and Maurice Meisner, *Mao's China and After: A History of the People's Republic* (New York: Free Press, 1986), pp. 217–64. See also Carl Riskin, *China's Political Economy: The Quest for Development Since 1949* (Oxford: Oxford University Press, 1987), pp. 114–47, and Nicholas Lardy, "The Chinese Economy," in *The People's Republic of China*, ed. MacFarquhar and Fairbank, pp. 360–90.

12. The best articulated alternative strategies were those advanced by Chen Yun and Deng Zihui. Chen Yun, minister of commerce, and Deng Zihui, head of the party's Rural Work Department and a principal proponent of gradual transition, were most sensitive to issues of peasant welfare in the inner-party struggles over collectivization and the Great Leap Forward. While Chen sought to prevent the annihilation of markets, Deng was a central figure urging gradual, voluntary cooperation and the most important advocate of the household contract systems that emerged in the early 1960s; he is, in important respects, the forefather of the agrarian reforms of the 1980s. See Jiang Boying, *Deng Zihui zhuan* (Biography of Deng Zihui) (Shanghai: People's Publishing House, 1986); Nicholas Lardy and Kenneth Lieberthal, *Chen Yun's Strategy for China's Economic Development: A Non-Maoist Alternative* (Armonk, N.Y.: M. E. Sharpe, 1983).

13. "Model Regulations for an Agricultural Producers' Cooperative," in *Agricultural Cooperation in China*, ed. Tung Talin (Beijing: Foreign Languages Press, 1959), p. 99.

14. The dimensions of the Great Leap famine are explored in Thomas Bernstein, "Stalinism, Famine and Chinese Peasants," *Theory and Society* 13 (May 3, 1984): 339–77. My critique of Maoist political economy in the collective era, underlining the

disjuncture between goals and reality, is spelled out in *The Political Economy of Contemporary China* (Armonk, N.Y.: M. E. Sharpe, 1988). The theme is further explored in Edward Friedman, Paul Pickowicz, and Mark Selden with Kay Johnson, *Chinese Village, Socialist State* (forthcoming).

15. Howe and Walker, "The Economist," p. 191. The issue of extraction of the rural surplus is explored in Chih-ming Ka and Mark Selden, "Original Accumulation, Equity and Late Industrialization: The Cases of Socialist China and Capitalist Taiwan," *World Development* 14, 10/11 (October 1986): 1293–1310.

16. Steve Reglar's interesting essay, "Mao Zedong as a Marxist Political Economist: A Critique," on this point follows a long tradition of theoretical work in confining the analysis to discussion of Marxist and Maoist texts and ignoring policy and its consequences, even when the two are diametrically opposite. Reglar finds, for example, that "The necessary manipulation of exchanges between industry and agriculture to promote a Stalinist unequal exchange in favour of industry was rejected by Mao, as was a policy of granting light industrial development a low priority." *Journal of Contemporary Asia* 17, 2 (1987): 209. The points noted by Reglar, based on a reading of Mao's "Ten Major Relationships" and "Reading Notes on the Soviet Union's Political Economy," are virtual mirror images of Chinese policy implemented throughout the period of Mao's rule. Indeed, on these points, Chinese practice was even more extreme, and more costly, than was that of the Soviet Union in the Stalin era.

4

ON THE ORGANIZATION OF PRODUCTION UNDER SOCIALISM

Peter Schran

Mao Zedong's successors have done away with the great helmsman's legacy in theory and practice to an extent and at a pace that hardly any student of things Chinese thought likely ten years ago. Yet in retrospect, their drastic modification of his relentless efforts to devise and force China's transition to socialism and communism must ring bells of déjà vu in the minds of many students of Marxism and Soviet socialism elsewhere in the world, where similar changes have been made on comparable occasions during earlier years. This is true in particular of ideas and policies relating to the organization of production, which are central and critical to any attempt to remake society in Marx's image.

It is possible to argue that all of these responses, in China as well as elsewhere, were inevitable because the strategies they corrected were exercises in futility. From a different ideological vantage point, such a critique might extend to the fundamentals of Marxism.[1] Short of this comprehensive rejection, it could be held within the confines of doctrine that at some point in the evolution of thought and action, errors were introduced that produced the deviations that had to be reversed. Communist reformers, in China and elsewhere, typically have taken this latter approach, without always succeeding in legitimating their revisions.

In the end, the issue of doctrinal legitimacy reduces to what can be rendered compatible in one form or the other with the ideas of the founders of "scientific socialism," Karl Marx and Friedrich Engels, and with the commentaries of those principal disciples, notably Lenin, who are not being doubted. The following pages will explore these possibilities and the use that has been made of them, first elsewhere and eventually in China.

The Views of the Founding Fathers

It is well known that Marx and Engels chose to say very little about the characteristics of socialism and communism. The principal features of the future order followed antithetically from their critique of capitalism, but in their opinion its numerous details could not be predicted with any confidence. They felt compelled to comment on such matters only to rebut the "utopian" views of other critics of capitalism, whom they considered mistaken on various grounds. For this reason, their statements tended to be selective and unsystematic in terms of issues as well as negatively phrased and polemical, frequently leaving it to the reader to make the proper inferences with respect to the "true" future state of affairs.

Marx's assertions about the characteristics of communism and the socialist transition to this final stage have been collected, systematized, and analyzed by Fred Gottheil.[2] Together with related statements from Engels' *Anti-Dühring*,[3] which offers more details about the founders' vision of the future, they support the following scenario:

1. Socialism and communism would originate not in the abstract, unrelated to any other phenomenon, but in response and as solutions to the problems posed by the process of capitalist development. Socialist and communist forms of organization therefore could not be imagined freely, as the "utopian" socialists were prone to do, but would be implied by this process, to be inferred "scientifically."

2. Capitalism would perish because its characteristic form of organization, the market, which facilitated commodity economy and the capitalists' drive to accumulate, would be unable to sustain the further development of the productive forces. Its "anarchy" and the chaos it produced therefore would have to be replaced by a system of macroeconomic planning, which would coordinate the activities of all formerly private enterprises consciously in the common interest.

3. The transition to central coordination at the national level would be the culmination of a process of economic concentration under capitalism. The development of the productive forces had led already to the emergence of "large-scale industry," owned by a few coupon-clipping capitalists and run for them by hired employees. The former were to be expropriated, the latter to be placed under the new central direction and control.

4. The new forms of appropriation and organization could be cooperative as well as societal. The workers' cooperative had appeared already in capitalist times as a positive step toward more advanced forms of "association." The farmers' cooperative was a similarly useful device in moving beyond small-scale production in agriculture. Capitalist state monopolies were sure to remain in the hands of the state, and means of production

generally would have to be owned by society at large, as represented at first by the state, to prevent the exercise of special interests, notably by the cooperatives.

5. The forms of management, about which Marx and Engels had least to say, apparently would be determined by the technical requirements of production, which would change with the further development of the productive forces, as follows: The increasing mechanization of production would serve to simplify most work, and the improving education of the workers would qualify them for more assignments, so that specialization and permanent division of labor would diminish and disappear.

6. Labor and work incentive would be assured in this new situation first, under socialism, by "distribution according to labor," which would force everyone—former capitalists as well as proletarians—to work for a living, but which would also allow for unequal labor shares in recognition of the continuing inequality of labor power. With the development of production and diminishing division of labor, labor would become a "joy" instead of a "burden" for all, and it would be possible to change to "distribution according to need" as the form appropriate for communism.

In short, based on their analysis of capitalist development, Marx and Engels hypothesized dialectically a future economy that would be behaviorally cooperative rather than competitive, with central coordination (as long) as needed, oriented at meeting common human needs rather than individual profit objectives. Essential for this state of relations would be the appropriation of all means of production to all people collectively. A more limited socialization and the preservation of competition in any sphere à la Dühring would be incompatible with it:

> There will therefore be rich and poor economic communes, and the leveling out takes place through the population crowding into the rich communes and leaving the poor ones. Thus although Herr Dühring wants to eliminate competition in products between the individual communes by means of the national organisation of trade, he calmly allows competition among the producers to continue. Things are removed from the sphere of competition, but men remain subject to it.
>
> In any case the economic commune has instruments of labor at its disposal for the purpose of production. How is this production carried on? Judging by all Herr Dühring has told us, precisely as in the past, except that the commune takes the place of the capitalists. The most we are told is that for the first time everyone will be free to choose his occupation, and that there will be equal obligation to work.
>
> We have already seen that Dühringian economics comes down to the following proposition: the capitalist mode of *production* is quite good and can remain in existence, but the capitalist mode of *distribution* is evil and must disappear. We now find that Herr Dühring's "socialitarian" system is nothing more than

> the application of this principle in fantasy.[4]

Lenin endorsed the Marx-Engels vision of the future in his *Notebook: Marxism on the State* and in *The State and Revolution.*[5] Although he was preoccupied with the future of the state in these writings, he followed Marx and Engels in relating its "withering away" to changes in the economic base, in production and distribution, which were to be induced by the complete socialization of all means of production after capitalism had created the preconditions. He demanded the "strictest" social and state control of labor and consumption during the transition to ultimate communism, and he outdid Marx and Engels in making light of the managerial problems involved in this process, under the influence of revolutionary optimism in 1917:

> Given these *economic* premises [of universal literacy, of the "training and disciplining" of the labor force, etc.] it is quite possible, after the overthrow of the capitalists and bureaucrats, to proceed immediately, overnight, to supersede them in the *control* of production and distribution, in the work of *keeping account* of labor and products by the armed workers, by the whole of the armed population. (The question of control and accounting must not be confused with the question of the scientifically trained staff of engineers, agronomists and so on. These gentlemen are working today and obey the capitalists; they will work even better tomorrow and obey the armed workers.)
>
> Accounting and control—that is the *main* thing required for the "setting up" and correct functioning of the *first phase* of communist society. *All* citizens are transformed into the salaried employees of the state, which consists of the armed workers. *All* citizens become employees and workers of a *single* national state "syndicate." All that is required is that they should work equally—do their proper share of the work—and get paid equally. The accounting and control necessary for this have been *simplified* by capitalism to an extreme and reduced to the extraordinarily simple operations—which any literate person can perform—of checking and recording, knowledge of the four rules of arithmetic, and issuing receipts.
>
> When the *majority* of the people begin independently and everywhere to keep such accounts and maintain such control over the capitalists (now converted into employees) and over the intellectual gentry who preserve their capitalist habits, this control will really become universal, general, national: and there will be no way of getting away from it, there will be "nowhere to go." The whole of society will have become a single office and a single factory with equality of labor and equality of pay.[6]

Lenin did not go beyond the problem of control in this context. Moreover, his statement may imply that the appropriate forms of national economic planning and direction of production were largely technical issues, to be addressed by the "scientifically trained staff" referred to in the quotation, which would include the managerial personnel of the formerly capitalistic enterprises and state. The development, for example, of wartime economic planning in imperial Germany under von Neurath and of "scientific management" in America by Taylor and others impressed him as relevant advances in this perspective, just as Marx had attributed positive value to piece work. The constructs of Proudhon, Dühring, and others, with their inklings of "market socialism," apparently did not concern him at all.

The Soviet Experience

Soon after the October Revolution, the transition to socialism began to appear much more complicated and protracted. In backward circumstances that did not fit Lenin's earlier premises and which had been aggravated by years of war, the newly formed soviets were not very successful in keeping accounts and controlling production and distribution. For this reason, the move to natural economy under War Communism appeared retrospectively as an excessive advance, even though it had served to achieve victory in the field under chaotic conditions. The great sacrifices that War Communism had imposed on the supporters and prospective beneficiaries of the revolution could not go on for long. Since natural economy evidently could not alleviate these burdens and improve the living of both workers and peasants notably soon, its institution had to be reinterpreted as a premature event, which had to be reversed.

The proper step back was not a return to bourgeois democracy and unrestricted capitalism, Lenin argued, but the adoption of a New Economic Policy (NEP) under Soviet state capitalistic auspices.[7] He called for the restoration of commodity relations in order to reactivate performance incentives among the remnant nonproletarian classes, and especially among the peasants, who accounted for the majority of the Russian population. This return to market economy was to be accomplished, however, without reprivatization of the principal means of production. In particular, land was to remain fully nationalized while the peasant proprietors were to be accorded part of the surplus:

> Why must we replace surplus appropriation by a tax? Surplus appropriation implied confiscation of all surpluses and establishment of a compulsory state monopoly. We could not do otherwise, for our need was extreme. Theoretically speaking, state monopoly is not necessarily the best system from the standpoint of the interests of socialism. A system of taxation and free exchange can be employed as a transitional measure in a peasant country possessing an industry—if this industry is running—and if there is a certain quantity of goods available.
>
> The exchange is an incentive, a spur to the peasant. The proprietor can and will surely make an effort in his own interest when he knows that all his surplus

> produce will not be taken away from him and that he will only have to pay a tax, which should whenever possible be fixed in advance. The basic thing is to give the small farmer an incentive and a spur to till the soil. We must adapt our state economy to the economy of the middle peasant, which we have not managed to remake in three years and will not be able to remake in another ten.[8]

The manufactured goods demanded by the peasants in exchange for their reprivatized surplus could not be provided adequately at once by "large-scale socialist state industry," which remained seriously impaired by the war. Increases in their supply therefore depended in part on the restoration of various forms of "*small* industry" and trade that matched small-scale farming in terms of development.

Lenin understood and accepted in 1921 that this "revival of the petty bourgeoisie and of capitalism on the basis of some freedom of trade (if only local)" would last for some time. Instead of permitting it to proliferate uncontrolled, however, he proposed to "channel it into *state capitalism*," which he considered economically possible. Two avenues in particular appeared promising to him: Concessions to foreign capitalists were to bring much needed capital and technology for the development of large-scale industry, which would reduce supply problems, gradually displace small-scale producers, and eventually become the property of the Soviet state. Fostering "cooperative capitalism," that is, the cooperative organization of small-scale producers and traders, would facilitate "accounting, control, supervision and the establishment of contractual relations between the state (in this case the Soviet state) and the capitalist."[9]

Channeling capitalistic activities in these and other ways[10] could not and was not meant to preclude that the restoration of commodity relations would affect practically all parts of Russia's economy. State enterprises were to be put on a profit basis and become competitive. The consequent reemergence of conflicts of interest between management and labor would necessitate revisions in the role of the trade unions in the state enterprise sector.[11] Above all, state administrative regulations and practices needed to be reformed drastically to assure the effective implementation of the new policies.[12]

Although the return to commodity production and capitalist management practice was thus nearly all-pervasive, the NEP did not ever figure as a permanent retreat in Lenin's thinking. Instead, Soviet state capitalism became an intermediate phase during the transition from early capitalist or even precapitalist formations to socialism, which the Second Congress of the Communist International had declared possible elsewhere as well.[13] As an alternative to private capitalism, it had to phase out like the latter in response to the development of the productive forces and their concentration in ever larger organizations of production, which in imperial Germany, for example, had given rise to bourgeois state capitalism.[14]

For this reason, Lenin proclaimed that "Communism is Soviet power plus the electrification of the whole country"[15] and called further for the formulation of an Integrated Economic Plan for Russia's technical transformation along lines initiated with the Plan for the Electrification of the RSFSR.[16] In addition, however, he considered it possible that "the cooperative policy, if successful, will result in raising the small economy and in facilitating its transition, within an indefinite period, to large-scale production on the basis of voluntary association" without specification of the technical requisites. Accordingly, "cooperative trade is more advantageous and useful than private trade not only for the above-mentioned reasons, but also because it facilitates the association and organization of millions of people, and eventually of the entire population, and this in turn is an enormous gain from the standpoint of the subsequent transition from state capitalism to socialism."[17]

On the eve of Lenin's incapacitation in early 1923, the impact of the NEP had become apparent. Consumer goods production and living conditions were improving notably thanks to the restoration of market economy, but profiteering, speculation, and other objectionable petty bourgeois transgressions were flourishing as well. The foreign capitalists' interest in concessions was disappointingly limited, and the domestic small producers' attraction to cooperatives was far from encouraging. The latter fact moved Lenin to conclude that the step back had been too great:

> We went too far when we introduced NEP, but not because we attached too much importance to the principle of free enterprise and trade—we went too far because we lost sight of the cooperatives, because we now underrate the cooperatives, because we are already beginning to forget the vast importance of the cooperatives from the above two points of view.[18]

To provide more incentive for joining a cause during its infancy, Lenin insisted that the cooperatives be favored politically and privileged financially. Yet he also predicted that in addition to this support, it would take a "veritable revolution," a "period of cultural development," a "distinct historical epoch" of at least one or two decades to transform the entire population into genuine cooperators. Eventually, however, "and given social ownership of the means of production, given the class victory of the proletariat over the bourgeoisie, the system of civilized cooperators is the system of socialism."[19]

The "epoch" of state capitalism and the NEP came to an end in Russia long before this cultural revolution could be achieved. To accelerate the transition to socialism once more, Stalin forced the institution of state planning and the collectivization of farming—with predictions of economies of scale that generally failed to materialize in the circumstances. The market sphere contracted sharply as a consequence. But it did not disappear altogether:

> [T]he state disposes only of the product of the state enterprises, while the *product* of the collective farms being their property, is disposed of only by them. But the collective farms are unwilling to alienate their product except in the form of commodities, in exchange for which they desire to receive the commodities they need. At present the collective farms will not recognize any other economic relation with the town except the commodity relation—exchange through purchase and sale. Because of this, commodity production and trade are as much a necessity with us today as they were thirty years ago, say, when Lenin spoke of the necessity of developing trade to the utmost.
>
> Of course, when instead of the two basic production sectors, the state sector and the collective-farm sector, there will be only one all-embracing production sector, with the right to dispose of all the consumer goods produced in the country, commodity circulation, with its "money economy," will disappear, as being an unnecessary element in the national economy.[20]

Needless to add, this limited justification of commodity production ignored the more fundamental reason for its preservation in all spheres, which Stalin rejected explicitly in his comments on the law of value under socialism.[21] Marx and Engels had tied the emergence of communism to an advanced state of development of the productive forces, which would assure the requisite equality of labor power and abundance of products for distribution according to need. Until then, scarcity would prevail and call for rational (scarcity-conscious) allocation everywhere.

The Western Academic Debate

Until the Russian revolution gave it empirical relevance, the organization of production under socialism was a highly esoteric topic that attracted assorted political visionaries but few academic economists. The *German Verein für Sozialpolitik* debated the issue of socialization for the first time in 1919, when it was a popular political demand in the wake of the lost war. Proponents of the capitalist market system who favored various social reforms argued then as well as at other times that national economic planning and centralized management would probably involve a return to natural economy, organizational diseconomies of scale, work incentive problems, public costs in excess of public benefits and other negative consequences, which would assure the lower productivity and the lesser efficiency of socialism. Most academic socialists agreed with these assertions and joined in the verdict as it applied to the Soviet case. Emil Lederer, for example, held:

> In the most favorite case, when the creation of goods would not experience interruptions and reductions, when the manufacture of means of production would be assured, this method nevertheless would lead to natural economy, viz. to the guarantee of minima. In this bolshevism fatally resembles war economy, and because it has existed until now historically only in a state of war, it leads to regulated autarky; in a state of political peace, it would have to lead to worker mercantilism. Nowhere are its operating conditions such as to enable it to really organize the national economy as a whole. In the contest with the economic machine of international capitalism, which would remain superior for the time being (and which would have the tendency to checkmate it), it therefore would have to succumb or to try to offset capitalism's lead by mercantilistic measures. The method of bolshevism is that of an isolated socialism.[22]

Lederer and others, however, did not accept the proposition that any comprehensive systemic modification would by necessity entail sacrifices of efficiency and wealth. Those with social democratic leanings and an affinity to Marxian thought advocated instead alternative forms of socialization, notably that of managerial power through the institution of codetermination or industrial democracy. Others, especially scholars in Britain and the United States who were more firmly rooted in Marshallian economics, took up the contention of Ludwig von Mises that "a socialist economy must fail because the absence of a free market and a price system would preclude the application of any economic criteria. Against them, others, such as Mr. Dickinson, have proclaimed the possibility of combining a socialist economy with a price-system: a combination which, it is alleged, would provide superior criteria of costs and of demand to those which rule in a capitalist world."[23]

The responses of Oskar Lange, Abba Lerner, and others generated a prolonged debate that eventually established to most everyone's—though not to Mises'—satisfaction that it was conceivable and perhaps practicable to have a system in which all means of production were owned publicly but allocated competitively, like all other factors and products. Workers and managers of socialized enterprises would be expected and instructed to act like their forebears under capitalism as utility and profit maximizing price takers. Wages and prices would be determined through market interactions, which perhaps could be simulated by a planning board or left to occur in actuality. The returns to socialized capital and the profits of socialist enterprises would fund additional investment as well as a "social dividend" that would pay for the collective consumption of cultural, educational, and health services. Aggregate public investment and collective consumption would be decided by the Central Planning Board.

There were arguments over whether it was reasonable to assume that a socialist manager could effectively replace a capitalist entrepreneur, whether this was indeed the alternative, whether the planning of prices would be any easier than the planning of product quantities, whether the socialist market—simulated or actual—could be more "perfect" than the capitalist market with its concentration of power, uncertainty about the future, and so forth. The positions taken on all of these issues reflected in the end conflicting ideological commitments. Libertarians, like Marxists, presumed a correspondence between forms of ownership and forms of organization that made capitalism and a market economy as inseparable from each other as socialism and a centrally planned economy. By negating this link, "market socialists" came into conflict with both.

Unlike the libertarians, socialists of orthodox Marxist or Marxist-Leninist persuasion paid little attention to this tour de force then. A few academics in the West, notably Dobb, questioned the neoclassical premises of the argument.[24] To the Soviets, of course, the construct had to appear as anathema, comparable to the aberrations of Proudhon and of Dühring, which Oskar Lange had to recant when he returned to Poland after the Second World War.

The Expansion of the Soviet System

The establishment of additional people's republics in Eastern Europe and in East Asia after the Second World War put the Soviet Union's "advanced experiences" with socialist transformation to a second test. All of these countries followed the standard pattern which the Soviets had refined through their trials and errors along the road, with few organizational modifications and with variations primarily in their timing of the same transitional steps. Although lip service was paid at first to "national roads to socialism" in recognition of cultural particularities, practically all active proponents of deviations from the Soviet course soon lost their political positions and influence everywhere but in Yugoslavia. Uprisings in East Germany, Poland, and Hungary did little to change the course; far-reaching managerial reforms followed in Hungary much later. In the Soviet Union, interest in Khrushchev's administrative reforms and Liberman's reorganization proposals was short-lived. Moreover, the Soviets' reaction to the "Prague Spring" indicated subsequently that in their dominant opinion, the approved road to socialism remained narrowly defined and prescribed.

Among the newcomers, Mao's China appeared at first as a model student of Marxism-Leninism and Soviet precedents, in spite of its unusual revolutionary history. The essentials of the Soviet system of socialized ownership of the means of production and centralized management of the economy were instituted during an extremely brief period of seven years.[25] The added intermediate phase of people's democracy, which—like Soviet state capitalism—allowed for the transitory existence not only of individual small-scale production in agriculture and handicraft industry but also of traditional retail trade and service establishments, with more limited state ownership and planning, was cut short, contrary to earlier anticipations and pronouncements.

The acceleration of China's socialist transformation halfway through the First Five-Year Plan period appeared to be rational on certain premises. If social change was to set free productive forces, economic development in excess of the forecast could be attributed to people's ideological progress beyond previous expectations, which could be taken to justify even more reorganization in turn, notably the Socialist High Tide in 1956 and the formation of rural people's communes in 1958. The attribution, of course, could be mistaken. Significant exaggerations of such improvements, which had to become visible in unexpected performance problems for no other evident reason, could be corrected correspondingly by appropriate steps back in organization, such as the adjustments of 1957 and the return to a similar pattern during the Three Hard Years.[26]

There were differences of opinion about the correct interpretation of real accomplishments and the speed at which the socialist transformation should be carried out, about the appropriate degree of administrative integration or centralization in planning and management, and so forth. Until the fiasco of the Great Leap Forward and the formation of the rural people's communes were induced in this way, however, there appeared little disagreement about the systemic prototype and the proper directions of change.[27] This became evident especially in the response to Tito's Yugoslavia during its departure from the soviet path. The dismantling of the collectives in favor of reprivatized small-scale farms, crafts, and trades, the transformation of large-scale enterprises into communally (municipally) owned and worker-managed entities, and the reduction of state planning, direction, and control were in the Soviet view "Proudhonist" aberrations. By reinforcing self-seeking behavior in individual as well as in collective units and by reintroducing the anarchy of the market place, the reforms jeopardized progress toward "true" socialism in the near future.

Unlike the Soviets and many Chinese state planners, Mao Zedong was not opposed to limitations on the bureaucratic process, decentralization, and the masses' involvement in management.[28] But he propagated such changes in the context of an effort to move beyond socialism toward communism, away from the market and competition to more comprehensive cooperation and emulation, away from permanent division of labor and state domination to "work for the sake of working" in both production and administration, away from "distribution according to labor" to "distribution according to need." Moreover, he expected this simply fundamentalist vision of social change to become reality in most unlikely technical circumstances, beginning with the Great Leap Forward. The Soviets expressed their consternation and disagreement through charges of "voluntarism" and leftist deviation.[29]

The campaigns of 1958–1959, waged as a "war to conquer nature" that obviously could not be won, gave rise to disruptions and disasters not unlike those encountered under War Communism in Soviet Russia. To cope with these unintended consequences and the people's demoralization, rehabilitative measures in the spirit of the NEP were needed. The first step back in Mao's China was a return not to individual farming and largely free markets but to the organizational arrangements of the First Five-Year Plan period, in fact if not fully in name. Central planning functions were restored and indeed strengthened. The rural people's communes remained in existence but shrank in size and delegated most of their functions in production and distribution to the former cooperatives. Collective consumption was once again restricted in the main to health, education, and welfare services. Private plots and farm markets reappeared, individual material incentive regained importance in the state enterprise sector, and so on.

The reversion to soviet-type planning evidently helped to regenerate China's economic growth. Yet it also reactivated previous concerns that by design, this system could not achieve adequate allocative efficiency. On the eve of the Socialist High Tide of 1956, critics of the accelerated transition therefore had argued for the continuation of "people's democratic" forms of state capitalism and NEP-like policies until the productive forces could develop to the advanced state that the move to socialist relations of production required, according to Marx-Engels and even Lenin. After their premature institution by this criterion, the objection appeared in a new and more fundamental form. So long as the productive forces had yet to develop fully, there would be scarcity and therefore need for scarcity-conscious or rational resource use, irrespective of the form of appropriation of the means of production. Sun Yefang in particular, who had pioneered this interpretation of the Law of Value during the late 1950s, derived from it reform proposals that recommended as the appropriate form of organization a variant of market socialism, generally speaking.[30]

In the Maoist view, which rejected this interpretation as a "bourgeois" aberration, Sun's call constituted a more substantial and more consequential step back toward capitalism. Against it, the "proletarian line" reasserted the primacy of the social relations of production and social consciousness. In explaining the obvious failure of the leap to yield the predicted results, attention was shifted from the limited production possibilities to the failure of the masses and especially of their cadres to demonstrate the ideological progress that had been expected of them. So long as this expectation was upheld as justified, there consequently was cause for a campaign to raise the people's consciousness so that it would match the socialist institutions—rather than for institutional retrogression to fit their less developed state of mind, irrespective of the state of the productive forces.

The Maoist view prevailed.[31] The Socialist Education Campaign and even more so the Great Proletarian Cultural Revolution were instituted to bring about this ideological uplift and adaptation, by all indications to little avail. As a consequence, however, soviet-type socialism persisted, and alternative forms of organization remained anathema for more than a decade.

The Space for Doctrinal Innovation

This cursory review suggests that in Marxist-Leninist thought as well as in soviet-type practice, the organization of production under socialism has remained unchanged in its fundamentals most everywhere until recently. The efficacy of socializing all means of production, centralizing the planning, direction, and control of all economic activities, and distributing according to labor in order to eliminate commodity production has been disputed from the beginning. But the arguments in favor of more limited cooperation, market socialism, worker management, and so forth were ignored or dismissed because they came from outsiders such as "bourgeois vulgar economists" or from comrades who were accused of various rightist aberrations for waging them. In the extreme, Tito's Yugoslavia broke with Stalin's Russia over this issue, and Mao destroyed Liu Shaoqi.

In view of this evident orthodoxy, anyone claiming adherence to the creed and camp has very little latitude in modifying the organization of production. The principal opportunities for doctrinal innovation within the confines established by Marx, Engels, Lenin, Stalin, and the earlier Mao appear to be as follows:

First, it is possible to argue that because the proper correspondences between the social relations of production and the productive forces were ignored or misperceived in the past, social change outpaced economic development so that not only the initiation of the movement toward communism during the Great Leap Forward but even the preceding acceleration of the socialist transformation occurred prematurely. The correction of this "leftist" error would call for the retrogression to "people's democratic" relations of production, which would permit the restitution of individual small-scale farming, manufacturing, and commerce, the reintroduction of joint state-private ventures, the reopening of factor and product markets, and the restriction of state activities in planning, directing, and controlling the operations of all kinds of enterprises, as well as the transactions between them.

Because of the target value of socialism, such a retrogression may have to occur in fact more than in name. Just as the rural people's communes were deprived of most of their systemic functions long before they were abolished, so the collective ownership of land may be preserved formally while it is being eroded substantially by the introduction of tenancy-like responsibility contracts, which may even be viewed as forms of piece work representing distribution according to labor. Correspondingly, the nominal ownership of an enterprise by the entire people may become more and more of a fiction as its profit becomes increasingly the benefit of its labor force and thus comparable to cooperative earnings.

In support of such semantic variations, it is possible to argue in addition that particular institutions or organizational instruments need not have the same significance in different social systems. Just as Engels noted and Lenin stressed that the socialist state was really unlike the capitalist state because of its performance of communal functions,[32] so it could be said, for example, that the socialist market is unlike the capitalist market in that it allows commodity production not to accommodate the private acquisition of surplus value but to facilitate the satisfaction of human needs under conditions of distribution according to labor.[33] Moreover, the change in meaning could be indicated by a new label, in analogy to Engels' proposal to call the future state *Gemeinwesen* or *commune*.

Further, numerous managerial devices and procedures could be treated as purely technical instruments which are essentially part of the productive forces, irrespective of the social context within which they were first used. Shorn of their capitalistic trappings and possibly renamed to fit the new system, they may be accepted as instrumental to the development of socialism so long as they enhance the efficiency of production and distribution. Like piece work, "scientific management," and material balances planning before, and like the interest rate, which was reintroduced after Stalin's death as the coefficient of relative effectiveness in investment decisions, the organization and rules of economic decision making as formulated by Oskar Lange and others and approximated, to cite one instance, by Hungary's "new economic mechanism" (NEM) could be adopted as promising state-of-the-art techniques for conditions of scarcity and scarcity consciousness which the founding fathers could or would not envisage.[34]

To remain within the fold, of course, anyone making any or all of the preceding points would have to stress as well their temporary, transitory significance. Contrary to Maoist charges, the return to previous relations of production would not be the first step on the road to capitalism but a remedial measure. It therefore would not affect the expectation that the development of the productive forces eventually will create the conditions for a transition to full-fledged socialism and then communism, which will pose anew the problems of complete cooperative integration, work for the sake of working, and distribution according to need. That future world of emerging abundance may have little use for scarcity economics. But that will have to be decided then, the revised expectation being that "then" will be many years away.

The Justification of Reform in Post-Mao China

The economic reforms that were initiated during the late 1970s had to be explained in Marxist-Leninist terms, with due attention to Mao Zedong Thought—or at least the part of it that appeared to fit the new circumstances and revised perceptions. The indications are that such explanations were given generally within the frame of reference outlined above. Many of the planners and theorists who had been advocates of the 1961–1965 reforms and who therefore had been branded by Mao's protagonists as "rightists" at the beginning of the Cultural Revolution, now took aim at the "leftist" transgressions of Lin Biao and the Gang of Four as stand-ins for the inviolate Mao, within the same doctrinal context.

The reformers' contentions are nevertheless difficult to summarize. Whereas they all agreed that the changes in organization had gone too far, there was much less consensus on when, where, and how mistakes had been made that needed to be corrected. Moreover, the calls for and justifications of successive changes appeared gradually, as effective support for ever more far-reaching modifications could be mustered. The most comprehensive statements on the issues, which appeared quite early in order to give direction to the reorientation, are therefore likely to be outdated in numerous details.

Xue Muqiao, perhaps the most authoritative and prolific pen on the subject,[35] noted in 1980–1981 that the socialist transformation was carried out at too great a speed, especially during the "socialist high tide" of 1956. Yet he also accepted that result as a fait accompli. Instead of a return to people's democracy, he envisaged a more limited step back by dividing the first phase of communism into two subphases of less developed and more developed socialism, the former characterized by the coexistence of ownership by the whole people with collective ownership.

Xue thereby left little room for the resurgence of individual enterprises and of joint state-private ventures with foreign capitalists, which he acknowledged as helpful and nonthreatening a few years later, in words reminiscent of Lenin's advocacy of Soviet state capitalism.[36] But he justified the need for renewed commodity production more broadly than Stalin had conceived it.[37] In addition, he implied on orthodox Marxist grounds a long duration of this "immature" phase of socialism by stressing that the full socialization of all means of production and the uniform application of the principle of "equal pay for equal work" everywhere would require the elevation of technology, productivity, and income in collective agricultural production to the levels common in state-operated industries.

Ownership entitling to management, Xue noted the principal difference between the loci of managerial authority in the collective and the fully socialized sectors and charged that this facet had often been ignored in past practice. Instead of the previous unified planning of all activities, he proposed for the collective sector state guidance, coordination, and education in combination with market manipulation through price and tax policies to reconcile differences of interest between the collectives or their members and the state. In the fully socialized sector, he objected to the "undue emphasis on centralized leadership" along Soviet lines, which stymied the opportunities and incentives for grass-roots initiatives, and suggested instead in a more organistic perspective the delegation of more authority to the enterprises as well as the "democratization" of its exercise, without being specific.

Given that the survival of the collective sector as well as division of and distribution according to labor also necessitated the continuation of commodity exchange, Xue argued for an appropriate restructuring of the planning institutions and procedures. Bureaucratic forms of allocation should be simplified at least and replaced by market relations between enterprises whenever practicable, even in the exchange of producer goods between state enterprises. Instead of balancing supply and demand by decree through rationing and other means, which had been wasteful and ineffective, flexible prices should be used to reconcile society's needs and production possibilities. Because of their incentive functions, commodity prices could be expected to tend toward their values, that is, the socially necessary labor time expended on them.

To economize the use of labor time and increase its productivity, Xue advocated numerous improvements in distribution according to labor. The wage system in state enterprises, which had been affected by the egalitarian policies of the past, needed to be restructured so that it would provide incentive to work more and better, to improve skills, and so forth. Appropriate changes were more piece work, better bonuses, greater skill differentials, and total enterprise achievement. Corresponding changes were advisable in the determination of collective earnings shares, including the resort to labor quotas under responsibility contracts. In addition, state enterprises needed some freedom to hire and fire, and the people some freedom to choose their jobs. But there was no call for a labor market in analogy to the product sphere, in spite of the evidence of waste of talent through bureaucratic allocation.

With properly manipulated prices and wages, it would be possible, in Xue's opinion, to rely on the enterprises to use their authority correctly, especially if additional incentive were provided in the form of a profit share. Profits would have to be determined carefully in this case by deducting "differential rents" attributable to resource endowments, and by charging interest on the funds invested by the state. In addition, it would be necessary to reform enterprise leadership so that the role of the party committee would be limited to political and ideological work while the director, chief engineer, and treasurer would be more personally responsible for production and business operations, under the supervision of a newly formed workers' congress.

In such circumstances, the state, according to Xue, would still prepare a unified plan. But this document would be much more the result of projections at lower levels, and it would be implemented much more by indirect measures than before. The plan's objective should be maintenance of economic stability while competition served to improve allocative efficiency, he added recently in terms familiar to Western economics: "While it is necessary to exercise macroeconomic control, it is also necessary to leave as much leeway as possible for microeconomic activities."[38]

Xue's emphasis on the use of regulation through the market conflicted with proposals that concentrated solely on administrative reforms, either by restoring a purer variant of the Soviet system of centralized decision making or by delegating much more authority to lower administrative divisions à la Khrushchev. Evidently, the arguments in favor of more market economy prevailed,[39] with consequences that were difficult to imagine even five years ago and may have caused some initial advocates, such as Chen Yun, to revise their position.[40]

Conclusion

This review has shown that the Marxist classics were quite explicit in defining socialism as a behaviorally cooperative system with fully socialized means of production, national economic planning under state direction instead of commodity economy, and distribution according to labor. Any Chinese Communist claiming adherence to Marxism-Leninism and Mao Zedong Thought has to respect this vision. If he also wishes to retain or reintroduce competitive elements into the allocative process, which the market socialists have shown to be conceivable and perhaps practicable, he has to argue that the state of development of the productive forces does not yet call for socialism as defined by Marx and Engels. Any attempt to realize it and begin to move on toward communism is therefore premature and doomed to failure. More advisable is the transitory preservation or return to earlier forms of organization, which allow for competitive behavior as a response appropriate to scarcity and scarcity consciousness. Without questioning the October Revolution once it had taken place, Lenin himself followed this line of reasoning when he advocated the NEP in the Soviet Union and the fundamentals of people's democracy as an additional intermediate phase. The present Chinese leadership as represented by Xue argues in the same vein that the socialist transformation is a fait accompli in a sense, but that there are two phases of socialism to be distinguished, the first "immature" one requiring both planning and the market as organizational instruments. Like Lenin at the time of the NEP, when he talked about an "epoch," the Chinese now envisage that this first phase will require a long gestation period. Of course, such predictions may be revised in the future. They have been in the past.

Notes

1. For a recent essay in this perspective see Robert F. Dernberger, "The State-Planned, Centralized System: China, North Korea, Vietnam," in *Asian Economic Development—Present and Future*, ed. Robert A. Scalapino et al., Research and Policy Studies no. 14 (Berkeley: Institute of East Asian Studies, University of California, 1985), pp. 13ff.

2. Fred M. Gottheil, *Marx's Economic Predictions* (Evanston: Northwestern University Press, 1966), esp. chap. 12, pp. 171–90.

3. Note that the Foreign Languages Press, Beijing, has published an improved translation of the third German edition. See Frederick Engels, *Anti-Dühring (Herr Eugen Dühring's Revolution in Science)* (Beijing: Foreign Languages Press, 1976), esp. part 3, pp. 327–422.

4. Ibid., pp. 375–76, 388.

5. The relevant excerpts from Lenin's writings appear as appendices to Karl Marx, *Critique of the Gotha Programme* (New York: International Publishers, 1938). See esp. pp. 56–59 and 77–88.

6. Ibid., pp. 86–87.

7. Lenin based this call for an intermediate transition to socialism on an explication of Russia's class structure and economic situation, which he made public first in 1918 in his pamphlet on *The Chief Task of Our Day: "Left-Wing" Childishness and the Petty-Bourgeois Mentality*. Most statements of the NEP period refer back to this basic document, which Lenin himself valued highly.

8. V. I. Lenin, "Report on the Substitution of a Tax in Kind for the Surplus-Grain Appropriation System," Tenth Congress of the RCP (B), March 15, 1921, reprinted in *Selected Works* (Moscow: Progress Publishers, 1967), 3:572–73.

9. V. I. Lenin, "The Tax in Kind," ibid., pp. 596, 599.

10. Note that Lenin also mentioned state agency contracts and the leasing of state enterprises as possible state capitalist arrangements.

11. V. I. Lenin, "The Role and Functions of the Trade Unions Under the New Economic Policy," ibid., pp. 651–61.

12. Lenin, "The Tax in Kind," ibid., p. 612, and Political Report of the Central Committee of the RCP (B), Eleventh Congress of the RCP (B), March 27, 1922, ibid., pp. 683ff.

13. *Report of the Commission on the National and the Colonial Questions, Second Congress of the Communist International*, July 26, 1920, ibid., p. 459.

14. Lenin, "The Tax in Kind," ibid., p. 587.

15. Report on the Work of the Council of People's Commissars, Eighth All-Russia Congress of Soviets, December 22, 1920, ibid., p. 512.

16. Ibid., and Lenin, "Integrated Economic Plan," ibid., pp. 549–56.

17. Lenin, "The Tax in Kind," pp. 599, 600.

18. Lenin, "On Cooperation," p. 759. The two points referred to are state ownership of the means of production and ease of transition to socialism.

19. Ibid., p. 761.

20. J. Stalin, *Economic Problems of Socialism in the USSR* (Moscow: Foreign Languages Publishing House, 1952), pp. 19–20.

21. Ibid., pp. 23–29.

22. *Schriften des Vereins für Sozialpolitik* (Leipzig: Duncker and Humblot, 1920), pp. 106–107.

23. Maurice Dobb, *On Economic Theory and Socialism* (London: Routledge and Kegan Paul, 1955), p. 35.

24. Ibid., chap. 3, "Three Articles on the Problem of Economic Calculation in a Socialist Economy."

25. Note, however, two modifications: Land was not nationalized at once, as in the Soviet Union, and merely collectivized during the process of socialist transformation. Moreover, the "national bourgeoisie" of small industrialists and merchants were compensated in part when their enterprises became joint state-private ventures.

26. For a more detailed explanation of this perspective, see Peter Schran, "On the Rationality of the Great Leap Forward and Rural People's Communes," *Ventures* 5, 1 (Winter 1965): 31–38.

27. For a discussion of the disagreements over the socialist transformation of agriculture, see Kang Chao, *Agricultural Production in Communist China 1949–1965* (Madison: University of Wisconsin Press, 1970), chap. 1, pp. 11–35, and chap. 3, pp. 75–90.

28. The contrast between Lenin's and Mao's views is made explicit in Charles Bettelheim, *Cultural Revolution and Industrial Organization in China* (New York: Monthly Review Press, 1974), esp. chap. 3, pp. 60ff.

29. Note that the Russian revolutionaries had experimented with communes during the War Communism period, evidently unsuccessfully. Elements of collective consumption and living have not been characteristic of the collective farms since the late 1920s.

30. For a comprehensive review of the debates, see Cyril Chihren Lin, "The

Reinstatement of Economics in China Today," *China Quarterly* 85 (March 1981): 1ff., esp. 8–9, 14–16.

31. For a brief description of the confrontation, see Dwight H. Perkins, "Economic Growth in China and the Cultural Revolution (1960–April 1967)," *China Quarterly* 30 (April–June 1967): 833ff., esp. 843–46 on the opposing forces.

32. See Karl Marx, *Critique of the Gotha Programme*, app. 2, "Lenin on the Critique of the Gotha Programme," esp. pp. 47–48.

33. See Stalin, *Economic Problems*, pp. 17–18.

34. Note that this is in essence the implication of Sun Yefang's reasoning, which he supported with references to Engels. See Lin, "Restatement of Economics."

35. For the most comprehensive statement of his ideas, see Xue Muqiao, *China's Socialist Economy* (Beijing: Foreign Languages Press, 1981). The following pages summarize this work.

36. Xue Muqiao, "Socialism and Planned Commodity Economy," *Beijing Review* 30, 33 (August 17, 1987): 19.

37. For an explicit critique of Stalin's view, see ibid., p. 15.

38. Ibid., p. 18.

39. See Dong Fureng, "Some Problems Concerning the Chinese Economy," *China Quarterly* 84 (December 1980): 727–36, esp. 732–33, for this characterization of the conflicting positions.

40. Note that *Beijing Review* 29, 29 (July 1986): 14–15, published the outline of a talk given by Chen Yun on March 8, 1979, on "Planning and the Market," which called attention to the latter's role with comparable arguments.

5

MARX, MAO, AND DENG ON THE DIVISION OF LABOR IN HISTORY

Maurice Meisner

> The subdivision of a labour is the assassination of a people.
> —Karl Marx

It is no longer fashionable, either in the official circles of Beijing or in the conventional circles of Western scholarship, to take Mao Zedong seriously as a Marxist. Ten years after his death, Mao's ideas (even if not yet his physical remains and his historical image) have been safely put to rest, some in the silence of the museum, others buried beneath layers of a new orthodox ideological canon composed by his successors. Mao, of course, is still officially portrayed as a great nationalist and revolutionary leader—but only until the mid-1950s. The more critical ideas and theories he set forth over the final two decades of his life, according to his official assessors, suffer from "leftist," "idealist," and "utopian" deviations—and thus might best be forgotten.

Foreign scholars have proved eager to join, and embellish, Beijing's criticisms of Mao. Many Western observers who found so many virtues in Maoism when Mao was alive now have come to see the errors of their ways and hasten to laud China's current leaders as true "Marxist materialists" and "socialist democratizers." Some who once praised Mao for formulating a distinctive version of Marxism and forging a unique path of socialist development today belatedly discover that he was simply "China's Stalin," so much the easier then to ignore the questions Mao and Maoism posed, questions they formerly regarded as matters of burning relevance for the history of our time.

It would be interesting, if not necessarily instructive, to compare what

Western scholars now write about Mao with what they wrote during the Maoist era. But such exegetical exercises, while tempting to perform, would likely prove more useful for the study of the ideology of Western scholarship than for the understanding of Mao's Marxism. However that may be, there clearly has been a great deal of "forgetting" of Mao's ideas over the past decade, as Arif Dirlik has observed. The cause of this amnesia is not difficult to divine. For Mao, especially over the last twenty years of his life, raised questions about the means and ends of socialism that are profoundly unsettling for those who prize social normalcy, bureaucratic rationality, and familiar processes of modernization. That easy equation between Maoism and Stalinism buries such questions and thus proves politically and intellectually comforting to conservative minds in this post-Maoist era. But it is a historically false equation, no less so today than it was generally recognized to be a decade ago. Mao, after all, did not convert to Stalinism after his death. And it is thus time, as Dirlik has reminded us, to reconsider seriously some of the broader issues that Mao raised, and to bring an end to the decade-long ideological "suppression of memories of Mao's Marxism."

A reconsideration of Mao Zedong's Marxism does not call for an uncritical celebration of his standing in the Marxist-Leninist theoretical tradition, much less a celebration of his political practice. I long have argued (and long before the advent of Deng Xiaoping) that Mao's departures from Marxism, both in theory and in practice, were enormous, and that many of those departures were indeed "utopian" in the conventional Marxian sense of that term. I have also suggested that many of these utopian features of Maoism, however uneasily they rest with the premises of Marxist theory, were necessary prerequisites for the making of revolution in a modern Chinese historical situation where a revolution was needed. Whatever the merits or deficiencies of that view, it would prove no more fruitful now than it did in years gone by to indulge in scholastic controversies over whether the distinctively "Maoist" features of Mao's version of Marxism were ideological heresies or creative innovations. Happily, it is no longer the fashion to portray Mao Zedong as the twentieth-century reincarnation of Karl Marx. But having been relieved of that burden, we are by no means relieved of the responsibility of considering the issues raised in Mao's thought, and understanding their meaning for the history of contemporary Chinese society and for the fate of Marxism in the modern world.

Prominent among those issues was Mao's concern with the social consequences of the division of labor, especially as it manifests itself in occupational specialization. This is a critical issue in any society, but especially so for a rapidly modernizing country whose leaders profess to be striving for socialist goals. Before turning to Mao's concern and briefly contrasting it with the concerns of his successors, it might be useful to recall (for it is so often ignored or misunderstood) the central historical importance assigned to the division of labor and occupational specialization in the writings of Marx and Engels.

Classical Marxist Theory on the Division of Labor and Occupational Specialization in History

History, for Karl Marx, was not simply the story of human progress. Indeed, he held profoundly ambiguous attitudes about the "progressiveness" of historical development. On the one hand, Marx viewed human beings essentially as producers, and he thus placed a positive value on the development of the productive resources of society. On the other hand, he recognized that the development of productive forces exacted increasingly heavy human and social costs, more and more separating human beings from each other and from their own essential human selves. History was at once the story of people's productive achievements and the story of people's ever-increasing alienation in the world they built, the story of their growing bondage to the social, material, and ideological products of their own creation. In Marx's view, in contrast to the positivist interpretation that later was often imposed upon his views, economic and technological progress in history did not necessarily translate itself into human and social progress. As Engels put it, "every advance is likewise a relative regression."[1]

This irony of history is nowhere more apparent than in Marx's treatment of the division of labor. The social division of labor is essential for creating the necessary material conditions for human life; yet it is also the principal evil in history, the major cause of all forms of antagonism, conflict, alienation, and enslavement. The dual function of the division of labor is emphasized throughout the writings of Marx. In his early philosophical manuscripts, Marx refers to the division of labor both as "a major driving force in the production of wealth" and as the source of an "estranged and alienated form of human activity."[2] And in *Capital*, to take but one of innumerable examples, he writes: "If, therefore, on the one hand, it [the division of labor] presents itself historically as progress and as a necessary phase in the economic development of society, on the other hand, it is a refined and civilized method of exploitation." The capitalist division of labor, he notes, begets surplus value (or what bourgeois economists prefer to call "social wealth"), but it does so only "by crippling the individual labourers."[3] Thus the division of labor, however economically efficacious throughout most of human history, stands condemned as a barrier to human liberation. Communism, the realization of humankind's leap to the realm of freedom, therefore demands the abolition of the division of labor, or at least its abolition in all the forms in which until now it has historically been known. As Marx proclaims in *Critique of the Gotha Program*, the advent of the higher phase of communist society will bring to a definitive end "the enslaving subordination of the individual to the division of labour."[4]

Yet how can the Marxian demand for the abolition of the division of labor be accomplished? How can a social device that has been essential for yielding the material conditions for human existence be done away with? If the division of labor is inherently evil, and the primary source of most social evils, is it not a necessary evil, necessary for the maintenance of human life itself? Thus is not the call for the abolition of the division of labor the most utopian of all Marxist goals—and "utopian" in the conventional sense, which is to say, impossible in principle?

Marxist theory does not readily yield answers to these questions. But insofar as answers can be found, they must be sought in Marx's analysis of the qualitative transformation of the processes of production and the character of the division of labor wrought by modern capitalism. For understanding that transformation, it is necessary to review, albeit very briefly and superficially, Marx's lengthy discussion of the role of the division of labor in historical development.

The division of labor, for Marx, is a universal fact of human history, characteristic of every known mode of production, whether it be a self-sufficient communal village or a highly developed commodity economy.[5] The social division of labor originates in what Marx describes as a "natural" and "spontaneous" fashion, called forth to satisfy elemental biological and material needs. It initially "springs up naturally," Marx writes, "on a purely physiological foundation," based on differences in sex and age.[6] Indeed, "the first division of labour is that between man and woman for child breeding."[7] But the division of labor, once in existence, begins to lose its "natural" character (although it retains its "spontaneous" character well into the capitalist age) and soon becomes the main source of social antagonism and oppression. The sexual division of labor, originally an entirely natural phenomenon, develops into "the antagonism between man and woman in monogamian marriage," which Engels identifies as "the first class oppression"—that of women by men.[8] What Marx characterizes as "the natural division of labour in the family" soon results in "the separation of society into individual families opposed to another" and "the unequal distribution, both quantitative and qualitative, of labour and its products." One consequence of this is private property, "the nucleus, the first form of which lies in the family, where wife and children are the slaves of the husband."[9]

The further development of the division of labor—propelled by such factors as increases in population and the growth of commerce—soon finds social expression in the emergence of caste and class divisions, and the antagonism between them, the division between the owners of the means of production and the immediate laborers, between the exploiters and the exploited. It is "the law of the division of labour," Engels writes, "which lies at the root of the division of society into classes."[10] And it is the development of the division of labor, Marx and Engels argue, that is mainly responsible for changes in modes of production. Thus an unchanging division of labor, which Marx believed to be the central feature of societies burdened by the "Asiatic mode of production," results in social and historical stagnation.[11] In the Western line of historical evolution, by contrast, it has been a changing division of labor that brought changes in modes of production—from antiquity to feudalism to capitalism. "The various stages of the development of the division of labour," Marx writes, "are just so many different forms of ownership, i.e., the existing stage in the division of labour determines also the relations of individuals to one another with reference to the material, instrument, and product of labour."[12]

The development of the division of labor, while yielding new and presumably more progressive modes of production,[13] also produces regressive social tendencies and has dehumanizing effects on the people upon whom it impinges. Among the negative consequences of the division of labor, Marx and Engels particularly emphasize the division between mental and manual labor and the antagonistic distinction between town and countryside. The age-old division between mental and manual labor,[14] ever more intensified by an increasingly specialized division of labor, is seen as stunting both the intellectual and physical development of the individual. A no less odious result of the division of labor is the separation between town and countryside. While the antagonism between town and country "runs through the whole history of civilisation," it becomes a prime social evil only when the division of labor develops to the point where industrial and commercial labor is separated from agricultural labor.[15] The modern historical importance Marx assigned to the phenomenon is suggested in the following passage in *Capital*: "The foundation of every division of labor that is well developed, and brought about by the exchange of commodities, is the separation between town and country. It may be said that the whole economic history of society is summed up in the movement of this antithesis."[16] It is an antithesis for which the founding fathers of Marxism reserved some of their strongest moral and social condemnations. In the words of Marx: "The antagonism of town and country can only exist as a result of private property. It is the most crass expression of the individual under the division of labour, under a definite activity forced upon him—a subjection which makes one man into a restricted town-animal, the other into a restricted country-animal, and daily creates anew the conflict between their interests."[17] And as Engels later wrote: "The first great division of labour, the separation of town and country, condemned the rural population to thousands of years of mental torpidity, and the people of the towns each to subjection to his own individual trade. It destroyed the basis of the intellectual development of the former and the physical development of the latter."[18]

The two most general—and the most pernicious—results of the division of labor are "alienated labor" (as Marx termed it in his early writings and described it in appalling detail in his later writings, especially *Capital*) and occupational specialization. These closely related phenomena, while present in embryonic forms through most of human history, only fully reveal their terrifying dehumanizing potential under the modern capitalist mode of production. For capitalism, driven by a "werewolf hunger" for surplus value, carries the division of labor to horrifying extremes.[19] Marx's lengthy analysis of the intensification of the division of labor that takes place as medieval handicrafts production and the guild system are transformed into the manufacturing system of early capitalism and then into the factory system of the machine age is well known, and there is neither the need nor the space to summarize that analysis here.[20] What needs to be noted is that Marx viewed the last of these stages, the advent of the factory system of the machine age, as marking a qualitative transformation of the division of labor and its social effects. The rise of the manufacturing system in early capitalism, to be sure, marks an enormous change in the mode of production, bringing as it does the old social division of labor to the workshop itself and separating the laborer from his means of production, and converting the latter into capital. But it is "big industry," as Marx early termed the modern factory system, that "took from the division of labour the last semblance of its natural character."[21] In the capitalist factory, Marx writes, the old division of labor is "systematically re-moulded and established in a more hideous form by capital, as a means of exploiting labour-power. The life-long speciality of handling one and the same tool now becomes the life-long speciality of serving one and the same machine."[22] Modern industry, Marx continues, "sweeps away by technical means the manufacturing division of labour, under which each man is bound hand and foot for life to a single detail-operation. At the same time, the capitalistic form of that industry reproduces this same division of labor in a still more monstrous shape; in the factory proper, by converting the workman into a living appendage of the machine."[23]

If the material results of capitalist production are impressive, the social and human consequences are a ghastly tragedy. For the capitalist intensification of the division of labor in "hideous forms" and "monstrous shape" creates what Marx calls "a social anarchy which turns every economic progress into a social calamity."[24] That calamity is first and most obviously visited upon workers, for whom the capitalistic factory division of labor spells total alienation and dehumanization. Marx's description of these dehumanizing effects in *Capital* are among the most chilling passages to be found in all of modern literature, and they firmly link his early concept of "alienated labor" to his "mature" critique of capitalism. Under capitalist production, Marx says in his early manuscripts,

> the worker sinks to the level of a commodity and becomes indeed the most wretched of commodities. . . . The wretchedness of the worker is in inverse proportion to the power and magnitude of his production. . . . The worker becomes all the poorer the more wealth he produces, the more his production increases in power and range. The worker becomes an ever cheaper commodity the more commodities he creates. With the increasing value of the world of things proceeds in direct proportion the devaluation of the world of men . . . the object which labour produces—labour's product—confronts it as something alien, as a power independent of the producer. . . . The alienation of the worker in his product means not only that his labour becomes an object, an external existence, but that it exists outside him, independently, as something alien to him, and that it becomes a power of its own confronting him; it means that the life which he has conferred on the object confronts him as something hostile and alien.[25]

In *Capital* Marx writes that, for the worker, the factory division of labor

> does away with the many-sided play of muscles, and confiscates every atom of freedom, both in bodily and intellectual activity. The lightening of labour, even, becomes a sort of torture, since the machine does not free the labourers from work, but deprives the work of all interest. . . . It is not the workman that employs the instruments of labour, but the instruments of labour that employ the workman. . . . By means of its conversion into an automaton, the instrument of labour confronts the labourer, during the labour process, in the shape of capital, of dead labour, that dominates and pumps dry living labour-power.[26]

Marx leaves no doubt that this alien domination of the workers by the products of their own labor, this debasement and fragmentation of the individual human personality, this deprivation of all joy in work—these modern forms of slavery—are to be attributed primarily to what he terms "the evil effects of the division of labour."[27] "As the chosen people bore in their features the sign manual of Jehovah," Marx remarked, "so division of labour brands the manufacturing workman as the property of capital."[28] He goes on to write: "Some crippling of body and mind is inseparable even from division of labour in society as a whole. Since, however, manufacture carries this social separation of branches of labour much further, and also, by its peculiar division, attacks the individual at the very roots of his life, it is the first to afford the materials for, and to give a start to, industrial pathology."[29]

If the division of labor was seen by Marx and Engels as the enemy of human freedom, then it is hardly surprising that they leveled many of their most impassioned critiques against occupational specialization—the most ubiquitous and pernicious social manifestation of the capitalist division of labor. For Marx it was inherent in the nature of human beings to strive to become "all-round" individuals freely engaged in a vast variety of labors and pursuits, to strive, as he put it in *Capital*, to become "the fully developed individual, fit for a variety of labours, ready to face any change of production, and to whom the different social functions he performs are but so many modes of giving free scope to his own natural and acquired powers."[30] But this natural development of the human personality is precluded by occupational specialization whereby, by virtue of economic necessity and social custom, people are forced to spend the whole of their lives engaged in one form of activity. This is particularly, and unnaturally, the case under the capitalist mode of production, which develops and enforces occupational specialization to an intolerable and inhumane degree. That occupational specialization was viewed by Marx as but a refined form of slavery is made clear in *Capital*, where he comments on how the capitalist division of labor "seizes upon, not only the economic, but every sphere of society, and everywhere lays the foundation of that all engrossing system of specializing and sorting men, that development in a man of one single faculty, at the expense of all other faculties, which caused A. Ferguson, the master of Adam Smith, to exclaim: 'We make a nation of Helots, and have no free citizens.' "[31]

The capitalist mania for specialization, Marx writes, "converts the labourer into a crippled monstrosity, by forcing his detail dexterity at the expense of a world of productive capabilities and instincts; just as in the States of La Plata they butcher a whole beast for the sake of his hide or his tallow. Not only is the detail work distributed to the different individuals, but the individual himself is made the automatic motor of a fractional operation, and the absurd fable of Menenius Agrippa, which makes man a mere fragment of his own body, becomes realized."[32] Marx observes that "constant labour of one uniform kind disturbs the intensity and flow of a man's animal spirits, which find recreation and delight in mere change of activity." But such elemental human delight cannot be enjoyed by the modern worker, "The one-sidedness and the deficiencies of the detail labourer become perfections when he is part of the collective labourer. The habit of doing only one thing converts him into a never failing instrument, while his connection with the whole mechanism compels him to work with the regularity of the parts of a machine."[33]

It is not only the workers who are victimized and dehumanized by occupational specialization, but the exploiting classes as well, whose members, as Engels wrote, "are made subject, through the division of labor, to the tool of their function: the empty-minded bourgeois to his own capital and his own insane craving for profits; the lawyer to his fossilized legal conceptions, which dominate him as an independent power; the 'educated classes' in general to their manifold species of local narrow-mindedness and one-sidedness, to their own physical and mental short-sightedness, to their stunted growth due to their narrow specialized education and their being chained for life to this specialized activity—even when this specialized activity is merely to do nothing."[34]

Marx's classic statement of the tyranny of the division of labor as manifested in the enslavement of occupational specialization—which, at the same time, expresses his most idyllic vision of communism—is to be found in *The German Ideology*. Under the division of labor, he observes,

> each man has a particular, exclusive sphere of activity, which is forced upon him and from which he cannot escape. He is a hunter, a fisherman, a shepherd, or a critical critic, and must remain so if he does not want to lose his means of livelihood; while in communist society, where nobody has one exclusive sphere of activity but each can become accomplished in any branch he wishes, society regulates the general production and thus makes it possible for me to do one thing today and another tomorrow, to hunt in the morning, fish in the afternoon, rear cattle in the evening, criticize after dinner, just as I have a mind, without ever becoming hunter, fisherman, shepherd or critic.[35]

Thus the arrival of the future communist society demands an end to the slavery of occupational specialization and the abolition of the division of labor as a whole, at least the division of labor as it has been known in history until now, a demand which Marx and Engels repeatedly emphasized throughout their writings. As Engels put it: "It goes without saying that society cannot free itself unless every individual is freed. The old mode of production must therefore be revolutionized from top to bottom, and in particular the former division of labor must disappear."[36]

The Marxist call for the abolition of the division of labor in all of its forms and manifestations (including occupational specialization, alienated labor, and the distinctions between town and countryside and between mental and manual labor), however "utopian" a goal this may appear at first sight, is an entirely logical and necessary demand in light of the premises of Marxist theory. For Marx, it should again be emphasized, began with the proposition that human beings were essentially producers, that the creative realization of their truly human potentialities, their true joys and pleasures in life, resided not in the consumption of goods but rather in their work—but work freely and creatively undertaken. The Marxian critique of capitalism rests less on the inequities of capitalism as a mode of distribution than on its inhumaneness as a mode of production.[37] Capitalism is condemned primarily because it is an unnatural and dehumanizing way for people to live their lives as producers, one that robs the workers not only of the products of their labor but also of self-fulfillment in producing them.[38] The primary sources of this alienated and dehumanizing form of labor are the twin evils of occupational specialization and the division of labor, both of which capitalism develops to monstrous extremes—and both of which must be abolished if communism is to be realized.

The demand for the abolition of the division of labor does not imply the end of social cooperation in production. What is to be abolished is involuntary labor, or "wage slavery," as Marx called its predominant capitalist form, which is to be replaced by productive activities freely undertaken and collectively performed by the free association of producers. This new mode of production, whereby, in Engels' words, "productive labour will become a pleasure instead of being a burden,"[39] which would distinguish the communist future, was seen by Marx and Engels not only as a moral imperative but also as an economic and historical necessity. Modern industrial technology, Marx believed, had made the existing division of labor—inherited from the early manufacturing period—both economically and socially outmoded, an anachronistic barrier to economic as well as human progress. As Engels later summarized: "Nor is the abolition of the old division of labour a demand which could be carried through to the detriment of the productivity of labour. On the contrary. Thanks to modern industry it has become a condition of production itself. . . . But while the capitalist mode of employment of machinery necessarily perpetuates the old division of labour with its fossilized specialization, although it has become superfluous from a technical standpoint, the machinery itself rebels against this anachronism."[40]

There is thus a material basis, indeed a material prerequisite, for the abolition of the division of labor and its replacement by a communist system of voluntary labor and socially cooperative production. Necessary are both the technical requirements of modern productive forces and the conditions (or potential conditions) of material abundance yielded by those forces. As Marx writes, the end of "the enslaving subordination of the individual to the division of labor" requires a society where "all the springs of cooperative wealth flow more abundantly."[41] But this will not come about through the development of productive forces alone. There are human as well as economic preconditions, Marxism teaches, for the abolition of the division of labor and the realization of communism. A society based on voluntary labor and true social cooperation in production presupposes a transformation of human nature that brings about people who regard labor as "life's prime want" and not simply a means of life. All history, Marx says, "is but the continuous transformation of human nature,"[42] and thus the new society presupposes the emergence of "new men" who will have changed themselves in the process of changing their material and social world through what Marx called "revolutionizing practice."[43] In addition to the technological conditions for material abundance, therefore, the abolition of the division of labor and occupational specialization requires transformed human beings who desire to work together to create not simply wealth but "cooperative wealth."

While original Marxist theory sets forth necessary historical prerequisites (both material and human) for the abolition of the old division of labor, it cannot be too strongly emphasized that Marx and Engels envisioned the creation of a new communist mode of production as a lengthy historical process, not as a sudden event that would occur at some distant time in the future once all the economic preconditions had fully matured. Thus, following a successful socialist revolution, they advocated immediate steps to begin the process of abolishing the division of labor and to mitigate the social consequences of occupational specialization. In the *Manifesto* they propose, once the proletariat achieves power, a number of initial, concrete measures to begin "revolutionizing the mode of production." These include measures aimed at negating two of the more obvious manifestations of the division of labor—the divisions between town and countryside and between mental and manual labor. To bring about the "gradual abolition of the distinction between town and country," Marx and Engels propose a "combination of agriculture with manufacturing industries" and "a more equable distribution of the population over the country." To begin to break down the separation between mental and manual labor, they propose a public school system based on the "combination of education with industrial production."[44]

In *Capital*, Marx discusses at length the need to combine education with productive labor, to integrate mental and manual tasks. He notes, for example, that "From the factory system budded, as Robert Owen has shown us in detail, an education that will, in the case of every child over a given age, combine productive labour with instruction and gymnastics, not only as one of the methods of adding to the efficiency of production, but as the only method of producing fully developed human beings."[45] On the desirability of combining education with work, he further comments: "there can be no doubt that when the working-class comes into power, as inevitably it must, technical instruction, both theoretical and practical, will take its proper place in the working-class schools. There is also no doubt that such revolutionary ferment, the final result of which is the abolition of the old division of labour, is diametrically opposed to the capitalistic form of production, and to the economic status of the labourer corresponding to that form."[46]

Engels, in his later writings, as Marx had done earlier, devotes considerable attention to the social benefits to be yielded by combining industrial with agricultural production, and thereby eventually eliminating the distinction between cities and rural areas. Arguing that modern industry has largely "freed production from restrictions of locality," he advocates "one single vast plan [that] can allow industry to be distributed over the whole country." "Accordingly, abolition of the antithesis between town and country is not merely possible. It has become a direct necessity of industrial production itself, just as it has become a necessity of agricultural production and, beside, of public health. The present poisoning of the air, water and land can be put an end to only by the fusion of town and country; and only such fusion will change the situation of the masses now languishing in the towns, and enable their excrement to be used for the production of plants instead of for the production of disease." "The abolition of the separation of town and country is therefore not utopian," he continues, "in so far as it is conditioned on the most equal distribution possible of modern industry over the whole country. It is true that in the huge towns civilization has bequeathed us a heritage which it will take much time and trouble to get rid of. But it must and will be got rid of, however protracted a process it may be . . . the great towns will perish." It is in the conditions of modern industry itself that Engels finds, in embryonic form, the revolutionary elements that "will do away with the old division of labour, along with the separation of town and country, and will revolutionize the whole of production."[47]

Chinese Marxism and the Issue of Occupational Specialization

It is ironic that Marxism, a doctrine that teaches that the division of labor and occupational specialization are enemies of human freedom, has been fashioned into official ideologies of contemporary postrevolutionary societies where the division of labor (and all its social consequences) has been developed with a rapidity unprecedented in all human history. Thus, in the countries that prefer to call themselves "socialist" today, occupational specialization has become no less a way of life than it is in their capitalist counterparts.

This paradox, if a paradox it be, is not difficult to unravel. Marxist-led revolutions thus far have been successful only in economically backward lands, where, on the morrow of political success, victorious revolutionaries turned rulers have been confronted with the task of developing backward economies barely emerging from precapitalist modes of production. Modern economic development, and especially rapid industrialization, historical imperatives on both political and social grounds, naturally demand an intensification of the division of labor and increasing occupational specialization. These processes are both necessary to construct the economic preconditions for socialism and incongruous with the socialist and communist goals that modern economic development is originally intended to serve. In the end, it thus far has been universally the case, the means of economic development have proved more lasting than the socialist ends that were once sought—and the proclaimed socialist and communist goals, consequently, are first postponed and then subjected to familiar processes of ritualization, duly proclaimed on appropriate occasions but severed from any meaningful tie to social practice. In the meantime, "socialist" societies mimic capitalist ones in intensifying the division of labor and occupational specialization—and reproducing the inevitable social consequences of these phenomena.

The Soviet Union was the first to encounter the dilemma—and the first to bury it. On the issue of occupational specialization, the decisive steps were taken by Stalin in the 1930s, although not without the benefit of precedents established by Lenin, in placing an enormous emphasis (both in theory and in practice) on the virtues of expertise, specialization, and professionalism. This found its social expression in the creation of what Moshe Lewin has called "a strong layer of bosses," privileged strata of factory managers, technicians, professionalized intellectuals, and professional bureaucrats. And it found political expression in Stalin's efforts, continued by his successors, to recruit technical specialists and professionals into the Soviet Communist Party. The position and privileges of these groups have been refined and institutionalized for over half a century in an unbroken and largely unchallenged line of social (but hardly socialist) continuity.

Soviet Marxist theory has accommodated itself to Soviet social reality. Marx's views on the division of labor, much less his demand for its abolition, are little noted in Soviet Marxist writings. Although there have been voices to the contrary, official Soviet ideology denies that Marx opposed occupational specialization as a way of life, which, as Robert Tucker has said, "is to deny the undeniable."[48] The abolition of occupational specialization, in any event, is no longer even a ritualized goal in orthodox Soviet theory, and the whole Soviet historical experience offers little to suggest that simply "laying the material foundations for socialism" (as Soviet leaders have long proclaimed they are doing) will actually yield a socialist society. What experience does suggest is that the rapid intensification of the division of labor and the uninhibited development of occupational specialization inevitably lead to the emergence and solidification of new and privileged social strata and the institutionalization of new forms of social and economic inequality.

In postrevolutionary China, acceptance of occupational specialization as the necessary consequence of "modernization" did not come so easily or quickly as it did in the Soviet Union. It has, in fact, been a protracted and agonizing process marked by varied and strenuous efforts to mitigate the social consequences of the division of labor and an enormous reluctance to accept occupational specialization as the way of life in the new society. That resistance can be attributed, in part, to the unique nature of the Chinese Communist Revolution and the heritage it bequeathed to the leaders of the People's Republic after 1949; and, in part, to the intellectual orientations of Mao Zedong, who played no small part in forging that heritage.

Among those orientations was a hostility to occupational specialization, an antipathy that appears in Mao's earliest writings and becomes an abiding feature of the Maoist mentality. This strain in Mao's thought finds one of its early expressions in a certain hostility to intellectuals, especially those who fail to merge with the masses.[49] Eventually it grew into a general distrust of specialization, experts (but not necessarily expertise), and professionalism. The Maoist distrust of occupational specialization is well known and has been frequently noted, but there is considerable debate and confusion over its origins. Most commonly, it is simply dismissed as a sort of Luddite reaction to "modernity," a view almost ludicrous in its simplistic ignorance of the history of the People's Republic during the Maoist era, which is one of the most notable cases in world history of rapid modernization among nations that are latecomers on the industrial scene.[50]

More seriously, it has been argued that Mao's hostility to occupational specialization, and correspondingly, his preference for the "generalist" and the "all-round" man, derive from traditional Chinese sources.[51] In particular, it has been suggested that the Maoist antipathy to specialization reflects the Confucian contempt for professionalism and echoes the "amateur ideal" of the traditional scholar-gentry who, as Etienne Balazs has written, did not wish to "impoverish their personalities in specialization."[52] However appealing the analogy (which implies, in effect, that Maoism can be seen as a precapitalist rejection of capitalism), there is little evidence to support the alleged affinity and many reasons to doubt its validity. For while Mao was attracted to aspects of traditional culture, it was mostly popular peasant traditions he found appealing; for gentry traditions, he held a profoundly iconoclastic contempt. Furthermore, the Confucian preference for "the amateur style" and the ideal of the "well-rounded man" have been greatly romanticized in Western literature. They were, after all, the ideals of a small elite founded upon a particularly sharp and deeply ingrained distinction between mental and manual labor. As classically formulated by Mencius:

> Great men have their proper business, and little men have their proper business. . . . Hence, there is the saying, "Some labor with their minds, and some labor with their strength. Those who labor with their minds govern others; those who labor with their strength are governed by others. Those who are governed by others, support them; those who govern others are supported by them." This is a principle universally recognized.[53]

The separation between mental and manual labor, and thereby the distinction between rulers and ruled, was indeed "a principle universally recognized" in traditional Chinese society, not only in Confucian ideology but also in social reality. And there was no aspect of the traditional heritage that Mao Zedong found more distasteful from the outset of his mature intellectual life. As early as 1917, in his first published article, Mao condemned the traditional disdain for physical activity, which he wrote produced one-sided and feeble men with "white and slender hands" and had resulted in national weakness.[54] This first, embryonic expression of his hostility to occupational specialization derived neither from any elemental Luddism nor from the influences of traditional culture. And although Mao's opposition to occupational specialization was eventually to mesh with, and be formulated in terms of, the Marxist goal of abolishing the distinction between mental and manual work, it long predated his reading of Marxist texts. Rather, it was originally a populist-inspired hostility, closely related to "the great union of the people" he envisioned at the beginning of his revolutionary career.[55] In typically populist fashion, Mao tended to conceive of "the people" as an organic and ideally united entity, and he was opposed to all things that tended to divide people, and especially the division between "brain" and "brawn" workers. His desire to eliminate that pernicious distinction was to be reinforced by Marxist writings, but his vision, as he later put it, that "a man should work in many fields and have contact with all sorts of people,"[56] was a belief he held long before Marxian influences made themselves felt.

That Maoist belief was first translated into Maoist social practice in a rural environment over the long revolutionary era. During the civil war waged by the Chinese Communist Party, more so than in any other Marxist-led revolution, many of the socialist features of the envisioned new society were forged in the course of the revolutionary struggle itself, at least in embryonic form. It is particularly noteworthy that many of the distinctively Maoist values and practices of the revolutionary years, and especially of the celebrated Yan'an era, were highly antithetical to all forms of occupational specialization. The growth of a professionalized bureaucratic civilian and military apparatus was inhibited, although not entirely precluded, by the much celebrated principles of the "mass line," which demanded a close and reciprocal relationship between leaders and led; by campaigns for "simple administration"; and by various *xiafang* and *xiaxiang* policies that required party cadres, government officials, and intellectuals to participate regularly in productive work together with the laboring masses. The harsh and precarious conditions of rural revolutionary warfare, as well as Maoist ideological preference, demanded economic self-sufficiency in local areas, self-reliance, and cooperative forms of work organization—and these principles, necessary for sheer survival, became Chinese Communist ideals that found expression in economic policies that promoted the combination of industrial with agricultural production, and educational policies that centered on the combination of learning with productive labor in various part-time and work-study schools.

The Maoist revolution produced not only new institutional and political patterns but also new social values—and, indeed, a conception of the "new man" who embodied those egalitarian values, the ideal Yan'an guerrilla leader who was capable of performing a variety of military, political, economic, and social tasks, a "jack of all trades" who was able to switch from one job to another, as social and political needs dictated. It was a conception that bore remarkably strong affinities to Marx's vision of the new "all-round man" of the communist future, and it was the prototype for the later Maoist ideal of the "red and expert."[57]

It is paradoxical that the Chinese Communist Revolution, so incongruous with Marx's conception of a modern revolution, and indeed so far removed from any revolutionary process that Lenin could have imagined, should have yielded institutions and values that facilitated the pursuit of such ultimate Marxist goals as abolishing the distinctions between mental and manual labor, between town and countryside, and between worker and peasant. Yet it remains the ironic case that a modern socialist vision was forged in the most backward rural areas of a backward land. As Mark Selden once argued, the Maoist practice of "people's war," as Chinese Communist revolutionary strategy came to be known, "involves not merely a way of fighting but a way of life. It embodies a vision of man and society and an approach to development built on foundations of popular participation and egalitarian values." "In the military, political, social, and economic experiments which collectively represent the Yenan Way," Selden continues, "we find the genesis of revolutionary China's major contributions to the development of man and society." The experience of these revolutionary years, Selden observes, "substantially shaped the characteristic vision of Mao and much of the top leadership of the resistance. And the lessons and legacy of the Yenan era have subsequently inspired many of the boldest and most significant developments of the Chinese revolution."[58]

Although this may be a somewhat romanticized portrait of the Yan'an era and its legacy, there can be little doubt that from the Chinese Communist revolutionary experience there emerged values and institutions that harmonized in remarkable ways with Marxian socialist goals—and which, therefore, were fundamentally in opposition to occupational specialization, and, indeed, to all the social manifestations of the division of labor.

Yet it is most unlikely that the "Yan'an legacy," however powerful and attractive, would long have remained a significant force in the history of the People's Republic had it not been for the particular intellectual orientations of Mao Zedong and the manner in which they conditioned his response to the social consequences of economic development in postrevolutionary China. For in the early years of the People's Republic many of the protosocialist institutions and values of the revolutionary era seemed incongruous with the immediate tasks that confronted the revolutionaries who had come to rule one of the worlds' most backward lands: the building of a strong centralized state and the building of modern industry.[59] The revolutionary heritage was particularly incongruous with the Soviet model of development the Chinese Communists pursued during the period of the First Five-Year Plan, which placed enormous emphasis on the rapid building of heavy industry in urban areas and demanded the establishment of centralized political and economic structures. Among the results of, and preconditions for, rapid industrialization—especially Soviet-style industrialization—was a rapid intensification of the division of labor. As in the case of the Soviet Union, economic and social policies promoted occupational specialization and an acceptance of the new social inequalities that this inevitably entailed. The social manifestations of occupational specialization were entirely familiar: the creation of increasingly specialized economic ministries and planning organs, staffed by professional bureaucrats, to direct the industrialization process; the emergence of new urban administrative and technological elites; the recruitment of factory workers for ever more detailed tasks, and thus an increasingly sharp distinction between mental and manual labor; and a growing gulf (cultural and political as well as social and economic) between the modernizing cities and the backward countryside. These tendencies were reinforced by the establishment of a partly Soviet-style education system designed to train a professionalized technological intelligentsia. Accordingly, the number of scientists and technical personnel grew at an extraordinarily rapid pace, increasing from 50,000 in 1949 (and 425,000 in 1952) to 2,500,000 in the mid-1960s, according to official figures.[60] The figures can be taken as an indicator of the rapidity of the growth of specialization in work—and of social differentiation—in the urban industrial sector of the economy during the early years of the People's Republic. They also reflect the decline of the Yan'an ideal of the "generalist." As Soviet-style industrialization proceeded, the more egalitarian features of the "Yan'an legacy" became ritualized, and Marxian social goals were postponed on the assumption that it was first necessary, as Soviet ideology counseled, to construct the "material base" for their eventual realization.

Mao Zedong's response to the social and ideological consequences of the Stalinist model—whose uncritical adoption he later was to attribute to Chinese inexperience, ignorance, and "dogmatism"[61]—was not to slow the pace of industrialization (indeed, he urged an even more rapid rate of industrial development), but rather to attempt to mitigate the social effects of the division of labor. That attempt centered, in large measure, on a wholesale assault on occupational specialization which was to be pursued both through efforts to bring about radical social change and through political-ideological measures. The assault found its most radical expression in the policies of the Great Leap Forward campaign.

The Great Leap attack on occupational specialization involved radical social measures and proclaimed utopian goals that are well known and need only be briefly outlined here. The organizational heart of the ill-fated movement was the rural people's commune, which, as it was originally conceived and ideally portrayed in 1958, was to be a more or less autonomous and self-sufficient social and political unit that combined "industry, agriculture, trade, education, and military affairs." As an embryonic structure of a future communist society, the commune was assigned the task of abolishing occupational specialization and all social manifestations of the division of labor; as repeatedly proclaimed at the time, the commune was to lead the way to "the gradual diminution and final elimination of the differences between rural and urban areas, between worker and peasant and between mental and manual labor."[62] To Mao Zedong himself, at the outset of the campaign, was attributed the injunction to organize "industry, agriculture, commerce, education and soldiers into a big commune, thereby to form the basic units of society."[63]

The Marxian inspiration for this vision is apparent. It reflected itself, among many other reflections, in the choice of the term "commune," which occupies so hallowed a place in the Marxist tradition. Indeed, much was made at the time of the political similarities between the people's communes and Marx's description of the Paris Commune of 1871, and especially noted was Marx's praise of the Communards' policy of having ordinary working people perform administrative functions in place of professional bureaucrats. Nothing was more frequently reproduced in the Maoist literature of the Great Leap than the passage in *The German Ideology* where Marx condemned the despotism of occupational specialization in existing society where "each man has a particular, exclusive sphere of activity, which is forced upon him and from which he cannot escape," and envisioned the communist revolution in terms of the abolition of the tyranny of the division of labor:

> In communist society, where nobody has one exclusive sphere of activity but each can become accomplished in any branch he wishes, society regulates the general production and thus makes it possible for me to do one thing today and another tomorrow, to hunt in the morning, fish in the afternoon, rear cattle in the evening, criticize after dinner, just as I have a mind, without ever becoming hunter, fisherman, shepherd or critic.[64]

The Maoist antipathy to the division of labor was further reflected in a disdain for experts and specialists. Among the more prominent ideological currents in the Great Leap campaign was the popular injunction that "the masses must make themselves masters of science and technology," thereby, it was believed, doing away with the need for a technical intelligentsia separated from the laboring masses. Educational policies followed in accordance with this demand, emphasizing (as had Marx) the principle of combining education with productive labor through the establishment of a variety of "half-work and half-study" programs, part-time and evening schools, and what were called "red and expert" universities. These were advertised as a means to eliminate the distinction between mental and manual labor. What proved to be one of the more successful and lasting of the Great Leap policies, the program for rural industrialization, was celebrated as a step to narrow the gap between town and countryside and eliminate the differences between workers and peasants. As Mao Zedong enjoined: "Don't crowd into the cities. Vigorously develop industry in the countryside and turn peasants into workers on the spot."[65]

One Great Leap policy that was specifically intended to break down occupational specialization was the "three-unification movement," which attempted to unite cadres, technicians, and workers into single, integrated work units. As Franz Schurmann has observed: "Cadres are leaders; technicians are intellectuals; and workers are the masses. Judging from . . . Mao's speech ['On the Correct Handling of Contradictions Among the People,' 1957], each must be seen as in a contradictory relationship to the others. The three-unification movement launched by the Party was aimed at resolving these contradictions and thereby creating a unity of opposites. Resolution was not just the product of putting the three together. Rather, each was expected in effect to become the other: workers becoming technicians, technicians becoming workers, and both sharing leadership with the cadres."[66]

In the urban industrial sector of the economy, Great Leap policies attacked (albeit with little success) the rigorous division of labor that was demanded by the borrowed Soviet system of industrial organization and management, primarily through policies of social mobilization based on group solidarity and a collectivistic spirit. In wage policy, for example, the principle of payment of material rewards according to individual performance, which prevailed during the period of the First Five-Year Plan, was replaced by a system of collective rewards; piece-rate wages were replaced by time wages; and eventually, at least in theory, wages in general were renounced in favor of payment by "distribution."

Yet between the principles and the practice of the Great Leap, between the intentions and the results of the movement, there was an enormous chasm. Much of the celebrated social radicalism of the campaign was never widely put into practice, many of the policies that were put into effect were implemented in distorted form and irrational ways, and the end result was an economic and human disaster of monumental proportions. But the contradictions of the Great Leap were not only between its theory and practice. The very conception of the campaign was fraught with contradictions from the outset, and nowhere were they more evident than on the issue of the social division of labor. On the one hand, many of the policies of the Great Leap, and certainly Mao's intentions, sought to reduce (or at least mitigate) the human separations and social distinctions wrought by occupational specialization and the existing division of labor. On the other hand, the leaders of the campaign called for an intensification of the division of labor to achieve its proclaimed goals. At the outset of the Great Leap, in the mobilization of peasants for new modes of production, leaders of the campaign demanded more complex forms of work organization in the villages and a more "rational" division of labor. The model agricultural cooperatives, which were being amalgamated into communes in the summer of 1958, were praised by leaders in Beijing for "being administered like a factory," and the official press called for efforts to "organize village work like that of a factory."[67] Party cadres organized peasants and villages into "specialized brigades," and such brigades, according to official party policy, were to have "a specialized division of labor under unified leadership."[68] As Franz Schurmann has described labor mobilization policies in the early phases of the Great Leap: "Concretely the radical transformation of traditional work organization meant that every peasant was recruited into a rationally designed work team which performed specialized rather than general, specific rather than diffuse tasks."[69]

This newly introduced specialized division of labor was profoundly antithetical to the communist social vision the movement projected. In launching the Great Leap, Mao had prophesied both an economic miracle and a social one, both a "great leap" in productive forces that would enable China to overtake the advanced industrialized countries within a few decades and a rapid "transition from socialism and communism." If the two goals as such were not necessarily inherently contradictory, there was certainly an abundance of contradictions in the methods employed to pursue them, both in conception and reality. Mao and Maoists had attempted to use the commune structure to reconcile rapid economic development with radical social change, but in the end the Great Leap furthered neither the economic goals nor the social visions of the movement.

Despite early labor mobilization policies that demanded an increasingly specialized division of labor, the overall thrust of Great Leap policies was highly antithetical to occupational specialization. And this strand in Maoism survived the debacle, finding its main ideological expression in the

Maoist notion of "red and expert."

The dichotomy between "red" and "expert" is one of the most prominent themes in the history of Chinese Communism, and it has appeared in various guises and roles over the decades. The notion, or the "contradiction," if one prefers, variously has been seen as an antagonism between cadres and intellectuals; as a contradiction among old cadres; as a contradiction among intellectuals; as a clash between two competing social ideals and value systems; as a reflection of the "bifurcation of elites" in postrevolutionary society; as a struggle between personal and institutional modes of authority; and as a reflection of the clash between "tradition" and "modernity." But however it is viewed, the history of the "red and expert" formula is intimately intertwined with changing and conflicting Chinese Communist views on the issues of the division of labor and occupational specialization. An emphasis on the "expert" half of the notion has been associated with policies promoting a rational division of labor and the acceptance of occupational specialization as a way of life. The stress on "redness," on the other hand, has been associated with efforts to break down occupational specialization, or at least to limit its extremes.

During the period of the First Five-Year Plan the emphasis was on the value of expertise, and the policies of Beijing's economic planners aimed to develop a highly specialized division of labor in the industrial sector along with rigorously specified lines of responsibility. Much in the fashion that Stalin had created a privileged technological intelligentsia in the Soviet Union two decades before, Chinese leaders fostered a new elite that was to be both red and expert; party cadres were to be professionalized whereas professionals were to be politically and ideologically educated. These elitist tendencies were reflected in party recruitment policies, which favored intellectuals, technicians, and skilled workers.

Until the mid-1950s, Mao was apparently willing to accept the social consequences of Soviet-style industrialization as the necessary price of economic progress. This was clearly not the case by 1956, when he made known his opposition to the eminently Soviet-type formulations of the Eighth Party Congress and to the wage reform act of that year. Yet his views on occupational specialization remained contradictory and ambiguous. In 1957, for example, he advised a group of professionals: "Wisdom comes from the masses. I have always said that intellectuals have the least knowledge. Workers should be the decision-makers."[70] But several months later he acknowledged that "intellectuals are indispensable," providing as they did professors, teachers, scientists, and engineers, and he warned party cadres that they were "in danger of being red but not expert and therefore out of touch with reality."[71] With the launching of the Great Leap Forward campaign, however, Mao transformed the red/expert formula from a conception of the ideal elite into an egalitarian ideal to be realized by all of "the people." Now the masses of workers and peasants themselves were to become scientists and engineers, mastering modern technology and learning the necessary expertise in the course of their daily productive activities. They were to study while they worked, and apply their newly acquired knowledge to immediate productive needs. There was thus to be no separate stratum of experts and intellectuals, but only "reds and experts," a new generation of politically conscious *duomianshou* ("many-sided hands") or "jacks of all trades" emerging from the masses, who were to combine mental with manual labor and who were capable of engaging in "scientific and cultural undertakings as well as physical labor," as the Maoist literature of the time proclaimed. This would soon result in the creation of a whole nation of what Mao called "socialist-conscious, cultured laborers." Everyone, it was said, "will be mental laborer and at the same time a physical laborer; everyone can be a philosopher, scientist, writer, and artist." The "red and expert" notion was thus radically reinterpreted. It no longer simply meant "red" cadres acquiring expertise or experts acquiring "redness," but rather was now transformed into a universal ideal to be universally realized.

With the collapse of the Great Leap campaign and the efforts of the Liu regime to overcome the consequent economic crisis in the early 1960s, party policy and ideology once again emphasized expertise and specialization, as had been the case in the early 1950s. The "master of one technique," not the "jack of all trades," was celebrated as the ideal worker, and, as Schurmann has noted, power at all levels passed from "red" cadres to experts, especially state administrators, factory managers, and experienced old peasants.[72]

For Mao Zedong during these years, the party's stress on specialization and its promotion of experts were symptoms of "revisionism," which, in turn, portended a Soviet-style "restoration of capitalism." As Benjamin Schwartz once observed, whereas Stalin in the 1930s had found the Communist Party insufficiently expert, Mao in the 1960s found the Chinese Party insufficiently red.[73] Mao continued to champion the Great Leap version of the red and expert ideal, but with an increasing emphasis on redness. He repeatedly insisted that the politically conscious "generalist" or "outsider" was to lead the expert.[74] For political and professional elites, he demanded the reinstitution of the old remedy of regular participation in physical labor with the masses. "Without participation in labor," he warned, "party cadres will become separated from the working masses, which entails revisionism."[75] "Most official personnel should work (at their desks) half-time and labor (with the masses) half-time," he counseled. "Laziness is one of the sources of revisionism," he added.[76]

In the years immediately preceding the Cultural Revolution, Mao became convinced that the main site and source of the revisionist infection was

China's hierarchical political system, especially the cadre-ranking system and the work-grade system, which fostered elitism and specialization. He had made known his distaste for the grade-level system at the beginning of the Great Leap: "Bourgeois right must be destroyed every day, such as stressing qualifications or grade levels and not stressing the benefits of the supply system. . . . In 1953 we changed the supply system to a wage system. This method was basically correct. We had to compromise. But there were defects. On grade levels we also compromised. . . . The grade-level system is a father-son relationship, a cat-mouse relationship."[77] The implications of these comments, as Joseph Esherick has pointed out, suggest that Mao was less concerned with economic inequalities (although he continually called for narrowing wage and other economic differentials) than he was with the social distinctions in status and authority conferred by political power.

After the collapse of the Great Leap, Mao grew increasingly harsh in his criticisms of the privileges and attitudes of cadres and bureaucrats, of the new forms of social stratification generated by the postrevolutionary political system, and of occupational specialization in general. He spoke of socialist societies producing "vested interest groups" who "are content with the existing system and do not want to change it."[78] He was bitterly critical of party cadres who, he charged, had abandoned their revolutionary ideals and become conservative bureaucrats, seeking only power, social status, and luxuries.[79] And the children of cadres offered little hope for the future:

> The higher salaried strata of a socialist society have a bit more cultural knowledge but tend to be a trifle slow when compared to the lower strata. Thus our cadres' sons and daughters do not quite compare with the children of non-cadres.
>
> The children of cadres are a cause of discouragement. They lack experience of life and society, yet their airs are considerable and they have a great sense of superiority.[80]

Of particular significance was Mao's critique of Stalin's celebrated injunction that "cadres decide everything," a slogan identified in Soviet history with the Stalinist drive to widen and sanction differences in social status and occupation, especially the privileged status of the technological intelligentsia, and with the general institutionalization of socioeconomic inequality. On this Mao wrote in 1962: "Stalin's book from first to last says nothing about the superstructure. It is not concerned with people; it considers things not people. . . . They [the Soviets] believe that technology decides everything, that cadres decide everything, speaking only of 'expert,' never of 'red,' only of cadres, never of the masses."[81]

Further, taking issue with the Soviet orthodoxy that contradictions under socialism are reconcilable, Mao noted the continued existence of the major social manifestations of the division of labor and occupational specialization. In a socialist society, he warned, "there are still conservative strata and something like 'vested interest groups.' There still remain differences between mental and manual labor, city and countryside, worker and peasant. Although these are not antagonistic contradictions they cannot be resolved without struggle."[82]

Partly responsible for the production and perpetuation of these "conservative strata" and "vested interest groups" was China's elitist educational system, which Mao condemned as "exceedingly destructive of people."[83] To remedy a specialized education system that produced only experts and created divisions and separations among people, Mao proposed in 1964—and not for the first time—putting into practice the old Marxist principle of "the union of education with productive labor."[84] And to illustrate the virtues of abolishing the distinction between mental and manual labor, he set forth as historical examples Benjamin Franklin and James Watt: "Franklin of America was originally a newspaper seller, yet he discovered electricity. Watt was a worker, yet he invented the steam engine."[85]

Over the post-Great Leap years Mao Zedong retained and promoted a vision of the red and expert as a universalist ideal of the politically conscious "jack of all trades" who combined "brain work with brawn work," who could switch from one task to another as social needs dictated, and who mastered modern technology in the course of everyday productive activities. It was an ideal that at once harked back to a romanticized memory of the "generalist" revolutionary cadre of the heroic Yan'an era and projected a utopian Marxist image of the future "all-round communist man"—however incongruent this ideal was with the social realities of postrevolutionary China, and particularly with Chinese society in the early 1960s. It was of course an ideal that was highly antithetical to occupational specialization as a way of life, and in that sense, perhaps, incompatible with the immediate needs of modern economic development. But it did reflect Mao's abiding belief that "a man should work in many fields [and] have contact with all sorts of people."[86]

The Cultural Revolution began with a wholesale attack on occupational specialization and the existing division of labor. At the outset of the upheaval, Mao, in his "May 7th Directive" of 1966, counseled that all people working in what he identified as the seven main sectors of China's economic and political structure—industry, agriculture, military, education, commerce, service, and government—should acquire the skills necessary for work in sectors other than their own, and do so by practical experience in a variety of productive activities. Thus soldiers, as in the heroic Yan'an days, were to engage in agricultural production and operate small factories. Peasants were to work in industry and engage in educational and military activities as well as in agricultural production. Factory workers, "while mainly engaging in industrial activity . . . should also study military affairs and politics and raise their education level [and] where conditions permit, they should also engage in agriculture and side-occupations, just as people do in the Daqing Oilfield."[87] Those working in commerce were urged to gain experience in the production of the goods they sold: "Cloth-dealers should learn to weave cloth; vegetable-mongers should learn to grow vegetables."[88]

The national models for industry and agriculture celebrated and popularized during the Cultural Revolution were ones where occupational specialization had been downgraded and the social effects of the division of labor reduced. Thus, the Daqing Oilfield was praised not only for its contribution to national "self-reliance" but also because oil workers had achieved self-sufficiency in food by engaging in agricultural production, thereby moving toward the goals of eliminating the distinctions between town and countryside and between worker and peasant. Daqing was further celebrated because, it was claimed, professional managers had been replaced by a new "division of labor responsibility system under the collective leadership of the Party Committee."[89] Similarly, the constitution of the Anshan Iron and Steel Works, first promulgated in 1960, was widely praised during the Cultural Revolution for rejecting the Soviet "one-man management" system, reducing distinctions between workers and technocratic elites, and providing for workers' participation in management, planning, and technological development—thereby reducing the distinction between mental and manual labor. In agriculture, the Cultural Revolution model was the relatively egalitarian Dazhai brigade, also hailed for integrating "brain work" with "brawn labor."

The Cultural Revolution critique of occupational specialization was accompanied by Maoist attacks on wage differentials and the prevailing work-grade system. As Mao reportedly declared in 1967:

> Why should we practice the wage system? This is a concession to the bourgeoisie and would discredit us by ridiculing the "style of the countryside" and the "habits of the guerrilla" and lead to the development of individualism. . . . How about letting the military lead in restoring the supply system? The bourgeois conception of law should be relinquished. For example, rank, extra pay for extra working hours, and the theory that mental labor should be more highly paid than physical labor are all remnants of the bourgeoisie. . . . Our Party members in general lived a life of egalitarianism, worked diligently, and fought bravely up until the period of liberation. They did not depend on material stimulation at all but were inspired by the revolutionary spirit.[90]

During the Cultural Revolution, and indeed throughout what is now somewhat misleadingly termed "the Cultural Revolution decade," there was an enormous ideological emphasis on eliminating the "three great differences"—between mental and manual labor, town and countryside, and worker and peasant.

Yet while the ideology of the Cultural Revolution seemingly called for a fundamental transformation in the division of labor, the actual social results of the great upheaval were meager. There were, in fact, no significant changes in the existing division of labor or in prevailing patterns of work organization. The hierarchical work-grade system remained intact in its pre–Cultural Revolution form. The old wage system for workers, technicians, and cadres (with its large differentials between and among them) was largely untouched, save for the partial and temporary elimination of individual bonuses and prizes and ideological campaigns emphasizing the virtues of moral rather than material incentives. The relationship between town and countryside remained basically as it had been; while the Cultural Revolution yielded a greater emphasis on education and medical care in the rural areas, the urban-based state bureaucracy continued to exploit the villages much in the fashion as it has in earlier years. The more radical and egalitarian demands for fundamental changes in the prevailing system of industrial organization, issuing from certain sectors of the working class movement and voiced by some of the more radical leaders in Beijing, were denounced as "ultra-leftist" well before the Cultural Revolution had run its tragic course.

Such changes as the Cultural Revolution yielded in the industrial sector, such as measures to permit limited worker participation in management and technical innovation, were at best reformist in character. Many of these were far less than they were advertised to be at the time, and most were gradually abandoned in the early 1970s in favor of pre–Cultural Revolution forms of managerial authority, factory work rules, and labor discipline. Cultural Revolution policies that required managers and technical personnel to descend to labor periodically on factory benches (and cadres to labor in the fields) were, among other things, an expression of Mao Zedong's distaste for occupational specialization; but they did little, in the end, to alter the division of labor or even reduce status differentials. Such measures perhaps had a certain symbolic significance, but their effects on the consciousness of those involved were problematic in the short term and negligible over the long term, and they certainly did not reach to the structural roots of occupational specialization. There is little in the practice of the Cultural Revolution—as distinguished from its radical rhetoric and perhaps the intentions of its authors—to support the argument that the upheaval initiated a process of the revolutionary transformation of the industrial division of labor.[91]

How should we go about evaluating—and on the basis of what standards of judgment—the Maoist attempt to limit the development of the division of labor and mitigate its social consequences, especially occupational specialization and growing social inequality? The judgment of Mao's successors is quite clear, and quite clearly based on orthodox Marxist-Leninist perspectives. Mao Zedong's efforts to introduce socialist relations of production were pushed too far and too hastily in view of China's low level of economic development, it is now said in Beijing, and thus Maoist attempts to limit the development of the division of labor and occupational specialization were economically detrimental and socially irresponsible. Mao's policies, at least over the final two decades of his life, were therefore "utopian," in the traditionally pejorative Marxist sense of that term. For this critique, based on the assumption that stages of social development follow from levels of economic development, copious support can of course be found in classical Marxist writings. Marx and Engels often warned of the futility, and indeed the dangers, of "premature" attempts to create socialism in historical situations where modern productive forces were ill-developed. "Right can never be higher than the economic structure of society and its cultural development conditioned thereby," Marx wrote.[92] And Engels cautioned: "Only at a certain level of development of the productive forces of society, an even very high level for our modern conditions, does it become possible to raise production to such an extent that the abolition of class distinctions can be a real progress, can be lasting without bringing about stagnation or even decline in the mode of social production."[93]

Yet Marx and Engels did not anticipate—nor could they possibly have foreseen—that modern socialist revolutions proceeding under Marxist banners would take place not in the advanced industrialized countries of the West but rather in the agrarian and largely precapitalist lands of the East. But this is the course that twentieth-century history has taken, and there is little to suggest that it will reverse itself in the foreseeable future. While Western Marxists may bemoan this irony of history (and non-Marxists may savor it), the Marxist revolutionaries who successfully struggled for power in economically backward lands have been confronted with a cruel paradox on the morrow of their political victories. For the will to achieve socialism has been repeatedly frustrated by the absence of socialism's essential material and cultural preconditions. They thus have been forced to turn their energies, and harness the energies of the populations over whom they came to rule, to the task not of building socialism but of constructing its economic preconditions, to developing the productive forces abortive capitalist regimes failed to provide. This, in turn, has involved agonizing moral and practical dilemmas, not the least of them, the dilemma of building a modern economy without surrendering the socialist goals and spirit of the revolution in the process.

The Soviet response to this dilemma, foreshadowed by Lenin and made explicit by Stalin and his successors, was (and remains) an easy and comforting formula. The nationalization of the key means of production by a presumably "socialist" state, combined with rapid industrialization, as the Soviet orthodoxy has it, will more or less automatically and inevitably yield ever higher levels of socialism and eventually the arrival of communism. The social results of the policies ideologically rationalized by this now hoary notion are well known—and they offer little comfort or inspiration to those who still hope that socialist revolutions will yield socialist societies. As Mao Zedong diagnosed the matter, Stalin was concerned only with "things, not people." "This [Soviet] textbook addresses itself only to material preconditions and seldom engages the question of the superstructure, i.e., the class nature of the state, philosophy, and science." "Again and again the text emphasizes how important machinery is for the transformation [to socialism]. But if the consciousness of the peasantry is not raised, if ideology is not transformed, and you are depending on nothing but machinery—what good will it be?"[94] Socialist societies, Mao argued time and again, produce "vested interest groups" which become solidified as conservative barriers to the realization of socialist ideals.

What distinguished Mao's Marxism was a unique attempt, however flawed in practice, to reconcile the means of modern economic development with the ends of socialism. Socialism, for Mao, was not the predetermined outcome of the development of the productive forces, nor was it dependent on any given level of economic development in general. People, he believed, were free to choose their ends, and therefore they had an obligation to choose means consistent with the ends they sought. Thus, if modern economic development was to lead to a socialist historical outcome, the construction of socialist institutions and the socialist transformation of human beings were tasks to be undertaken in the here and now, as part of the process of building the material foundations for a socialist society. "If a socialist society does not promote socially collectivistic aims," Mao once asked, "then what of socialism still remains?"[95] It is in the perspective of this recognition that the search for socialist ends could not be separated from socialist means that one ultimately must view Mao's attempts to limit the intensification of the division of labor and the growth of occupational specialization. That attempt reflected not an old Confucian bias but an eminently socialist concern—more precisely, a concern growing out of a confrontation with the perhaps irresolvable dilemmas of attempting to build a socialist society in conditions of economic scarcity.

Post-Mao Chinese Marxist Ideology

Mao Zedong's concern with the division of labor and occupational specialization might also be viewed, in hindsight, from the perspective of how his successors have treated these issues in the post-Mao era. One of the more prominent features of recent Chinese Marxist theory is praise for the virtues of the division of labor and occupational specialization. This is wholly in accord with the economically deterministic version of Marxism that has become the official ideology of the post-Mao regime—and with the enormous emphasis in that ideology on the historically progressive character of capitalism. Deng Xiaoping, shortly after his achievement of supreme power, took the lead in promoting occupational specialization, which he coupled with an effort to depoliticize social and economic life in general. Early in 1979 Deng advised the masses that their business was production, not politics, and production within their own respective occupational spheres: "Extracting more oil is the politics of the petroleum industry, producing more coal is the politics of coal miners, growing more grain is the politics of peasants, defending the frontiers is the politics of soldiers, and working hard in study is the politics of students. The only criterion for the results of political education is its utility in improving the economic situation."[96]

At the same time, Deng moved to secure the privileged socioeconomic status and professional autonomy of technical specialists, intellectuals, and bureaucrats by reviving the formula he first had set forth (and Mao had opposed) at the Eighth Party Congress in 1956, decreeing that intellectuals "are part of the proletariat. The difference between them and the manual workers lies only in a different role in the social division of labor."[97] Beyond revealing an astonishing ignorance of Marxism—"*only* a matter of division of labor within the same class" was the way Deng originally put it[98]—the new orthodoxy classifying intellectuals as members of the working class served to bury the question of the distinction between mental and manual labor, thereby concealing the conflicting social class interests inevitably produced by that distinction. It hardly needs to be noted that the revived formula proved highly attractive to bureaucrats, intellectuals, and other "brain workers." No less appealing were additional decrees proclaiming that class divisions in Chinese society had virtually ceased to exist, and others condemning the theory of a "bureaucratic ruling class," a notion heard during the Cultural Revolution and revived by many Democracy Movement activists in the years 1979–1981.

These ideological pronouncements have supported social policies promoting professionalism and orderly careerism, serving to consolidate and institutionalize the privileged position of urban elites. The post-Mao regime has endeavored (with considerable success) to raise the material conditions of life and work and the social status of intellectuals, technical specialists, factory managers, and professionals, and to grant them considerable autonomy within their respective spheres of expertise in exchange for political loyalty (or, for that matter, apolitical loyalty). As a result, these groups have become the most reliable political supporters of the current government—indeed, one might say they constitute the regime's essential social base—and occupational specialization has been firmly established as the way of life in post-Mao China.

Chinese Marxist theoreticians have risen to the occasion by producing a voluminous body of literature calling for (and ideologically rationalizing) a more specialized division of labor in social production in general. The dominant argument currently pursued, with minor variations, begins with the now well-established orthodoxy that "the relations of production must conform to the character of productive forces." It is further argued that China is still largely mired in what is termed a more or less self-sufficient "natural economy." That allegedly being the case, the only and necessary way to overcome this condition of backwardness is the rapid development of a commodity economy. The growth of commodity exchange, together with the general development of productive forces, demands, in turn, an ever more specialized division of labor. As typically put: "In the present period [the development of productive forces requires] great changes in the level of the socialization of production, a more intensified social division of labor, more and more departments and trades, [and] an ever greater variety of products."[99] To be sure, the negative aspects of the division of labor are sometimes noted, that is to say, its dehumanizing effects on the laborers, but that is a problem that can be resolved only in the distant future, when a very high level of modern productive forces has been achieved.[100] In the meantime, and for the foreseeable future, it is the economic efficacy of occupational specialization and an intensified division of labor that is stressed and prized. Moreover, the suppression of discussion of Marx's concept of alienation (and the notion of "socialist alienation") since the 1983–84 campaign against "spiritual pollution" largely precludes discourse on the division of labor as a source of alienation.

Just as the post-Mao regime fosters specialization in economic life and social roles, so it attempts to do so in China's political structure. The essential aim of what is advertised as "political reform," at least insofar as higher party leaders are concerned, is not "socialist democracy" but rather the more prosaic goal of making the bureaucratic corps "better educated, professionally more competent, and younger," as Deng Xiaoping candidly put it.[101] In refashioning the political apparatus, the watchword is professionalism, and thus there is an enormous emphasis on the standard bureaucratic virtues of occupational and functional specialization, clearly defined responsibilities, strict subordination to higher administrative levels, and adherence to "rational" rules and regulations that promote efficiency, precision, predictability, and impersonality. The authors of most treatises on "political reform" seem more like disciples of Max Weber than of Karl

Marx. And insofar as plans to professionalize the bureaucracy are successful, they will serve to make bureaucrats a more distinct social group, more fully conscious of their status and interests—and thereby the already enormous gulf between rulers and ruled in Chinese society will be widened, as will the distinction between mental and manual labor.

The virtues of specialization and professionalism brought to the "modernization" of the bureaucracy in general have also been applied to the Chinese Communist Party itself. Here, beyond reestablishing firm Leninist principles of organization and discipline in party life, Deng Xiaoping has added a Stalinist tinge. In a speech delivered in January 1980 (and on subsequent occasions), Deng complained that party members lacked specialized knowledge and modern technical skills.[102] His solution for this red/expert dilemma was less to bring expertise to current party members than to bring experts into the party, replacing millions of purged "leftists." It was the same remedy Stalin had discovered a half-century before. In the 1920s the Soviet party had recruited its membership primarily among industrial workers, and to a lesser degree among people from peasant social backgrounds. Under Stalin in the 1930s, the new recruits were mostly professionals, technicians, and intellectuals. Stalin, as Benjamin Schwartz has observed, emphasized the "social engineering" function of the party rather than its moral virtues. "If Mao was to find the Party insufficiently Red, Stalin found it insufficiently expert," Schwartz wrote.[103]

Deng, like Stalin, also stresses the "social engineering" role of the party in his pursuit of modernization, and he has found the party insufficiently expert to perform the task. He has therefore instructed it to emphasize the recruitment of professionals and intellectuals who possess specialized knowledge and technical skills, and to give priority for promotion to those who graduated from universities and senior middle schools prior to the Cultural Revolution. Thus, the long-standing and agonizing red/expert contradiction has been resolved in eminently Soviet fashion.

The official ideology of the post-Mao regime sanctions policies that foster an intensified division of labor and increasing occupational specialization—and ones that produce the inevitable social consequences of these phenomena, such as growing socioeconomic inequalities and a greater distinction between mental and manual labor. That these social and ideological tendencies are incongruous with socialism, and antithetical to what so long has been hailed as China's "transition to socialism," is hardly a point that need be belabored. Marx, after all, defined socialism (or what he called "the lower phase of communism") as a transitional period that demanded progressive transformations of existing production relations (and especially measures to abolish gradually the inherited capitalist division of labor and its various social manifestations), which would be replaced, initially in embryonic form, by new communist productive relations.

The incongruity between Marxist theory and Chinese reality is officially explained by China's continued economic backwardness, and the resulting contradiction between the country's relatively "advanced" productive relations and its low level of productive forces. Thus, to resolve the contradiction, all energies are to be devoted to developing modern productive forces in the most rapid fashion possible through the most efficient means available, thereby establishing what are assumed to be the necessary economic prerequisites for socialism. Here post-Mao China follows the Soviet path, both economically and ideologically, albeit with variations in economic methods and forms. The Bolsheviks, beginning with Lenin, confronted with the unanticipated problem of a socialist revolution confined to a single backward country, expediently (perhaps out of historical necessity) accepted and built upon an existing capitalist mode of production, perforce intensifying the division of labor and occupational specialization in the process. The rationale for this mimicry of capitalism was that it was necessary to "lay the material foundations for socialism," as Soviet ideologies so long and so loudly proclaimed. The material foundations have been laid, but a socialist society has not issued from the process, and the prospects that it might do so in the foreseeable historical future are dim indeed.

The Maoist regime in China first embarked on a Soviet path. But Mao Zedong soon recognized that capitalist means could not be used to serve socialist ends. His concern, especially in his still officially unpublished critiques of the Stalinist pattern of development, turned to what he termed "relations among people in productive labor," rather than simply to the production and consumption of goods. He thus attempted to limit the development of the division of labor and occupational specialization, along with the inequalities they generated. Yet, in the end, Mao produced no viable solutions for the problem of reconciling the means and ends of socialism in an economically backward land.

Perhaps the intensification of the division of labor and the acceptance of occupational specialization as a way of life, and the alienating work these phenomena produce, should be counted as part of the social price that must be paid for modernization, or what Chinese ideologists prefer to call "socialist modernization." But the Soviet historical experience suggests that paying the price does not necessarily purchase the desired social results. It seems most doubtful that the present course being pursued by China's post-Mao regime, mimicking as it does its capitalist and Soviet predecessors, is likely to yield a society any more "socialist" than the one produced by Soviet modernization.

From both the Russian and Chinese historical records, it is easy enough to conclude that socialism is historically impossible, or at least a futile endeavor in lands burdened by conditions of material scarcity. It is tempting to dispose of the whole matter by invoking Karl Marx, who, in one of his more deterministic moments, declared: "The country that is more developed industrially only shows, to the less developed, the image of its own future."[104] But those who still hope for a socialist future for humankind might prefer to believe that the dilemmas of the means and ends of socialism in the modern world have yet to be fully historically explored. It cannot be taken for granted, and certainly not in the light of either modern or premodern historical experience, that modes of production and forms of work organization are technologically rather than socially (or politically) determined. As Mao Zedong once noted: "Much remains to be written about human relations in the course of labor."[105] It was precisely by challenging the technical determinism that pervades so much of contemporary thought, Marxist and non-Marxist alike, that Mao raised critical questions about the means and ends of socialism, and its human and social prerequisites, challenging conventional Marxist-Leninist orthodoxies on the economic preconditions for socialism and communism. The difficulty is not so much that Mao lacked answers for the questions he posed, but rather that his successors no longer pose the questions at all.

Notes

1. Frederick Engels, *The Origin of the Family, Private Property and the State*, in Marx and Engels, *Selected Works* (Moscow, 1949), 2:205.

2. Marx and Engels, *Collected Works* (New York: International Publishers, 1975), 3:317.

3. Marx, *Capital* (Chicago: Kerr, 1906), 1:400.

4. Marx and Engels, *Selected Works*, 2:23.

5. As Marx observed in *Capital*: "This division of labour is a necessary condition for the production of commodities, but it does not follow, conversely, that the production of commodities is a necessary condition for the division of labour. In the primitive Indian community, there is social division of labour without production of commodities."

6. Marx, *Capital*, 1:386.

7. Marx and Engels, *The German Ideology* (New York: International Publishers, 1960).

8. Engels, *Origin of the Family*, in Marx and Engels, *Selected Works*, 2:205.

9. Marx and Engels, *The German Ideology*.

10. Engels, *Herr Eugen Dühring's Revolution in Science (Anti-Dühring)* (Moscow, 1947), p. 418.

11. Socioeconomic life in so-called Asiatic societies, according to Marx, revolves about isolated and self-sufficient communal villages based on the "domestic union" of agriculture and handicrafts, i.e., a fixed division of labor, the condition responsible for

the alleged stagnation of such societies. See, for example, Marx, "The British Rule in India," in Marx and Engels, *Selected Works*, 1:312–18.

12. Marx and Engels, *The German Ideology*.

13. It is by no means the case that Marx viewed successive modes of production as necessarily progressive historical developments, even in strictly economic terms. For example, he offers the following description of the origins of Western feudalism: "If antiquity started out from the town and its territory, the Middle Ages started out from the country. This different starting point was determined by the sparseness of the population at that time. . . . In contrast to Greece and Rome, feudal development therefore extends over a much wider field. . . . The last centuries of the declining Roman Empire and its conquest by the barbarians destroyed a number of productive forces; agriculture had declined, industry had decayed for want of a market, trade had died out or been violently suspended, the rural and urban population had decreased. From these conditions and the mode of organization of the conquest determined by them, feudal property developed under the influence of the Germanic military constitution." (*The German Ideology*, pp. 11–12). This is hardly a portrait of economic progress, much less historical progress in general.

14. "Division of labour only becomes truly such," Marx remarks, "from the moment when a division of material and mental labour appears." Ibid.

15. Ibid.

16. Marx, *Capital*, 1:387.

17. *The German Ideology*, p. 44.

18. Engels, *Anti-Dühring*, pp. 434–35.

19. The reasons for the continual intensification of the division of labor under capitalism are not difficult to understand. As Marx explains, "the productive power of labour is raised, above all, by a greater division of labour, by a more universal introduction and continual improvement of machinery. The greater the labour army among whom labour is divided, the more gigantic the scale on which machinery is introduced, the more does the cost of production proportionately decrease, the more fruitful is labour. Hence, a general rivalry arises among the capitalists to increase the division of labour and machinery and to exploit them on the greatest possible scale." Marx, "Wage Labour and Capital," in Marx and Engels, *Selected Works*, 1:92.

20. See *Capital*, 1:385–556.

21. *The German Ideology*.

22. *Capital*, 1:461.

23. Ibid., vol. 1.

24. Ibid.

25. Marx, "Economic and Philosophic Manuscripts," in *The Marx-Engels Reader*, ed. Robert C. Tucker (New York: Norton, 1978), pp. 70–72. Marx goes on to observe: "Political economy conceals the estrangement inherent in the nature of labour by not considering the direct relationship between the worker (labour) and production. It is true that labour produces for the rich wonderful things—but for the worker it produces privation. It produces palaces—but for the worker, hovels. It produces beauty—but for the worker, deformity. It replaces labour by machines—but some of the workers it throws back to a barbarous type of labour, and the other workers it turns into machines. It produces intelligence—but for the worker, idiocy, cretinism."

26. Marx, *Capital*, 1:462.
27. Marx, "Wage Labour and Capital," p. 95.
28. Marx, *Capital*, 1:396.
29. Ibid., 1:399.
30. Ibid., 1:534.
31. Ibid., 1:389.
32. Ibid., 1:396.
33. Ibid., 1:374, 383–84.
34. Engels, *Anti-Dühring*, pp. 435–36.
35. Marx and Engels, *The German Ideology*, p. 22.
36. Engels, *Anti-Dühring*, pp. 437–38.
37. The point is superbly argued by Robert C. Tucker, *The Marxian Revolutionary Idea* (New York: Norton, 1969), chaps. 1, 2.
38. Of the products of capitalist industry, Engels observes, "No one person could say of them: 'I made that; this is my product.' " Engels, "Socialism: Utopian and Scientific," Marx and Engels, *Selected Works*, 2:127.
39. Engels, *Anti-Dühring*, p. 438.
40. Ibid., pp. 438–39.
41. Marx, "Critique of the Gotha Program," in Marx and Engels, *Selected Works*, 2:23.
42. Marx, *The Poverty of Philosophy* (New York: International Publishers, 1963), p. 147.
43. As Marx formulates it in the third of the "Theses on Feuerbach": "The materialist doctrine that men are products of circumstances and upbringing, and that therefore changed men are the product of other circumstances and changed upbringing, forgets that it is men who change circumstances and that the educator himself must be educated. . . . The coincidence of the changing of circumstances and human activity can be conceived and rationally understood only as revolutionizing practice."
44. Marx and Engels, *Selected Works*, 1:50–51.
45. Marx, *Capital*, 1:529–30.
46. Ibid., 1:534.
47. Engels, *Anti-Dühring*, pp. 441, 442–44.
48. Tucker, *The Marxian Revolutionary Idea*, p. 21.
49. As, for example, in the 1927 "Hunan Report" with its contempt for urban intellectuals, and where Mao contrasts "the futile clamour of the intelligentsia and so-called 'educators' for 'popular education' " with the innate wisdom and creativity of the peasantry. *Selected Works of Mao Tse-tung* (London: Lawrence & Wishart, 1954), 1:56–57.
50. As I have noted elsewhere, China's decadal rate of industrial growth under the Maoist regime compares favorably with the most intensive periods of industrialization in Germany, Japan, and the Soviet Union, however much the Maoist economic record is flawed in other respects. See Maurice Meisner, *Mao's China and After* (New York: Free Press, 1986), chap. 22.
51. For example, Mary C. Wright, "The Pre-Revolutionary Intellectuals of China and Russia," *China Quarterly* (April–June 1961): 179.
52. Quoted in Joseph Levenson, *Confucian China and Its Modern Fate* (Berkeley:

University of California Press, 1968), 1:16.

53. *The Works of Mencius*, book 3, part 1, chap. 4, Legge, 2:125–26.

54. Mao Zedong, "A Study of Physical Culture," *Xin qingnian* (April 1917).

55. Mao, "The Great Union of the Popular Masses," extract translated in Stuart R. Schram, *The Political Thought of Mao Tse-tung* (New York: Praeger, 1969), pp. 162–64.

56. Mao Zedong, "Speech at Hangchow," (December 1965), in *Mao Tse-tung Unrehearsed: Talks and Letters, 1956–1971*, ed. Stuart R. Schram (Middlesex, England: Penguin, 1974), p. 239.

57. On the relationship between the Yan'an ideal and the post-1949 "red and expert" notion, and the tension between "reds" and "experts," see Franz Schurmann, *Ideology and Organization in Communist China* (Berkeley: University of California Press, 1968), pp. 163–72.

58. Mark Selden, *The Yenan Way in Revolutionary China* (Cambridge: Harvard University Press, 1971), pp. vii–ix.

59. These were the two "present" tasks Mao set forth on the eve of the founding of the People's Republic in his 1949 treatise "On People's Democratic Dictatorship," while at the same time both reaffirming and postponing Marxian socialist goals. *Selected Works of Mao Tse-tung* (Beijing: Foreign Languages Press, 1961), 4:411–24.

60. Tong Dalin and Hu Ping, "Science and Technology," in *China's Socialist Modernization*, ed. Yu Guangyuan (Beijing: Foreign Languages Press, 1984), p. 644.

61. "We lacked understanding of the whole economic situation, and understood still less the economic differences between the Soviet Union and China. So all we could do was to follow blindly," Mao commented in 1958. Mao, "Talks at Chengtu" (March 10, 1958), in *Mao Tse-tung Unrehearsed*, ed. Schram, p. 99.

62. "Resolution on Questions Concerning People's Communes," Sixth Plenary Session of the Eighth Central Committee of the Chinese Communist Party, December 10, 1958.

63. The words were attributed to Mao by Chen Boda. See *Hongqi* (Red flag) 4 (July 16, 1958)

64. Marx and Engels, *The German Ideology*, p. 22.

65. *Mao Zedong sixiang wan sui* (Taipei: n.p., 1969), p. 389.

66. Schurmann, *Ideology and Organization*, pp. 75–76.

67. *Renmin ribao* (People's daily), July 4, 1958. Cited in Schurmann, *Ideology and Organization*, p. 467.

68. Ibid., p. 469.

69. Ibid., p. 471.

70. *Mao Zedong sixiang wan sui*, p. 121.

71. Ibid., pp. 131, 146.

72. Schurmann, *Ideology and Organization*, p. 534.

73. Benjamin Schwartz, "The Reign of Virtue: Some Broad Perspectives on Leader and Party in the Cultural Revolution," in *Party Leadership and Revolutionary Power in China*, ed. John W. Lewis (Cambridge: Cambridge University Press, 1970), p. 164.

74. *Mao Zedong sixiang wan sui*, p. 221.

75. Ibid., p. 445.

76. Ibid., p. 499.

77. Cited in Joseph W. Esherick, "On the 'Restoration of Capitalism': Mao and Marxist Theory," *Modern China* 5, 1 (January 1979): 61.

78. *Mao Zedong sixiang wan sui*, p. 344.

79. As early as 1957 Mao complained that "some cadres now scramble for fame and fortune and are interested only in personal gain." Mao, *Selected Works of Mao Tse-tung* (Beijing: Foreign Languages Press, 1977), 5:350–51. His condemnation of cadre greed became increasingly frequent and harsh in the early 1960s.

80. Mao, "Reading Notes on the Soviet Text 'Political Economy,' " in *A Critique of Soviet Economics* (New York: Monthly Review Press, 1977), pp. 117, 71.

81. Mao, "Critique of Stalin's 'Economic Problems of Socialism in the USSR,' " in *A Critique of Soviet Economics*, p. 135.

82. Mao, "Reading Notes on the Soviet Text 'Political Economy,' " p. 71.

83. Mao, "Remarks at the Spring Festival" (February 13, 1964), in *Mao Tse-tung Unrehearsed*, ed. Schram, p. 208.

84. Ibid., p. 206.

85. Ibid., p. 208. "Both in ancient and modern times, in China and abroad," Mao added, "many scientists trained themselves in the course of practice."

86. Mao, "Speech at Hangchow" (December 21, 1965), in *Mao Tse-tung Unrehearsed*, ed. Schram, p. 239.

87. *Beijing Review*, May 14, 1976, p. 9.

88. *Shanghai wenhui bao*, September 5, 1968. Cited in Richard Kraus, *Class Conflict in Chinese Socialism* (New York: Columbia University Press, 1981), p. 151.

89. On the Daqing model, see Stephen Andors, *China's Industrial Revolution: Politics, Planning, and Management, 1949 to the Present* (New York: Pantheon, 1977), pp. 143–47.

90. "Mao's Latest Instruction," in *Chinese Communist Affairs: Facts and Features* 1 (November 1, 1967): 18–19; cited in Lowell Dittmer, *Liu Shao-ch'i and the Chinese Cultural Revolution* (Berkeley: University of California Press, 1974), p. 193.

91. The argument was presented in its most sophisticated version by Charles Bettleheim in *Cultural Revolution and Industrial Organization in China: Changes in Management and the Division of Labor* (New York: Monthly Review Press, 1974). See especially the section entitled "Transformations in the Social Division of Labor," pp. 69–89.

92. Marx, "Critique of the Gotha Program," in Marx and Engels, *Selected Works*, 2:23.

93. Engels, "On Social Relations in Russia," in Marx and Engels, *Selected Works*, 2:46.

94. Mao, "Reading Notes on the Soviet Text 'Political Economy,' " p. 55.

95. *Mao Zedong sixiang wan sui*, p. 197.

96. *Renmin ribao*, April 11, 1979.

97. *Beijing Review*, March 24, 1978.

98. Deng Xiaoping, "Report of the Revision of the Constitution of the Communist Party of China," *Eighth National Congress of the Communist Party of China: Documents* (Beijing, 1956), 1:213. (Emphasis added.)

99. Yu Zuyao, "Shehuizhuyi shangpin jingji lun" (On the socialist commodity

economy), *Jingji yanjiu* (Economic research) 11 (1984): 14.

100. Ibid., p. 11.

101. Deng Xiaoping, Speech to the party Politburo delivered August 15, 1980. Text in *Issues and Studies* (March 1981): 81–103.

102. Deng Xiaoping, Report of January 16, 1980.

103. Schwartz, "The Reign of Virtue," p. 164.

104. Marx, *Capital*, 1:13.

105. Mao, "Reading Notes on the Soviet Text 'Political Economy,' " p. 67.

6

MAO, SCIENCE, TECHNOLOGY, AND HUMANITY

Bill Brugger

Science and Technology: Are They Different?

China is currently pursuing its "four modernizations." Of these, the third is "science and technology." These two terms are lumped together now as they were in Mao's day. How do they differ? No philosopher has as yet come up with a satisfactory definition of science, nor has even solved successfully Popper's problem of demarcating it from nonscience or pseudoscience. It is generally agreed, however, that, though science may never be totally value-free, it differs from technology in its greater distance from social determinants and purposes of human emancipation. In the Marxian couplet, science helps to interpret the world and technology to change it.

If, however, one adheres to the Marxian view that understanding and changing the world are unified dialectically, then the two concepts have to be seen as part of a totality, constantly informing and transforming each other. Herein lies a major problem. It is crucial to the Marxist project to know what is socially constructed and what is not. If one may not draw a line between science and socially constructed technology, then one can be led to one of two ludicrous (but, unfortunately, respectable) poles.

On the one hand, one can be led to the view that everything is socially constructed and, therefore, there can be no "essences." This "post-Marxist" social-Einsteinism (holding that everything is relative), so popular nowadays in the discipline of sociology, deprives one of any standards from which to take a moral position. For a Marxist, this analysis is calamitous because there is no way of arguing why socialism might in any respect be better than capitalism, or for that matter why colonialism or racism ought to be opposed—other than appealing to convention.

On the other hand, one can be led to the view, implicit among the present Chinese leadership and common in the West, that neither science nor technology is socially constructed. In Western terms, they are "independent," and in Marxist terms they are part of the "productive forces." But surely a kidney dialysis machine is not the same in Bangladesh and New York, and the Baoshan Steel complex is not the same kind of operation as Nippon Steel. If, as Marxists claim, a policy is correct so long as it "liberates the productive forces," and if both science and technology are simply productive forces, then most sober observers have to agree that so far capitalism does the job better.

I maintain the view (old-fashioned nowadays) that science and technology are different. I argue that technology, by its very nature, has to be seen and justified in social context. Science, however, is much more (though never completely) autonomous. There are probably a few inappropriate sciences, but there are many more inappropriate technologies. I am not saying that any scientific experiment should be allowed to proceed regardless of human cost. On the contrary, human values should inform the procedures of science. My point is simply that science should proceed outside a utilitarian calculus and should be permitted, so long as one cannot envisage a violation of humanity. Technology, on the other hand, should proceed only if it maximizes human goals. I wish to criticize Mao Zedong, as I wish to criticize Margaret Thatcher and the "New Right," for denigrating pure science. One recalls the fate of pure mathematics in the Cultural Revolution and the protests in 1972 of Zhou Peiyuan, then head of the Revolutionary Committee of Beijing University, against the charge that all knowledge that does not lead to increasing production is useless.[1] Nevertheless, I wish to assess Mao positively for articulating a view of technology geared to emancipatory purposes.

A consideration of technology is important when one categorizes Marxism. In his famous book *The Two Marxisms*, Gouldner distinguished between "scientific" Marxism (exemplified in the Soviet Union) and "critical" Marxism, which included a hotch-potch of thinkers ranging from the Frankfurt School to Mao Zedong.[2] The inadequacy of this all-inclusive second category is obvious. While both the Frankfurt School and Mao wished to restore the human dimension to scientistic orthodox Marxism, they clearly had different views concerning technology. In this essay I shall try to shed light on the problem by comparing the Soviet orthodoxy with the approach of Mao. To underscore the range of views occupying Gouldner's critical camp, I compare briefly Mao Zedong and Herbert Marcuse. I conclude by suggesting that Mao's treatment of the subject, far from reflecting nostalgia for a lost freedom, actually prefigured some modern thinking in science. Mao, however, never sufficiently escaped from the influence of Engels. Far from being too "utopian," Mao was not utopian enough.

The Soviet View

The original Soviet model, articulated most clearly in 1936 by Stalin, gave priority to science (even though some of the scientific formulations were strange if not false). One can imagine Soviet planners agreeing with Laplace:

> One must envisage the present state of the universe as the effect of its previous state, and as the cause of that which will follow. An intelligence that could know, at a given instant, all the forces governing the natural world, and the respective positions of the entities which compose it, if in addition it was great enough to analyze all this information, would be able to embrace in a single formula the movements of the largest bodies in the universe and those of the lightest atom: nothing would be uncertain for it, and the future, like the past, would be directly present to its observations.[3]

Such a view is similar to the old view of St. Thomas Aquinas, that human beings, by "right reason," may come to understand the rational order created by God and the objective laws governing that rational totality.

This was the view that informed Stalin in 1936 when he announced the basic achievement of "socialism," cast as a distinctive mode of production (though the translation used the term "form of production").[4] I have argued elsewhere that this formulation had more in common with Weber's "ideal type" than what was usually considered to be a mode of production in the Marxian sense.[5] Nevertheless, the view presented was that socialism had basically been "achieved" because of the inexorable development of the productive forces, and that the relations of production had been brought in conformity with them.

> First the productive forces of society change and develop, and then, depending on these changes and in conformity with them, men's relations of production, their economic relations change. . . . However much the relations of production may lag behind the development of the productive forces, they must, sooner or later, come into correspondence with, and actually do come into correspondence with, the level of the development of the productive forces, the character of the productive forces.[6]

For Marx, there was a glaring contradiction between the brilliantly rational and efficient forces of production, exemplified in the modern capitalist factory, and the backward and chaotic relations of production characterized by boom and depression. This is why Lenin could praise the Taylor system while condemning the system that produced it.[7] Now, according to

Stalin, conformity between forces and relations of production had been achieved in the Soviet Union. The economy was seen as a factory writ-large, and its operations might be seen in terms of "objective economic laws" of a "universal" character. All that remained was to perfect the productive forces and the relations of production would change in conformity with them. The future was assured and could be scientifically planned.

At least that was the theory. Trotsky was not slow to point out that the model of socialism presented by Stalin was a pretty miserable one. After all, the productive forces were way behind the level of development of capitalism.[8] The planning system, moreover, was hardly as rational and coordinated as the model supposed. But that is beside the point. I wish merely to argue that the scientific mode of thinking predicated social development on the logic of productive forces which programmed humans out of history. The communist telos was seen less and less as a human telos. Indeed, one should not be surprised at the view of the aspiring textbook writer Yaroshenko, who declared that communism was no more than rational organization—a view that even Stalin had to criticize.[9]

Mao's "Lutheran" Response

The Stalinist picture of science, therefore, was a modern atheist version of understanding through "right reason" of the way God had created the world. But one should recall the comment of William of Ockham that, although Aristotle "knew everything," God had created Aristotle, and God could change things. Ockham went on to denounce the pope as an "Antichrist." Replace God by humanity and the pope by the Soviet leadership and one has a hint of Mao's "promethean" streak. Consider "Ockham's razor" and Mao's belief that scientific theories were amenable to all people if expressed simply with an economy of words. Then consider Ockham's most famous follower, Martin Luther, cast as a quasi-pope, used by careerists to justify "independent kingdoms," and pronouncing against the peasant disorder he had helped to foment. Here we have Mao's dilemma in the Cultural Revolution. In the end, Luther, who originally wanted everyone (aided by their pastor) to work out "the correct line," had to pronounce on "God's law" (an earlier form of "supreme directives") but was never sure whether he had been misled by Satan.[10] (Remember Mao's remark in a moment of doubt: "Don't put all the blame on Comrade Liu Shaoqi."[11])

Mao had several Satans, all misled by an "idealism" Mao had helped to promote. I am not too worried by such a charge (any more than Meisner is worried by Mao's "utopianism") and do not see how one can avoid idealism. Just read Engels' comments on how the German working class inherited classical German philosophy[12] in the work Wang Ruoshui felt should be translated as "Feuerbach and the Outcome [*Ausgang*, Chinese *jieguo*] of Classical German Philosophy," rather than the normal and misleading title of "Ludwig Feuerbach and the End [*zongjie*] of Classical German Philosophy."[13] To dispense completely with idealism is to render technology without a telos. Mao's "idealist" deviation was, on the contrary, a source of strength.

Let me repeat an earlier comment and underline Meisner's contribution to this volume. Mao criticized Stalin's mechanistic world for neglecting humans. For Mao (in an Aristotelian vein different from the reference above), it was politics that had to be added to the Stalinist view in order to realize the human telos:

> Stalin's two slogans lack dialectics. [If you say] technology decides everything, what about politics? [If you say] cadres decide everything, what about the masses? Lenin said it well: the soviets plus electrification is communism. The soviets are politics, and electrification is technology. The unity of professional work and politics produces communism.[14]

Although I will not go as far as Andors in his optimistic view of Mao's industrial management policies in the Great Leap,[15] one should recall Andors' stress on Mao's attempt to unite "politics, policy, and operations." It is a commonplace that the policy-operations dichotomy, stressed in older books on management, is about as incoherent as the Westminster parliamentary system, though like that parliamentary system it is useful as an ideal standard. Mao set himself the task of uniting policy and operations, and indeed going beyond them by stressing politics.

This was a noble attempt and cannot be dismissed just because Mao premised the task on principles of "class struggle" that could not be operationalized on the shop floor. Contemporary critics are undoubtedly correct that the Cultural Revolution led to much inhumanity, and the desire to put a human telos back into the Stalinist machine led to tragedy. Perhaps the Cultural Revolution was the inevitable consequence of the early 1960s' stress on class struggle at all levels—inappropriate "politics" perhaps. But it was certainly not the inevitable consequence of a stress on politics per se. Liberals such as Pateman have stressed that primacy should be given to (a different kind of) politics.[16] So have neo-Aristotelians such as Hannah Arendt.[17] Surely only those of the old "antitotalitarian" school, who talk of the inevitable progression from Rousseau to Stalin[18] (even perhaps Medicare to Belsen), or neolibertarians such as Milton Friedman who talk of the reverse "political" hidden hand,[19] would disagree.

Marcuse and Mao: A Comparison

Of course, there were many ways other than Mao's of recovering human goals. Critical Marxism grew up in the West as a reaction against the non-dialectical, humanless socialism of the Soviet Union and, by drawing on the early Marx, sought to reintroduce some notion of the human telos into Marxism. Marcuse was the heir to that tradition. As Marcuse saw it, technology should not be seen as neutral. Technical processes, once geared to human ends, had distorted both liberal and socialist ideas to serve nonhuman ends. Consumption of the fruits of technology had totally corrupted the progressive forces of traditional Marxism (the proletariat), bringing about a totally administered society in which democracy was simply a formality. Socialist societies were ruled more by the technology of repression, while capitalist societies were distorted by the technology of "repressive tolerance." Culture was no longer a vehicle of protest but a consumer item. Philosophy was no longer the vehicle for the flowering of human reason but a technical guide to clear thinking. Science and technology were no longer vehicles of emancipation from domination and accommodation to nature. On the contrary, scientific method, "which led to the ever-more-effective domination of nature . . . came to provide the pure concepts for the ever-more-effective domination of man by man through the domination of nature."[20]

Here science and technology were simply ideologies legitimizing the power of those who controlled them. The world was that of the technical and social engineer, in which humans were no longer creative subjects but merely means to greater rationality. The only way out was appeal to marginalized groups or the wretched of the earth.

The Marxism of the Frankfurt School, or the quasi-Marxism of Marcuse and others, found little resonance in China, at least until the 1980s, and then they were roundly denounced as a form of "ultra-leftism" that negated everything including science and technology themselves. As Xia Jisong, one critic of the Frankfurt School, put it:

> As for science and technology, they are an important component of the culture of humankind; they have no class nature in themselves. Admittedly in class societies, for example in capitalist society, the use of science and technology in production is usually bound to cause harm to the workers; but the cause lies in the capitalist system of exploitation and not in science and technology themselves. . . . What the socialist system should negate is not science and technology but the decadent capitalist system of exploitation which impedes the development of science and technology and the development of the productive forces.[21]

I shall say little of such discussions here; I have written elsewhere on the similarities between Mao and what is nowadays called "the alienation school," which includes persons such as Wang Ruoshui.[22] Let me merely underline the point made above. The rejection of a humanless model of socialism, among the critical school, led eventually to an antitechnological view. Mao, however, while rejecting the humanless model, had extraordinary faith in technology. As Pischel has pointed out, the antitechnology stance of many European "Maoists" had little in common with Mao.[23] Those "Maoists" were the products of industrial society, not one struggling always to "catch up" with the technologically advanced nations. In the Great Leap Forward, it was precisely technology that was to transform the country in a short space of time. In the Cultural Revolution, tremendous efforts were made to promote institutions like the July Twenty-first Workers' Universities to broaden the base of technological education.

It is not just "Maoists" who doubt Mao's faith in technology. Many economists talk about Mao adopting an "ambivalent" approach to technology. Howe and Walker, for example, note a contradiction between the affirmation of "self-reliance" in the mid- to late 1960s and the imports of technology, which by the 1970s became very large indeed. "Campaigns against foreign technology in 1975 and 1976 appear to echo many of his feelings on the subject."[24] It is difficult to ascertain just what Mao's views actually were during the days of the so-called Gang of Four, but should one not suspect that the objections centered not so much on the importation of technology per se as on the importation of complete plants? Many non-Marxists worry about such moves on the ground of inadequate infrastructure to ensure full operation; many economists should be ambivalent. From a Marxist point of view, a major objection has been that complete plants embody the relations of production of their country of origin, or, to put it another way, forces of production only exist within given relations of production. This point of view, unfashionable among China's present leaders, was certainly one in which Mao believed. As to whether Mao extended this to worries about all technology, we cannot say. Suffice it to observe that only a strange theorist, believing that technology cannot be neutral, would not have such worries. As I type this essay on a computer, I am aware of the enormously liberating experience that electronics offers, while fearing the use that technology might be put to in curtailing freedom or producing (in Illich's words) a less "convivial" society.[25]

While affirming the positive role of technology, however, Mao, like the critical Marxists (as well as many critical non-Marxists), took a stand against what in the West would be called "technologism" or "technocratic ideology." This was the trend that collapsed the classical telos into techne, where technique became self-serving and emancipatory ends were lost. Mao was not to make the "revisionist" step (taken recently by critics in China) of talking about the appearance of human "alienation" in "socialist" society manifesting itself apparently in conditions different from those dominated by the commodified labor-power discussed by Marx. But surely, in moves such as his provisions for the Anshan Constitution,[26] Mao was trying to counter a similar trend.

Unlike Marcuse, Mao was optimistic; how otherwise would he have been found guilty of excessive faith in the human will to surmount obstacles (his alleged "voluntarism")? But it was always a qualified optimism. This was so not just because of Luther-like doubts but, indeed, befitted a dialectician who believed that in every success there must be failure. Unlike Marcuse, he was optimistic about the role of the proletariat. But again this optimism was qualified. In the late 1920s and early 1930s workers showed themselves unwilling to rise. In the 1950s Mao's Yan'an section of the party (Gao Gang's "Party of the Red Areas") remained contemptuous of the urban Communist underground (Gao Gang's "Party of the White Areas")—tensions that later manifested themselves in the Cultural Revolution. In that revolution Mao surely endorsed the criticism of the All-China Federation of Trade Unions, which had apparently responded to "the sugar-coated bullets of the bourgeoisie" in much the same way as Marcuse's malleable American workers. Indeed, Mao himself appealed at times to the marginalized—the "poor and blank" uncorrupted by the technology of consumption.

Both Mao's and Marcuse's critical reaction grew out of the view that technology, by its very nature, should be defined in terms of human ends. Marcuse spoke of the original (teleological) notion of "reason," whilst Mao was more earthy, supporting slogans like "humans before weapons."[27] Though they disagreed in terms of an optimistic/pessimistic appraisal, Mao and Marcuse would concur that, in Marxist terms, technology ought to be related to praxis.

But praxis has been a word much misused. There are a few strange Marxists in China nowadays who speculate about the role of praxis in relation to "black holes" in space and the like;[28] their comments demonstrate a continuing confusion in China between science and technology. Surely, praxis has meaning only in terms of the latter—how to combine science with human ends.

Of course, ontologically, science has to be prior to technology. But this need not be the case socially. Marcuse argued how, in capitalist (and "socialist") societies, means may swallow up ends. One could go on to argue that, after its victory, the so-called teleological school of Soviet planners became obsessed with working out a complex set of material balances and how well these fitted together rather than what ends they were to serve. Ironically, for a school called "teleological," technique became its own telos.[29]

Technology and Human Ends

Technology, however, should not be just how one uses science to pursue human ends, but how human ends may be linked to science. The first formulation sees nuclear technology geared to serving the needs of increasing energy. The second view postulates a complex causal relationship between means and the ends that gave rise to them. One may explain this in terms of the cybernetic language of inputs, outputs, and feedbacks if one likes. I prefer to see the relationship dialectically—nuclear technology is intrinsically contradictory and consistently demands a consideration of the whole range of human ends.

Mao was unwilling to see the argument above about nuclear energy. Indeed, when asked by Gu Mu and Yu Qiuli in 1965 whether China ought to catch up with and surpass international levels of technology, Mao replied: "Yes, we must . . . whatever the country, whatever the bomb, atomic bomb, hydrogen bomb, we must surpass them. I have said, if the atomic bomb goes off, even if half of humankind perishes, there will still be the other half."[30]

Here, surely (and alarmingly), Mao had lost sight of the human telos. But, time and again, whether criticizing the "purely military viewpoint" or arguing against mechanically copying the Soviet model, Mao affirmed the idea of technology in the original sense of a relation between scientific means and human ends. For example, only a tortuous logic could deduce the need to overcome the "three major differences" from the Stalinist argument about the primacy of the "productive forces." The scientific paradigm would surely say that one overcame the difference between worker and peasant when the productive forces were developed sufficiently to transfer resources to the poorer rural areas from the richer urban areas (or from areas where comparative advantage and economies of scale dictated that they be produced). Such is usually rationalized in Marxist-Leninist language as the "law of planned and proportionate development."[31]

On the contrary, Mao chose to advocate the local development of low-level technology. This, according to normal economic logic, might have been extremely wasteful at times, but such is debatable when one considers that many small industries turned into capital savings, which may have been impossible under conditions of less than "wasteful" mass mobilization. What few would deny, however, was the wastefulness of "third-line" industries that used modern technology, but alas without the infrastructural back-up to make it productive. But, had there been a major international war in the 1960s, we might now be praising Mao as far-sighted in that "wasteful" enterprise. An assessment of technology should demand an assessment of goals. What is technologically rational may be scientifically irrational (in this case according to straight cost-benefit analysis, measuring benefits simply in economic terms with an appropriate *ceteris paribus* clause that everyone pretends to know the meaning of but most people ignore).

Let me push the argument further. "Walking on two legs" might involve scientific mumbo-jumbo. At least such is the case in medicine. One uses traditional technologies for which the explanation is often metaphysical and incoherent. One uses them because they sometimes achieve the primary goal of health care. Here the pursuit of technology might fly in the face of what we know about science. Yet, on the other hand, engaging in a technology might help to produce science. For example, we are now beginning to test theories about the production of endogenous opiates as a result of Chinese experience with acupuncture.

Learning by doing can be immensely silly if everyone has to invent the wheel just for the sake of inventing the wheel. As stated earlier, the tendency to despise learning not geared immediately to practical goals in the Cultural Revolution was retrograde. But learning by doing is not necessarily silly provided one's human goals are clear.

The so-called scientific experimentation, which proceeds at the basic level, might be completely bogus. Few believe that peasants were everywhere inventing new high-yielding seed strains in the Cultural Revolution. They were more often than not learning to be familiar with strains imported originally from Mexico and the Philippines. They might genuinely have believed that they had achieved high yields because of an infusion of Mao Zedong Thought—a most dubious proposition from the perspective of science. What is important, however, is that the experimentation with new technology produced a willingness to take risks with the new genotypes which were known to be disease-prone and could result in short-term crop failure, while overall returns in the long run were outstanding. The aim was to make ordinary people accept risks rather than that being a cost born by a reified science. Peasants were not engaging here in science but developing the technology of reduced-risk cropping. They were engaging in "practice."

But when Mao said "practice is the sole criterion for evaluating truth"[32] he was wrong. As Wang Ruoshui has pointed out, practice only has relevance in terms of predetermined goals,[33] and revolutionary praxis only has meaning in terms of predetermined goals of revolutionary transformation. But Mao, the author of that inductivist essay "On Practice," did usually know what he was doing in stressing the importance of human goals in social policy. Of course, there were inconsistencies. Recently one school of thought on the praxis question has said that teleological concerns may not be the starting point in evaluating the success of practice because they are subjective. Rather, we would evaluate the success of practice in terms of "objective results"[34] (a silly tautology—if it works, it works). The scientistic legacy survives. Doubtless, to blow up the world would confirm the truth of scientific laws governing nuclear fusion and might validate current hypotheses about "nuclear winter." We do not need that kind of practice.

Mao and the Engelsian Paradox, Mao and Prigogine

That the latter school might find ammunition for its arguments in the works of Mao reveals a contradiction in his writing. Mao, after all, talked a lot about "objective laws." The point, however, is that Mao, despite his criticism of Engels' laws of dialectics,[35] still adhered to the Engelsian paradox put so succinctly by Nobel laureate Ilya Prigogine:

> Apparently there are two conflicting worlds, a world of trajectories and a world of processes, and there is no way of denying one by asserting the other. . . . To a certain extent there is an analogy between this conflict and the one that gave rise to dialectical materialism. We have described . . . a nature that might be called "historical"—that is capable of development and innovation. The idea of a history of nature as an integral part of materialism was asserted by Marx and, in greater detail by Engels. Contemporary developments in physics, the discovery of the constructive role played by irreversibility, have thus raised within the natural sciences a question that has long been asked by materialists. For them understanding nature meant understanding it as being capable of producing man and his societies. . . . But "mechanicism" [*sic*] remained a basic difficulty facing dialectical materialism. What are the relations between the general laws of dialectics and the equally universal laws of mechanical motion? Do the latter "cease" to apply after a certain stage has been reached, or are they simply false and incomplete? To come back to our previous question, how can the world of processes and trajectories ever be linked together?[36]

Coupled with attempts to rescue the human dimension from Soviet mechanical view, much of Mao's later life was concerned with the above problem of dialectics. He reacted constantly against those who remained only within the world of "processes." He reacted against that view of the world put so succinctly by Marcuse:

> The human world was presented as governed by objective laws, analogous or even identical with the laws of nature, and society was set forth as an objective entity more or less unyielding to subjective desires or goals. Men believed their relations to each other to result from objective laws that operate with the necessity of physical laws and their freedom to consist in adapting their private existence to this necessity.[37]

Yet the ghost of Engels remained, just as, when Mao came to see the Communist Party as a force for retrogression, the ghost of Lenin remained. But, before we simply dismiss the man as confused, let us explore the tension further. We must do this because what is at stake is a tension in all science and all technology—not just the Marxist kind—the tension between "processes" (expressed as general laws) and trajectories (expressed teleologically). Let me for a moment compare Mao and Prigogine.[38]

Unlike Mao, Prigogine is preoccupied with the concept of "system." There is a long tradition of denouncing "systems theory" in official Marxism, despite Khrushchev's flirtation with the subject. Critics, however, tend to focus on "closed" systems modeled on the steam engine. Here Prigogine's demolition of classical dynamics is most relevant.[39] For Prigogine, a steam engine is a near-equilibrium closed system. It is closed because it does not grow due to inputs of energy from the outside, and because it depends on an external engineer. It is far enough from equilibrium to maintain a difference between the hot and cold parts, but it is not allowed to get sufficiently away from equilibrium for entropy-producing irreversible processes fatally to impair efficiency. Transposing this model to society resulted in the arid analyses of social systems of the 1960s, which were echoed in the Soviet Union.

One may readily see the analogies with Mao's thinking. The Soviet model was seen as a closed system just like a steam engine. The external engineer was the planner. Its normal and necessary departures from equilibrium could be described as "internal contradictions," but the model denied Mao's belief that such contradictions were the motive force of progress. Departures too far from equilibrium and the appearance of entropy-producing features Mao saw at first as the development of new "antagonistic contradictions" (as in Hungary). Using the same analogy, one may see why the Soviet party saw the Great Leap as a similar departure too far from equilibrium, whereas Mao's theory of uninterrupted revolution aimed at a dynamic reappraisal of that development.

The machine analogy of a social totality replaced a much older analogy—the biological. In the 1960s, attempts were made in the Soviet Union to fuse together the machine analogy and the organic analogy celebrated in Soviet Marxism by Bogdanov.[40] Success was limited. Mao went a different way, as I shall explore. Meanwhile, let me note that now, with Prigogine, physics and biology are united in a novel approach to open systems (as they were with Mao, but he did not use the term "open system").

Open systems respond to the environment, take in energy, and grow. Classical thermodynamics had little to say about this form of "negative entropy." Prigogine's thermodynamics, however, attempt to unite both the second law of thermodynamics (the tendency toward entropy) and the development of order out of chaos. The argument is that the mechanics of the industrial revolution concentrated only on equilibrium or near to equilibrium situations. Clearly such situations always tended to break down, just as the archetypal steam engine wore out. One saw entropy everywhere. Mao put it differently: "Imbalance is a universal objective law. Things forever proceed from imbalance to equilibrium, and from equilibrium to imbalance, in endless cycles. It will forever be like this, but each cycle reaches a higher level. Imbalance is constant and absolute; equilibrium is temporary and relative."[41] Mao, like Prigogine, seems to be arguing that if one looks at far from equilibrium situations, one can see order being generated everywhere.

What most of us were taught in the 1960s was equilibrium science. In a chemical reaction, for example, the random collision of two sets of molecules, when sufficiently excited, causes bonding to occur. This regular reaction in equilibrium chemistry may be described in terms of universal laws, initial conditions, and consequences (Popper). But in a far from equilibrium chemical reaction, Prigogine argues, a specific occurrence causes massive oscillations in the reaction system. In this chaotic situation, fluctuations of larger and larger numbers of molecules take place until a critical point is reached (the bifurcation point—"turning point" in Chinese phraseology). At this point, a number of different potentialities exist within the system, and one cannot predict which will win out (though Mao, the optimist, tried). Suddenly, one potentiality dominates and a new order is established. Such a reaction may not be described in terms of universal laws; all one may talk about are tendencies (or "trajectories"). The initial conditions, moreover, are forgotten, or simply irrelevant, and the consequences are merely probabilistic.

What happens in far from equilibrium chemical reactions also occurs in biology. Prigogine calls the development of far from equilibrium forms "dissipative structures." Once formed, these structures, to keep their shape, need to dissipate entropy so that it will not build up within the system and kill it (or return it to equilibrium). Since they produce high levels of entropy, they require high inputs of matter and energy. They are literally structures that are maintained by the matter and energy flowing though them. This conceptualization is the opposite of the textbook approaches of the 1960s (Western or Soviet). Biological organisms are not structures maintained in a precarious equilibrium so that pathology becomes the study of disequilibrium. On the contrary, biological organisms are in a far from equilibrium state and need to remain so to prevent the development of entropy—the tendency toward chaos, the ultimate equilibrium.

The above discussion of dissipative structures is relevant, Prigogine tells us, not only to physics, chemistry, and biology but also to society. When we consider that a biological cell, a person, a city, and a society are all dissipative structures, we confront the problem of levels, not of analysis but of reality itself.

For Prigogine, a dissipative structure, undergoing massive fluctuations, might escape into a higher order, or might generate new dissipative structures within itself, at a lower level, to compensate for the growth of entropy. If one accepts this, then the traditional hierarchy of sciences, with physics at the base, proceeding through chemistry, biology, physiology, sociology, and so forth, breaks down. Everything is in dynamic interaction, and no science is basic. No level of reality has priority. The laws appropriate to each level are different yet feed into and modify each other.

Add to that the view that human consciousness (embracing technology) is itself a dissipative structure that brings to the totality an ability to appreciate irreversible processes (that is the difference between past and future, or simply time), then we have a rich view of the totality. A universe, once seen as governed by dynamics that were in principle reversible and which once had to be seen by a "demon," a God or some functionally equivalent external observer in their place, now may be seen from within by a dissipative structure that may appreciate irreversibility. The observer is the observed in a complex network of dissipative and nondissipative structures. We have broken away from the world of Aquinas, transcended the problems of Ockham and Luther and, for that matter, humanism cast as religion. Even more important, we have transcended Engels.

One hopes that the reader has kept in mind Mao's theory of "uninterrupted revolution" of the Great Leap Forward. Many contemporary Chinese observers are constantly mindful of that, and they warn that enthusiasts for Prigogine should not use his theories for advocating disequilibrium in economics.[42] They remember the economic chaos of the early 1960s. Mao would not agree that society reorganized itself at a lower level in the 1960s; but surely, were he alive, he would have found solace in Prigogine's eloquent denunciation of the old axiom that there are no leaps in nature.

One may see why the works of Prigogine have been attractive to many Chinese Marxists. Deng Weizhi complains that those who promote the current fashion for systems theory, cybernetics, and information theory usually fail to realize that Prigogine's theory of dissipative structures has already made all these other approaches out of date.[43] Dare one add that Mao, in his amateurish way, prefigured that. As Chen Kuide argues, the development of science has gone through three phases.[44] The first treated science as a branch of philosophy: that philosophy sought to grasp the totality (and one might add a social telos). The second phase started as an attack on mysticism and led to an atomistic, deterministic, and mechanistic science. The third stage, epitomized so well by Prigogine (and, dare I add, shared in rudimentary form by Mao), once again unites science, technology, and philosophy. This "negation of the negation" (a notion that Mao explicitly rejected)[45] transcends the traditional Chinese conception of totality, producing a new totality that can incorporate the great achievements of what has normally been called science during the past three hundred years. The new approach to totality, moreover, dissolves the old dichotomy between humans and the natural world. If, in the world of nature, there occurs movement from disorder to order through what Prigogine calls "fluctuations," and if structures reform themselves to fulfill functions, then there is teleology in nature itself. Humans, as goal-seeking entities, are simply complex forms of natural processes. Such is heady stuff! But is it too mystical?

Memories of the Great Leap Forward might lead one to that conclusion. But one should note that Prigogine's teleology was prefigured by Mao's old mentor Li Dazhao, who, like Prigogine, absorbed ideas from the works of Bergson.[46] There is a strong antideterminist stream in Chinese Marxism which, we now see, may be reconciled with materialism. Mao derived much from traditional Chinese cosmology. So perhaps did Prigogine. In Beijing in August 1978, Prigogine spoke of the coming of an "excellent alliance between Western science and the understanding of totality and harmony in Chinese culture," leading to a new philosophy of nature.[47] This was duly noted by Chen Kuide, who took "totality" and "harmony" to refer to the "spontaneous dialectical elements in Chinese thought, which had emphasized interconnection and interdependence."[48]

Now consider Prigogine's following point:

> A system far from equilibrium may be described as organised not because it realizes a plan alien to elementary activities, or transcending them but, on the contrary, because of the amplification of a microscopic fluctuation occurring at the "right moment" resulted in favouring one reaction path over other equally possible paths. Under certain circumstances, therefore, the role played by individual behaviour can be decisive.[49]

"Individual behaviour" here may refer in an economy to enterprises, in society to classes—or, at another level of analysis, to biological individuals.[50] The relevance for Mao is clear. Consider that when reading the "Resolution on Certain Questions in the History of our Party," which (in my view correctly) denounces the Maoist cult of personality.[51]

Now what has all this to do with technology? It is simply this. Prigogine, like Mao, is arguing that there is no essential difference between science and technology. I am reluctant to argue, as Prigogine does, that science and technology are closer than ever before.[52] I still wish to make the distinction I outlined at the beginning of this essay. But my point is that Mao prefigured what has become a respectable branch of the scientific endeavor. Both Mao and Prigogine have to be seen in a teleological context.

Conclusion

Mao, despite his training in Engels (or maybe because of it, since Engels was as confused as he was on the relationship between Hegelianism and positivism), has to be seen as a person who affirmed the importance of "trajectories" over processes, as well as a person who was ever reluctant to lose sight of a human telos. In the Great Leap, he supported a cavalier attitude toward science. But his antiscientific behavior has to be seen in a technological light (as I have used the word)—he has to be seen as a technological Marxist struggling against a technocratic orthodoxy that Marcuse (or Ellul or even Galbraith) would immediately recognize. In Gouldner's formulation, Mao was a "critical" Marxist, though, unlike others in Gouldner's category called "critical," he did not proceed from the criticism of technocracy to the criticism of technology itself.

Moreover, though there is remarkable affinity between Mao and the later works of Prigogine, there are annoying contradictions in Mao. These are logical contradictions rather than social contradictions—an understanding of which is the only way to understand the dialectical nature of trajectories. While Mao sometimes harked back to the old Chinese notion of totality, he still talked occasionally about "making war against nature." That is, he sometimes wanted to employ technology to attain human ends at the expense of nature rather than to link nature, science, and human goals through technology. One might expect nature, in Engels' words, "to exact a revenge." To be sure, Mao was sometimes guilty of "draining the pond dry to catch the fish." For all that, he should be understood as one who offered a human critique of mechanistic Marxist orthodoxy, which was rooted in reality—the need to overcome mindless scientism, "objective economic laws" seen only as "processes."

Mao, of course, does not merit a Nobel prize like Prigogine. But he should be taken seriously as a person who was concerned to solve the Engelsian contradiction between processes and trajectories, a Marxist groping, semiconsciously, for the new world of nonequilibrium science and indeterminacy, rather than as the pre-industrial throw-back, as some modern "scientists" and "technologists" cast him.

Notes

1. Zhou Peiyuan, *Guangming ribao*, October 6, 1972, pp. 1–2.
2. A. Gouldner, *The Two Marxisms* (New York: Seabury Press, 1980).
3. S. de Laplace, cited in J. Bernstein, *Einstein* (London: Fontana/Collins, 1973), p. 33.
4. J. V. Stalin, "On the Draft Constitution of the USSR," November 25, 1936, in J. V. Stalin, *Problems of Leninism* (Moscow: Foreign Languages Publishing House, 1947), pp. 540–68.
5. B. Brugger, "Soviet and Chinese Views on Revolution and Socialism—Some Thoughts on the Problems of Diachrony and Synchrony," *Journal of Contemporary Asia* 11, 3 (1981): 311–32.
6. J. V. Stalin, "Dialectical and Historical Materialism" (September 1938), in

Stalin, *Problems of Leninism*, pp. 585–86.

7. V. I. Lenin, "The Immediate Tasks of the Soviet Government" (April 1918), in V. I. Lenin, *Selected Works* (1967), 2:664.

8. L. Trotsky, *The Revolution Betrayed: What Is the Soviet Union and Where Is It Going?* (New York: Pathfinder Press, 1970), pp. 62–63.

9. J. V. Stalin, *Economic Problems of Socialism in the USSR* (1951) (Beijing: Foreign Languages Press, 1972), p. 62.

10. See E. Erikson, *Young Man Luther: A Study in Psychoanalysis and History* (London: Faber and Faber, 1959).

11. Mao Zedong, "Talk at the Central Work Conference" (October 25, 1966), in *Mao Tse-tung Unrehearsed*, ed. S. Schram (Harmondsworth, England: Penguin, 1974), p. 274.

12. F. Engels, "Ludwig Feuerbach and the End of Classical German Philosophy" (1888), in K. Marx and F. Engels, *Selected Works* (Moscow: Progress Publishers, 1970), 3:375–76.

13. Wang Ruoshui, "Deguo gudian zhexue jiandan de 'zongjie' le ma," *Guangming ribao*, April, 24, 1982, p. 3.

14. JPRS, *Miscellany of Mao Tse-tung Thought* (Arlington, Va., 1974), p. 115; my translation from Mao Zedong, *Mao Zedong sixiang wansui* (hereafter *Wansui*), 1st collection (n.p., August 1969), p. 216.

15. S. Andors, *China's Industrial Revolution: Politics, Planning and Management, 1949 to the Present* (New York: Pantheon, 1977).

16. C. Pateman, *Participation and Democratic Theory* (Cambridge: Cambridge University Press, 1970).

17. H. Arendt, *On Revolution* (London: Faber, 1963).

18. J. Talmon, *The Origins of Totalitarian Democracy* (New York: Praeger, 1960).

19. M. and R. Friedman, *Free to Choose* (New York: Harcourt, Brace Jovanovich, 1980), p. 292.

20. H. Marcuse, *One Dimensional Man: The Ideology of Industrial Society*, 2d ed. (London: Sphere Books, 1968), p. 130.

21. Xia Jisong, "Dangqian liuxing de xifang makesizhuyi zhi yi—Falankefu xuepai," *Zhexue yanjiu* 4 (1980): 78.

22. B. Brugger and D. Kelly, *Considerations on Chinese Marxism* (forthcoming).

23. E. C. Pischel, "The Teacher," in *Mao Tse-tung in the Scales of History*, ed. D. Wilson (Cambridge: Cambridge University Press, 1977), p. 166.

24. C. Howe and K. Walker, "The Economist," in ibid., p. 222.

25. I. Illich, *Tools for Conviviality* (New York: Harper and Row, 1973).

26. *Beijing Review* 16 (April 17, 1970): 3; 14 (April 3, 1970): 11.

27. Mao Zedong, "On Protracted War" (May 1938), in *Selected Works* (Beijing: Foreign Languages Press, 1965), 2:143.

28. Zha Ruqiang, "Practice Is the Unique and Ultimate Criterion of the Truth of Knowledge," paper presented to the 16th International Congress of the History of Science, Bucharest, 1981.

29. This kind of argument is best explicated in J. Ellul, *The Technological Society* (New York: Knopf, 1967). For a summary of this way of thinking, see B. Brugger and G. Stokes, "The Technocratic Challenge to Democratic Theory," in *Liberal Demo-*

cratic Theory and Its Critics, ed. N. Wintrop (London: Croom Helm, 1983), pp. 361–405. On the Soviet Union and China, see the discussion in B. Brugger, "Undeveloped Socialism and Intensive Development," in *Chinese Marxism in Flux*, ed. B. Brugger (London: Croom Helm, 1985), pp. 103–104.

30. Mao Zedong, "Tingqu Gu Mu, Yu Qiuli huibao jihua gongzuo shi de zhishi" (January 1965), in *Wansui*, p. 606.

31. For a criticism of this "law," see B. Brugger, "Once Again 'Making the Past Serve the Present': A Critique of the Chinese Communist Party's New Official History," in *China's Changed Road to Development*, ed. N. Maxwell and B. McFarlane (Oxford: Pergamon Press, 1984), p. 173; see also B. Brugger, "Undeveloped Socialism and Intensive Development," in *Chinese Marxism in Flux*, pp. 98–118.

32. Mao Zedong, "On Practice" (1937), in *Selected Works*, 1:296.

33. Wang Ruoshui, "Shijian de mudi shi hengliang shijian chengbai de biaojun," *Guangming ribao*, May 12, 1980, p. 3.

34. Li Minsheng, "Shijian de mudi shi hengliang shijian chengbai de biaojun ma?" *Guangming ribao*, August 7, 1980, p. 4. See Wang's reply, "Renshilun bu yao wangdiaole ren," *Guangming ribao*, February 12, 1981, p. 4. Translated as "Epistemology Must Not Lose Sight of Man," in "Wang Ruoshui: Writings on Humanism, Alienation, and Philosophy," ed. D. Kelly *Chinese Studies in Philosophy* 16, 3 (Spring 1985): 101–12. See also the critical comment by Li Jingrui, "'Shijian de mudi shi hengliang shijian chengbai de biaojun' bushi makesizhuyi renshilun," *Shehui kexue jikan* 4 (1981): 29–33.

35. Mao Zedong, "Talk on Problems of Philosophy" (August 18, 1964), in *Miscellany*, p. 393; *Wansui*, p. 558.

36. I. Prigogine and I. Stengers, *Order Out of Chaos: Man's New Dialogue with Nature* (London: Fontana, 1985), pp. 252–53.

37. H. Marcuse, *Reason and Revolution: Hegel and the Rise of Social Theory*, 2d ed. (London: Routledge, 1955), p. 256.

38. This is taken from Brugger and Kelly, *Considerations on Chinese Marxism*.

39. Prigogine and Stengers, *Order Out of Chaos*.

40. P. Ludz, "Marxism and Systems Theory in a Bureaucratic Society," *Social Research* 42, 4 (Winter 1975): 670. See also Ludz, *The Changing Party Elite in East Germany* (Cambridge: MIT Press, 1972), pp. 341ff., 351ff.

41. Mao Zedong, February 19, 1958. This is taken from an untitled Red Guard source. Another translation may be found in *Current Background* 892 (October 21, 1969): 7. For an earlier formulation, see Mao Zedong (January 1957), in *Miscellany*, p. 49, and for a later one (May 10, 1958), ibid., p. 112.

42. Shen Xiaofeng, "Haosan jiegou lilun yu shehui shenghuo," *Guangming ribao*, November 6, 1985, p. 3, a continuation of an article in *Guangming ribao*, October 9, 1985, p. 3.

43. Deng Weizhi, "Makesizhuyi yanjiu zhong de tupo," *Renmin ribao*, March 14, 1986, p. 5.

44. Chen Kuide, "Dangdai kexue de xin sichao: haosan jiegou de qidi," *Fudan xuebao (Shehui kexue ban)* 2 (1982): 25–33.

45. Mao Zedong, "Talk on Problems of Philosophy," p. 393.

46. Prigogine and Stengers, *Order Out of Chaos*, pp. 89–93, 173–74; W. Bauer,

China and the Search for Happiness: Recurring Themes in Four Thousand Years of Chinese Cultural History, tr. M. Shaw (New York: Seabury Press, 1976), p. 375. See also M. Meisner, *Li Tachao and the Origins of Chinese Marxism* (Cambridge: Harvard University Press, 1967). I am indebted to D. Kelly for this observation.

47. I. Prigogine, "Cong cunzai dao yanhua," *Ziran zazhi* 3, 1 (January 1980), esp. p. 14.

48. Chen Kuide, "Dangdai kexue de xin sichao," p. 28.

49. Prigogine and Stengers, *Order Out of Chaos*, p. 176.

50. This point by D. Kelly.

51. Chinese Communist Party, Sixth Plenum of the Eleventh Central Committee, "Resolution on Certain Questions in the History of Our Party Since the Founding of the People's Republic of China," June 27, 1981, *Beijing Review* 27 (July 6, 1981): 10–39.

52. Prigogine, "Cong cunzai dao yanhua," p. 1, passim.

7

SOCIALISM AND ECONOMIC DEVELOPMENT: THE POLITICS OF ACCUMULATION IN CHINA

Penelope B. Prime

China's experience with socialist economic development created an irony from which two perspectives spring.[1] From one perspective, China under Mao's leadership did respectably well, achieving economic growth and providing basic needs. From a second perspective, including that of the post-Mao regime, the Maoist approach to development was an economic disaster that the Chinese people want to put behind them. One explanation of the coexistence of these two seemingly contradictory perspectives is that the Maoist approach to socialist accumulation, typified by the Cultural Revolution, glorified austerity to achieve rapid industrialization.

A basic economic problem for China, as indeed for all countries that wish to industrialize, is capital accumulation. The higher the rate of growth, the more difficult it is to achieve sufficient accumulation while maintaining a balance with the rest of the economy.[2] Sources of accumulation within a socialist strategy of accumulation are substantially fewer than in capitalist societies. Reliance on capitalists, landlords, or multinationals is eliminated from the list of options once land reform and nationalization have occurred. Reliance on export markets to generate surplus also entails a risky dependence on the international capitalist economy which a socialist approach to development typically tries to avoid.[3] Reliance on agriculture for accumulation by setting agricultural prices low relative to industrial goods is also problematic; for Mao, for example, decreasing the differences between urban and rural areas to strengthen the worker-peasant alliance imposed constraints on this option, as did agriculture's urgent need for modern inputs.[4] Two accumulation options left, then, are to raise output per worker and reinvest the increment, or to restrict consumption. Raising productivity, while more desirable, is especially difficult in low technology, agrarian economies in which the increases that can be achieved may be inadequate for rapid industrialization. The temptation to pursue the remaining option, restricting consumption, is therefore great, but it is feasible only in proportion to the willingness of people to make sacrifices or to the state's success with coercion.

Accumulation options in China were limited further by socialist ideology, as well as by existing economic conditions. Under Mao's leadership China chose an approach to accumulation that in rhetoric adhered to a non-elitist "mass line" socialist agenda, but in practice made rapid industrialization the priority.[5] Rapid industrialization was to be achieved without "capitalist" methods of specialization, without hierarchy in management, and without too much dependence on technology. China was also not going to rely on foreigners or international markets, which in effect ruled out export promotion, foreign investment, and foreign borrowing as accumulation options. Instead, a socialist, self-reliant approach was to be followed. This approach included concurrent promotion of small, medium, and large enterprises; a worker-peasant alliance through the integration of state ownership and mechanization; and a call to political consciousness to augment, and temporarily replace if necessary, material incentive.[6] Maoists condemned bourgeois economists' concern with profits and accounting and instead espoused the socialist struggle for production through a variety of well-publicized slogans: "self-reliance," "grasp revolution, promote production," "put politics in command," "red" over "expert," "proletarian revolutionary" principles for enterprise management. The Maoist approach emphasized the importance of relations of production as a determinant of the forces of production, replacing a concern with the technological base per se with an attempt to transform social relations through class struggle.[7] "Economism" was attacked for giving priority to production and profits at the expense of people, ideology, and politics. A 1967 critique of Liu Shaoqi in *People's Daily* is a good example:

> According to China's Khrushchev, in economic construction we can rely on a handful of "experts," "rely on directors, engineers, and technicians" who give orders. The revolutionary masses are only "labor" and "ignorant masses" who only obediently take orders from the top. He and his followers taxed their brains to work out a series of revisionist regulations in order to exercise bourgeois dictatorship over the workers.[8]

Slogans that targeted class struggle as a way to achieve socialist development began to define China's revolutionary culture and were expressed over and over in art, literature, film, education, and emulation campaigns. In the words of a *Liberation Army Daily* editorial in May 1966, "We must pay great attention to the reaction of the superstructure on the economic base and to the class struggle in the ideological sphere"[9]—and so the Cultural Revolution did.

Viewed in terms of the problems of production and consumption during these years, this revolutionary fervor and the emphasis on class struggle in culture assume another significance than that which the revolutionaries claimed for them: they helped produce the acquiescence essential to limit increases in consumption and leisure time in the cause of economic development.[10] The economic meaning of Mao's class struggle was that everyone had to sacrifice in the short run to achieve rapid growth—a presumed prerequisite for the attainment of communism. The Cultural Revolution was extremely successful at suppressing conspicuous consumption and discouraging "bourgeois" expenditure of even modest amounts of time and money on clothes, houses, the fine arts, hobbies, and ceremonies. The Cultural Revolution also called for decreases in the state's commitment to cultural, educational, and health projects that would instead be supplied, on a much simpler basis, by local communities and work units. The attack on professionals and intellectuals was partly a consequence of a desire to curtail social interests tied to expenditures on formal education, institutions, and advanced equipment. In short, the Cultural Revolution resulted in an attack on consumption throughout society in the name of class struggle to achieve rapid industrialization.

Austerity was not sustainable, however. Rapid growth was achieved, but at the cost of inefficiencies and incentive problems, thereby exacerbating the accumulation problem. In addition, contrary to rhetoric, the state made production and consumption decisions, leaving meaningful worker and peasant participation unimplemented. The role of the masses, it could be argued, was reduced to policing each other's consumption, creating alienation and bitterness. In the end, by insisting on rapid industrialization, the nonelitist, mass-line socialist agenda was compromised.

This interpretation helps explain the current critique in China of the Cultural Revolution—despite its economic achievements—and the post-Mao government's concern with providing consumer goods and higher wages. The sections that follow reevaluate the economics of the Cultural Revolution period by first examining economic growth in these years, especially its sectoral biases, and then relating these outcomes to three key facets of accumulation during the Cultural Revolution.

Economic Growth During the Cultural Revolution

Despite China's current criticisms of the economics of the "ten years of chaos," substantial growth occurred during the Cultural Revolution, particularly in industry.[11] The Chinese date the Cultural Revolution period as 1966 to 1976, and it is true that the first three years, 1966 to 1968, saw extensive violence, work stoppages, and distribution problems, all of which hurt economic performance. In 1969, however, there began an investment and growth period that has continued, except for a few years, well into the 1980s. If the Cultural Revolution is defined as 1966 to 1968, the years when the ideological stage was set for more than a decade, then, economic chaos is an appropriate description; if, however, the broader period lasting until 1976 with the death of Mao or 1978 with the end of Maoist policies is considered, economic growth was substantial.

China's own statistics reveal that respectable advances occurred during the Cultural Revolution even if the poor performance years between 1966 and 1968 are included. Some indicators of growth are given in table 1.[12] National income, China's measure of total net output value, grew at an average annual rate of 6.9 percent between 1966 and 1975. This rate of growth was below the 8.9 percent rate of the First Five-Year Plan when China received substantial Soviet aid, as well as the 14.7 percent of the 1963–1965 period, when the economy was recovering from the Great Leap Forward. Growth during the Cultural Revolution, however, was slightly higher than the 6.6 percent average annual growth for the thirty-three years between 1953 and 1985, which includes the high growth of the first seven years of the post-1978 reform period. Per capita national income also increased from 216 yuan in 1966 to 273 yuan in 1975.[13] If the first three years of poor performance are not included, the growth rate of national income was 8.5 percent between 1969 and 1978, well above the thirty-three year average, and by 1978 per capita national income increased to 315 yuan.[14]

Growth in sectoral net output value followed a similar pattern to national income. Net value of agricultural output grew at an average annual rate of 3.2 percent between 1966 and 1975, just under the 3.4 percent growth rate for the entire thirty-three-year period. Net value of industrial output increased an average of 10.3 percent per year in the Cultural Revolution years, with gross value of heavy industry increasing an average of 12.4 percent and light industry increasing 8.1 percent. In all of these cases except agriculture, the rates of growth between 1969 and 1978 were substantially higher than the thirty-three-year average. Average annual growth of national income and heavy industry between 1966 and 1975 approximated that of the thirty-three-year average.

Thus, far from being a total economic disaster, there were substantial increases in production capacity and output during the Cultural Revolution period, and especially after 1969. The particular composition of these increases, however, gives an indication of the problems inherent in the Maoist approach. Economic expansion favored industry over all other sectors and,

Table 1

Economic Growth Indicators, 1953–1983

	National income	Agricultural output	Industrial output	Light industrial gross output	Heavy industrial gross output
1953–1957	8.9	3.7	19.6	12.9	25.4
1958–1962	–3.1	–5.8	1.8	1.1	6.6
1963–1965	14.7	11.5	21.4	21.2	14.9
1966–1970	8.3	3.0	12.3	8.4	14.7
1971–1975	5.5	3.5	8.3	7.7	10.2
1976–1980	6.0	2.2	8.5	11.0	7.8
1981–1985	9.7	9.9	9.2	12.0	9.6
1953–1985	6.6	4.7	11.0	9.9	12.5
1966–1975	6.9	3.2	10.3	8.1	12.4
1966–1968	0.5	2.3	1.3	0.4	–1.1
1969–1978	8.5	2.9	13.4	10.8	16.0

Source: *China's Statistical Yearbook, 1986*, pp. 53–54 for national income, net agricultural and industrial output, and pp. 44–45 for gross value of light and heavy industrial output.
Note: These average period growth rates are based on annual growth rates calculated from indices in comparable prices.

within industry, growth was biased toward heavy industry at the expense of consumer goods. Both were a consequence of trying to achieve rapid industrialization, and both contributed to poor productivity performance.

The bias toward industrial development is underscored in tables 2 and 3. Table 2 shows the contribution to national income by sector for selected years. The most striking change shown by these figures is the rising proportion of industry in the production structure (from 19.5 percent in 1952 to 45.8 in 1980 to 41.5 percent in 1985) while agriculture, construction, transportation, and commerce all fell or stagnated. Although a decline in the importance of agriculture has commonly occurred in developing countries as they industrialize, the absence of development in construction, transport, and commerce is unusual and has contributed to serious imbalances geographically and between sectors.[15] Within industry the bias toward increasing heavy industrial output over light, apparent in table 3, exacerbated balance problems and contributed to scarcities of consumer goods. The per-

Table 2

Percentage of National Income by Economic Sector

	Agricul-ture	Indus-try	Construc-tion	Trans-port	Com-merce
1952	57.7	19.5	3.6	4.3	14.9
1957	46.8	28.3	5.0	4.3	15.6
1962	48.0	32.8	3.5	4.1	11.6
1965	46.2	36.4	3.8	4.2	9.4
1970	41.3	40.1	4.1	3.8	10.7
1975	39.4	44.5	4.5	3.8	7.8
1980	39.1	45.8	5.0	3.4	6.7
1983	44.3	41.4	5.5	3.4	5.4
1985	41.4	41.5	5.5	3.5	8.1

Source: *China's Statistical Yearbook, 1986*, p. 55.
Note: Percentages are based on figures for national income (*guomin shouru*) given in current prices.

Table 3

Relative Percentages of Light and Heavy Industrial Gross Output Value in Industrial Production

	Light industry	Heavy industry
1952	64.5	35.5
1957	56.0	45.0
1965	51.6	48.4
1970	46.2	53.8
1975	44.1	55.9
1978	43.1	56.9
1980	47.2	52.8
1983	48.5	51.5
1985	46.7	53.3

Source: Calculated from figures based on current prices published in *China's Statistical Yearbook, 1986*, p. 46.

centage of heavy industrial output in total industrial output peaked as a result of the Cultural Revolution years, with heavy industrial output value reaching 56.9 percent in 1978, up from 35.5 percent in 1952.

Encouragement of small-scale enterprises added to the bias toward heavy industry. This was a key component of the Maoist approach. Rural enterprises were set up both as state enterprises, primarily as the "five small" rural industries, and as collective enterprises.[16] Counting just the collective industrial enterprises at the commune level and above, between 1965 and 1976 the number increased from 12,200 to 106,200.[17] The five small industries, which were targeted at agricultural inputs and therefore oriented toward heavy industry, included farm machinery, cement, chemical fertilizer, iron and steel, and energy.[18] Development of the five small industries began in 1968, and by the end of the Cultural Revolution period contributed substantially to total output. By 1977, for example, there were 4,300 farm machinery manufacturing and repair plants at the county level, and 495,000 assembly and repair stations at the commune and brigade level.[19] The output of these enterprises represented all of the simple farm tools and almost 100 percent of all small and medium farm machines produced in China. Nitrogenous fertilizer plants numbered approximately 1,350 and produced over 43 percent of total output from all plants. There were over 1,000 small-scale phosphorus fertilizer plants, producing over 50 percent of the total, and over 3,000 cement plants, producing 64 percent of China's cement output. Total small hydroelectric plant capacity grew from 200,000 kilowatts in 1966 to 3,000,000 kilowatts in 1975, increasing to 6,330,000 kilowatts by 1979.[20]

In sum, due in part to contributions from small-scale production, total output including national income, agriculture, and industry increased at respectable rates beginning in 1969. But this growth was highly skewed toward heavy industry at the expense of all other sectors. At the same time, despite potential improvements in technology embodied in heavy industry, Chinese leaders and scholars often comment on China's poor total factor productivity performance in both industry and agriculture. Calculations by some foreign scholars have also shown poor results.[21] For example, China's highest productivity growth in state industry occurred during the First Five-Year Plan and between 1963 and 1965. Most calculations have shown that since 1965 productivity increases in this sector have been very low, possibly even offsetting all gains. During some years of the Great Leap Forward and the Cultural Revolution, inputs increased more than outputs, causing negative productivity change. Without substantial improvements in productivity, continued accumulation becomes more and more difficult.

Implementation of Maoist Economic Strategy

In the face of severe economic constraints made worse by productivity problems, how was the rapid industrial growth of the Cultural Revolution period achieved? Three complementary facets of the Maoist approach to accumulation explain both the successes in achieving growth and the inevitable failure to sustain or legitimize the Cultural Revolution socialist experiment. First, the leadership allocated via the plan a high proportion of national income to accumulation, stimulating growth but leaving little room for growth in consumption or other sectors. Second, the contribution to accumulation from the local sector increased substantially with the implementation of "self-reliance," adding to growth but also to inefficiencies. And third, the dynamics of the Cultural Revolution were such that people were enticed and coerced into sacrificing consumption and working long hours, often without monetary rewards. Hence, nonmaterial incentives to contribute to production complemented the plan's bias against consumer goods, but such low payoffs were unsustainable. These three facets of the Maoist approach to accumulation will be discussed in turn.

China's high accumulation rate generally, and especially during the Great Leap Forward and the Cultural Revolution, has been well publicized, in part as a critique of the Maoist approach.[22] *China's Statistical Yearbook, 1984* published the division of national income between accumulation and consumption annually between 1952 and 1983.[23] The two years with the highest accumulation were 1959 and 1960, with 43.8 percent and 39.6 percent, the very years when China's economy collapsed with famine. Not surprisingly, for the four years after, the accumulation rate fell substantially. In 1965 the percentage rose again to 27.1 percent, and then to 30.6 percent in 1966. After falling some between 1967 and 1969, accumulation in 1970 rose to 32.9 percent and remained above 30 percent into the early 1980s. The peak occurred in 1978 at 36.5 percent. Since the amount of national income available for consumption is inversely related to accumulation, China's high rate of accumulation generally, and especially during the Great Leap Forward and for the greater part of the Cultural Revolution, meant total output devoted to consumption was low and exhibited a declining trend over time.[24]

The breakdown of productive and nonproductive uses within accumulation is also indicative of the emphasis on accumulation during the Cultural Revolution. There was an emphasis on productive investment, meaning that machinery and machine tools received top priority, while "nonproductive" assets such as housing were at the end of the queue. Productive investment was highest during the Great Leap, reaching 97.4 percent in 1960. The 1966–1975 period, and then continuing to 1978, also had very high percentages, ranging between 68.9 and 82.2 percent and averaging 75.5 percent between 1966 and 1975.[25]

Corresponding to the high rates of accumulation were high investment levels, especially in heavy industry, which partly explain the speed and composition of growth. The tilt toward giving priority to heavy industrial investment began during the First Five-Year Plan but was pushed to extremes during the Great Leap Forward and Cultural Revolution. For example, the amount of basic construction investment going to heavy industry between 1966 and 1970 was 51.1 percent, and between 1971 and 1975, 49.6 percent, compared with 36.1 percent during the First Five-Year Plan.[26] In contrast, only 4.4 percent was invested in light industry and 10.7 percent in agriculture between 1966 and 1970, and 5.8 percent and 9.8 percent respectively between 1971 and 1975. Consequently, other sectors such as construction, transport, education, and health also received relatively little investment.[27] This is consistent with their stagnation or decline observed in the previous section.

The second facet of Maoist accumulation, self-reliance, explains the increasing contribution of localities and small-scale enterprises to total output. Internationally, especially after the Sino-Soviet split in 1960, self-reliance meant that China imported goods and technology on a highly selected basis. Within the domestic economy, self-reliance meant that each province was to move toward producing its own grain, energy, and industrial needs; within provinces, counties were to do the same.[28] The decentralization presupposed by the Maoist development model, expressed in this geographical, spatial way, reinforced the development of small-scale production in rural areas. Since provinces and counties could not rely on either central allocation or market purchases, there was strong incentive to produce for their own needs whenever possible. Further, since rural industrialization was initially aimed at increasing modern inputs into agriculture, and because agricultural output used in light industry continued to be tightly controlled by the center, rural industrial development was also skewed toward the producer goods sector.[29]

Self-reliance, then, was intimately tied to the development of rural small-scale industry, which contributed to China's overall rapid industrial growth, and to the heavy industrial bias in production. This local industrial development resulted in the accumulation and investment of local, often marginal, resources since state supplies were reserved for larger enterprises. But as a result of using marginal resources, duplication of facilities, and mechanization, total inputs per unit of output increased markedly. Two examples of increased use of inputs are energy and labor.

In terms of energy consumption, the percentage of total national primary, modern energy consumed in the agricultural sector was 3.1 in 1965. This increased to 6.4 percent by 1975.[30] The percentage of China's electricity consumed in agriculture increased from 4.4 percent in 1965 to 6.5 percent in 1975, and to 10.1 percent in 1978.[31] Part of this increased electricity use was due to increased mechanization. For example, land irrigated with electrical machinery increased from 8,093,000 ha in 1965 to 24,895,000 ha in 1978, representing an increase from 24.5 percent of the total irrigated land to 55.4 percent.[32] But part was also due to the use of equipment and processes that utilized energy inefficiently. For example, the average rate of energy consumption in small ammonia plants was as much as 2.4 times higher than that in large plants. As a result, small nitrogenous fertilizer plants, while producing about 60 percent of the nation's total using mostly local supplies of coal, also consumed as much energy as was utilized directly in agricultural production in 1978.[33] Further, the mining of coal and petroleum tended to be inefficient since even small deposits in mineral-scarce areas were tapped.[34]

With respect to labor input, rural mechanization during the Cultural Revolution allowed double and triple cropping, leading to substantial increases in human labor input. This was especially true in rice-growing areas where much of the transplanting and harvesting was still done by hand.[35] In addition, many labor hours were employed in tasks such as collecting and distributing organic fertilizer, leveling land and other construction projects, and sideline activities. To illustrate, Shigeru Ishikawa has estimated that in the Yangzi River Valley in 1956, the labor input per crop per hectare of rice land was about 200 eight-hour days; by the end of the 1970s it had increased to between 500 and 800 work days, and it was as high as 1,500 work days in some areas that sustained three crops per year.[36]

The contribution to accumulation of regional self-reliance, then, took the form of bringing into production previously unutilized resources, such as small mineral deposits, marginal cultivatable land, and labor time, but often to the point of overutilization, frustrating efficiency and productivity gains and, therefore, consumption.

The final facet of the Maoist approach to accumulation—curtailed consumption and leisure—provided the foundation for the first two. The increase in labor time needed for agriculture has already been mentioned. Leisure itself, of course, associated as it was with a "leisure class," was not deemed virtuous. The number of restaurants and other daily-use services was severely curtailed. The deemphasis on consumer goods and services generally within the plan was consistent with achieving higher accumulation and was legitimized through the promulgation of values of frugality and stoicism. Simultaneously, wages rose very slowly, especially in rural areas, dampening household demand.[37]

To be sure, China's leaders under Mao were concerned with providing basic needs to its large populace, and they were fairly successful in achieving this, although the food shortages resulting from the Great Leap Forward are an obvious exception. With respect to life expectancy and nutrition, for example, China in the 1970s compared favorably with other countries, controlling for income per capita.[38] Mao's call to "plant grain everywhere," however, was achieved partly at the cost of slower increases in other foodstuffs such as fruit, vegetables, bean curd, meat, and fish,[39] so that average per capita calorie intake did not improve between 1957 and 1977.[40] Another example of the trade-offs involved in providing basic needs is that provision of inexpensive housing resulted in severe crowding. In other words, people had access to a minimum of basic needs, but consumption beyond these minimums was checked both by investment in other sectors and by public surveillance over those who tried to consume more than their share.[41]

In the realm of public consumption, expenditures on culture, health, and education increasingly became the responsibility of local communities rather than the state budget.[42] For example, the number of hospital beds at the commune and brigade levels increased from 308,000 in 1965 to 1,140,000 in 1978, and health personnel increased from 880,000 to 1,321,000 during the same period.[43] The ability of communities to invest in these items, however, varied by their economic circumstances, leading to unequal distribution and quality of these services.[44] In education, also, while the number of students and schools increased substantially, many argue that the quality of education and research suffered, adversely affecting other aspects of society, including the economy.[45]

Thus, although Chinese development concentrated on heavy industrial growth, the leaders agreed that certain basic needs should be provided; the provision of these needs, however, came at a very high price to individuals, families, and communities generally. This price was paid in stagnant wages, scarcity of many consumer goods and services, and increasing work loads. These conditions affected all groups in China but probably were the most severe in the countryside, where double and triple cropping and construction projects raised the number of working hours tremendously while consumption possibilities were kept low. The line between coercion and voluntary choice is difficult to draw here, especially as "class struggle" is not recalled with pleasure in China today.[46] But the fact remains that these sacrifices were the basis for much of what post-1949 China has accomplished in terms of economic growth and distribution.

Socialist Development and the Chinese Experience

Part of the test of socialism in Mao's China was achieving rapid growth. With constraints resulting from the low development level of the economy combined with limited options of a socialist approach to accumulation, as Mao defined it, there was continual pressure for austerity to achieve high growth. During the Cultural Revolution the virtue of austerity reached its pinnacle.

Such a savings ethos is, of course, not unprecedented—high savings rates in modern Japan and the so-called Protestant ethic of Northern Europe are just two examples. Periods of high national savings rates are helpful for countries to become, or even remain, advanced industrial economies, whether socialist or capitalist.

Why, then, the backlash in China? A complete answer to what went wrong would need the perspectives of a number of disciplines; here, by way of suggestion only, the implications of some of the economic factors are raised.

First, perhaps austerity under Mao's China went too far in how much was sacrificed to achieve growth. It is one thing to live modestly with hopes for a better future; it is another to store grain until the barrels are overflowing and still not be allowed substantially to improve and vary one's diet. Basic foods such as bean curd became rare; wages remained virtually stagnant for two decades; and the enjoyment of even simple pleasures like potted house plants was criticized. China's leaders promised a great deal in terms of economic success, but prolonged austerity—made worse by low productivity—eventually became incongruous with high expectations.

Second, austerity and high savings during the Cultural Revolution were not the decision of individual households, but rather were imposed from above. Perhaps this, combined with the anxiety and results of monitoring each other's behavior, thoughts, and consumption, contributed to both the extremes in implementation and the bitter memories of the process. To the extent that people believed that high-level cadres who decided in favor of austerity for the general populace themselves lived well, the bitterness would have been accentuated.

Finally, despite deserved criticism of the Maoist approach to development in China, the achievements upon which Deng's regime is now building should also be recognized. For example, China's international policies under Mao avoided debt problems and capital flight. Without these concerns, and with a substantial domestic industrial base, Deng no doubt found it easier to reenter international markets without fear of compromising China's national autonomy.[47] Also, the roots of China's current success with rural and small-town development lie with the Cultural Revolution's small-scale industry policies. Other ways of achieving these results exist, but the fact that it has happened as a result of the Maoist development approach should not be overlooked.

In conclusion, China's experience with socialist economic development leaves us with two lessons: the costs of rapid industrialization in a poor, agriculturally based economy, and the perils of believing in a benevolent state. China's economy under Mao's leadership made progress toward development measured by a variety of indicators. This approach to development, however, best articulated during the Cultural Revolution, contained its own contradiction in which the critique of economism's neglect for humanity itself compromised revolution in the cause of production.

This Maoist contradiction has led to a crisis of Marxism, and perhaps of socialism, in China. Discussing the possibility of establishing a "feasible socialism" without using Stalinist methods, Alec Nove has said: "Appeals in the name of national development and socialist aims to defer current consumption would be essential, and would (one hopes) be rendered more acceptable by heavier taxes on high incomes and avoidance of conspicuous consumption."[48] As the Chinese case shows, this too can be taken too far. The fruits of Chinese socialism must be shared with the Chinese people. In the words of Su Shaozhi, former director of the Marxism-Leninism-Mao Zedong Thought Institute in Beijing: "It is not only through propaganda and education [that we must raise the prestige of Marxism]—the basic thing we have to do is to show our people we succeeded because we put Marxism into practice correctly, which includes the development of productivity, the realization of the four modernizations, and the raising of the people's material and cultural living standards. These are more persuasive than words."[49]

Notes

1. The initial idea for this essay came about through a series of lively discussions with Arif Dirlik, which resulted in our coauthoring the first draft. I wish to acknowledge gratefully Arif's contributions, but also to release him of any responsibility for the final interpretation and any errors within.

2. For Mao's views on the necessity and difficulties of rapid industrialization, see, for example, Mao Tse-tung, *A Critique of Soviet Economics*, tr. Moss Roberts (New York: Monthly Review Press, 1977), pp. 52–53.

3. In some cases, however, reducing export dependency is economically difficult despite political and ideological goals. For example, Cuba tried to lessen its dependence on sugar exports, but when it did the constraints on alternative sources of accumulation became painfully clear. For an analysis of Cuba's attempts at domestic accumulation that is similar to the one made here for China, reflecting the fact that Cuba borrowed liberally from the "Maoist model," see Andrew Zimbalist and Susan Eckstein, "Patterns of Cuban Development: The First Twenty-five Years," *World Development* 15, 1 (January 1987): 5–22.

4. Mao, *A Critique*, pp. 46–47, 77.

5. Mao's intent is not at issue here; the consequences are. In this essay China's development policies until Mao's death are referred to as "Maoist" because of Mao's clear influence on them, especially during the Cultural Revolution period. This is not to say that Mao personally orchestrated the economy, nor that the set of policies collectively were consistent, since other leaders, objective conditions, and the system itself also played their parts.

6. Mao, *A Critique*, pp. 46–47, 53, 83.

7. Ibid., pp. 65–66.

8. "Two Diametrically Opposed Lines in Building the Economy," *Renmin ribao*, August 25, 1967, p. 8, tr. in *Chinese Economic Studies* 1, 2 (Winter 1967–68): 3.

9. "Never Forget the Class Struggle," *Jiefangjun bao*, May 4, 1966, tr. in *The Great Socialist Cultural Revolution in China (1)* (Beijing: Foreign Languages Press, 1966), p. 25.

10. For several other interpretations and approaches to this issue, see Mark Selden, "The Logic—and Limits—of Chinese Socialist Development," *World Development* 11, 8 (1983): 631–37; Bruce McFarlane, "Political Economy of Class Struggle and Economic Growth in China, 1950–1982," *World Development* 11, 8 (1983): 659–72; and Kojima Reiitsu, "Accumulation, Technology, and China's Economic Development," in *The Transition to Socialism in China*, ed. Mark Selden and Victor Lippit (Armonk, N.Y.: M. E. Sharpe, 1982), pp. 238–65.

11. Amidst the critiques, a few Chinese and foreign scholars have recently acknowledged these gains. See, for example, Li Chengrui, "Shinian nei luan qijian woguo jingji qingkuang fenxi" (Analysis of China's economic situation during the ten years of internal disorder), *Jingji yanjiu* 1 (January 1984): 23–31, tr. in Foreign Broadcast Information Service, *China Daily Report*, March 7, 1984, pp. K2–K15; and Robert Michael Field, "The Performance of Industry During the Cultural Revolution: Second Thoughts," *China Quarterly* 108 (December 1986): 625–42.

12. The average rates of annual growth for each period are based on annual growth figures published in China. No attempt is made to estimate biases due to valuation or output quality problems. Therefore these figures reflect the Cultural Revolution record as shown by Chinese statistics themselves. Further, it is unlikely that reconstruction would significantly alter the argument concerning growth made here. For example, even though Field's careful estimates are slightly different than the official figures, his figures still represent substantial growth during the Cultural Revolution period ("Performance of Industry," pp. 625–27). Taking into consideration the impact of changes in the structure of industry on the price index, Field's estimate of the average annual rate of growth of total gross industrial output value between 1966 and 1975 is 10.6 percent per year, compared with 10.4 calculated directly from the Chinese figures and given in table 1. For light industry Field's figure is 7.9 instead of 8.8, and for heavy industry, 13.5 instead of 12.4.

13. Zhongguo Tongji Ju, *Zhongguo tongji nianjian, 1984* (China's statistical yearbook, 1984) (Beijing: Zhongguo Tongji Chubanshe, 1984), p. 29.

14. Ibid., and table 1.

15. Thomas P. Lyons, "China's Cellular Economy: A Test of the Fragmentation Hypothesis," *Journal of Comparative Economics* 9 (1985): 125–44.

16. For a discussion of the development of the five small industries, see Christine Wong, "Rural Industrialization in China: Development of the 'Five Small Industries,' " Ph.D. dissertation, University of California, Berkeley, 1979.

17. *China's Statistical Yearbook, 1984*, p. 193.

18. Wong, "Rural Industrialization," p. 5.

19. Ibid. p. 5, table I–1.

20. Robert P. Taylor, *Rural Energy Development in China* (Washington, D.C.: Resources for the Future, 1981), p. 164, table 7–1.

21. See, for example, Robert Michael Field, "Slow Growth of Labour Productivity in Chinese Industry, 1952–1981," *China Quarterly* 96 (December 1983): 641–64, and Gene Tidrick, "Productivity Growth and Technological Change in Chinese Industry," World Bank Staff Working Papers no. 761 (Washington, D.C.: World Bank, 1986). At least one study has questioned these results, suggesting that problems with methodology and data have led to underestimates of change in China's industrial productivity (K. Chen et al., "Productivity Change in Chinese Industry: 1953–1985," Department of Economics Working Paper, University of Pittsburgh, October 1987). Even in this study, however, during the Cultural Revolution "productivity fluctuates considerably but with no distinct trend," and it is not until 1985 "that productivity moves decisively above its 1957 and 1970–72 peaks" (p. 18).

22. See, for example, Li Chengrui, "Analysis of China's Economic Situation," p. 29.

23. *China's Statistical Yearbook, 1984*, p. 32.

24. When these figures are put in Western terms of gross domestic product, China's rate of savings by 1979 was higher than that in many middle-income countries as well as being far above that in other low-income countries (World Bank, *China: Socialist Economic Development*, main report [Washington, D.C.: World Bank, 1981], pp. 48–49).

25. Ibid., p. 34.

26. Ibid., p. 308.

27. Ibid., p. 307.

28. Nicholas R. Lardy, *Agriculture in China's Modern Economic Development* (Cambridge: Cambridge University Press, 1983), pp. 49–50, and Christine P. W. Wong, "Ownership and Control in Chinese Industry: The Maoist Legacy and Prospects for the 1980s," in U. S. Congress, Joint Economic Committee, *China's Economy Looks Toward the Year 2000* (Washington, D.C.: Government Printing Office, 1986), 1:571–603, esp. 574–76.

29. Christine Wong, "Material Allocation and Decentralization: Impact of the Local Sector on Industrial Reform," in *The Political Economy of Reform in Post-Mao China*, ed. Elizabeth J. Perry and Christine Wong (Cambridge: Council on East Asian Studies, Harvard University, 1985), pp. 253–80, esp. pp. 257–66.

30. Taylor, *Rural Energy*, p. 63, table 3–6. These figures do not include the energy needed to produce chemical fertilizer.

31. Ibid., p. 64, table 3–7.

32. *China's Statistical Yearbook, 1984*, p. 175.

33. Taylor, *Rural Energy*, pp. 62–63.

34. For example, northern Jiangsu province has rich coal deposits, but investment in coal mines in the south was undertaken at great expense. "Calculated one way, in the construction of coal mines in southern Jiangsu, 24 pairs of shafts were declared worthless, a waste of 234 million yuan. Calculated another way, total accumulative investment and deficit subsidies amounted to 700 million yuan, which have produced an annual capacity of about 2 million tons. . . . If these funds had been invested in the coal-rich Xuzhou area, an annual production capacity of almost 10 million tons would have been added." Wu Jinglian and Chen Jiyuan, "Establishing a Rational Industrial

Structure According to Local Characteristics," *Social Sciences in China* 3 (September 1980): 231.

35. Taylor, *Rural Energy*, pp. 60–61.

36. Shigeru Ishikawa, "Labour Absorption in China's Agriculture," in *Labour Absorption and Growth in Agriculture: China and Japan*, ed. Shigeru Ishikawa, Saburo Yamada, and S. Hirashima (Bangkok: International Labour Organization Asian Employment Program, 1982), pp. 12–14; Thomas B. Weins, "The Limits to Agricultural Intensification: The Suzhou Experience," in Joint Economic Committee, U.S. Congress, *China under the Four Modernizations, Part I* (Washington, D.C.: Government Printing Office, 1982), pp. 462–74.

37. See, e.g., S. Lee Travers, "Getting Rich Through Diligence: Peasant Income After the Reforms," in *The Political Economy of Reform*, ed. Perry and Wong, pp. 111–30.

38. World Bank, *China*, main report, pp. 67–71.

39. Ibid., pp. 53, 71. See also Lardy, *Agriculture in China's Modern Economic Development*, pp. 52–54, for a discussion of aggregate costs of ignoring comparative advantage in agricultural crops and using pasture lands to grow grain.

40. World Bank, *China*, main report, p. 71.

41. There are many examples of such surveillance during the Cultural Revolution, especially in the 1966–1969 period. See, for example, Gao Yuan, *Born Red* (Stanford: Stanford University Press, 1987), for a description of attacks on party personnel, teachers, and administrators for their access to grain coupons, cigarettes, and other consumer goods, and for eating better than the students (pp. 67–76). "Socialist morality" was to conquer those with "bourgeois lifestyles."

42. For a discussion of local financing of education, for example, see Stanley Rosen, "Recentralization, Decentralization, and Rationalization: Deng Xiaoping's Bifurcated Education Policy," *Modern China* 11, 3 (July 1985): 327–35.

43. *China's Statistical Yearbook, 1984*, p. 519. Note that these figures are given for *xiang* and *cun*, the new names for commune and brigade.

44. World Bank, *China*, main report, p. 69.

45. Rosen, "Recentralization," pp. 324–31; Richard Conroy, "Technological Innovation in China's Recent Industrialization," *China Quarterly* 97 (March 1984): 7.

46. See Ishikawa, "Labour Absorption," pp. 23–25, for a discussion of the varieties and likelihood of coercion in the Chinese countryside.

47. This sense of confidence is frequently conveyed in editorials and speeches. For example, Deng Xiaoping, "On Upholding the Four Cardinal Principles," March 30, 1979, reprinted in *Beijing Review* (February 9, 1987): 29–36, and Dai Yannian, "Cultural, Material Advances: Hand in Hand," *Beijing Review* (October 20, 1986): 4–5.

48. Alec Nove, *The Economics of Feasible Socialism* (London: George Allen and Unwin, 1983), p. 195.

49. Gordon H. Chang, "Perspectives on Marxism in China Today: An Interview with Su Shaozhi, Director of the Marxism-Leninism-Mao Zedong Thought Institute, Academy of Social Sciences, Beijing, China," *Monthly Review* (September 1986): 25–26.

8

RESTRUCTURING THE WORKING CLASS: LABOR REFORM IN POST-MAO CHINA

Gordon White

Over the past decade economic reformers have undertaken a series of changes in China's labor system with the aim of raising labor productivity in the state sector and increasing the flexibility and dynamism of the urban-industrial economy as a whole. At the macro (national) and meso (local) levels, they have taken steps to dismantle the previous system of direct administrative control over urban labor; at the micro level, they have sought to redefine the work change status of state workers. These measures undermine the system of de facto job security, stimulate workers to move between enterprises, and give managers greater powers over the recruitment and disposition of their workers. The overall direction of these measures is toward a more "flexible" labor system working along lines comparable to the "labor markets" familiar to Western economists.

In political terms, labor reform is a particularly sensitive policy area. It raises important ideological issues about the nature of a "socialist" as opposed to "capitalist" mode of production within the Marxist canon. Policies that seek to introduce the instabilities and insecurity associated with a "labor market" appear to contradict the conventional socialist commitment to full employment and job security. Labor reforms are directed at the urban working class, which, in terms of the official ideology, is the main political underpinning of Chinese communism. The reforms embody potentially fundamental changes in the socioeconomic position of Chinese workers and in their relationship to their managerial superiors. As such, they threaten to disrupt established interests and understandings that accumulated in China's enterprises over the first three decades after Liberation. Hence, it would not be surprising to find that the reforms run into considerable resistance.

This essay explores how these reforms have been conceived and put into practice and assesses their impact on China's urban industrial economy, looking at the subject from a political rather than an economic perspective. I shall deal mainly with industrial labor in the state sector, which has been the primary target of labor reforms. Though the state sector only makes up a small proportion of industrial enterprises (20.2 percent in 1985), it produces the bulk of industrial output (70.4 percent in 1985) and owns most of industry's fixed assets (87.8 percent in 1984).[1]

While the state work force as a whole (including the nonindustrial) is a small proportion (18 percent in 1985) of the nation's total work force (including agriculture), it made up roughly 70 percent of the urban work force in 1985 and enjoyed a higher average wage-level than the urban collective sector (1,166 yuan per annum in 1985 compared to 925 yuan).[2]

Labor reform in the state sector should be viewed in the broader context of China's overall employment situation where the government faces severe problems: a chronic urban labor surplus and the increasingly worrisome issues of rural surplus labor and rural-urban and interregional migration.[3] Systematic discussion of these issues is outside the scope of this article, but relevant information will be included where necessary.

The Previous Labor System and the Reform Critique

On the eve of the reform era, which began with the cardinal Third Plenum of the CCP Central Committee in December 1978, the Chinese system of labor allocation was heavily *dirigiste*, even in comparison with its Soviet and Eastern European counterparts. It was organized on the administrative principle of "unified allocation," which in the early years after 1949 had been introduced to deal with certain groups with scarce specialized skills of strategic importance for the new planned economy (notably graduates of colleges and specialized middle schools). Over time, the practice of "unified allocation" was extended to include virtually all members of the urban labor force including both state and collective sectors.[4]

Along with this statist system of labor allocation there developed a system of de facto job tenure, not only for workers and staff in state enterprises but also in larger "collective" enterprises which operated in reality as part of the state sector. As late as 1983, 96.8 percent of the state work force were "fixed workers" who enjoyed the right to remain in their initial enterprise for life.[5] This also gave them privileged access to certain welfare benefits provided by the enterprise itself, such as medical and labor insurance, housing, child-care facilities, pensions, and guaranteed jobs for their children through the increasing practice of occupational inheritance. In fact, large state enterprises tended to turn into "small societies" with mini "welfare states," and smaller ones operated like large families regulated by particularistic relationships.[6] In consequence, state work forces tended to be very stable, with increasingly high levels of overmanning (to use Janos Kornai's term, "unemployment on the job")[7] and low levels of interenterprise, intersectoral, or interregional mobility, and with seniority as a prime criterion for payment and promotion within the firm. Economic reformers now refer to the guarantees under this system derogatorily as the "iron rice-bowl," which they have taken as one of their tasks to make more fragile (indeed converting it into a "porcelain rice bowl" which the worker must treat with greater care and caution).

The existence of these phenomena of rigidity and overmanning is well established and can be attributed to certain basic economic and political factors. First, of considerable importance has been the long-standing structural dualism of the urban economy, that is, the socioeconomic gap between a relatively privileged state sector (incorporating the so-called big collectives) and the small-collective sector run by urban neighborhoods, in terms of wages, welfare benefits, economic security, political access, and social status.[8] Urban job-seekers reacted rationally to this dualistic divide by trying to get "real jobs" in the state sector; once there, they had little incentive to move out into the small-collective sector.

Second, the CCP has been committed since the 1950s to providing jobs for all urban job-seekers, and it has been sensitive to the political dangers posed by urban employment. During the Cultural Revolution era, the attempt to solve the problem by sending urban graduates to the countryside proved very unpopular, providing much political fuel for Dengist forces after Mao's death. The new leadership attached high priority to this problem from the outset, and, year after year, official spokespeople have pointed proudly to their record of bringing down the urban unemployment rate. According to official statistics, the "job-waiting rate" (the euphemistic term for unemployment) has been reduced from a peak of 5.3 percent in 1978 to 1.8 percent in 1985.[9]

These statistics underestimate the problem, however, since they only include people formally registered as job-seekers and do not include illegal or semilegal rural immigrants whose numbers have swelled in recent years. This immigration reflects a growing problem of rural surplus labor which in 1982 was estimated to be about 35 percent of total rural labor.[10] Under the commune system, local labor surpluses tended to be absorbed by the redistributive mechanisms of the collectives at team, brigade, and commune levels, but the spread of household-based responsibility system in the 1980s has extruded labor from agriculture. Although it is planned to absorb most of the surplus through local diversification and industrialization in villages and small towns within the countryside, it is also recognized that a certain—and probably growing—number will have to be admitted to the larger towns and cities.[11] In overall terms, the World Bank estimates that the total labor force will increase by about 180 million between 1981 and 2000, requiring about 10 million additional jobs per annum.[12] This places heavy pressure on state labor authorities, which can be expected to persist until the end of the millennium.

The pressure of surplus labor further reduces the motivation of workers to leave state jobs and provide a political impetus for administrative controls motivated by the desire of a socialist government to avoid unemployment.[13] However, much of the CCP's apparent success in reducing urban employment has been achieved by converting open unemployment into "unemployment on the job."

China's reform economists have argued that this labor system posed a serious obstacle to growth, particularly "intensive" as opposed to "extensive" growth. In their view, it was too rigid and bureaucratic, constraining the flexibility of the economy, perpetuating poor labor productivity, and retarding technical change. Changes were necessary, they argued, to increase the flexibility of movement of the labor work force, give managers more power over their work-force labor, and break the iron rice-bowl of state workers.[14]

Specifically, they have argued that the degree of direct administrative control over urban labor has been excessive, rendering the economic actors themselves—both managers and workers—inert. Official overemphasis on the need to reduce unemployment, moreover, brought direct costs through overmanning and even greater opportunity costs in that surplus labor in the state sector could be employed more productively in the collective and private sectors. Though increasing labor mobility would lead to a certain amount of frictional unemployment, this could be cushioned by state welfare provisions (a dole, retraining, and relocation) and eventually absorbed by a more dynamic and diverse economic system. At the enterprise level, the introduction of labor contracts for state employees would provide greater flexibility by allowing "two choices" or "two freedoms" (more opportunities for workers to change jobs and more powers for managers in handling labor) and would raise labor productivity since workers would work harder to ensure that their labor contracts were renewed.

Labor Reform Policies and Policy Debate

The specific reform policies adopted after the Third Plenum reflect the above critique. While the principle of state labor planning was to remain intact, state labor agencies were to play a more limited and indirect role. They would still regulate the overall structure of the nonagricultural labor force without as much resort to administrative control. New labor agencies (called companies) would be set up outside the state sphere; enterprise managers would have more power to recruit and dismiss workers; workers would be encouraged to seek to create their own jobs; the iron rice-bowl would be broken by employing state workers on renewable labor contracts. The end-product was to be a more flexible labor system, in effect a regulated labor market.

This paradigm of labor reform has received support from foreign economists and agencies, most importantly the World Bank, which sent a mission to China in early 1984 and published an exhaustive report on the current situation and future prospects of the Chinese economy in 1985. The report in the main agreed with both the Chinese reform critique of the previous labor system and the measures proposed to remedy the situation. Specifically, this meant more opportunity for workers to move jobs and greater discretionary power for personal managers, particularly the power to dismiss workers either for incompetence or in response to changing production and market conditions. In the bank's view, the economic costs of frictional unemployment would be less than those resulting from "unemployment on the job." Temporary unemployment could be eased by state provision and by an economy being restructured in ways that generated employment outside industry and the state sector. The report thus echoed the rationale of the Chinese reformers and probably strengthened their hand within China.

Has the reformist analysis of labor policy been unchallenged in China? There has been a debate on the issue, but this has been limited in several ways. First, it has not fully reflected the wide spectrum of opinions on the issue because the views of the disgraced radical Maoists have been excluded. Second, while there has been public disagreement on labor issues, the paradigm outlined above has dominated the debate. No well-articulated alternative position has emerged with a different diagnosis and solution. Partly this reflects the fact that the dominant section of the CCP leadership, led by Deng Xiaoping, has thrown its weight behind the reform analysis, converting it into orthodoxy; partly it reflects the (as yet) apparent absence of such an alternative.

Most participants in the debate recognize that there were problems in the previous labor system: rigidity, bureaucratic arbitrariness, waste of scarce skills, slack labor discipline, low levels of labor productivity. However, they vary in their evaluation of the seriousness of these problems, their weight relative to other policy issues, and the kind of measures appropriate to solving them. Opponents or skeptics of the reform program have laid heavy stress on political and social as opposed to economic issues. They argue that the policy objectives of full employment and job security are basic commitments that distinguish a socialist from a nonsocialist regime and must be maintained even though they may bring some economic costs. In this view, the goals of reducing unemployment and raising labor productivity are, in the short term at least, contradictory. The iron rice-bowl is thus seen less as an expression of inefficient featherbedding or sectoral privilege and more of a socialist concern for workers' welfare. The author of one rare public critique felt the need "to cry out for the iron rice-bowl system with a heavy heart" since "many of our revolutionary comrades struggled all their lives so that the people of the whole country could each have an iron rice-bowl."[15] The author probably spoke for many, particularly state and party cadres and state industrial workers, when he argued that job security was part of "the superiority of socialism" while attempts to undermine it, such as the labor contract system, were comparable to a capitalist "wage labor" system.

Critics have warned that labor reforms would be politically divisive and socially harmful: for example, they could lead to invidious divisions between "fixed" and "contract" workers, or between the employed and the unemployed. Open unemployment would also lead to juvenile delinquency and a decline in moral standards.[16]

There has been some concern, furthermore, about the effects of labor reform on the nature of the enterprise. One can detect three themes here. First, there is a "neotraditional" position that sees the firm as a family, operating through quasi-kinship relations of loyalty and solidarity. Changes that rupture these may cause social disorientation and economic damage.[17] Second, there is a recognition that lifelong job security appears to have been a factor in the superlative performance of Japanese enterprises; if this was not incompatible with capitalism, why should it not be compatible with socialism? Third, there is a more directly socialist concern that a stable work force is necessary to enable workers to exercise their rights within the enterprise, particularly in the context of any move toward worker self-management. In the view of one noted economist, for example, comprehensive adoption of the labor contract system to counter the iron rice-bowl would intensify an already evident shift of power within the enterprise in favor of managers, workers becoming "hired laborers" rather than "masters" of the enterprise.[18]

Views of this kind do not usually signify total opposition to reform; they tend to counsel caution in the implementation of policy or advocate a watering down of policy (for example, accepting a partial application of the labor contract system). But these critics do suggest that the productivity goals of the reformers can be met by other means: by tightening labor discipline, introducing more effective wage and job responsibility systems, improved training facilities, more advanced technology, and better relations between managers and workers.[19]

The views of these critics do highlight problems in the reformist approach and cannot be dismissed as "dogmatism" or special pleading. Reformers would do well to heed their warnings about the potential political repercussions of labor reform. Moreover, reform prescriptions do not as yet rest on sophisticated analyses of the internal social relations of enterprises and thus cannot answer questions about the extent to which the iron rice-bowl may, along Japanese lines, be economically productive in certain contexts. However, the economic arguments of the critics are less convincing, partly because they are not coherent, and partly because they do not appear to work very well, judging from disappointing attempts over the past decade to improve economic performance by strengthening managerial controls or setting up wage incentive schemes. The reform argument does have considerable force, namely, that such measures cannot be effective as long as workers have guaranteed employment in a given firm, nor can firms operate effectively in a market environment without greater managerial freedom to redeploy and if necessary prune their work force. That this will create unemployment is undeniable, but the key question is whether such movement toward a labor market can be squared with continuing socialist commitments. I shall return to this issue in the conclusion.

Ideological Issues in Wage Reform

Since the reform paradigm leads labor policy in a market direction, policy makers have had to confront the question of how a "market in labor power" fits into their official ideology. In the Marxist canon, this notion implies that labor power is a commodity; since this perhaps is the definitive characteristic of a capitalist economic system, it would seem to be fundamentally incompatible with the role of labor in an avowedly socialist economy. The previous administrative system of state labor allocation rested on the idea that labor power was not a commodity. Existing ideology thus provides a theoretical rationale for previous practice and poses problems for the reformers. In an "ideocratic" policy of the Chinese kind, economic policies must be clothed in suitable ideological garb; radical changes in policy thus require congruent changes in ideology that can provoke charges of "revisionism" from opponents. In essence these debates reflect different conceptions of socialism—the "traditional" Marxist-Leninist view and a reform view of a society based on the notion of a "socialist commodity economy." The Talmudic tussle over the ideological status of labor power markets reflects this basic political divide.

This ideological debate both among the reformers and between them and their opponents has reflected more concrete disagreements over labor policy. As reform leaders gradually gained political predominance in the mid-1980s, the ideological frontiers have been pushed back, and previously heretical ideas have received a public airing. The range of views reflected in the public debate, conducted in both academic journals and mass circulation organs, has been surprisingly wide and reflects the political sensitivity of labor issues. Answers to the basic question "Is labor power a commodity under socialist conditions?" have ranged from an emphatic no to an equally emphatic yes, with various shades of opinion in between. There has been debate about whether workers should enjoy guaranteed employment and job security as social rights.

The traditional ideological position, that labor power cannot be a commodity under a socialist economy, retains support among both analysts and officials. Hu Chen, for example, argues that labor power is not a commodity under socialism for two reasons: first, "public ownership is practiced and the laborers jointly possess the means of production and are the masters of the means of production. We cannot say that laborers are selling labor power to themselves"; second, the worker's wage does not represent the value of his or her labor power but "the value of income distributed according to work," including not merely the value of the laborer's means of subsistence but also the value of enjoying and developing such means as well as collective welfare, awards, bonuses, and so on.[20]

However, while denying that labor power is a commodity, Hu Chen does admit that a labor power market can exist. Other analysts have been more squeamish about the term "market in labor power," preferring more neutral terms such as "labor services market," "job market," "labor market," or "labor resources market."[21]

Other reformers wish to go further in revising the ideology to fit a new policy regime, arguing that it is important to recognize that labor is also a commodity in the new socialist commodity economy. They criticize as naive the traditional view that since workers own the means of production, they can hardly sell labor power to themselves. Zhuang Hongxiang, for example, argues that in a socialist economy the seller and buyer of labor power are two different legal persons. For Zhuang, labor power remains a commodity because of "objective economic law."[22]

Other reformers, notably Zhao Guoliang and Dong Fureng, take a more practical position, arguing that the answer to the question of whether or not labor power is a commodity depends on the actual nature of the labor system in operation at any particular time.[23] In the previous system, since there was very little in the way of free exchange between worker and employer, there was thus no labor market and labor power was not a commodity. However, if this situation changed, in particular with the adoption of a system of renewable labor contracts, labor power would then become a commodity. It is the task of the reforms they argue, to transform labor power into commodity, with the prior recognition that this is an essential element of the type of economy they seek to establish.

In essence, these theoretical differences between more radical and moderate reformers reflect different responses to a basic political challenge: the establishment of a new congruence between three levels of political analysis: Marxist economic theory, operational ideology, and specific policies. The first level is that of the Marxian economic canon, which is in theory immutable but in practice malleable, thanks to its lacunae and inconsistencies. The second level is the reigning operational ideology of the day, a more specified derivation of the first which varies according to country, historical phase, or nature of the dominant leadership and is the terrain of debate and conflict in the higher reaches of the party. The reformers are in effect trying to create a new operational ideology that links high theory with practical policy and legitimates changes in economic policy.

This attempt to reconstitute the relationship among theory, ideology, and policy is complicated by two important political factors. First, there is another level of ideology which one might call small-i as opposed to big-I ideology, that is, the values of mass publics shaped by decades of Communist rule. As will be seen later, many, perhaps most, state industrial workers hold "traditional" socialist views about the need to protect job security under socialism and are skeptical about the labor reforms. Second, ideological disagreements at both elite and mass levels tend to be linked with specific clashes of social interests. At the elite level, the "traditional" view that labor power is not a commodity reflects and reinforces the power of party and state officials responsible for organizing the previous labor system. At the popular level, for example, the "traditional" view reflects the interests of workers in the relatively privileged state sector who have enjoyed an iron rice-bowl in the past. Both groups pose powerful political obstacles to the reform process.[24]

Ideological debate thus reflects deeper political disagreement among the party leadership and the clash of attitudes and interests within the state and in society at large. As of 1988, the economic reformers have yet to arrive at a new definition of the role of labor in a new form of "socialism." Are they offering state industrial workers a better deal in the new "socialist commodity economy" than in the traditional system? If they are unable to carry this conviction, they are politically vulnerable to their conservative opponents. Influential reformers such as the economist Dong Fureng are aware of this problem and are careful to point out that, though labor may be a commodity in the postreform economy, this has fundamentally different meanings under capitalism and the new form of socialism. There are similarities—notably the separation of interests between seller and buyer, their separate legal identities, and their freedom to enter into a contractual exchange. But these are outweighed by one fundamental difference—to whom the surplus products belong and whose interests they serve.[25]

The key political problem here may rest on in the realities of labor's position in the postreform society, both within the enterprise and in the economy at large. Will it be better off than before, and what will be the key "socialist" institutions and policies that serve to differentiate the new labor system from that characteristic of capitalism? Before returning to this issue in the conclusion, I shall briefly assess the extent to which China's labor reforms have actually made a difference as of 1987.

The Impact of Labor Reform Policy

At the macro level, the central aim of the reform policy has been to reduce the direct involvement of the state. This process has had three aspects. First, it involved a redefinition of the regulatory role of state agencies. This meant an attempt to devolve decisions over labor allocation from state labor bureaus to nonstate agencies of various types, notably new "labor service companies." Though the state would continue to engage in labor planning, this was seen in terms comparable to the kind of "manpower planning" characteristic of mixed economies. Though direct controls over certain strategic categories of specialized labor might be retained (notably college graduates), their numbers would be reduced, and greater power over their disposition was to be given to training and hiring institutions and to individuals themselves. Regulation of other categories of labor was to become more indirect. Moreover, state labor bureaus would take on new roles to facilitate labor mobility between enterprises and to "cushion" frictional unemployment. They would take responsibility for labor shed by enterprises, arranging interim welfare benefits and retraining and eventual reassignment to other units. Second, deregulation was to be accompanied by a corresponding increase in the labor allocation powers of enterprise managers, as part of the wider move to increase the operational autonomy of basic units of production. If enterprises needed more workers, they should be allowed to advertise, deal with applicants directly (not via the local labor bureau), and use their own recruitment procedures. They should also be able to lure away labor from other units, using their increased power to offer wage and other incentives. Even more crucial, argued the reformers, was the right of enterprise managers to dismiss workers—without this, any attempt to put the economy on a market footing would come to naught. Third, the reforms attempted to increase the choice and opportunities available to individual workers and professional staff. Greater freedom, it was argued, would increase the general efficiency of labor utilization and in particular protect specialized personnel against the arbitrary dictates of personnel cadres in enterprises or state organs.

As of early 1987, though there had been some movement in these directions, reform economists regarded progress as disappointing. To the extent that urban labor circulation has become more flexible, it is for reasons other than labor reform policies themselves. The previous system of labor allocation has been slow to change. The degree of administrative direction has remained high, most notably in the state sector but also in the urban economy as a whole. State labor bureaus at various levels continue to dominate labor allocation, though some of their previous responsibility for details has increasingly been devolved to other institutions, notably labor service companies and enterprises.

Though control over the disposition of strategic groups and labor in centrally managed enterprises remains in the hands of the central labor authorities, local governments have gained power over the disposition of urban labor outside these two sectors. However, the directive element in local labor allocation is still dominant. In Beijing municipality, for example, the process of drawing up the city's labor plan has not changed since 1979. It is based on an estimate of the needs of enterprises and offices within the city, each of which submits its labor requirements to the labor and wages office of its superior bureau, which then communicates with the municipal labor bureau. The ensuing recruitment plan draws on three sources of labor: the strategic groups under centralized "unified allocation" who must be given priority; junior and senior middle-school graduates from the city (and left-over graduates from the previous year who are "waiting employment"); and people with jobs who want to move. The actual process of assignment to a state enterprise is handled by three agencies in concert: the enterprise, the relevant functional bureau's labor office, and the city labor bureau (or its affiliate labor service company).

Particularly at the stage of initial recruitment, there have been significant changes since 1979. Previously, local labor bureaus not only assigned a numerical quota to a state enterprise but also chose and dispatched the individual workers. Since 1979, the enterprise has been given greater say in evaluating and choosing individual workers. Job seekers can apply through a local labor bureau, through one of the new labor service companies, or directly to the enterprise. Local labor bureaus do retain some controls: for example, they may enforce a rule of gender equity if an enterprise refuses to accept female labor for no defensible reason.[26]

Another significant change has been the rise of the labor service company.[27] Though LSCs were originally set up to find jobs and provide training for entrants into the labor force, many have developed into a sort of holding company with their own enterprises, operating in the interstices of the urban economy, creating rather than merely finding jobs. Though all LSCs are dependent on their sponsoring agencies, be they government bureaus or enterprises, they do enjoy a degree of operational independence. This gives them greater scope to weave their way through the highways and byways of the planning system and the urban economy than their sponsoring organs.

If the LSCs are evaluated in the overall system of labor allocation, however, their value as an instrument of economic reform is ambiguous. As agencies of labor management, they act to extend the power of the state labor bureaucracy and the principle of nonmarket allocation into the urban collective sector. As such, they are an integral element of the state labor system. Rather than facilitating the operation of labor markets, they contribute to a kind of "state pluralism" in a system of nonmarket allocation. On the other hand, they have brought an element of decentralization and flexibility into urban labor allocation.

Clearly, labor reforms, to be effective, depend for their success on other areas of reform policy. The continuing pressure of surplus labor and the maintenance of a political commitment to full employment still act to impede the progress of labor reform. The chronic overmanning of Chinese state enterprises reflects both sets of pressures. However, recent changes in the structure of the urban economy are bringing about the increase in labor mobility that the reformers desire. On the other hand, limited progress in introducing wage reforms in the state sector means, among other things, that wages still do not serve as signals to channel labor (notably from low- to high-performance state enterprises). Nonetheless, there are some indications that the previously rigid dualism between state and collective enterprise is breaking down to some extent. The greater freedoms enjoyed by urban collectives and private businesses have opened up opportunities and increased incentives for state workers to leave the security of their iron rice-bowls. Research in China in mid-1987 suggests that, in sectors such as textiles, state enterprises are having trouble both attracting and keeping labor: in some textile mills, for example, workers are often prevented from leaving when they wish.[28]

These trends may be accelerated by changes in the status of labor within the enterprise. As we have seen, reformers view the existence of a virtual tenure system to be a major constraint on increasing labor productivity and encouraging labor flexibility. However, their attempts to weaken the principle of the iron rice-bowl by putting state workers on labor contracts have run into a great deal of resistance from those workers, and from some managers who view the reform as disruptive or administratively burdensome.[29] Though the policy was launched in 1982, progress has been very slow: by the end of 1986, only 5.24 million state workers were on contracts, about 5.6 percent of the total. Although a new policy offensive to introduce labor contracts was launched in mid-1986, progress has not been rapid. This means that enterprise managers still have limited ability to lay off workers, either in response to the enterprise's changing labor requirements or to workers' bad performance. According to statistics for 1986 drawn from fourteen provinces and cities, only 0.007 percent of the state work force were fired for "violation of discipline."[30]

To sum up for both macro and micro levels, labor reform has encountered a good deal of skepticism and resistance, and overall progress has been disappointingly slow from the viewpoint of the reformers. To a considerable extent, this can be attributed to certain political factors that have played an important role in conditioning the reform process. These will be discussed in the concluding section.

Conclusions: On the Politics of Labor Reform

Why have labor reforms run into such heavy weather and made so little progress? One factor is clearly bureaucratic inertia and resistance. State labor agencies have been reluctant to devolve anything but relatively marginal powers to lower-level units. Moreover, the new ancillary agencies, the labor service companies, have a marked tendency to behave like state agencies. Clearly, the principle and practice of comprehensive state labor regulation is still firmly in place, though more pluralistic. Once such a complex institutional network has been established and consolidated over more than two decades, it is difficult to shift.

However, state labor authorities are themselves subject to strong external pressures both pro- and antireform. Pressure for reform comes from party leaders bent on improving the nation's economic performance; from enterprise managers who would like greater power over their own work force and resent bureaucratic interference; from part of the work force itself, notably young, skilled (and potentially mobile) workers, or highly trained professionals, who dislike being told where to work after graduation and resent the lack of freedom to move on to better jobs. On the other side, there are powerful pressures to blunt the impact of reform or retain the status quo. The key factor here is the continuing problem of surplus labor which threatens politically unacceptable levels of unemployment. These circumstances, and the fears they inspire, produce widespread skepticism when reform economists praise the putative benefits of labor markets, or the virtues of unemployment as a stimulus to productive effort. It would be very difficult for the party to revoke its commitment to maintaining full employment to the greatest extent feasible.

This commitment has created over the past two and a half decades a kind of institutionalized patron-client relationship between the Chinese state and its urban constituents: the state takes on the role of provider and the clientele comes to depend on the state and expect its bounty. There is thus a mass constituency to retain state labor control that coincides with and reinforces the institutional interests of state labor agencies.

The antireform influence of this political relationship is buttressed by certain interests within state enterprises, who see dangers in any expansion of a labor market: enterprise managers who fear losing their best workers to more successful enterprises—state, collective, or private; workers who fear that the reforms will threaten their jobs or conditions of work. Within state enterprises, an implicit social contract has developed over the past three decades whereby workers exchange their quiescence and cooperation for managerial or state guarantees of job security and material welfare. Thus the basic character of Chinese enterprises is a powerful brake on current labor reforms.

If these implicit social contracts—between state and society at large and between managers and workers within enterprises—are threatened, the legitimacy of the state is called into question and there is the danger of mass discontent and resistance. Policy makers are keenly aware of this latter prospect and talk of the need to proceed cautiously with labor reforms for fear of disturbing "social peace."

One strong message from the preceding analysis is that, if the reformers are to succeed, they must carry with them those whose interests are affected and whose values are challenged. Do the reforms really offer a "new deal" for Chinese labor (and managers) compared to the traditional labor system? Reform economists may well enthuse about "labor flexibility" or speculate on the economic advantages of unemployment,[31] but they will not be the ones to bear the brunt of adjustment. At the broadest level, this is a question of whether they can offer a practical vision of a "socialist commodity economy" wherein the advantages of markets can be combined effectively with the advantages of socialist planning and institutions, that is, an economically more dynamic and productive, less bureaucratic form of socialism that offers faster income growth and greater socioeconomic opportunity while retaining the basic distinctive socialist concern for full employment and job security. Alternative future scenarios are not unlikely: either a "halfway home" that encounters the characteristic problems of a market economy while retaining many of the negative features of the old administrative planning system, or a "postradical market reform" in which workers are prey to powerful managers and the vicissitudes of a labor market.

In the short and medium term, it is the basic economic and political realities analyzed earlier that will continue to determine the pace and direction of the reform and maintain a balance between certain features of the old and new labor systems. Political leaders will continue to lend one ear to reformist paeans of the market and the other to their own political values and the demands of their various political constituencies. The most favorable environment for rapid reform is a situation in which incomes and opportunities are expanding rapidly, thereby minimizing the zero-sum element of adjustments in the labor system. But, though the performance of the Chinese economy over the past eight years has been impressive, labor officials are sober about the problem ahead. The normal increase in urban labor force will be swelled by labor "shaken out" by industrial rationalization (particularly if the bankruptcy law is allowed to bite) and the increasing flow of labor from the countryside. Political pressures to expand employment through state action will remain high. Other social objectives, such as correcting regional inequalities, will also prompt labor planners to retain some direct controls (particularly over the employment of college graduates).

At the same time, the reform policies designed to encourage greater labor flexibility will also be pursued, at both macro and micro levels. Frictional unemployment will probably increase as industry restructures and the labor contract system is extended within state enterprises. Recent experience suggests, however, that these measures will be introduced cautiously and with the accompaniment of complementary policies to cushion their impact, notably a state welfare system to retrain and reallocate the unemployed and a system of legal and institutional safeguards to protect the rights of workers involved in labor contracts. One theoretical expression of this attempt to combine elements of traditional socialist concern with greater labor flexibility is the redefinition of the notion of the right to employment: it involves the basic right to a job, but not any particular job in any particular firm (one writer refers to this distinction in terms of the difference between "major and minor concepts of the iron rice-bowl").[32]

There are signs, moreover, that as the labor system takes on certain market attributes, such as differential wages and contractual exchanges, hitherto dormant worker organizations will step in to defend the rights of their members—the trade unions and "workers' representative congresses" within enterprises.[33] While they do not figure largely in the program of the reform economists, such organizations would seem to be natural products of a commodity economy, capitalist or socialist. This is but one aspect of a wider process of institutional growth or regeneration stimulated by the reforms, finding its counterpart on the managerial side in the rise of trade associations, entrepreneurs' associations, and chambers of commerce. There are signs of the birth of a new form of "civil society" in response to the advance of market socialism. This should be a priority area for research on the politics of China's economic reform.

Notes

1. State Statistical Bureau, *Statistical Yearbook of China, 1985 and 1986* (Hong Kong: Hong Kong Economic Information and Agency).

2. These statistics should be used with caution since an unidentifiable proportion of so-called collective enterprises (the big collectives, *da jiti*) have become de facto state enterprises and thus should strictly be included in the state sector.

3. Feng Lanrui, "Six Questions Concerning the Problem of Employment," in *Selected Writing on Studies of Marxism*, no. 1 (Beijing: Institute of Marxism-Leninism-Mao Zedong Thought, Chinese Academy of Social Sciences, 1982).

4. Gordon White, "Urban Unemployment and Labor Allocation Policies in Post-Mao China," *World Development* 10, 8 (1982): 613–32.

5. This statistic was estimated by Prof. Wu Dingcheng of the Chinese Academy of Social Sciences, Institute of Economics. See Gordon White, *Labor Allocation and Employment Policy in Contemporary China* (Brighton: Institute of Development Studies, University of Sussex, 1985), p. 7.

6. For this "neotraditional" character of Chinese enterprises, see Andrew Walder, *Communist Neo-traditionalism: Work and Authority in Chinese Industry* (Berkeley: University of California Press, 1986). Chinese managers recognize these phenomena, and their view of industrial relations reflects their influence. See, e.g., the comments by a personnel manager of the Jaiyuan Iron and Steel Company about the large industry as a "small society" in White, *Labor Allocation*, p. 33, and by the manager of the Shanghai High-Pressure Oil Pump Company, a small-scale enterprise visited in 1983, who repeatedly referred to his firm as a "family" (*jia*), in Gordon White, *Industrial Planning and Administration in Contemporary China* (Brighton: Institute of Development Studies, University of Sussex, 1983), pp. 57ff.

7. Janos Kornai, *Economics of Shortage* (N.Y.: North-Holland, 1980), A:254.

8. For these differences, see Martin Lockett, "Small Business and Socialism in Urban China," *Development and Change* 17,1 (January 1986): 35–67.

9. State Statistical Bureau, *Statistical Yearbook, 1986*, p. 104.

10. White, *Labor Allocation*, p. 3. The figure was provided by Prof. Feng Lanrui of the Chinese Academy of Social Sciences.

11. For a discussion of this process by Shanxi social scientists, see ibid., p. 39–41; for plans in Jiangsu province as presented by local experts, see ibid., pp. 42–44.

12. World Bank, *China: Long Term Development Issues and Options* (Baltimore: Johns Hopkins University Press, 1985), p. 127.

13. For a Chinese discussion of the impact of surplus labor, see Zhao Lukuan, "On China's Employment Problem Under Conditions of Relative Labor Surplus," *Renmin ribao* (People's daily), March 2, 1982, cited in Foreign Broadcast Information Service (FBIS) 048, p. 5.

14. For an example of reformers' arguments, see Ye Ming, "In Making the Best Possible Use of Manpower, Put the Stresses on 'Flexibility,' " *Guangming ribao* (Guangming daily), August 7, 1980, in Joint Publications Research Service (JPRS), *China Report: Economic Affairs* 84 (1980).

15. Yi Duming, "In Defence of the 'Iron Rice-Bowl' System," *Yangcheng wanbao* (Guangzhou evening news), February 23, 1986, in JPRS, *China Report: Economic Affairs* 347 (1986).

16. See the interview with a veteran army officer in Hong Kong's *Zhengming Daily*, July 24, 1981, who linked growing unemployment with increasing prostitution and criminal violence. Cited in FBIS, July 27, 1981.

17. Cheng Tizhong, "An Inquiry into Certain Problems Concerning a Comprehensive Implementation of the Contract System," *Zhongguo laodong kexue* (Chinese labor science) 5 (May 1986): 10–12.

18. Jiang Yiwei, "If All Workers Are on the Contract System, It Will Not be Conducive to the Socialist Character of the Enterprise," *Jingji tizhi gaige* (Economic structural reform) 1 (1985): 11–13.

19. Yi Duming makes these points, as does a local labor bureau official from Hebei province in *Hebei ribao* (Hebei daily), April 13, 1982, in FBIS, April 26, 1982.

20. Hu Chen, "Opening Up a Labor-Power Market Is Not Based on Regarding Labor-Power as a Commodity," *Guangming ribao*, October 25, 1986, in BBC, *Summary of World Broadcasts: Far East* (SWB:FE) 8412 (1986).

21. Ibid. For advocacy of a "job market," see Wei Jie, "A Socalist Job Market Should Be Established," *Guangming ribao*, August 10, 1985. For use of the term "labor resources market," see Wang Jie and Xiao Xiu, "Tentative Analysis of the Labor Resources Market," *Guangming ribao*, July 12, 1986.

22. Zhuang Hongxiang, "Recognizing Labour Power as a Commodity Will Not Cause the Negation of the Socialist System," *Guangming ribao*, September 7, 1986, in SWB:FE 8368 (1986).

23. Dong Fureng, "A Brief Discourse on the Labour System and Labour Power as a Commodity," *Guangming ribao*, October 4, 1986, in SWB:FE (1986); Zhao Guoliang, "A Brief Discussion of Socialist Labour as a Commodity," *Guangming ribao*, August 23, 1986, in SWB:FE 8357 (1986).

24. Gordon White, "The Politics of Economic Reform in Chinese Industry: The Introduction of the Labour Contract System," *China Quarterly* 111 (September 1987).

25. Dong, "Brief Discourse on the Labour System."

26. For examples of job discrimination against women, see Chi Yuhua and Chen Jin, "Zhang Guoying, Vice-President of the All-China Women's Federation, Calls for Eliminating Discrimination Against Women," *Renmin ribao*, July 31, 1987, in SWB:FE 3640.

27. Gordon White, "The Changing Role of the Chinese State in Labour Allocation: Towards the Market?" *Journal of Communist Studies* 3, 2 (June 1987).

28. Gordon White and Paul Bowles, *Towards a Capital Market? Reforms in the Chinese Banking System*, China Research Report no. 6 (Brighton: Institute of Development Studies, University of Sussex, 1987).

29. White, "The Politics of Economic Reform."

30. China News Agency (Beijing), August 5, 1987, in SWB:FE 8643.

31. Cheng Feng, "A Fresh Understanding of the 'Waiting for Employment' Problem," *Jingji ribao* (Economic daily), April 18, 1987, in SWB:FE 8569.

32. Commentator, "Is the 'Iron Rice-Bowl' Something We Cannot Bear to Part With? On Reform of the Labour System," *Renmin ribao*, November 18, 1986, in SWB:FE 8428.

33. Note, for example, complaints about extension of working hours by the vice-chairman of the All-China Federation of Trade Unions, in *Gongren ribao* (Workers daily), March 4, 1987, in SWB:FE 8520.

Part III
Social Relations, Political Power, and Culture

9

THEORIZING THE DEMOCRATIZATION OF CHINA'S LENINIST STATE

Edward Friedman

For most of that one-third of the earth's people living in Leninist states, ruling groups have declared an intention to reform and democratize the Leninist system. In China, the Deng Xiaoping administration has steered a zig-zag course. Every political opening has been quickly followed by a tightening. But political closure causes economic losses, the correction of which requires a reopening that in turn carries political costs that cause another closure. Is China caught in a vicious circle or is it gradually freeing itself from undemocratic trammels?

This essay argues that it is best to conceive of these contradictions as inherent in Leninist dynamics, and not to apply analytic categories invented for other situations and systems. The Marxist categories of secular progress from capitalism through socialism to communism do not apprehend the actual forces unleashed by Leninist states. Similarly, the democratization of a Leninist party-state is inconceivable within the anti-Marxist framework of totalitarian theory. A totalitarian state is, by definition, a self-enforcing power structure that cannot be reformed or transformed into something fundamentally better by its own contained, demobilized, and repressed social forces. Foreign intervention may overthrow such a regime, but supposedly self-sustaining systems cannot, in totalitarian theory, democratize themselves from within.

Yet scholars of the post-Stalin Soviet Union regularly describe these states as merely authoritarian.[1] Most theorists of authoritarian dynamics conclude that authoritarian states can reform themselves into democratic polities. Hence, if, as even many former theorists of totalitarianism now acknowledge, the regimes of Stalin and Mao can swiftly become authoritarian in the years following the death of the great tyrant, then these Leninist states must, in reality, have an inherent potential for democratization. The notion of an unchanging totalitarian stasis has been exploded and emptied of meaning.

The deeply entrenched conservatism of Leninist systems leads an increasing number of students of Leninist systems to comprehend those states not as radical instances but as forms of quite traditional rule.[2] Conceiving of such systems as traditional invites consideration of a democratic transition from perspectives of modernization. In that perspective, in contrast to Marxism, democracy is not the self-interested act of a power-grabbing bourgeoisie, but a political form through which society liberates itself from traditional or feudal forms of domination to participate as an agency in its own self-definition.[3] Democracy is a universal, as are toleration and human rights. Leninist states and their development are thus no longer conceived as unique, fixed isolates, but as integral, albeit complex and contradictory, parts of the partial human passage to diverse forms of modernity.

The notion that is rendered problematic by this reconsideration is socialism. Leninist socialism appears from this perspective as the ideology of power holders that nourishes premodern social habits and practices rather than preparing a transcendence of merely bourgeois democracy for a yet more liberating project. To see the Leninist system not as the consolidation of liberating, progressive socialism but as the fortress of an outmoded order is, for all but Leninist conservatives, traditionalists, and fundamentalists, to conceive the need to reform that party-state so that the people of the nation-state can enjoy the blessing of the modern world.

For Leninist rulers, the imperative of economic reform has placed democratization high on the political agenda. Yet China is not the Soviet Union. Looking at diverse histories reveals that conceptualizing the problem of democratization in terms of an abstract and uniform Leninist party-state, imagined as totalistic institutions of dictatorship, omits major differences among states. Each nation-state has its own history. This crucial variety will make for diverse reform paths.

The particular history of peasantry and intelligentsia in China may be potentially more democratic than in Soviet Russia. As the Swedish peasantry, in contrast to the French, served democratizing purposes, so social groups which in the development of the Soviet Union may lack a strong democratic dynamic may, in China or elsewhere, have a more liberating potential. On the other hand, in contrast to the Soviet Union, Mao's economic irrationality has left in place many more unprofitable state-sector enterprises whose managers feel threatened by reforms premised on profitability. Also in contrast to the Soviet Union, Mao's continuous use of the conservative military has made that chauvinistic institution a more formidable barrier to reform. Thus democratization must be theorized in terms of cultural and historical particulars as well as institutional universals.[4]

Although the Chinese peasantry's deep involvement with and loyalty to Mao's conservative armies leads China's democrats to slight them, that peasantry could contribute to the democratic forces. The dominant Han Chinese peasantry grabbed on to market reforms and the household economy; tillers seemed quite capable of playing the role of independent yeomen who could, in a corporate sense, be a pillar of democracy. Chinese democratic reform theorist Liao Gailong reportedly suggested to a Central Committee work meeting at the end of the 1970s that rural workers who join in marketing, credit, purchasing, or other co-ops should be allowed to organize politically to represent their own interests. The party should not substitute for genuine democratic representation of the diverse and conflicting concerns of the immediate producers. The matter, however, was not put on the agenda of the party's Central Committee. Democratization was thwarted. No great struggle followed. Reformers were so alienated by Mao's insistence that it was imperative to learn from the backward peasantry that urban democrats in the post-Mao era usually do not see any progressive potential in the peasantry.

As China's peasantry could play a democratic role, similarly China's intelligentsia seems far more capable of acting to further democracy than does the intelligentsia of the Soviet Union. Stalin co-opted and corrupted many in the group, making them more a part of the privileged state orbit. Mao, seeing this trend in the Soviet Union, treated intellectuals in China as enemies, ironically turning them into strong believers in an independent judiciary, legal due process, political toleration, and free speech. In the antidemocratic reversals of 1983 and 1987, most intellectuals courageously refused to join in the party center's politically motivated attacks on democratic personages. By 1989 they began to sign letters of democratic petition. Such heroic acts contribute to the experience of ruling groups of being isolated and vulnerable unless they reform. Thus, it may well be that the democratization of China's Leninist state is, at the level of social forces, a much easier task than that confronting democrats in the Soviet Union. The diverse and dynamic histories of groups, interests, and experiences show the error of explaining too much by a theory of institutions.

Most uniquely, China is different in its ambiguous Maoist legacy. However much Maoism shares with Stalinism, Maoism is distinguished by an attempt to avoid certain evils perpetuated in Stalinism. Maoism, however, misidentifies the source of those evils.

Maoism, as Stalinism, involves an extraordinary concentration and centralization of power, ready use of state terror, and a party-run nationalized economy with collectivized agriculture. But Stalinism combined these with crucial concessions to the imperatives of rational economic development: top-notch modern education, co-opting technocrats, and permitting private plots for peasants. In contrast, Maoism involves a war on these Stalinist concessions to rationality plus a sundering of centralized bureaucracies, thereby detracting from the one economic strength of Leninism, the power to coordinate and mobilize national resources. Hence the many segmented monopolies at local levels in Maoist China are far more economically wasteful and irrational than the partial modernization of Stalinism.

If there is a healthy partial inheritance in Maoism, it is legitimating an understanding of the Leninist system as so undemocratic that not to find means of democratizing the polity is to guarantee the vitiating of all the noble purposes in whose name so many good people died to win a new world in the original revolutionary civil war. It is even possible to imagine a Chinese future in which democratic reformers who cite Mao's attacks on bureaucratic privilege oppose traditional Leninist conservatives who cite his attacks on capitalism, meaning by capitalism all the rational reforms that would undermine the dictatorial power of the Leninist state.

Relying on Marxist categories to legitimate a democratic reform project is no easy task. In the Marxist world view, the bourgeoisie builds the institutions of political democracy. But the Leninist ruling party is supposed to implement a proletarian project that negates the bourgeois agenda. Hence for Marxists to claim that China still needs that democratic construction forces them to acknowledge that China is at a more backward stage than capitalism, that China is still burdened by a precapitalist mode of production.[5] The official notion of the late 1980s that China is in a prolonged early stage of socialism papers over this most evident contradiction.

Given national pride, which seeks dignity by ranking China among the top nations of the world, reformers cannot woo superpatriots by insisting that China remains very backward. From gymnastics to ping pong, Chinese patriots want to be number one. The conservatives who point to the Mao era's high production results in heavy industry and to military and space science achievements can better stir patriotic pride than reformers who point out that the consumption standards of most citizens stagnated in that era. China's enormously popular muckraking writer, journalist Liu Binyan, who was purged at the end of 1986, wisely insisted that the leadership had to dampen the dangerous chauvinism it had fostered. That chauvinism, which Mao kept inflamed, is a major obstacle to democratization. It produces popular riots when a Chinese soccer team loses to Hong Kong. That chauvinism turns a policy of openness to the outside world into an experience of inviting polluting foreigners to corrupt pure Chinese. Such pollution is seen as an evil source of everything from more divorces and spoiled children to an individualism that undermines the hierarchical, patriarchal, conservative Confucian social order which undergirds authoritarian rule.

Post-Mao reformers in China have boldly initiated policies toward a project of democratizing the state. Yet, at the same time, Leninist continuity produces propaganda from China that often reads as socialist realism. Since the future is always glorious for Leninist power holders, their claims read as if the democratizing agenda and the democratic goals are, if not already a living reality, in place and guaranteed. Such propaganda ignores the institutionalized, corrupt, and dictatorial organization of the entrenched Leninist state. In the post-Mao era, as in the Mao era, party propagandists are adept at creating a dramaturgy to persuade the audience of a new, true plot leading to the bliss of a uniquely happy ending. The analyst must respond with critical intelligence, not mindless applause. One must look closely at the forces making or breaking the democratic prospect. These forces are powerful and entrenched.

Yet, independent, critical and thoughtful analysts immersed in the theoretical writings—or daily newspaper editorials—of China's reform democrats conclude that an extraordinary democratic breakthrough is in the offing.[6] With virtually all Leninist party-states, even the traditionally Stalinist ones such as North Korea, Albania, and the Soviet Union, initiating reforms away from the traditional version of socialism, it is possible to be optimistic. The waste of the command economy and the incompetence institutionalized by the nomenklatura that promotes the politically loyal instead of the competent make global economic and military competition well-nigh impossible in an era of fast-changing technologies with high capital costs. Even the Soviet Union must seek out capitalist joint ventures freed of command economy constraints. If basic reforms are not carried out, a Leninist nation will grow more economically dependent, its military will become weaker, and ruling groups will be incapable of delivering the legitimating goods of the modern consumer world to the nation. This has been the fate of Cuba and Vietnam, Mozambique and Ethiopia.

The most vital interests or ruling groups impose the reform agenda. The traditional command economy of the prereform era rationalizes, solidifies, and freezes the technological moment of big steel and big hydroelectric dams. It is Russia racing to keep up with Bismarck's Prussia and Ford's assembly lines. In the 1950s India could welcome Soviet steel. But by the 1980s, Soviet industrial exports to India had drastically declined because the traditional Soviet steel economy could not meet the high-technology needs of India.[7] In the much transformed world at the end of the twentieth century, Leninist reformers are compelled to rethink the basics of Leninist Marxism because ever-changing "capitalism" has turned out to be technologically and economically dynamic while what the Soviet Union's command economy originally conceived seems ever more in place, that is, out of place for the transformed world. Everything needs changing, yet nothing seems to change.

While analysts note how reforms of the party in the post-Mao era have advanced swiftly, most Chinese experience how the party has gotten around the reforms, how sons replace fathers while the system remains. There is a popular experience that the reforms are so antithetical to the interests of the privileged state that it is only a matter of time and timing before all the political achievements of the post-Mao era are canceled and the remaining exciting agenda items are abandoned. Peasants act as if even the successful rural reforms could be reversed. The state is compelled to make ever more concessions to the peasantry to persuade them that the reform agenda is set and unchanging. But given the turmoil of the Mao era, nothing short of decades of reform persistence will persuade rationally cynical peasants and others.

What is rational and inevitable also seems suicidal and impossible. The system blocks the reforms the system demands. Yet movement in the reform direction seems inescapable. It is difficult for Leninist ruling groups to ignore their nation's military technology gaps, inability to compete in the international economy, or inability to satisfy popular consumer demand. Before reforms, ruling groups witness a popular consumer demand. Before reforms, ruling groups witness a popular expansion of smuggling, a vital second economy, and the black market. Elite children ridicule the traditional rationalizations of parents. Except for overrewarded privileged state sectors, the rulers can see that people mainly work hard and well outside of the collectivized or nationalized economy. But they can also see that a labor market—even unemployment (a reserve army of labor) and unemployment insurance—are inevitable once one permits the prod of efficiency to dominate the labor market.

It is not easy for committed Marxist socialists to grapple with such an explosive reality that leaves little left to the Marxist notion that exploited proletarian labor is the unique source of modern value and that exchange value in labor is the essence of capitalist exploitation. Yet reformers rightly point out that most modern wealth is created not by a surplus stolen from manual laborers, but by science, by everything from managerial efficiency to technological innovation. Beyond the core notion that a labor market is exploitation, reformers must also abandon the idea that the proletarian workers at the steel furnace symbolize the production of modern value. Scientists, in genetic research, seed improvement, or discovering cheaper plastics or synthetics or substitutes, add far more value than do the ever-declining percentage of manual factory laborers. The entire ideological scaffolding seems in need of reconstruction once one tries to reform a Leninist state. Consequently, what is at issue is the rulers' claim that by the scientific understanding of Marx, Lenin, and Stalin, they discover the path to the future. The very legitimation of Leninist party dictatorship is at issue. That is why matters of theory and ideology remain far more central to the ongoing power struggle in Leninist systems than many Kremlinologists will acknowledge.

China's reformers are courageously confronting these contradictions between Leninist theory and economic reality. Honest theoreticians are vulnerable to attack by conservatives and fundamentalists who insist on the literal truth of the written word of the great Marxist prophets of old. Democratic reformers adopt the language of those whom Leninists have long denounced as merely bourgeois democrats. Consequently, issues such as Bukharin, the united front, nonclass interests, pluralism and the Menshevik-Bolshevik debates, Bernstein, Kautsky, and Luxemburg remain contested matters.

Hence, it is quite typical, and yet extraordinary, that in China democratic reformers by 1986, in stark contrast to self-interested formulas and irrational dogmas on the inherent superiority of Leninist democratic centralism, confronted the analyses of Hannah Arendt on totalitarianism and Milovan Djilas on Yugoslavia. Perhaps most significantly, from the perspective of democratic legitimation within a Marxist socialism, are the positive analyses of the work of Luxemburg, Kautsky, and the revisionists, that is, Marxist democrats who argued that the institutionalization in state power of the dictatorial, hierarchical, overly centralized system of secrecy, military obedience, and concentrated initiative of the Leninist party would turn the promise of socialism into the practice of extreme personal despotism.

Lenin's achievement must be challenged or reinterpreted. The revisionist insistence that socialism cannot be built without the democratic achievements of what Marx considered the bourgeois stage is increasingly legitimate in the reform perspective. Yet that is precisely the central illegitimate item to rulers insisting that the Leninist party is the dictatorship of the proletariat, that the party inherently represents the interests of the exploited proletarian majority, that party dictatorship, therefore, is already more democratic than mere bourgeois democracy, which hides a monopoly of power for a small minority. Marx himself must be challenged or passed over if political democracy is to be institutionalized in an economic world never envisioned by Karl Marx.

Some analysts find in the economic reforms a basis for successful political democratization. The dictatorial Leninist political superstructure is taken as a reflection of the Leninist command economy. Hence, to break up the statist concentration of economic power will permit the growth of plural space for individuals to act and live more freely and fearlessly. To live all one's life in a unit of the command economy that controls jobs, army service, travel, bonuses, promotions, political memberships, rationing, housing, and so on is to live in awe of the unit's masters.[8] Political democratization therefore requires an end to the command economy. Economic reform, in this perspective, creates political space, legitimates competition in politics as in economics, and builds a system of legality, contracts, and rights as it disperses power. Fundamental economic change thus leads to fundamental political reform.

In the Chinese countryside the post-Mao economic reforms have gotten some of the burden of local despots off the backs of villagers. Not only has land been decollectivized and the rural market freed, but households now control their own labor time. They no longer have to answer to a party boss who can command when to work, what to do, and how to do it. As long as the household meets minimal crop-equivalent tax responsibilities to the state, rural people are free to work and sell as they please. The rural reforms have remade the Chinese countryside into a happier and more vibrant world. There is far less violence by local tyrants against previously powerless and absolutely dependent local people.

Putting aside the extraordinary productive efficiency entailed in this freeing of rural workers from the collective's feudal-like enserfment, there is also a personal and political experience of liberation and empowerment. Travel can follow from individual wishes rather than state fiat. Money is a universal solvent that is destroying the need for place-specific grain ration coupons, thereby eroding the oppressive control of the local echelon of the heavy state bureaucracy. These rural reforms must be conceived, not as a retreat from socialism, but as progress out of something resembling feudalism, progress from something less humane than bourgeois democracy. Once again the whole notion of equating Leninism with socialism is rendered problematical. The happy reform fruits of this liberating growth away from political controls toward autonomy and independence include everything from hostels and eateries to honeymoon travel, a spectrum of possibilities that weaken the reach of the police state and enhance the prospect of fulfilling needs and desires, of pursuing interests and happiness. Individualism and empowerment are positive political consequences of dismantling even part of the Leninist command economy.

Whether the space created by reform will be filled by democratic political action is a question not answered without investigating the reform of other elements of the institutional nexus of the Leninist state. The notion that domestic economic reform leads directly to democratic political reform not only omits too much of Leninist reality, it also ignores the surging force of the powerful capitalist world market.

After all, what does make for successful economic progress in the contemporary epoch? Students of the so-called East Asian miracles offer diverse answers to this problem. For analytic purposes, these answers can be divided into two groups. One sees China as incapable of doing what Japan, South Korea, Taiwan, Hong Kong, and Singapore have done. The other finds no inherent obstacles to China succeeding economically as have these other places. The debate is not a right-left divergence.

Analysts who accept much of dependency theory or world-system theory see the earlier advance of the East Asian peoples as a result of a unique and already passed historical conjuncture.[9] Hence, the Chinese cannot take a train that is already gone. Other analysts who agree that China cannot ride on the miracle road focus, however, not on the infrequent opportunities granted by world capitalism but on the inherent incompatibility of the economically irrational system of Leninism with the success requirements of market rationality. In this latter view, the Leninist state is so rutted in another logic, a nonmarket-regarding logic, that there is no way Leninist China can pull out of its sad rut to move on to the better path of reasoned growth.[10] In the former argument, world capitalism inherently leaves little space in which socialists can progress. In the latter argument, Leninist states inherently deny themselves the means of progress as only market systems can. Without denying the insights won in studying the constraints, both of the world market and of Leninist states, both these negative judgments seem too absolute and unidimensional given gains that already have indubitably occurred.

Two other very different perspectives, in contrast, agree in finding no inherent obstacles to China advancing as have other parts of Pacific East Asia. In one perspective, it is all a matter of the proper institutions.[11] With China building a MOFERT to emulate MITI, a Shenzhen Special Economic Zone to do as Gaoxiong in Taiwan, targeting and aiding export industries, using financial inducements to reward exports, and so forth, China too will do well in world market competition as have others who emulated Japan's formula. Since China broke with the notion of minimal involvement in the world market, its exports have grown from a level equal to India's to an extraordinary 400 percent better than India, which has not instituted such practices. China's hard-currency foreign exchange earnings exceed those of the Soviet Union and its East European dependencies combined. China's GNP per capita has risen at a rate more than twice that of the Soviet bloc.

In a second view that shares the conclusion that China can take the East Asian success road once it abandons its unwillingness to benefit from the world market, the focus is not on particular new correct policies but on the inherited strengths of history and culture shared by all members of Confucian East Asia.[12] Similar families, saving structures, stress on education, and so forth will permit China too to succeed. In the reform period of 1978–1985, not only has growth been much faster than in other Leninist states, but gains in productivity challenge the rates of Pacific rim miracle economies. The actual successes of the post-Mao period would seem to throw doubt on the dogmatic pessimism of both the antimarket and promarket negativity. On the other hand, given a lack of increased productivity in industry, the post-Mao boom could turn out to reflect gains in agriculture and the tertiary sector away from the extraordinary economic irrationality of wasteful Maoism, gains which cannot be sustained without further reforms of prices, subsidies, industry, and so on. But do such economic reforms presuppose political democratization?

If China can indeed forge ahead economically even with a dictatorial Leninist system, then politically democracy will not naturally fall as the ripe fruit of a rich economic tree. Indeed it has been argued that authoritarianism is actually conducive to the success of Pacific East Asia in temporarily repressing labor demands for higher wages and permitting long-term industrial planning by entrenched power holders.[13] It was under strong dictatorship that great economic strides were taken by Meiji Japan and Bismarck's Germany. It is therefore doubtful if economic reforms in themselves can close the monumental gap in Leninist systems between state and citizenry, powerful and powerless, those in monopoly control of the means of state power and those who have no rights to political tools that produce legitimate political consequences.

And yet the evolution of Franco's fascist Spain into a strong and stable democracy in the 1970s forces one to take seriously the possibility that over a generation China's open integration with a democratized East Asia could facilitate democratization in China. At least that is what happened as Spain opened itself to integration with the democratic European Community. For similar forces to work, democratization must be institutionalized in Taiwan and South Korea and perhaps Hong Kong.

Meanwhile, China's Leninist dictatorship will continue to delegitimate itself and thereby prod democratizers to act. The pervasive police system of the Leninist state combines with files that serve nomenklatura promotion on the basis of networks of personal and factional loyalty so as to keep ties between the embedded party-state and the alienated citizenry at the level of hypocrisy. Citizens grumble to each other, while lying and fawning in the presence of the powerful. As in Spain, Portugal, Greece, Argentina, and Taiwan, democracy will have to be fought for and won in its own right. The noneconomic obstructions to democracy must be confronted and removed. A major obstacle to democratization has been an authoritarian and politically powerful military. In contrast, nations such as the United States or Australia, said to be born free, tended to develop without the burden of powerful, politically involved standing armies. Sometimes these antidemocratic militaries in dictatorial states are defeated or discredited in war.

Nations that have democratized have had to get their militaries out of power.

Theoretical literature on the military and democratization suggests that China's military will not be readily amenable to democratization. It has in the reform era time and again thrown its weight on the side of conservatism, or pure obstructionism. Militaries tend to be hardest to get out of the way of democracy when they are engaged in numerous nonprofessional activities, when they engage in corrupt practices, when they have a historical legitimation as referees and saviors. All of these features characterize China's military. Clearly, given the entrenched antidemocratic statist institutions, one cannot expect economic reform in an evolutionary way smoothly to clear a path into a state of political democracy.

And yet one must make seriously the reform view that economic deconcentration can serve the purposes of political democratization. Conservative, entrenched, and neo-Stalinist power holders in Leninist states treat economic reforms as threats to their privileged position, or, as they prefer to express it, to socialism itself. The main meaning of socialism in an institutionalized Leninist state is the institutions of that state. Surely the command economy, pervasive police, nomenklatura, and so on are not what socialism is all about. An autonomous state cannot be democratic, that is, openly and competitively determined by society, when its essence is to know for society and to act in place of society. Ending both private ownership and a competitive market, as Leninists do, does not advance socialism if economic wealth and political power are then concentrated in hands that do not move as society wishes. Economic democracy combined with political democracy would capture more of the content of socialism. Diverse political representation requires prior economic differentiation and some state neutrality, a rule of law, a move away from the Leninist command economy. The economic reforms therefore are a necessity but an insufficient prod to democratization.

Meanwhile the zig-zag path of partial reform shaped by the contradictions of the Leninist state keeps the citizenry simmering without boiling over. There is no doubt that Deng Xiaoping, who greatly admires Poland's military dictator, has stability as his number one priority. Deng fears workers joining with intellectuals to attack the system. He wants a quiescent population and a quiescent, conservative party. In that quiet, Deng would advance economic and administrative reforms that replace incompetents with specialists, produce desired commodities instead of planned waste, and offer an experienced link between effort and reward. These reforms are intended to keep the regime and its policies legitimate.

But Deng's insistence on tranquility instead of boldness has meant that large political reforms have been frustrated. As with the era before the death of Mao, opposition forces remain just below the surface. Conservative power remains institutionally strong, while, at the same time, the forces insisting on democratization are growing. China's future could be marked by popular democratic explosions and police repression. What would keep the antidemocratic forces of coercion from throwing their weight onto the balance?

Should one assume that democratic forces must be defeated by party dictatorship? Perhaps Chinese Confucian culture so legitimates an exam-based meritocracy that it will be easier in China (and Vietnam and North Korea) than in Europe, Africa, and Latin America to replace the Leninist nomenklatura with systems guaranteeing jobs and promotion by proven merit. The Thirteenth Party Congress in October 1987 proposed moving to a civil service system.[14] Surely it is a truism, in a world of spreading fundamentalism, that the impact of deep and strong cultural and religious forces should not be underestimated.

More to the point, it is difficult to imagine the alienating Leninist state surviving were merit systems to replace the nomenklatura, were due process of law—made legitimate even in China's ruling party by Mao's vigilantism—to replace the pervasive police, and were the command economy to be dismantled. As Stalin proved in the great purge and Mao in the similarly great Cultural Revolution, the party can be rendered vulnerable to other societal and state forces. Hence, particulars of history and culture might over time conspire with the economic reforms to enhance greatly the strength of democratic forces in China's internal balance of power. The post-Mao focus by intellectuals only on the negative, backward, antidemocratic elements in China's heritage, as with its peasantry, may prove quite misleading. Chinese culture is not a seamless cloth; the fabric is full of strands that may yet be seen as a democratic part of the pattern. But it is the economy that has taken the lead in post-Mao changes.

China's economic reforms have been far-reaching. A stock market is growing. Special economic zones welcome the laws and logic of capitalist productive efficiency. Commodities, which Marx, Engels, Lenin, Stalin, and Mao all took as the essence of the capitalist mode of production, have been redefined by China's post-Mao rulers as necessary and healthy elements. The ruling party has reconceptualized China as a socialist commodity economy in a prolonged era of very early socialism. In the economic realm at least, both Stalinism and Maoism—which are referred to in orthodox Chinese writings as the traditional Soviet model and as ultra-leftism—have been negated in theory and stalemated in practice. The legitimate debate is about how far and fast to move with needed reforms.

If we analyze the factional debate within ruling groups in post-Mao China—putting aside the weighty matter of the relative autonomy of the institutions of coercion—after the removal of Mao's anointed heir Hua Guofeng, then three opinion groupings are manifest, often referred to as conservatives, moderate (or partial) reformers, and radical (or all-out) reformers. Some people see two factions, with the radical reformers a segment of one large reform coalition. Some join the conservatives and moderates as opponents of democratization. In fact, the factional struggle is complex, in flux, and multifacted.

The titular leader of the conservatives in the 1980s has been Chen Yun. He was the highest-ranking leader in 1956 and again in the early 1960s most sympathetic to Titoist and Leiberman reforms. Thus the political spectrum in China, even in its most conservative moment, begins with people who would take economic reform beyond early Tito or late Khrushchev. China's political debate and policy struggle are among reformers. Which is not to say that were the conservatives or military to win total victory they would avoid unleashing nasty semifascist or neo-Stalinist forces. There is much at stake in the ongoing struggle.

The moderate reformers wish to fulfill the promise of the reform program initiated in East and Central Europe. The present economic agenda in China promises at least to achieve that. It already is based on a more liberating consensus than the maximum reforms projected in the mid-1980s by Gorbachev.

Only the all-out reformers argue both that the economic reforms cannot be fully realized without political reforms and that democratization is a goal in itself. The 1986 return to print, to legitimacy, and to centrality in the political debate of radical reformers Li Honglin and Wang Ruoshui from external and internal exile symbolizes the reality that political initiative can be seized by the democratizers. By late 1986 democratic reformers dominated all party committees working on political reform. Yet their subsequent blacklisting in 1987 is evidence that the weight of conservatives and the military and their spokesman Wang Zhen in the ongoing political struggle is large. Victory for either side is far from decided.

That continuing power struggle in China is also experienced as part of a major succession crisis, a generational succession. A little discussed but most important obstacle to democratic reform is the succession to patriarchal charismatic power to the third echelon, the technocratic grandchildren of the old revolutionary elite. If one accepts an understanding of Leninist states as institutionalizing a form of traditional power such that ruptures and modernizing departures require charismatic leadership, then Deng Xiaoping is wise to woo and win the party patriarchs, to buy them off or coopt them by promoting their heirs. This third echelon increasingly commands the resources of technical competence. But its rise is systematically facilitated by personal networks of corrupt Leninist power. It is princes who are now rising. Chinese people call them princes or high cadres' kids. A key question, then, is, will the third echelon of rising princes further reform sufficient to democratically empower the citizenry, or will the princes merely manage moderate reforms to make permanent their own privileged power?

Put another way, has Deng Xiaoping, by cautious co-optation of the elite, lost a unique and fleeting opportunity provided in 1977–78 by the surging emotions and massive support following the arrest of the Jiang Qing group and the replacement of hated, economically irrational fundamentalist policies with popular and productive reforms? In 1977 he could have had people temporarily tighten their belts while they enjoyed the blessings of new openness, of culture come to life, of families reunited, and of political labels lifted. It was a joyous moment. Is it no longer possible to mobilize the citizenry for a democratic breakthrough? Are they now so suspicious about politics that they insist first and foremost on getting theirs? Have the compromises engendered too much cynicism? Has popular political passion turned into the narrowest of short-term calculations? Most Chinese I have talked with answer in the affirmative to these unhappy prospects.

Put in terms of the nexus of institutions that constitute the autonomous power of the Leninist state, the question is, will a nomenklatura system of promotion give way to a civil service premised on criteria of technical competence, exams, and merit? Depoliticizing a politicized system threatens to change the winners and the losers. To be sure, the heirs of the apparatus with first access to the best schools at home and abroad have a clear advantage even in a merit system. The race does not begin for all at the same starting line. The educational advantages of ruling families in a more democratic world where careers were open to talents could lead such power holders not to block the reforms. As with local party people who seize the best economic opportunities in the era of market reform, for higher party people to seize the best educational opportunities for their families is a two-edged sword. It creates the appearance that nothing has changed for the better. It intensifies corruption and enhances popular cynicism, which can, in the short run, be used by the conservatives to discredit the all-out reformers. But it also facilitates basic change. It creates time and stability for the reformers to institutionalize themselves and build ever broader and more insistent support for genuine democratization in the continuing political struggle. All of this suggests that politics—matters of leadership, timing, coalition building, and strategies—may prove decisive.

Even to legitimate the issue of competence or election instead of the nomenklatura as the bases for selection and promotion begins to make the entrenched Leninist system seem illegitimate. Already the political agenda of reform demands independent governmental administrative authority and independent economic management authority. The party is incompetent. As with the delegitimation of a feudal nobility by enlightenment criteria, loyalty must give way to rational merit. Feudal lords seem a useless excrescence. If the party and its ideological criteria, which mask the purposes of replicating personal power, no longer could secretly decide economic and governmental appointments and promotions, then people could begin to grow economically secure. They could see the possibility of a good life even in opposition to the party. Basic reform that goes beyond mere economic reform greatly strengthens the force of democratization.

To be sure, the pervasiveness of the other integral institutions of the Leninist state, such as the politicized police apparatus, could strongly limit such cultural and individual independence. Hence, establishing an independent judiciary with genuine due process of law, which is already on the political agenda, is crucial to the success of the democratization project. Yet none of this chain of logic reaches to the issue of the military, which must be grappled with, as usual, as a complete, somewhat separate, dangerously implosive and decisive issue.

The dictatorial Leninist party, if removed by reforms from control of the command economy and the nomenklatura, would be tempted to hold onto power by making greater use of its police power (or of military allies). The full reform project is a risky one. Not only does it produce a whole set of unwanted negative side effects (e.g., greater cynicism and corruption), but it also increases the likelihood of a reactionary police or military takeover in the name of patriotism and dignity. Conservative party and military people sincerely believe, not that their institutions are black, but that reformers such as Liu Binyan unfairly blackened them in the service of causes such as Western-style democratization which deny the unique achievements of Chinese socialism. The military conservatives promote tough, patriotic martyrs, who slight bourgeois values, as modal personalities. The protofascism inherent in this military chauvinism is palpable. It is so weighty that no Chinese political force can soon deal it out of the power game. Party Secretary Hu Yaobang, who challenged the size, purpose, and funding of the military, was defeated by that military. Reformers who would change the mission, status, and budget share of the military end up losing or surrendering leaders, arenas, budgets, and political power to this most weighty military. The established veto power of the military has been strong enough to reject all candidates suggested to replace Deng Xiaoping as chairman of the party's Military Affairs Commission.

There is no easy success formula for defanging the military or dismantling the institutions that constitute the Leninist party-state in order to guarantee the achievement of democracy. But there is in the ongoing struggle in post-Mao China a popular tendency in no way similar to democratic challenges in Central Europe. The party apparatus may be illegitimate, but the notion of a socialist state, including a government doing everything from running nationalized industry to providing high social welfare floors, remains legitimate. The issue in Central Europe for most democrats is a democratized socialist state. But in China, market and household forces and logic seem peculiarly strong. Many reformers have quietly concluded that capitalism is superior to socialism. Perhaps this particularity is a reflection of the extraordinary economic disaster of Maoism.

Individuals in the Mao era were left to be self-reliant. Welfare was provided to rural individuals by families. In addition, state enterprises were inefficient in the extreme and were experienced as corrupt and also closed as an avenue of mobility for most people. State payrolls seemed unsavory ways by which the privileged could succor state-favored individuals. Hence, both the welfare state and nationalized enterprises seem to most people in China empty, fraudulent, worthless, corrupt, and wasteful rather than partial achievements that should be preserved, cleansed, and strengthened, as in East Europe where Stalinism delivered at least some economic benefits. The peculiarly large number of money-losing enterprises spawned by Maoist China makes even the economic reform of a bankruptcy law seem threatening to especially large numbers of Chinese power holders, thus blocking urban and enterprise reforms. The inordinate institutionalized wastefulness of the Mao era has left a heritage that blocks reform, yet cries out for reform. The schizophrenia continues; of the impossible being the imperative.

This theoretical reconsideration which forces one to confront how poorly Maoism served China's poor and powerless leads us to come to grips with the most fundamental misapprehension of Maoism outside of China. In the 1960s Maoism was experienced among many Western progressives as the negation of Stalinism, as true democracy, something similar to Paris May, the Prague Spring, and the participatory democracy of SDS in the United States. The anti-Titoist, anti-capitalist, anti-export content of Maoism was thought of as opposition to the Soviet system, not noticing that in treating Khrushchev as another Tito, Mao actually was embracing core elements of Stalinism and then, in the name of dogmatic orthodoxy, extending and expanding economic irrationality and political inhumanity. It is the experienced need in China to negate that combination of tragic consequences that gives to the project of democratization a less statist, more capitalist, and more democratic bent than is the case among reformers in Central Europe. Although so far the democrats have been defeated on such issues, China's all-out reformers have argued for legitimating large-scale employment which acknowledges labor as a commodity, a universalization of stockholding in major enterprises, competition in large-scale enterprises, and a generalization of the practices of the special economic zones. In theory the reforms have gone very far indeed.

The conservative opposition has defeated democratic reform initiatives by appealing to popular envy of those who prosper first, to Maoist slogans legitimating common prosperity, to superpatriotism, to traditional values, and to a Marxist ideology that has no place for the commodification of labor in a socialist system. Even in urbanized Hungary in 1986, after a generation of successful economic reform, barely half the population unreservedly embraced the reform project which, as in China, has been most successful in the countryside. Perhaps further democratic reform in China and other Leninist states will have to find a way to build more on those rural beneficiaries whose gains are greatly resented by the privileged of the urbanized Leninist state. And the ironical issue of where the proletariat will stand is far from decided. Conservatives can rely, in opposition to the reformers, not only on the self-interested privileged apparatus and its beneficiaries (including urban workers?) but also on popular, patriotic, antireform sentiments among the more traditional peasantry, and on legitimating antimarket Maoist ideas. The results could well be a continuation of a struggle and a process that could build support for a democratic breakthrough or a conservative military backlash.

If there can be no easy answer to the question of political outcomes, there at least can be some clarification of how to comprehend theoretically the problematic of democratization. American social scientists increasingly envision post-Mao China as just another authoritarian system. The literature on the democratization of authoritarian regimes forcefully calls attention to the role of the military. Indeed, in China—as in Peter the Great's Russia, Bismarck's Germany, and Meiji Japan—state involvement in the economy is inseparable from the creation of military strength. The Manchu monarchy was delegitimated and destroyed in China in large part when it failed to defend the nation, wastefully built a summer palace with naval funds, was humiliated in wars with foreign nations, and disgracefully bankrupted and betrayed the nation with foreign loans and indemnities.

The military in China today has had its authority gravely undermined with politicized urban elites for its unjust privileges, failure in Vietnam, discrediting participation in the Cultural Revolution, and monumentally wasteful spending on third-front construction. Yet the Leninist state remains as stable as ever. If similar, serious delegitimation would have at least shaken a nonparty authoritarian regime, then the democratization dynamics of the Leninist system should be conceived of in its own terms, that is, not as just another traditional military authoritarianism.

Whether the weight of the military and other coercive instruments in post-Solidarity Poland, Stalin's Soviet Union, Lin Biao's China, and Pol Pot's Kampuchea suggests unique trajectories for militarized Leninism must be considered. Whereas heavy steel and heavy industry facilitated not only

Stalin's war machine but also the traditional institutions of Leninist socialism, the new, rapidly changing information, electronic, and computer technologies legitimate the anti-Stalinism of reform communism to foster a society with lateral ties, flexible response, rapid feedback, and individual creativity. This new mentality may actually woo the military for, and win patriots to, the reform project, at least in this particular technological era. In this era, these technological imperatives of national strength may join with the hopeful possibilities already displayed in democratized Hungary (1956), Czechoslovakia (1967–68), and Poland's Solidarity movement to build a uniquely democratized socialism. Categories are being turned right side up. What was once denounced as revisionist is revealed as democratic. The conservative military and the traditional peasantry could yet join a democratic coalition. It is crucial that rather than suffering from political arteriosclerosis, unpredictable energies are flowing in the Leninist body politic. For more and more people living in a Leninist state, the future is open and democracy is worth working for.

As Stalin's star falls and Bukharin's rises, so a different Mao may emerge in China, the one who championed a united front and cared about the question as to why the religious wars of Europe helped give birth to toleration. So the bloody vigilante violence of Mao's Cultural Revolution may give birth to new and creative democratizations. The courageous struggles of reformers in China and other socialist states compel us to try to theorize that democratic praxis where Mao failed.

Notes

1. A perusal of the mainstream scholarly literature shows that "authoritarian" is the standard label applied to China's post-Mao government. See Harry Harding, "Political Development in Post-Mao China," in *Modernizing China*, ed. A. Doak Barnett and Ralph N. Clough (Boulder: Westview Press, 1986), p. 33.

2. Kenneth Jowett, *The Leninist Response to National Dependency* (Berkeley: Institute of International Studies, 1978). That approach is developed for China by Andrew Walder, *Communist Neo-traditionalism: Work and Authority in Chinese Industry* (Berkeley: University of California Press, 1986), and Barrett McCormick, "Leninist Implementation: The Election Campaign," in *Policy Implementation in Post-Mao China*, ed. David Lampton (Berkeley: University of California Press, 1987).

3. The most insightful works on democratization in Leninist states have come from democrats living in those systems. See Ladislav Hejdanek, "Prospects for Democracy and Socialism in Eastern Europe," in *The Power of the Powerless*, ed. Václav Havel et al. (London: Hutchinson, 1985), pp. 141–51.

4. One attempt to do this is Andrew Nathan, *Chinese Democracy* (New York: Alfred Knopf, 1985), especially chs. 3 and 6. Nathan contends that democracy has flourished both in countries as Confucian as China and in nations as poor as China. Hence he does not grapple with the negative assessment made by Chinese democrats

that their culture is so fractious and the world so dangerous that unity must be imposed from above by a strong state, that individuals must give way to the group, especially to the nation conceived of as a race in a battle for survival against other races. Nathan does not inquire into the fascist elements manifest in Confucian nationalism that made the fascist militarization of Korea, Japan, and China's Chiang Kai-shek more likely than democratization.

5. The nub of the matter is not the analytic utility of treating China's Leninist state as a feudal form but the political disutility of such a claim which allows political opponents to brand one as a virtual traitor to the nation. For an example of the analytic utility of treating China as "feudal," see Tang Tsou, *The Cultural Revolution and Post-Mao Reforms* (Chicago: University of Chicago Press, 1986), pp. 144–88, and Lowell Dittmer, *China's Continuous Revolution* (Berkeley: University of California Press, 1987), pp. 58, 79, and 245, which treats China's Leninist state as a form of neofeudalism.

6. Roger Garside, *Coming Alive: China After Mao* (New York: McGraw Hill, 1981).

7. Elizabeth Valkenier, *The Soviet Union and the Third World: An Economic Bind* (New York: Praeger, 1983), p. 141.

8. The first systematic attempt to analyze the role of the unit was Fox Butterfield, *China: Alive in the Bitter Sea* (New York: Times Books, 1982).

9. Bruce Cumings, "The Origins and Development of the Northeast Asian Political Economy," in *The Political Economy of the New Asian Industrialism*, ed. Frederick Deyo (Ithaca: Cornell University Press, 1987), pp. 44–83.

10. Chalmers Johnson, "Political Institutions and Economic Performance: The Government-Business Relationship in Japan, South Korea, and Taiwan," in ibid., pp. 136–64.

11. See the essays in Robert Scalapino et al., eds., *Asian Economic Development—Present and Future* (Berkeley: Institute of East Asian Studies, 1985).

12. Dwight Perkins, *China: Asia's Next Giant?* (Seattle: University of Washington Press, 1986). Herman Kahn argued this in 1979. His "The Confucian Ethic and Economic Growth" is reproduced in *The Gap Between Rich and Poor*, ed. Mitchell Seligson (Boulder: Westview Press, 1984), pp. 78–80.

13. Chalmers Johnson has dubbed this the Taira theses since it was first elegantly painted in by Koji Taira, "Japan's Modern Economic Growth: Capitalist Development Under Absolutism," in *Japan Examined*, ed. Harry Wray and Hilary Conroy (Honolulu: University of Hawaii Press, 1983), pp. 34–41.

14. Cf. John Burns, "China's Nomenklatura System," *Problems of Communism* 36, 7 (1987): 36–51.

10

STRUCTURAL CHANGE AND THE POLITICAL ARTICULATION OF SOCIAL INTEREST IN REVOLUTIONARY AND SOCIALIST CHINA

Marc Blecher

In the village of Huitsaiyu in Hopei Province a farmer came home and told his wife: "We must release ourselves from the landlord." His wife replied: "We are accustomed to being oppressed. We can't speak as fluently as the landlords. We are too slow." The words of this farm wife expressed the mood of many peasants.

Ever since the Ching [*sic*] dynasty, Ma [Chiu-tze] revealed, his family had been poor tenants, renting land and never having any of their own. Every year he raised eight piculs of millet and every year he had to give four of these piculs to Landlord Wang. He could afford no medicine for his wife whom he feared was dying. Two years before, his father had died and he had not been able to buy the old man a coffin, but had to wrap him in straw. Now he was thirty-five and still poor and it looked as if he would always be poor. "I guess I have a bad brain," he would say in summing up the reasons for his poverty.

Then the cadres would ask: "Are you poor because you have a bad brain or because your father left you no property?"

"I guess that's the reason; my father left me no property."

"Really is that the reason?" asked the cadres. "Let us make an account. You pay four piculs of grain every year to the landlord. Your family has rented land for sixty years. That's 240 piculs of grain. If you had not given this to the landlord, you would be rich. The reason you are poor, then, is because you have been exploited by the landlord."

They would talk like this for hours and Ma would finally acknowledge that he was exploited by the landlord. . . .

For fifteen days the cadres talked with Ma. In this period they had twenty-three formal talks with him besides the numerous evening talks. . . . From this it can be seen it is not easy to move a Chinese peasant.[1]

I

In theory, socialism envisions two powerful but contradictory political transformations: the enhancement of state power, and increased popular participation and democratization. Theoretical efforts by Marx and leading Marxists like Engels and Lenin to deal with the contradiction through formulations such as the state losing its political character, the withering away of the state, or democratic centralism beg more questions than they resolve, and ultimately have proven unconvincing. They have also proven to be poor guides to praxis, which is a particularly damning indictment for Marxist theory.

In practice, most socialism has resolved the contradiction by developing state power at the expense of participation and democratization. China is perhaps the most outstanding example of a socialist country in which statist and participatory politics have coexisted, at least during the Maoist period. To be sure, political participation during the Maoist period was problematical. In practice it was by turns tightly circumscribed and then explosive (and sometimes violent). It was manipulated and spontaneous, sometimes simultaneously. It could be authoritarian in process and outcome even as it was at its most participatory; yet it could also take a more democratic and consensual form at the grass-roots levels. However contradictory a phenomenon it was, popular politics in state socialist China during the Maoist period was real, and as such demands attention. But the broad critique of the Maoist period both in China and in the West, combined with the basically nonparticipatory and nondemocratic character of actual socialism elsewhere, have resulted in analytical and evaluative short shrift being given to it. This is a phenomenon at once ideological and subversive of truth.

This chapter attempts to reopen analysis of popular politics in Maoist China a decade after its demise. It charts the development of political participation at the grass-roots level from the revolutionary period through the 1970s, highlighting the obstacles, identifying the factors involved in overcoming them, and emphasizing the sharp break made with the Chinese past. It also analyzes some of the contradictions immanent in the politics of Maoist period, which ultimately led to a crisis that paved the way for the less participatory politics of the Deng period.

II

China's revolution and socialism involved a historical break whose epochal proportions are easy to forget now that collectives are being dismantled, private markets have returned, depoliticization of social and political life is proceeding apace, and the Chinese leadership and its intellectual apparatus regard the Maoist period as having strong affinities with feudalism. Ways of thinking about and acting in the world appeared that were utterly at odds with those that had prevailed for millennia. The transformation involved nothing less than new forms of material and social life, a new phenomenology by which people experienced them, and a new epistéme for understanding them.

To grasp the dimensions of the discontinuities, some of the basic structures that preceded the revolution should be recalled. The state kept itself sharply distinct and distant from most of society. This was imprinted in the geography and architecture of state institutions. The lowest-level government offices were maintained only in the major town or city of the county, to which most Chinese rarely if ever traveled. These offices were sequestered inside walled, guarded compounds, and admission was tightly restricted.[2] The distance between state and society was also inscribed in language: state business was transacted and recorded in the unspoken, difficult classical language, command of which required years of formal education. Dress and decoration symbolized the gap: officials wore garments and surrounded themselves with emblems that indicated their position. The state set up strenuous and somewhat ritualistic barriers—the famous "examination hell"—for admission to its ranks. The chasm between state and society could only be traversed by those with considerable wealth: to finance a son's education in the hopes of his gaining an official post, to provide bribes to gatekeepers controlling access to state officials, to provide gifts to those officials once access were gained, to cultivate connections necessary to convert access into influence.

But such access was probably not experienced as terribly urgent to most members of society anyway, since the range of social concerns defined by the state and accepted in common understanding as "political," in the sense of subject to public or governmental determination, regulation and action, was narrow. It included mainly criminal justice, taxation, the provision of public works, and maintenance of order. Even on these matters, moreover, the state was rarely the primary focus of social interest. From the peasants' point of view, the key authority was usually the landowners, to whom the state delegated the performance of basic governmental functions—such as tax collection and public security—in the localities. The great distance between the state and society was, then, also built into the intermediated structure and circumscribed scope of government itself.

Thus most Chinese experienced and conceptualized the state as remote, bewildering, prepossessing, and largely irrelevant to their daily existential struggles and occasional joys. And if the landlords were the more immediately apparent political power for the peasants (including even those who did not rent land from them), they were for their proximity and familiarity no more appropriate a target of political articulation of social interest. Landowners normally comprised the sociopolitical elite of the village. They headed kinship and other kinds of local associations, controlled access to scarce commodities such as grain surpluses and credit, and in general dominated the social hierarchy and social and cultural life. Other classes had little in the way of institutional or political resources with which to challenge the landlord elite.

To sum up: before the Chinese Revolution the peasantry experienced the state as very remote, and the local landlord elite as nearly omnipotent. Moreover, the range of issues defined as political was narrow, and did not include most of the basic ones germane to the struggle for existence waged daily by most Chinese, such as rent, credit, income, health, or ability to marry and care for the dead. Even on issues that were both crucial to the peasantry and defined as political—such as taxation—the peasantry possessed almost no resources for articulating its views to the state or the landlords. Indeed, given the structures of political and economic power over the Chinese peasantry as well as the strength of the Confucian political culture of authoritarianism, it could be argued that few of them could even conceive of something we understand today as ordinary politics, that is, normal institutions, processes, and practices for deliberation and determination of public issues. If politics were conceptualized in less rationalistic or "modern" terms, there is still little evidence that Chinese peasants understood themselves as capable of participating in them.[3] Thus, when challenged to respond to their oppression, the farmer's wife and peasant Ma could only draw a blank.

III

Yet beginning with the land reform and continuing for at least the next generation, this political structure and epistéme began to be replaced by a local politics that was *unthinkable* at the outset. In the land reform, China's peasants suddenly found themselves denouncing their landlords at public meetings, and then violating the sacrosanct principle of private property by seizing and redistributing the land, tools, and animals of the landlords. In the early to mid-1950s, they began to erect public institutions, forums, and processes for deliberating about the most basic economic issues: production, interest, livelihood, and property. Once the formerly private, even secret realm of economic life had been opened to a public politics, it was not long before other facets of social, cultural, and ideological life followed: class relations, gender relations, family relations, sex and procreation, and the inner world of political ideology and consciousness. By the 1960s and 1970s, these matters were being debated and discussed in village meetings, political study sessions, informal but nonetheless purposively political settings (such as "bull sessions" with local officials or within earshot of them), and even textual forms such as "big-character posters." Linguistic change suggests that people even began to think about themselves and their social relations in radically new ways. In ordinary language, rural Chinese regularly referred to themselves and each other as "commune members," a conception whose public, political connotation goes beyond even the bourgeois democratic one of "citizen" (while also lacking the formalistic tone of "comrade"). Equally significant, millions of Chinese peasants—perhaps on the order of one in ten—acceded to positions of local leadership. Some of these, such as brigade or team leaders, were quite powerful in the local realm. Others were more routine but still involved responsibility for collective affairs and, concomitantly, an expression of public trust and an opportunity to take part in the local leadership's investigations, deliberations, and discharge of public affairs. Compared with the absence in prerevolutionary times of any practice of regularized or ordinary popular politics—and indeed with the apparent absence even of any *conception* of such a politics in the minds of many Chinese—the changes wrought by China's revolution and socialism were a sea-change, an epistemological, phenomenological and practical break of breathtaking proportions.

The development of a popular politics in rural China involved many elements. One was a shift in the *scale and venue of political activity*. Where in the past political activity required access to the county government, during and after the revolution the scale of political activity and administration was reduced with the creation of village-level Communist Party branches, township (*xiang*) governments, cooperatives and production teams (organized along the contours of local settlements), and mass organizations such as women's association branches, poor and lower-middle peasant associations, militia platoons, Youth League branches, and study groups. Though recently the language of state *penetration* of local society has become predominant among analysts to describe the effects of the new political structure,[4] increased *access* of local society to the state, or at least increased proximity of state and society, also resulted.

Along with the devolution in scale came an expansion in the *substance* of local politics. As befits socialism, the most basic economic issues with which all peasants were familiar and concerned—including production, income, credit, ownership, investment, labor and planning—came to be defined explicitly as public, political ones. The material concerns and productive relations that for centuries had been privatized (which had held a key to the domination and exploitation of the peasantry) now became politicized at the local level, first in rent and interest reduction campaigns, then in land reform, and finally in the collectivization of agriculture. China's peasants, who in the past were not involved in politics partly because it dealt only indirectly or in a mystified way with their basic existential concerns, now were drawn into it because of those very same concerns.

This change in the substance of politics was perforce accompanied by changes in its *form*. The day-to-day issues that now entered the political realm and drew the peasantry into it could only be discussed in the vernacular, which replaced classical Chinese as the lingua franca of politics. As ordinary speech entered politics, dialectically, politics entered ordinary speech, becoming a regular and accepted part of daily popular discourse. This had enormous phenomenological consequences. No longer was political discourse confined to venues or personages bedecked with prepossessing symbols of elite stature and culture. Politics took place within simple walls, or even in the outdoors, and its participants were usually illiterate, calloused, dirty, and disheveled.

These changes fundamentally altered the *resource requirements* for participation in local politics. In the past, local politics was elitist—it involved relations among landowners, occasionally a few wealthy merchants, and state officials. It was also a politics of mutual threats and promises, obligations and favors, and the formation and manipulation of patron-client relations, factions, and personal networks. Therefore participation in it required certain kinds of resources, such as wealth, connections with and access to office holders, privileged information, and spare time and energy. Most peasants lacked these. Such resources became less important as gateways to local political participation in revolutionary and postrevolutionary China. In the early revolutionary period—through the land reform—wealth was often viewed as a political liability that made one suspect. That aside, no material resources were required to speak at a village meeting or become a local "activist" or even a cadre. Indeed, they were often a liability in a politics that equated poverty with exploitation and therefore with political virtue, or at least with progressive political impulses and predispositions. In the language of social science, the correlation between economic status and political participation, which had been nearly perfect in prerevolutionary China, when only the wealthy could take part, dissipated in revolutionary and postrevolutionary China. By the early 1970s, the pattern of local political participation was not significantly related to income or wealth.[5] Partly this was because economic resources were no longer as useful in the new politics as they had been in the old, and partly it was the result of the great equalization of income that had occurred within the collective units that formed the boundaries and institutions of grass-roots politics. Now that meetings were held in the evenings or during breaks in the work day, and many informal modes of participation required little or no expenditure of time, leisure, which in China's peasant economy was largely a function of wealth, became less important a prerequisite for political participation.

Of course political resources go beyond the material level. Expressive skills and information are valuable in operating in the public realm. Before the revolution there was a folk saying that "a poor man has no right to talk," and early attempts at political mobilization often collapsed because peasants were unable to speak in public. Ma's wife said: "We can't speak as fluently as the landlords." But by the 1960s and 1970s peasants said in ordinary language that one had a "right to talk" in public deliberations if one possessed information or experience relevant to the issue at hand, or even just some basis for being concerned with the problem. Knowledge of agriculture and practical skills at management and human relations became qualities demanded for participation in local politics. Thus, for example, former rich peasants were often included in village discussions of agricultural matters.[6]

But changes in the scale, venue, substance, form, and resource requirements were not themselves sufficient to transform local politics. Peasants' *historically formed sense of social inferiority and political inefficacy* often prevented them from simply stepping forward to take the controls of the new, simplified political machinery erected during the revolution. Eric Hobsbawm has pointed to this problem in peasant societies generally: "The potential power of a traditional peasantry is enormous, but its actual power and influence are much more limited. The first major reason for this is its constant, and in general quite realistic, sense of its weakness and inferiority. . . . at bottom peasants are and feel themselves to be subaltern."[7] Hobsbawm's argument finds rich exemplification in the Chinese case. Ma Chiu-tze eventually did come to accept the conception put forward by the persistent cadres that he was exploited by his landlord. But his next remark is telling: "What can I do? Everyone looks down on me. When it's mealtime the landlord eats inside the house, but I must eat outside, standing up. I am not good enough. Everyone looks down on me."[8] Mau Ke-yeh, the cave-builder of Liulin, told Jan Myrdal that when the Red Army first came to the village in 1935, "we didn't think they had any real power. They did not look as though they had, and what could we poor farmers do? So we did nothing."[9]

The peasantry's sense of weakness and inefficacy was a correct reading of its own historical experience. As such, this form of self-consciousness could only be transformed when the peasants would experience their own effectiveness in transforming history and destroying the social classes to whom they felt inferior and against whom they felt weak—Marx's conception of "revolutionizing practice."[10] But not content to wait for the spontaneous outburst of such action by the peasants, the Communist Party took a number of steps to coax China's peasants into activity to transform their world *in advance of the peasantry's own confidence that it could do so.*

During the revolution, one obstacle to a confrontation by the peasants with their landlords had to do with physical security. Hobsbawm notes that peasants feel inferior and ineffective partly because they lack their own effective armed force.[11] This was an insight that Mao began to grasp as early as 1927, after the CCP was nearly destroyed by the Guomindang and Mao and others concluded that the party needed its own army. The party continued to recognize that peasant participation in revolutionary political change required a certain level of security from counterattacks by landlords, the Guomindang, and the Japanese. This was the real meaning of Mao's often misunderstood statement that "political power grows out of the barrel of a gun." Thus the party learned not to undertake land reform except in secure base areas.

Another way of helping peasants gain a feeling of political efficacy and power was to demonstrate concretely to them that the new leadership cared about their interests and wanted to have those interests articulated and acted upon in popular political practice and policy. This involved persuasion, but Chinese peasants are far too hard-headed to put much stock in words that are detached from experienced reality. The party thus developed a set of practices for seeking out the peasantry in intimate contacts with local cadres. It often tried to forge an empathetic basis for these contacts by having local officials live and work alongside the peasants. These contacts were designed to give party officials a grasp of the peasants' existential situations and problems, impart a sense of the ways in which the peasants perceived and thought about their world, and ascertain their views about it. They were also to provide a basis for the party to reinterpret the peasants' views and interests in terms of its own revolutionary Marxist ontology, and then formulate policy accordingly. Then these contacts with the peasantry were to be used in undertaking a process of concrete change by persuading peasants to participate in politics. This combined set of activities, involving political solicitation, reinterpretation, persuasion, and mobilization, came to be know in Chinese as the "mass line."[12]

The intensive efforts of the cadres of Stone Wall Village to get to Ma Chiu-tze—"twenty-three formal talks" and "numerous evening talks" over fifteen days—are a good example. They were the cadres' response to their failure to get the villagers to come forward through changes of the sort described above in the venue, content, form, and resource requirements of local politics.

> When Chou and his fellow workers [from the Hexian County Salvation Association] arrived in Stone Wall Village, they posted proclamations of the Shansi-Hopei-Honan-Shantung Border Region government, announcing that every village had the right to elect its own officials and that land rents and rates of interest should be reduced. Then they called a meeting to explain these proclamations, but the people listened only half-heartedly, kept their mouths

> tightly shut and went home without speaking further to the cadres.
>
> For several days the cadres went individually among the people asking them about local conditions and their own lives, but no one would talk. Whenever a cadre approached groups of people they would break apart and move away. One or two men cornered alone admitted they were afraid of the landlord.
>
> Under these conditions the cadres could not carry on with their work, so they decided to seek out one of the poorer men in the village and talk to him alone and in secret.[13]

Thus began their multitudinous discussions with Ma.

William Hinton relates a similar story about a public meeting called in Long Bow village by revolutionary cadres to criticize a corrupt village head. After the cadres made their accusations,

> The people in the square waited fascinated, as if watching a play. They did not realize that in order for the plot to unfold they themselves had to mount the stage and speak out what was on their minds. No one moved to carry forward what Kuei-ts'ai [one of the cadres] had begun.
>
> T'ien-ming [another cadre] was upset. Without the participation of hundreds, the record could never be set straight. He called a hasty conference of his fellow village officers. They decided to put off the meeting until the next day. . . .
>
> That evening T'ien-ming and Kuei-ts'ai called together small groups of poor peasants from various parts of the village and sought to learn what it was that was really holding them back. They soon found that the root of the trouble was fear. The landlords and the Kuomintang Party organization . . . had taken vigorous steps to forestall and divert the attack. They spread rumors to the effect that [infamous warlord] Yen Hsi-shan, with the help of the Japanese Army, would soon be back. . . . rumors were spread that women were nationalized in the Liberated Areas, ancestral graves violated and all peasants forced to eat *ta kuo fan* or "food out of one big pot."[14]

After soliciting the feelings and views of peasants who would not participate in local revolutionary politics, the next step in the mass line was to broaden the participatory base through persuasion. Ma Chiu-tze was encouraged to bring several equally oppressed neighbors to late-night chats with the cadres. One was murdered by the landlords on his way home, a terrible event that put a temporary stop to the movement but eventually was used to rally support against the landlord.[15] Likewise, in Long Bow:

> That evening, [the cadres] talked plain facts to the selected people in the small groups that they had called together. They discussed "change of sky." Could the Kuomintang troops or the Japanese ever come back? "Even if they do," T'ien-ming said, "we younger men can go off to the higher mountains with the Eighth Route Army, so why be afraid?". . . Emboldened by T'ien-ming's

> words, other peasants began to speak out. They recalled what Te-yu [the "puppet" village head] had done to them personally. Several vowed to speak up and accuse him in the morning....
>
> On the following day the meeting was livelier by far.[16]

This technique of political solicitation to investigate problems and ascertain popular views, followed by encouragement to mobilize political participation (on the basis of which policy could be revised) continued to be put to use throughout the 1950s, 1960s, and 1970s. Vivienne Shue has written of the mutual aid and cooperativization movements in the early 1950s:

> It became standard for each major policy thrust in the villages to be followed up with a period of investigation and rectification of local work done, during which errors and distortions of policy were deliberately sought out and discussed, and plans were made for correcting them. . . . An investigative work team was generally dispatched to each village. It heard reports from local cadres, carried out its own inspections, and usually called a series of small group meetings in which responsible peasants were encouraged to ask questions, raise problems, and voice complaints. . . . they generally elicited a critique of the current situation in the village. . . . The process of rectifying village work . . . tended to be a very lively affair marked by bitter and bawdy humor, desperate threats, and poignant excuses. The sort of give and take which was characteristic of the investigation and rectification process in rural communities *played an important part in redefining the nature and terms of village politics . . . [and] the possibilities for individual and group participation.*[17]

Here is a brand of grass-roots politics that would have been *unthinkable* a decade or two earlier.

We see the same phenomenon again a decade later:

> In late 1963 an outside work team came down to Chang's commune. . . . During the early period they asked selected peasants about their problems and the local situation . . . as in the earlier land reform campaign, they tried to find a few who were willing to speak out about their grievances. They tried to point out to such peasants the ways rural life had improved since 1949 and to convince them that all of these gains would be undone if the poorer peasants didn't speak out against capitalist and feudal tendencies which had re-emerged.[18]

This work resulted in an outpouring of new forms of political participation: small political mobilization meetings, rallies, organizational activities, public criticism campaigns, and recruitment of new leaders.

By the 1970s, political solicitation had become institutionalized in the Chinese countryside. As Michel Oksenberg has written:

> The higher levels do not wish to rely exclusively on the data they receive via

> written reports and oral briefings. They go themselves to the lower levels, either in groups or individually, for long or short periods. Over the past twenty-two years, cadres have learned about local affairs under a variety of different programs: cadres to the countryside (*ganbu xiaxiang*) in the 1950s; sending down (*xia fang*); "squatting at a point" (*dun dian*); and attending rural 7 May cadre schools. In addition to these special efforts are the more routine investigation (*diaocha*) and inspection (*jiancha*).[19]

Other modes of political solicitation were also regularly in use in the early 1970s: "interviewing the poor and miserable" (*fang pin wen ku*), the "four togethernesses" (*si tong*, under which higher-level cadres moved into the homes of peasants to eat, live, work, and consult with them), work teams, and "on-the-spot conferences" (*xian chang huiyi*). In addition, many local cadres up to at least the commune and sometimes even the county level made it a point to solicit opinions by asking detailed questions at formal collective meetings and also in informal settings such as evening "bull sessions," while working in the fields (under regular cadre labor participation programs), or when they ran into peasants by chance.[20]

Thus by the 1970s local life and the ways in which peasants spoke and appeared to think about it were eminently and indeed intensely political, and politics was understood to be a public process. With the coming of socialism, basic issues of daily existence, including income, production, and social relations not only among classes but also within families were subjects of public politics at the grass-roots level. The break from a past in which politics was a realm open almost exclusively to elites and conducted behind closed doors, and in which productive relations were privatized and not subjected to political determination either in public or in private, could not be greater.

IV

Explanation of this break demands a complex model of causality. For change took place at many levels, each of which served both as "cause" and "effect."[21] The development of a conception, a language, a set of institutions, and a repertoire of practices of local participatory, public politics in postrevolutionary rural China was inextricably linked with transformations of the mode of production, class relations, and popular epistemology, consciousness, and ideology. The sea-changes wrought by the Chinese revolution were, in a word, overdetermined.[22] They illustrate the massive scope, the complexity, and, as will be seen in the next section, ultimately the difficulties and contradictions of a transition to socialism.

The development of a popular politics in rural China was grounded in the move toward a socialist mode of production. It began in the struggles for reduced rent and interest and eventually for land reform. Later it came to revolve around the management of collective economic affairs in the agricultural cooperatives and then the communes. Economic life provided much of the substance of local participatory politics during the Maoist period: debates about workpoints, production planning and management, collective accumulation and investment, and so forth. But the mode of production was no mere "base" or "cause" in the story. Changes in the mode of production did not by themselves bring about political change in any direct or simple way. The emergence of a new kind of local politics was a process both tortuous and inextricably bound up with the struggles over new modes of production. Land reform, cooperativization, and even the creation of the people's communes (and most certainly their reorganization in the early 1960s) were products of participatory local politics (which, to be sure, had grown up around economic issues). In turn, changes in the mode of production reshaped local politics. For example, the great equalizations of income and wealth within production teams provided a context in which the pattern of political participation was not skewed by the uneven distribution of economic resources.

Likewise with social class. The preexisting class structure was simultaneously an object of and an obstacle to the rise of popular politics during the revolution. In Stone Wall and Long Bow villages, so long as the landlords dominated the villages, peasants were reluctant to enter into the uncharted and indeed unconceived realm of political struggle against them. But a dialectic of victimization operated too: it was the exploitation and depredations of that domination that provided the impulse—however trammeled—to do so. After the land reform, the struggle against rich peasants provided much of the text and subtext of the local politics and institution-building involved in cooperativization.[23] The continued use of former landlords as whipping-boys and political scapegoats through the 1960s and 1970s, however inappropriate and hurtful it might have been, should be seen as a product of their centrality in the process by which China's peasants began to develop and flex political muscles for the very first time. From the peasants' and local leaders' point of view, continued exorcism of the landlords was a symbolic way of reaffirming and even celebrating the existence of the new popular politics that had been forged in the struggle against former class enemies.

The transformation of local politics was also bound up with changes in popular phenomenology and epistemology. The cadres who came to Stone Wall Village undertook to transform the way Ma Chiu-tze comprehended the 240 piculs of grain he and his ancestors had paid Landlord Wang for sixty years. We will never know how the wretched Ma understood this before his encounter with the revolution: as part of a moral economic exchange, as a legal and therefore just prerogative of private property, as unavoidable given Ma's lack of political and economic power, or simply as a custom upon which reflection was not appropriate or undertaken at all. In any event, Belden's story makes it clear that an epistemological change involving a new understanding of rent as exploitation and, moreover, as key to the explanation of Ma's misery was a necessary condition of Ma's entry into a new politics. The depth of this change in Ma's way of thinking is indicated by the great difficulty and protractedness (fifteen days, twenty-three "formal talks") with which it was brought about.

Once the Ma Chiu-tzes of rural China had taken their first hesitant steps into the realm of local politics, those politics became experiences that in turn reshaped the nature of local politics. The cynical theory that in the Maoist period political participation became a kind of empty ritual played out by people who learned to manipulate ideological language and feign political interest or contrition is one example of a phenomenologically based explanation of the new politics.[24] But local politics was experienced in more positive ways, too, which could result in different effects on political activity. Hinton's account of Long Bow Village demonstrates how its people learned to participate in local politics by experiencing their own effectiveness therein. In the process of carrying out several rounds of public decision making and collective action, Long Bow peasants became much more adroit political actors. While at the beginning of *Fanshen* the village is plagued with insufficient attendance at meetings and recurring, alternating incidents of rashness or indecisiveness, by the end local politics begins to function much more smoothly and effectively. The second rounds of land reform, class classification, and cadre rectification were much more successful than the first.[25] This is not a matter of practice making perfect. It also has to do with a phenomenological change in which peasants experienced political efficaciousness. Result then became "cause." Precisely because of its view that the direct experience of political power was a prerequisite to consolidating the revolutionary transformation of local society and thence to constructing socialism, the party demanded that the land reform be carried out not simply by administrative fiat but instead through a more arduous politics in which poor peasants personally denounced their landlords. The continuing vilification of landlords in later years was, then, also a way for peasants and local leaders to remind themselves of the power they had exercised—a power which was unimaginable only two or three decades earlier. It was regularly used by local leaders in conjunction with appeals for popular participation in various new political movements. So was the practice of "speaking bitterness," which helped even crusty old peasants develop an interest in sometimes abstruse contemporary political affairs. As one young peasant said in 1975: "The older peasants were interested in the criticism of Lin

Biao because at every meeting to criticize him they could 'recall the bitter and think of the sweet' (*yiku sitian*). The old folks talked about how they had suffered from the landlords' oppression in the past [and linked this to the criticism of Lin]."[26]

Finally, the transformation of local politics had its roots in the political realm itself. Techniques of political solicitation and mobilization were absolutely indispensable in broadening the extent of local participation, as has been seen. Yet they too were not sufficient to bring about the new local politics. The campaigns to implement various elements of the left rural development program, such as collectivized private plots or brigade accounting, often fell on deaf ears where they did not correspond to the concrete and self-understood material interest of the local cadres and peasants.[27]

Thus the sea-changes in popular politics wrought by the Chinese revolution involved transformations of the mode of production, class structure, popular phenomenology and epistemology, and politics itself. Moreover, only a few examples have been given of the ways in which these various factors interacted with each other, depended on each other, and resonated back onto themselves. The Chinese revolution and socialist transition is a practical recognition of the complex interconnectedness of the spheres of economy. Chinese revolutionary and socialist praxis during the Maoist period involved a recognition that to bring about deep change anywhere, revolutions have to bring about change everywhere. *Plus ça change, plus ça change.*

V

The problem is, of course, that it did not do so. *Plus ça change, et plus c'est la même chose, avec une vengence.* The Chinese revolution and the socialism that flowed from it opened up a new world of grass-roots political activity, experience, and understanding. The boundaries were being vastly expanded. But they were not being abolished. The state dug a deep trench between itself and the grass roots. Or, perhaps more accurately, it failed to traverse, and may even have deepened, a trench system already dug doubly by China's own statist political culture and tradition and by the institutions and proclivities of Leninism (and especially Stalinism).

The rise of a popular, participatory politics was not spontaneous. The interlocking, hegemonic structure of prerevolutionary economy, class, politics, phenomenology, and epistemology prevented this from emerging on its own. It is probably not a deterministic excess to assert that the creation of the new politics required purposive leadership of the sort undertaken by the CCP; in any event, it was certainly a resultant of those actions. But the party also kept its own significant control over the new local participatory politics. Political solicitation and mobilization took place around issues decided upon and in terms defined by the party. If power is the ability to define the situation, then the party retained a great deal of power in grass-roots politics.

Agendas for local participation were set strictly, and there was no way to transcend them. As one key example, macroeconomic planning was never put up for public deliberation and debate even by leaders and experts (not to mention citizens). China's peasants were not given the opportunity to learn about or discuss, much less influence, issues that deeply affected them, such as the relationship between agriculture and industry, the proportion of consumption and accumulation, or the policy of local grain self-reliance. As the imperial polity had kept basic existential issues such as rent, interest, and gender relations from public discussion and action, the revolutionary socialist polity defined equally basic issues as not subject to public politics. The new political formation did not live up very well to socialist aspiration for democracy of the economy.

On a host of other issues, some role for grass-roots participation was preserved. Localities were in theory to be given discretion in deciding how to remunerate labor: by what mix of collective and individual distribution; by piece rates or time rates; if the latter, by frequent meetings stressing strict labor performance or by the more "progressive" Dazhai system of infrequent meetings and use of broader criteria that included public-spiritedness (which in practice often meant political rectitude). They were given narrowly specified ranges within which to set collective accumulation and welfare funds and allocations of private plots. They were given more latitude in selecting local leadership.[28] Elements of the radical program of rural transformation such as the enlargement of the basic unit of collective account or the collectivization of private plots, pig husbandry, and even housing were to be undertaken only when local conditions were determined to be appropriate and local people were willing to undertake them. But on all these matters the state made its wishes all too clearly known and exerted often heavy pressure on localities to comply with them. Cadres were told that they would be evaluated on their successes in securing local implementation of these policies, and political movements and policy "winds" were promulgated to help assure popular compliance.[29]

The politics here was in general not totalitarian. Production teams were indeed able to set the size of their accumulation funds as they wished (within the prescribed limits). They could choose their own workpoint systems (though if they insisted on piece rates they often had to demonstrate the unsuitability of time rates by trying them out and seeing them fail). Localities that stood their ground and opposed movements to enlarge the size of the collective unit of account or collectivize private plots were often successful in staving them off. Others coped with pressure on these and other issues by evasion or subterfuge, time-honored strategies used by peasants to resist the state.[30]

But the capacity to block the implementation of state policies or to alter them through implementation involves a qualitatively different politics from active participation in the formulation of those policies in the first place. The program of radical transformation first seen in the higher-stage cooperativization, then in the Great Leap, and finally in the Dazhai campaign was decided upon by the party leadership. The mass line was impressed into service in each case. Localities like Dazhai, which, often for locally specific reasons, were enthusiastic about elements of the program (or had actually generated such elements themselves), were found. Their actions were taken as evidence of general popular support (which if not yet active or conscious was, in the party's view, certainly in the offing once the peasants were made aware of their inherent "correctness"). They were also regarded as harbingers of the next phase of teleological progress toward communism. Once the policies were formulated and promulgated, campaigns of mass persuasion and mobilization were undertaken. They were presumed to be largely unproblematical since it was assumed that the content of the policies was congruent with the objective interests of the peasants (which only needed to be made subjective). At each stage the identification of those interests and interpretation of popular subjectivity was left exclusively to the party.

The coexistence of an emergent participatory local politics concerned with basic existential questions on the one hand and a statist politics affecting those same issues on the other led eventually to a political crisis. So long as material life was improving, as during the early and (with some slowing) mid-1950s, this could be averted. The disasters of the Great Leap did much to damage the peasantry's faith in the ability of the state to formulate policy wisely. The state's response was not to open the polity to broader participation, which would have shifted the responsibility for the formulation and effects of policy partly off itself. Instead, the contradictory situation was extended. Renewed emphasis was placed on local participation during the Socialist Education and Dazhai campaigns, while at the same time the state continued to insist on its prerogatives to set many of the parameters of policy making. The result was, insofar as one can tell, widespread disillusionment with local participatory processes and institutions that continued to be heavily influenced and circumscribed by the exercise of state power in directions and forms that did not accord with local interests or subjectivities. The stage was set for the Dengist climacteric.

There are two contrasting themes in it. One is fundamentally non- or antiparticipatory. Collective participatory institutions at the grass roots have been dismantled, and political processes (such as political solicitation, mobilization and propaganda campaigns, and political study classes) abolished. Political control of the economy has been criticized in the strongest terms. The basic existential issues of material life, whose collectivization was a key to the creation of the new participatory politics during the revolutionary and socialist periods, have now been privatized again. The socialist aspiration to democracy of the economy, which largely eluded China during the Maoist period because of overweening state control, continues to elude Dengist China as the local economy is depoliticized. Now there is much less to participate about, and fewer ways of participating on such issues as remain on the local agenda.

A second theme is the regularization, rationalization, and institutionalization of local political participation. Legal rights for participants are to be created and guaranteed. Local assemblies are to be established, complete with competitive elections, to deal with such local issues as remain in the public realm (e.g., management of collective enterprises and property) and the implementation at the local level of state policies (e.g., population control). The party is being urged to restrain itself in making, influencing, or administering local policy.

Of the two, the former has progressed much more rapidly. Politics has become passé to most peasants, who are now busying themselves more exclusively than at any time since 1949 with the opportunities and difficulties of making a living. It is not clear just who is participating in the new assemblies, or what they are participating about—which suggests that are not riveting the attention of China's peasants, who until so recently were intensely involved in local politics. Dengism seems to be creating (and perhaps is intent on creating) a small-holding peasantry with secure title to land—a class that, if comparative historical analysis is any guide, exhibits strong tendencies toward political passivity and conservatism.

Thus there is in Dengism a major structural change of mode of production, class structure, and the state and politics—the second within the span of less than half a century. The fact that the post-1978 changes are structural is itself a reflection of the structural character of the revolutionary transformations that preceded them and their attendant crises. The Dengist leadership is engaged in nothing so innocuous as "reform." One question worth debating as we look back on the Maoist period is whether and how it could have been reformed. For the moment this may appear as a purely academic exercise, since the revival of a reformed Maoism, or the adaptation of some of its elements within some other social formation, seems most unlikely. But the directions in which the Dengist leadership is taking China will eventually reveal their own contradictions. Like the contradictions of the early Maoist period, this will not happen until crises in economic and material life force them into the open.

One of these will revolve around the relationship of a still highly centralized and authoritarian state and an increasingly privatized economy. To be sure, the Dengists have declared themselves opposed to aspects of statism, especially as these affect the economy. But in other very basic respects the Dengist state is as authoritarian as its Maoist predecessor. Deng and the Dengists have, like Mao and the Maoists, assumed they know the objective interests of the Chinese people, and they continue to reserve for themselves the power to issue authoritative interpretations of popular subjectivity. Consequently they have set about what they see as the basically unproblematic process of mobilizing them to implement the reform program. But this has involved a very heavy hand of the state. For example, tremendous pressure has been exerted on many localities that sought to continue to farm collectively or to maintain other elements of the Maoist mode of production they had developed.[31] Can such a state leadership ever really give society the free reign inherent in the market forces that it is glorifying and unleashing?

Another contradiction is that between the participatory habits, impulses, and proclivities fostered during over three decades of Maoist political practice, on the one hand, and the present depoliticization, on the other. Though many of the Chinese who were drawn into the new politics have left it behind in disgust and disillusionment, others have from time to time sought to express discontent with the present policies, for example, by sitting in front of government offices or vandalizing collective property that has been contracted to individuals. For the moment their discontent is smoldering quietly, perhaps eventually to dissipate or perhaps simply awaiting the right climate of national politics to express itself.[32] But the political experiences and effects of the popular politics that emerged in the Maoist period ran very deep. It would be premature to write them off.

If the contradictions of Dengism reach crisis proportions—which could occur because of either economic difficulties or successes that engender new political pressures (as in South Korea in mid-1987)—the Maoist period may present itself as a source of inspiration or repository of policy measures. At that time its history will again be rewritten. One can only hope that when it is, a dispassionate reading of this passionate period will be possible—a feat which has thus far eluded Chinese and Westerners alike, to the detriment of serious understanding of the dynamics of socialist transition in the epoch when it was begun.

Notes

This essay has benefited from the help of several colleagues. Raymonde Carroll, Pat Day, Nelson DeJesus, and Mathis Szajiowski, all of Oberlin College, were kind enough to invite a social scientist to their reading group on the Marxist literary theory of Fredric Jameson, which provided the lively and stimulating setting that catalyzed my rethinking of these issues. Arif Dirlik and Jing Wang invited me to the conference for which the first draft of this paper was prepared. They and all the rest of the Institute staff upheld the highest standards of intellectuality, hospitality, and efficiency. The other conference participants—including, quite serendipitously, Prof. Jameson—provided three refreshing and valuable days of discussion and learning in an atmosphere that was uniquely unideological but also open to serious analysis of socialist transition and development. Subsequent written comments from Prof. Dirlik and from Harlan Wilson, my Oberlin colleague in political theory, were especially helpful in recasting and revising the paper.

1. Jack Belden, *China Shakes the World* (Harmondsworth: Penguin, 1973), pp. 244–45, 258.

2. This has remained the case, though to a lesser extent than in the past, at the county level and above since 1949. But at the grass-roots levels government offices are far more accessible and less prepossessing.

3. This is not to say that China's peasants never struck out against the oppression and exploitation that they experienced. China's long history of peasant-based rebellions shows that they did. But the fact that they resorted spasmodically to armed force—what might be called extraordinary politics—suggests the weakness of what I am calling ordinary politics.

4. See, for example, Tang Tsou, "Back from the Brink of Revolutionary-'Feudal' Totalitarianism," in *State and Society in Contemporary China*, ed. Victor Nee and David Mozingo (Ithaca: Cornell University Press, 1983), p. 54 and passim.

5. Marc Blecher, "Leader-Mass Relations in Rural Chinese Communities: Local Politics in a Revolutionary Society," Ph.D. dissertation, University of Chicago, 1978, pp. 123–26.

6. Ibid., ch. 4.

7. Eric Hobsbawm, "Peasants and Politics," *Journal of Peasant Studies* 1 (October 1973): 12.

8. Belden, *China Shakes the World*, p. 244.

9. Jan Myrdal, *Report from a Chinese Village* (New York: Signet, 1966), p. 97.

10. Karl Marx, "Theses on Feuerbach," in *Marx and Engels: Basic Writings on Politics and Philosophy*, ed. Lewis Feuer (New York: Anchor/Doubleday, 1959), p. 244.

11. Hobsbawm, "Peasants and Politics."

12. The absence of a single word or concept in English that would incorporate these various activities indicates the great differences in leader-mass relations between our own politics and that of revolutionary China. It also suggests the epistemological difficulties that must be overcome to apprehend the latter.

13. Belden, *China Shakes the World*, p. 243.

14. William Hinton, *Fanshen* (New York: Vintage, 1966), pp. 114–15.

15. Belden, *China Shakes the World*, pp. 246–48.

16. Hinton, *Fanshen*, p. 115.

17. Vivienne Shue, "Keypoints, Cadre Deviations, and the Rectification of Village Work: Some Aspects of Rural Local Political Leadership in China," paper presented at the California Regional Seminar on China, Center for Chinese Studies, University of California, Berkeley, May 22, 1976; my emphasis.

18. Martin Whyte, *Small Groups and Political Rituals in China* (Berkeley: Univer-

sity of California Press, 1974), pp. 147–48.

19. Michel Oksenberg, "Methods of Communication Within the Chinese Bureaucracy," *China Quarterly* 57 (January–March 1974): 21–22.

20. Blecher, "Leader-Mass Relations," pp. 178–95.

21. This conceptual dyad has probably done as much to set back social science explanation as to advance it. It is a good candidate for a dose of analytical deconstruction.

22. This term is one of the most misunderstood in social theory. It does not connote inevitability or ineluctability. Rather, it refers to the complex linkages between the aspects or analytical levels of a structured social object—here, the mode of production, class structure, state and politics, culture, ideology, and other forms of consciousness and thought, which taken together make up a social formation—in which changes in any one part reverberate throughout the whole, producing changes in all the others (that in turn react back upon itself). The English term, which originates from the French *surdetermination* and the German *uberdeterminierung*, might better be translated as superdetermination, in the sense of determination from above (though this too has problems, since "above" is not quite appropriate, and "determination" has a different and much looser, less "deterministic," meaning in the French and German). For a gloss on "overdetermination" that is even more inelegant than this, see Louis Althusser, *For Marx* (New York: Vintage, 1970), pp. 252–53.

23. Vivienne Shue, *Peasant China in Transition: The Dynamics of the Development Toward Socialism, 1949–1956* (Berkeley: University of California Press, 1980).

24. Whyte, *Small Groups*, p. 95 and passim; Lucian Pye, "Mass Participation in China: Its Limitations and the Continuity of Culture," in *China: Management of a Revolutionary Society*, ed. John Lindbeck (Seattle: University of Washington Press, 1971), pp. 3–33.

25. Hinton, *Fanshen*.

26. Blecher, "Leader-Mass Relations," p. 132.

27. David Zweig, "Agrarian Radicalism and the Chinese Countryside, 1968–1981," ms.

28. John Burns, "The Election of Production Team Cadres in Rural China, 1958–74," *China Quarterly* 74 (June 1978): 273–96.

29. Zweig, "Agrarian Radicalism."

30. Ibid.

31. Witness the sad, bitter plaint of Wang Jinhong, the village leader of Long Bow, over the pressure on his village to divide up its land into strips, with the attendant destruction of its well-developed capacity for agricultural mechanization, in Carma Hinton, *All Under Heaven* (New Day Films, 1986).

32. Significant criticism of the household responsibility system continued to find expression at least through the latter part of 1980, almost two years after the triumph of the Dengists at the Third Plenum of the Eleventh Party Central Committee (Xue Muqiao, "Socialism and the Planned Commodity Economy," *Beijing Review* 30, 33 [August 17, 1987]: 16). It was again attacked in mid-1987, when the political climate shifted after the fall of Party Chairman Hu Yaobang (Robert Delfs, "A Summer Peace," *Far Eastern Economic Review* 137, 29 [July 16, 1987]: 11).

11

PROSPERITY AND COUNTERPROSPERITY: THE MORAL DISCOURSE ON WEALTH IN POST-MAO CHINA

Ann Anagnost

In the years since 1978, a revolution in moral values appears to have taken place in the Chinese countryside. The egalitarian idea has been officially repudiated as the essence of leftist error. But even so, peasant households who dare to become wealthy suffer harassment that reasserts local norms of reciprocity. Furthermore, the identification of the party's own moral authority with the idea of economic equity is too close and too complex to be abandoned altogether. The following discussion will explore how ideas of economic equity appear (if only subterraneanly) in official discourse on the rural economy. More importantly it will explore the ways in which this official discourse both interweaves with popular practice and confronts it with a competing morality.

The economic changes in the Chinese countryside of the last ten years have been well documented so that I need not detail them here. Generally speaking, most of Chinese agricultural production is no longer organized collectively but on the basis of contracting collectively owned resources to individual households. "Contracting everything to the household" (*da baogan*) is only one of the many forms of the new responsibility system, but it appears at present to be the predominant form. This change in policy represents a radical departure from collective organization prior to 1978. In that year, the spontaneous movement toward household contracting had already begun the momentum that would finally be officially sanctioned in September 1980.[1]

Although it is important to remember this spontaneous groundswell of support for the responsibility system, the official promotion of this policy has led in some areas to its implementation in the face of local opposition, especially in wealthier collectives that have a more developed agricultural infrastructure. Even in more typical cases, resources better left collectively managed (such as large-scale farm machinery, nonrenewable resources, brigade industries, and social services, including the local health clinic) have been contracted to individual households.[2]

In most rural areas, the household has become the most important unit of agricultural production in the present rural economy. Along with its renewed importance, the household has become objectified in discourse in ways that, in the very process of individuating it, compromise its seeming autonomy. To understand this process fully, it must be set in the context of a continuing moral discourse by both official and unofficial voices that centers on the obligations of wealth and what the wealthy individual owes to the collectivity. This may subtly qualify the understanding of the extent to which a supposed revolution in moral values has led to the practice of untrammeled individualism in the Chinese countryside.

In the following pages, I wish to explore this discussion of wealth and morality but with the following caveats. First, although I have been following this discussion since 1981, more recently its intensity and ideological volume appear to have become somewhat subdued, at least insofar as its coverage in the Chinese media is concerned. Whether or not the discussion continues in popular discourse would be difficult to say without direct field research. My interpretation of it is dependent primarily on materials from Chinese newspapers, and this limits what I can say about its present importance in everyday affairs.[3] I suspect that it does remain important, and that the official discourse itself has changed. Conflict remains, but now it appears to be phrased more in terms of legal protection of the newly prosperous rather than in terms of a moral discourse.[4]

Second, I do not want to make any universal claims about the nature of a peasant morality in exploring these issues. I feel that these moral issues must be understood in their historical context and that any "essentialist" notion of a peasant mentality is to be rigorously avoided. It should not be surprising that the practical redefinition of socialism around what were formerly condemned as capitalist categories should produce stresses and strains that call into question all economic practice. At the same time, in the wake of the policies of the 1960s and 1970s, which were catastrophic for many areas, it may not be surprising that the idea of a socialist morality would be regarded with anything but a healthy measure of cynicism, but cynicism itself bears the trace of a former commitment. One should not expect a complete volte face in peasant consciousness to follow quickly on the heels of so fundamental a change in official policy as the dismantling of the collective and the seeming betrayal of a commitment to "mutual prosperity."

If indeed the activity of this moral discourse should prove to be only a transitional phenomenon, then its significance will lie precisely in its character of renegotiating the boundary between the proper and the heterodox in economic practice. This process of renegotiation should be intrinsically interesting for what it might say about changing relations of power and the transformation of ideologies in general.

The Moral Discourse of Wealth

The change in agricultural policy that began with the Third Plenum in 1978 is often referred to in the press as a repudiation of the egalitarian ideal in order to "liberate" the productive forces. This language is telling in itself because it means not just a change in economic policy but a radical reassessment of the nature of peasant society. The egalitarian ideal, which had previously held a favored place in the official ideology, is now seen as a negative aspect of a peasant world view that holds back the development of the rural economy.

The present status of the egalitarian ideal in the official discourse is, of course, that of a backward idea characteristic of a small-producer mentality. But it also carries with it a strong association with the ultraleftist thought of the Cultural Revolution and its aftermath. In fact the egalitarian ideal has become disvalued as the quintessence of leftist thought. As such it carries much of the onus for the problems that the rural economy has encountered in the last two decades. In practical terms, it is now defined as the antithesis of the current policy of compensation according to labor. In this light the image of the egalitarian idea appears as a large rice pot on which underproductive individuals can rely, producing a negative incentive for those capable of greater industry.

The current agricultural policies, based on a more direct return for one's labor, have led unavoidably to a measure of economic differentiation between households. Although the earlier policies insisted on everyone advancing toward prosperity at the same level and rate, the state now acknowledges the differences between households in their ability to become more productive (in terms of labor power, social connections, technical knowledge, and so forth). By allowing some households to get rich at a faster rate than others, these factors can be brought into play. This is what is meant by "liberation of the productive forces." However, the economic differences now reappearing in the countryside have led to fears of new class formation. These fears have been expressed by peasants and local leaders in ways that often compel prosperous members of the community to acknowledge their obligation to it by some act of generosity.

To understand how the egalitarian ideal continues to carry a moral weight in the Chinese countryside, despite its identification with agrarian radicalism and the economic mismanagement of the Cultural Revolution period, one must distinguish the concept as it has been used by elites from the forms it actually takes in peasant society. Peasant egalitarianism need not be reduced to a purely economic idea. It bears a social dimension that has been systematically ignored by the state. Its continued presence as a real social force is detectable in the Chinese press through its discussion of socially generated reciprocity in the countryside. Grumbling about public displays of reciprocity in rural villages (gift exchange and communal banqueting) is frequently grouped together in newspaper format with other negative categories such as folk ritual and gambling. Why should such innocently appearing acts of communal sharing be a focus for official concern? One might speculate that it is not only because they "hold back" economic development (it makes people afraid to assume the social obligations of wealth), but also because these rites of reciprocity reproduce social relations that challenge state authority and elude the controlling technologies of state power.

Although the customary forms that this communal sharing might take hearken back to a prerevolutionary ethic of personal relations that might be identified as Confucian, the extent to which they are generated from a concern that class divisions are reappearing is the product of a much more recent history. During the thirty years prior to the current decade of reform, the evolution of a socialist political culture emphasized the writing of a mythic history that detailed the horrors of the old class society and underscored the historical imperative for revolutionary change. This mythic history was constantly reinscribed onto the present: in the context of the struggle sessions that preceded land reform, in "speaking bitterness" rituals, in the intensification of class struggle during the 1960s. It was a history that was repeatedly put into performance and made pertinent to contemporary concerns. To the extent that this history in performance did indeed shape people's perception of the past, one can expect it to be an inevitable influence on present practice as a "fear of polarization" of class society and all that it represents. The fact that this fear appears to take form in ways that echo prevolutionary customary practice may have more to say about a disarticulation between official and popular ideas of the obligations of wealth and how these should be met, and less to say about the imperviousness of large agrarian states to change, and to revolutionary change in particular.

The significance of egalitarian sentiments need not be reduced to the desire for a strictly economic equality. They are also meaningful in terms of social equity. In this sense an egalitarian ideology can tolerate a certain amount of economic disparity between individuals as long as these differences do not become the basis for severing social ties to neighbors and kin. Claims on generosity are not necessarily a means by which poorer peasants victimize those who dare to get rich. Nor need they be viewed solely as a leveling mechanism meant to ensure absolute economic equality between households. Such claims are merely the functioning of one's social universe. The burden of the individual in maintaining social life is dependent on relative wealth, and indeed the shouldering of more than an equal share is what constitutes symbolic capital in rural society. In pre-Liberation China, one's relative wealth determined the amount one would contribute to local ritual activities. This manifestation of generosity on a material level was replicated on a more cosmological one. The wealthy man was believed to be unusually endowed with yang essence, which translated into economic luck. By contributing generously to the local temple cult or by assuming ritual offices, his yang power entered into the public domain to grace the entire community.

Despite the heavier social demands on the wealthy person's generosity, there are limits as to how far this generosity need be extended. The object is not to avoid becoming wealthy but to avoid accusations of miserliness. Gifts and favors are exchanged in the context of long-standing social relations. Reciprocity is required for continued sociality and is therefore a social expectation governed by village norms. To have a surplus and to have the ability to respond to a request is not sufficient in itself. One must also have the obligation to respond, and this network of obligation reproduces social life.[5]

When economic disparities develop to the point at which kin or neighbor asks a favor (within the village norms of what is an appropriate request) and is refused, the humiliation is deeply felt. A denial of generosity in this situation becomes a denial of the social tie. The refusal does violence to more than just this individual relationship; it throws into question the entire system of social relationships that define the community. It means simply that an individual no longer has any regard for his or her social reputation. Village gossip as a means of asserting community norms of reciprocity can no longer touch such persons. They have, in effect, cut themselves off from all claims of sociality. A failure of generosity brings the first awareness of classes in formation, and the difficulty we may have in understanding the magnitude of this break is perhaps a measure of our own alienation.

The expression of individualism to the point of social cleavage usually cannot be explained in terms of processes internal to peasant communities.[6] During the period of radical agrarian policies, the village had become encysted within the state economy. Individual efforts to participate in opportunities outside the collective organization were severely limited. During this time, the village resembled, in certain striking ways, the closed corporate communities of the Latin American highlands.[7] With the recent policies, however, the avenues to wealth within the village have become increasingly dependent on individual connections that extend outside the local community.[8] As access to the avenues of wealth becomes less equal, as divisive influences from outside the community become more and more difficult to control, the rituals of social exchange become even more important for reassurance that economic differences have not yet progressed to the point where mutuality is impossible.

As suggested above, the fear of polarization is based on a memory of the old society recreated in local histories that have been written and performed almost continuously since Liberation. In the political culture of the 1960s and 1970s, the emergence of a class of wealthier peasants signaled a "recrudescence" of the hardship and exploitation of the old class society.[9] This fear is still present, and it is shared not only by peasants but by certain elements in the party as well. For despite its new economic policies, the party is still concerned that the road to prosperity be accompanied by a more equitable distribution of wealth than would be true in an environment of untrammeled capitalism. In terms of official discourse, it is assumed that if a certain number of households are to be allowed to achieve prosperity ahead of the rest, they are expected to "carry" the others in ways that are not always clearly specified. To a certain extent this broadening of prosperity is expected to occur naturally through the enlivening of the rural economy resulting from the activity of these more enterprising households. At the same time, official voices do express an expectation that wealthy households bear some responsibility for those less successful, and that they should actively endeavor to help others prosper.

Hence the obligations of wealth enter into official discourse, although these obligations are stated differently from those that arise from communal norms of reciprocity, thereby resulting in a dialogue of competing moralities. For although peasant communities may use local rites of reciprocity to reproduce social relations, these local practices are dismissed by official voices as a form of "waste." Instead, the "spirit of the gift" can only be given in the name of the party as a gratuitous offering on the part of the enlightened individual. The forces that compel the "proper" expression of generosity emanate from the party and are not recognized as being socially generated. The "gift" becomes a means of "producing" hegemony for the party by reaffirming the party's commitment to an equitable distribution of wealth without negating its policy of encouraging economic autonomy.

Before turning to a discussion of the obligations of wealth, however, I would first like to digress a moment to a discussion of the household as an object of discourse that mirrors in diverse ways the economic changes of the post-Mao period.

The Household as an Object of Discourse

The abandonment of collective agriculture has put a new measure of importance on the individual household as the primary unit of production and consumption. This supposed economic individuation has been reflected in language in which the household has been reconstituted as an object of discourse. Not only does the household appear as the primary economic actor, but its relative success in the economic realm also relegates it to one of a number of named categories that place each individual unit on a scale of relative prosperity. This pinning to categories is no simple-minded process, and the politics that surround it are precisely what I hope to discuss in this chapter. A new set of named categories that measure one's present economic success in a positive light neatly displaces an older set of class categories, now abandoned, that were based on the comprehensive class analyses that preceded land reform, and once determined one's place in a reverse status hierarchy throughout the Maoist period.[10]

The labels currently in use, all of which are nominalized with the character *hu* (household), studiously avoid reference to earlier class statuses or moral judgments on the possession of wealth. Among these labels are those that locate each household on the path to prosperity in terms of its relative success. *Zhifu hu* (prospering household) refers to those households who are perceived to be well on the way to economic success through the proper exercise of the new economic freedoms. *Wanyuan hu* (10,000-yuan household) is the Chinese equivalent of a millionaire in rural society. Its application is often symbolic and not necessarily based on the objective attainment of a precisely measured accumulation of wealth. At the opposite end of the scale are the *kunnan hu* (hardship household) and the *wubao hu* (five guarantees household), who have not achieved prosperity for various reasons, usually attributed to insufficient resources, expertise, or household labor power.

Other labels mark the degree of specialization of the domestic unit in the current diversification of the rural economy and its reorientation to the market. *Zhongdian hu* (key household) refers to those households that are still linked to grain agriculture but have also diversified their household economy to include handicraft or agricultural sidelines. Even more specialized is the *zhuanye hu* (specialized household) that has abandoned grain agriculture altogether in pursuit of a specialized sideline. These two categories are especially important because they specify the newly opened avenues to peasant prosperity, and the number of households subscribing to these labels have become a measure of how well the new economic policies are succeeding in a local area.[11]

Parallel to this ranking and specification of household units in the context of the new economic policies, the household has also been reconstituted as an object of ideological control. The household or *hu* has a long history as a bureaucratic object in China. It was the basic unit for taxation and the exaction of corvée in the imperial period. In socialist China, especially since the population control law of 1958, the *hu* has continued to be a unit of bureaucratic control. A system of household registration fixed the household within a local collective organization that controlled its access to productive resources, grain rations, permission to have a child, and other essentials. By this means the spatial mobility of the household was effectively limited.

With the present decollectivization of agricultural production, the hold of the local collective organization over the household has loosened considerably. The household has not only regained considerable autonomy, but the community as a whole has become more permeable, allowing some movement of population in and out of its officially defined boundaries. Outsiders may outbid local people for contracts over locally owned productive resources. Peasant households who have the means to set up small service enterprises are encouraged to relocate in county towns. Official encouragement for the development of horizontal linkages between producers and their sources of supply and markets also contributes to a new measure of autonomy for the household.

Despite this greater autonomy, and perhaps even because of it, the household has also become more important, however, as an object of knowledge and control in the realm of ideological work. The collective organization of production can no longer serve as the basis for organizing groups for political study or for mobilization for ideological goals. Ideological work has been reorganized accordingly on the basis of the domestic unit by retailoring already familiar institutions such as the emulation campaign. Households, rather than individuals or collectively organized units, are now more likely to be ranked and judged in terms of their advance toward a specified behavior through emulation of an officially defined ideal. For instance, a local sanitation campaign might promote a competition between households to attain the status of "sanitary household" (*weisheng hu*). In a more comprehensive campaign, a cluster of behaviors that range from compliance with the birth policy to fulfilling responsibility contracts or perhaps the ordering of intrafamilial relationships might be targeted for reform through the designation of certain model households as "civilized households" (*wenming hu*).

Likewise, a social survey-style inquiry by the local leadership into locally defined problems is meant to define anomalies in the social body that will provide the targets for reform in a subsequent emulation campaign. Such a survey can then identify "problem households" (*dingzi hu*) that refuse to comply with official policies and that can then become the means through which power can be exercised and displayed. Borrowing from Foucault, this mechanism to specify and rank households in order to judge them might be called a "meticulous ritual of power," and as such it is essential in understanding the dialectic between official policy and popular practice, but for reasons of space I will not deal with the implications of this technology here.[12] My reason for introducing the topic at all is to underline the extent to which the household has been made into an object of discourse in official contexts. As suggested above, this objectification of the *hu* in official language is certainly not new, but its present elaboration is important for the discussion below.

Before leaving this topic, however, I would like to discuss one more pair of labels that also refer to household prosperity. Unlike the labels already discussed, which avoid reference to earlier class statuses or moral judgments on the possession of wealth, the contrasting pair *maojian hu* (conspicuous household) and *baofa hu* (nouveau riche) regulates a distinction drawn between proper and improper ways to household prosperity. The conspicuousness of wealth is implicit in the term *maojian*, which is used at times to designate prosperous households in the press and means literally "to stand out," or "to be conspicuous." The bestowal of such a label is not an unmitigated honor in that the heightened visibility it suggests is more than metaphoric. Such households are subject to the invidious gaze of their neighbors and of local officials who, in the latter case, carry the authority to define proper economic behavior. A great deal of uncertainty and anxiety results from this communal surveillance for the households subjected to it. This anxiety is in part a legacy of the past, when to stand out in this way was foolish if not dangerous, but it is also equally a product of the present. The line between proper and improper pathways to wealth has not remained fixed and continues to be defined in practice.

Prosperous households are often painfully aware of their ambiguous status. Their experience of earlier periods of economic liberalization warns them to hide their success for fear that a sudden policy reversal should leave them vulnerable in a new campaign. At the same time, however, local cadres are eager to recognize them as local models that demonstrate the success of the new policies in the area under their jurisdiction. Public recognition is publicly acknowledged by posting their names on a village honor roll or by broadcasting their success over the loudspeaker system. This publicity not only is meant to legitimate the prosperity of these households in the eyes of the local community, but in doing so it offers them as newly defined models of economic behavior for emulation by others too timid to expose themselves in this way. Unfortunately, this public approbation carries with it the negative result of making prosperous households even more conspicuous and thereby intensifying their anxiety that they not slip from the path of economic rectitude in a terrain that has no map.

The anxiety produced by public scrutiny of these households was depicted in a brief fictional account of a prosperous household in the *Fujian*

Daily (January 12, 1982). The head of this household is surnamed Shi, but he is called "Old Mao" by his neighbors. Here Mao is short for *maojian hu*; however, the identical ideograph is not only a Chinese surname but can also be interpreted to mean "to risk," "to be bold," "to falsely claim," all of which carry potential significance for this story. The story begins with the engagement of Old Mao's son, now over thirty years old. This event crowns the family's present prosperity, which has arrived finally after great hardship. According to custom, an engagement present of a wristwatch must be presented to the future daughter-in-law. Fashion dictates that this wristwatch be the stylish "Iron Anchor" brand, completely automatic, with a luminous dial that shows the date in both the Western and lunar calendars.

To purchase this highly desired item, Old Mao must go to the black market. When he demurs, his wife encourages him by insisting that even the cadres, who should know better, are not afraid to buy black market goods. The rest of the story describes Old Mao's path to the marketplace and his feelings of shame when he is observed and taunted by a man who formerly bore the label of "capitalist tail." As a result of his shame, he ends up not buying the watch, and the pressure to fulfill his social obligation with that particular gift is lifted when he discovers that the family of his son's future in-laws is even more ideologically correct than he. The story is pervaded by the old man's consciousness of people watching him and his concern over how he is perceived by them. What seems most real about the story is Old Mao's straining to fit the role of economic rectitude that has been placed on him.

Public scrutiny concerns not only how one chooses to spend one's newly acquired wealth but also how one obtains it. For the mirror image of the *maojian hu* is what the press often refers to as the *baofa hu*. This term translates freely as "upstart" or nouveau riche. More literally, however, *baofa* carries a meaning of explosive energy and force. A household so designated has gained its wealth with a speed that cannot be accounted for entirely as due to a natural increase produced by one's own labor. The implication is that dark economic forces have "produced" this wealth: exploitation, speculation, extortion, and fraud. The expressions *maojian hu* and *baofa hu* therefore mark the difference between honest labor and "economic crime." This suspicion of the unnatural growth of wealth is not simply a "primitive Marxism" that may be interpreted from certain folkways on the capitalist periphery.[13] In China, the consciousness of capital as an aspect of social relations has been actively cultivated through the writing of local histories on the exploitative nature of pre-Liberation class and market relations.[14] This carefully cultivated consciousness conditions the atmosphere surrounding economic activities that, although now legal, come dangerously close to what once defined capitalist relations, such as hired labor. Most of the anxiety attached to the designation of the *maojian hu* is, as I already suggested, its reversibility. Not only is there the possibility of a policy reversal (now increasingly distant), but there also have been cases in which locally admired *maojian hu* were subsequently revealed to have engaged in improper economic activities that not only reversed their status but also exposed them to legal action for economic crimes.

The Obligations of Wealth

The ambivalence attached to the status of *maojian hu* does not derive solely from official voices but conjoins with local sentiment regarding economic equity and the social obligations attendant on economic success. These sentiments do not arise from an "essential" peasant morality but are in part the residue of a socialist morality carefully cultivated during the previous two decades. The sudden wealth of a few households in a community where the means for achieving prosperity may be limited or felt to be unfairly distributed also may engender intense feelings of envy and resentment that can intensify the sentiments about wealth that derive from a socialist morality. In China these powerful emotions of envy and desire are referred to in the press and in everyday speech as "red eye disease." The present use of this expression in the press has made it into a means of dismissing popular discontent about widening economic differences between households as characteristic of a "small producer's mentality." This reduction is an attempt to deny the potential inequities in the present economic environment.

Prosperous households are not unaware of these sentiments among their neighbors and kin, and, in fact, the community has its own ways of making these sentiments known to those who are judged to be holding back on their obligations. In a discussion of village-level reciprocity, we may perhaps distinguish between rituals of sociability and those that acknowledge economic difference. Communal banqueting confirms and celebrates the already existing social relations that define the community. Many of these social rituals are concentrated during the New Year's holiday, and that is why in the weeks preceding it the frequency of items in the press discouraging large-scale banqueting and the giving of gifts rises dramatically. For instance, a letter from Heilongjiang complains of the local custom of circulating the obligation to donate a pig for the annual New Year's feast in one production team.[15] In this case, the writer states the official position on such customs that it is a burden on the household so obligated each year. "It's no small thing for peasants to raise a pig!" On a smaller scale, banqueting is also an important means of acknowledging a debt or soliciting a favor. Or it may be the expression of a network of social and economic relations involving several households. The *Chinese Peasant Gazette* (May 30, 1982) published a letter it had received from cadres in seven provinces, all complaining about the reciprocal banqueting among labor exchange groups, a form of mutual aid that has reappeared with the implementation of the responsibility system.

In contrast to these rituals of sociability, there are also customary rites through which the community recognizes individual prosperity. Folkways, which border on ritual, act as a form of gentle extortion on those who display the visible markers of prosperity. Again, many of these rites also occur during the New Year's season. One such custom in Hunan province is called "greeting the new house," when the dragon lanterns and lion dancers visit each new house in turn to revel until the master of the house distributes red envelopes containing money.[16] The amounts are small, but they too are defined by official voices as a heavy economic burden.[17] Yet another letter complains that with increasing prosperity, the obligation to give gifts to neighbors and kin to mark such traditional occasions as a baby's "full month" ceremony has also increased.[18] Failure to give or to give enough opens oneself up to accusations of miserliness or of "not following the custom of the neighborhood." The letter ends with the plaintive remark: "When will the meat be fully cooked in one's own pot?"

The revival of folkways and social obligations that require wealthy individuals to be generous in return for social recognition of their success is categorically condemned as a kind of "victimization" due to the backward ideology of their social environment. There are other forms as well: constant asking for handouts, borrowing of small loans which are never returned, taking tools or produce without asking, and outright sabotage of household enterprises are frequently cited in letters from disgruntled or worried peasants.[19] Their concern is not only for their material loss, but also for what these claims may ultimately portend. For the obverse side of the fear of polarization is the fear of policy reversal that may call into question their present economic practice.

Wealthy peasants are especially vulnerable to this fear when these claims come from local officials who have the power to obstruct their progress or to label them as negative examples. There can be no doubt that a certain breed of local officials takes advantage of this fear on the part of prosperous households to engage in a mild and continuous extortion of goods and favors from them. But this need not be true of those rural cadres who may act from a sense of conviction in exacting contributions from them for collective projects. In fact this sort of drama is frequently represented in press accounts of generous acts made by newly prosperous households in ways that are officially approved.[20]

One example provides a striking parallel to the more traditional process of a public subscription of wealthy individuals for ritual activities. The brigade party branch of a Hunan village called a meeting of the local leadership to discuss funding for the renovation of the local school. The meeting was interrupted by the arrival one by one of the more prosperous peasants of the community who came to offer their "unsolicited" contributions. The first to appear was a peasant, a "specialized household" in pen making, who handed over a red envelope containing 100 yuan. This act of public generosity was accompanied by his wife saying, "We are well-off because the party's policies are good. It is our duty to give a little money for the school." When another specialized household heard the news, he hurried to the meeting and gave 120 yuan to make up for being slow to contribute. Several key households followed, each contributing 100 yuan. Less prosperous households gave 5 or 10 yuan. Altogether the collection totaled almost twice the required sum.[21]

In the above account, the wealthier members of a community are seen competing with each other in matching or exceeding the contributions in a competitive display of generosity: the potlatch.[22] The first contributor may well have been an "activist" who consciously set up the conditions for competitive generosity. The others were quick to pick up the challenge, motivated by both political pressures and social expectations. In any case the pattern for ideal behavior had been set. Those households who had been perceived as benefiting in a special way from the new economic policies knew that they had better make a generous showing or suffer the consequences, either loss of face in the present or political problems in the indefinite future.

It is hard to determine the degree to which the officially sanctioned potlatch, performed in the name of the party, truly supersedes those forces that derive from a village morality. Some sort of negotiation between the two is being continually worked out. The impulse to generosity in the name of the party is perhaps quite often an indirect response to community expectation. The party clearly cannot completely disregard egalitarian sentiment in the countryside without losing an important element in its own prestige.

Officially approved acts of generosity need not always be displayed in such a public and overtly competitive way. Individual acts of generosity are often praised in the press. Often one sees the headline "After Getting Rich" with a description of ideal behavior. One such account commends a party member named Lin who had prospered in the development of household sidelines. His annual income grew to 8,000 yuan, which made him one of the wealthiest households in the county. But despite his success, he was always solicitous of households less well-off than himself. He helped other families get started in their own sidelines by lending them money.[23] In two years, he had lent out a total of 6,000 yuan. One neighbor helped by this man was moved to say, "He has cut off his own flesh to stick to mine" (an extremely graphic image of "leveling"). Others accused him of stupidity. Lin's response was simply that he became a party member in order to lead everybody to prosperity and enhance the glory of the party.[24]

Through the publication of such stories, the image of the wealthy peasant, victimized by the unwelcome demands of poorer kin and neighbors, is transformed into the image of the selfless individual, voluntarily casting aside self-interest for the good of the collectivity. This selflessness is represented as deriving from the knowledge of the greater good, a consciousness which is, of course, the product of the party's beneficent instruction. The party appropriates for itself the charisma of the gift in that what is owed to the community is given in its name. The important difference, of course, is that the guarantee of economic equity is no longer institutionalized through the organization of production but is now dependent on the party's ability to generate a moral climate in which individuals feel obligated to share their prosperity with others. The degree to which they are successful in doing this is difficult to measure from a distance. Perhaps it is only possible here to note that the attempt is made.

Socialist Realism and Lived Reality

The proliferation of labels that locate households in the current discourse on the rural economy is readily apparent in their widespread use in publicity that celebrates the success of the new policies. The *hu* has therefore become reconstituted as a publicity object in addition to its other objectifications in current use. However, households designated by these labels often experience their new status in sometimes surprising ways. The charisma of success (or what appears as the promise of success) attracts to itself considerable attention that often provides an ironic gloss on the "conspicuousness" of the *maojian hu*.

Publicity by means of the official media as well as by word-of-mouth can spread the fame of a successful household over a wide area. Reference to individual households is made in the press by name and locale when they are designated as county-level or even provincial- or national-level models. This attention brings with it a number of problems for the households so designated. First of all, the publicity elicits a steady stream of curious individuals, official delegations from higher levels of administration, and others from nearby units or localities who are eager to "observe" the operation of successful household enterprises to learn the "secret" of their success. These visits not only hinder production but also become a serious drain on household resources to provide the cost of hospitality.

The notoriety of these households is also frequently accompanied by the sort of harassment often experienced by lottery winners in the United

States. Sudden wealth in a society that has only recently departed from an ideal of collective prosperity becomes the kind of wealth on which everyone feels they have some sort of a claim. However, due to the scale of the publicity surrounding these households, the claims made on their generosity far exceed those that derive from community norms of reciprocity. Letters and requests pour in from petitioners throughout the country asking for financial help.

Yet another effect of this process of objectification is the appearance of the model without the substance. A letter to the *People's Daily* (January 29, 1984) describes the experience of a young peasant who found himself propelled into the role of a highly publicized specialized household due to the expectations that were raised by his initiative in contracting 40 *mou* of fishpond. The news of his venture was out before he was able to stock the pond, drawing the attention of radio and newspaper reporters. The intensity of this media exposure made him elated and yet fearful of failure. He invested 2,000 yuan in stocking the pond and worked his entire household to the point of exhaustion. He began to wonder whether the designation of "specialized household" was worth the tremendous effort which made regular agricultural work look easy by comparison.

After six months of hard work, the yield was extremely low due to a number of unforeseen problems. Despite this poor showing, however, the brigade party secretary reported good results to the higher-level authorities and delegations were sent from a number of government offices to observe for themselves. Somehow this failed enterprise was miraculously transformed into an astonishing success in its re-creation as a media event. Persons interested in learning the skills of fish production arrived in an endless stream. The annual income of this new "specialized household" totaled only 2,000 yuan in its second year of operation. This was duly reported to the county party headquarters, who then declared him a "10,000 yuan household." He was selected as a local model to represent other fish-producing "specialized households" and was sent to meetings at the county, district, and provincial levels. His letter concludes sadly by stating that his is a very peculiar kind of achievement.

This story demonstrates rather convincingly that "socialist realism" is not a genre confined to art or literature but one that extends into the experience of one's lived reality. The designation of these labels is part of a fiction that the state creates about itself and the effectiveness of its policies.[25] The success of a model household depends to a certain extent on its ability to jump into this fiction and improvise. From the above case, one sees that these "false models" may not necessarily be willing to participate in the fiction, and yet they find themselves subject to a momentum they can no longer control. Despite their ability to maintain the guise of success, they may be only too aware of the duplicity of the charade they are performing. The situation demands a reconstitution of the self in relation to power, but the self that is created is a highly conscious, unauthentic self forced to play a role despite a constant fear of exposure.

This blurring of the line between authenticity and illusion is certainly not new; the creation of "false models" is well documented for the high tides of earlier campaigns. Hinton's account of the Great Leap and its aftermath provides plenty of ironic examples of the gap between official ambitions and the practical difficulties of realizing them.[26] In that earlier time, pressures to embody the ideal were imposed on entire communities, while now, individual households continue to be subject to this pressure.

A recent novella by Gu Hua documents the pressures placed on a small mountain community to take on the appearance of the Dazhai ideal, which proved monumentally unsuited to its economic difficulties. It abandoned its disastrous attempts to emulate a model impossible for them and reorganized production on the basis of household contracting. The year was 1968, ten years too early. The responsibility system was condemned at that time as "taking the capitalist road." The secret of their economic misbehavior involved the entire community in a conspiracy of silence. Their dramatic success in raising productivity attracted the attention of the "higher-ups." The village now had to assume the appearance of the model of the Dazhai type and became itself a local-level model for others to emulate. Higher-level cadres and study teams swarmed to Pagoda Ridge to "study" the success of this once-poor mountain community. The entire village engaged in an elaborate performance to sustain the fiction of the Dazhai ideal. The team leader was sent to distant conferences to talk about the success of Pagoda Ridge. When the truth was revealed, he was arrested and sent to labor camp for "setting up an independent kingdom."[27] The dynamic that engendered the imposture of Pagoda Ridge is not so different from the one that produces similar impostures today. This continuity perhaps mirrors a continuity in the relations of power despite the dramatic changes that have taken place in the economic domain.

The Golden Treasure of Leshan

Publicity that features households remarkable for their very "enterprisingness" also marks them as targets ripe for the fleecing through fraudulent enterprises. A story in *People's Daily* (March 23, 1984) is an especially novel instance of this phenomenon. A group of young people started a rumor that in 1937 Mao Renfeng, the Guomindang head of security, had buried a treasury of gold under the foot of the great Buddha of Leshan in Sichuan province. The secret was said to have been entrusted to a Buddhist monk who died at the venerable age of 108 years. By this time, however, the secret of the treasure had already been passed on to the ringleader of this scam operation while he had been imprisoned with the monk during the Cultural Revolution. This young man could produce four pieces of evidence as proof of his story: a tape recording of the monk's voice telling the story of the treasury as he lay dying, a photograph of the cave entrance, a set of three keys needed to gain entry to the cave, and a document reporting the existence of the treasury.

The scam worked as follows. The avowed intent of the group was to alert the state to the existence of the treasure. Presumably once it was recovered, the state would return 20–30 percent of its value to those who had reported its whereabouts. The young man in possession of the evidence claimed to be exhausted in his efforts to get the information into the hands of the proper authorities. He had written to various levels of government to report the treasure, but the state remained singularly unresponsive to his claims. Other problems intervened. Part of his difficulty was due, he said, to the presence of numerous Guomindang agents at all levels of government. In desperation the young man offered to reveal the secret of the treasure and all the particulars as to its location to certain celebrated peasant households in return for a share, paid in advance, of the expected reward, in hopes that they might succeed in getting the information into the proper bureaucratic channels.

Among the peasants who contributed large amounts was a "famous *maojian hu*" in Sichuan province who contributed a total of 9,700 yuan. A peasant from Shanxi contributed 4,000 yuan, and a Gansu herdsman paid 3,400 yuan. These are not insignificant sums. Others contributed smaller amounts, raising the money by borrowing or by selling what liquefiable assets they had available, such as lumber, a scarce resource made scarer still by the current rage for housebuilding. One can surmise from the character of the victims and their widely spaced places of origin that the group found their fattest marks through the publicity that surrounds the success of these model households.

In regarding this scam as a popular culture text, we must take into account certain of its elements that were borrowed from other developments in the heady environment of the liberalization. First of all, the theme of recovering buried gold was very much in the popular consciousness. One possible source of this theme was a film, immensely popular at the time, called "Shenmi de dafo" (The mysterious Great Buddha), the plot of which featured a fictional search for a valuable gold statue hidden somewhere in the Great Buddha of Leshan. As popular entertainment, the film clearly tested the extent to which cultural production would be allowed to depart from the canon of socialist realism and participate in more crass forms of commercial exploitation. For this reason, it drew considerable criticism from official voices in Peking who condemned it for aping *gongfu* movies, being, therefore, a form of "spiritual pollution" emanating out of the capitalist deformation of Chinese culture in Hong Kong.

Another source of this theme of buried gold was possibly the publicity surrounding the digging up of money and valuables hidden by peasant households during previous political campaigns.[28] Official encouragement to prosper has created an urgent need among more enterprising households for ready capital to set themselves up in sideline enterprises. At the same time, through these publicized cases, the state has delivered a message that the recovery of this hidden wealth would not be likely to bring official reprisals as long as a certain portion of it was surrendered to the state. In the new economic atmosphere, returns on the remaining capital would easily compensate for this loss and were incentive enough to take the risk of revealing hidden wealth. This theme of sharing the discovery or recovery of buried wealth with the state is replicated in the scam.

The most interesting aspect of the story, however, is the question of entitlement. No one seems to question the moral as well as the jural right of the state to the treasure; and in fact, this is precisely the premise upon which the scam operates. If one were to read this as a "folk" image of the state, then one would see a state authority, popularly perceived to have a moral right to hidden wealth (or at least, to a well-defined portion thereof), but through its sheer bureaucratic weight and corruption (the presence of Guomindang spies at every level), it displays a singular lack of responsiveness to repeated reports of the treasure. The scam provides us with an ironic commentary that counters Kafka's story "The Great Wall of China" in which the message sent from the capital is never received or received too late to prevent the wedding of the fabulous with the historical present. Perhaps in the distance created between a state and its people, when socialist realism blends with lived reality, there also opens up a space in which other fictions can be spun that derive from below.

The Post-Mao "Socialist Imaginary"

In the years since the death of Mao, there has been a tendency among foreign observers to overestimate the effects of the new economic policies on rural political culture. The degree to which the household has been granted autonomy in economic decisions has been somewhat overstated. As should be apparent above, the economic practice of the peasant household is, to a significant degree, conditioned by a political discourse that creates categories and retains the power to assign economic actors to them. This power to assign difference is still firmly in the hands of the state/party apparatus, providing it with a mechanism to control indirectly the pace and direction of change in economic practice.[29] This indirect control suggests that, although the organization of production has undergone dramatic changes, these have not been accompanied by any significant change in the relations of power between state and society. One could support this assertion by looking further to other areas where this marking of difference displays the power of the state. An obvious example would be the implementation of the one-child family which entails a surveillance so intensive that families are categorized by the way they comply or fail to comply with the policy. It is perhaps no accident that just when the state has chosen to "loosen" its hold on production, it has simultaneously chosen to tighten its grasp on reproduction with such force as to obliterate the rights of the individual for "the common good," making women's bodies the instruments of the state, subject to a number of disciplinary procedures, in reference to a plan.[30] Whereas the birth policy may well imply an important shifting of the locus of control, I would still insist that control over economic practice is far from being completely relaxed, and that indeed, the debate continues over the degree to which control may be relinquished in the economic sphere and the extent to which this relaxation threatens the definition of a "socialism with Chinese characteristics" as a socialism that allows the free development of the productive forces without relinquishing its own ideal of itself as a scientifically planned and ordered society, and therefore, one that cannot fall heir to the contradictions of untrammeled capitalism, its constituting "Other."

In exploring the issues of power and control implied above, one could perhaps evoke here Lefort's critique of Soviet totalitarianism, identified by him, not as a specific political regime (such as the dictatorship of a Stalin or Franco, or even a Mao), but as a newly evolved form of society, "a metamorphosis of society itself in which the political ceases to exist as a separate sphere."[31] The diffusion of politics throughout society is intended to create a fusion between state and civil society, but in effect it merely projects an imaginary unity, "the image of a society at one with itself."[32] In so doing it creates new forms of separation and alienation: "everywhere people run up against the norms of the party and confront it as an alien body whose power is imposed on society. The party thus creates new divisions, new lines of conflict, new forms of vulnerability, whereas it claims to abolish all division and to govern in the interests of society as a whole."[33] The discussion above offers two ways in which this alienation finds expression: in the socialist realist fictions of policy makers and in counterrepresentations emanating from below. The juxtaposition of the two offers an interesting perspective from which to view the dynamic of state power in the post-Mao period.

The image of the enlightened kulak as the vanguard of the new policies holds out a promise to those who are at present less privileged economically. Despite the reappearance of economic differentiation under the current policies, the party continues to propagate the image of a society "at one with itself," as one in which economic differences at this stage of socialism are qualitatively different than they were in the old society, or would be under a capitalist system. Economic differences are therefore "rewritten" as points along a trajectory toward an economic prosperity that all will share in time. What makes the difference is, of course, the enlightened leadership of the party whose sustained vigilance in economic matters is insurance against the reappearance of exploitative practices. Hence the constant need to define and redefine the difference between proper and improper economic practice, even as the difference between socialism and free-market economism becomes whittled gradually away.

This emphasis on the "imaginary" is the basis for the forms of imposture described above. Where the pressure to sustain the fiction of the efficacy of party policy overwhelms the material constraints on realizing them, the unfortunate individuals who get caught up in this fiction experience a curious form of alienation: a doubleness that denies their real material conditions of existence. This could be described as a communicational maladaptation, in which the party, in its effort to sustain the "social imaginary" of a society "at one with itself" insists on a hypercoherence of economic practice, across the board, with disregard for local conditions: what in China is referred to as "one cut of the knife."

This maladaptation is nothing less than a perversion of the mass line, through which information on the efficacy of party policy is meant to travel up to the central organs of control so that policies can be reformulated to fine tune them to material conditions. This maladaptation is just as egregious in the present as it was in the past. Just as collective organization was imposed on local economies which lacked the material conditions to sustain it successfully, so has decollectivization been forced on communities who prospered under collective organization and were loathe to give it up. Despite the present emphasis on "seeking truth from facts," the pressure from above for conformity with the prevailing policy continues. The situation described in *Pagoda Ridge*, in which a local team leader goes against the tide to institute a household contract system in opposition to the collective ideals of Dazhai, is replicated in the present. A more recent folk hero is Zhang Zhenliang, the party secretary of Doudian in a rural county near Beijing who was criticized for his refusal to decollectivize in order to preserve high levels of mechanization. His persistence has now paid off and he has been relabeled as a model, which demonstrates the value of collective organization now that the initial momentum of the responsibility system has given rise to new contradictions.[34]

This lack of responsiveness on the part of the central authorities does not mean that the mass line does not function. On the contrary, the early experimentation with various forms of contract systems is an explicit example of how it should work. In the early post-Mao years, when the economic reforms were still new, there was more of a dialectic between local practice and the reformulation of policy at the center.[35] Once this crisis of identity was, to some degree, resolved and a newly defined socialism gradually found its practical form, however, the push toward hyperconformity with a centrally defined model repeated the errors of the past. The image of the state as a massive bureaucracy unresponsive to local initiative thereby became the means by which the scam of the "Golden Treasure of Leshan" could operate. Despite the recent changes, the social imaginary of a society at one with itself is continuous with its Maoist past, and so are the specific forms of contradiction to which it gives rise. Sustaining the image of what the state dreams itself to be takes precedence over accommodation to local needs.

A return to the opening theme of this essay opens the question of where, in this discussion of the post-Mao social imaginary, can one situate a popular discourse on wealth and morality? To what extent does it derive from a prerevolutionary communal ideology or from the Maoist political culture that prevailed until 1976? Moreover, given the fact that I have made a distinction between popular ways of asserting communal claims on the individual that mirror traditional folkways and those that the state finds appropriate, does this distinction mirror a difference in origin, or does it bear a much more complex relationship to a prerevolutionary morality and its Maoist transformations? In addressing this question, I am of course observing my data from a great distance, picking out as best I can what appears to be a popular voice in texts that derive from the official media. Under conditions that push one's interpretive skills to the limit, theoretical biases cannot help but be made evident. My own interpretation rests on the idea that given the history of the past forty years of revolution and political activism, popular expressions that assert communal claims on the wealthy, no matter how traditional a form these claims may take, cannot help but be informed by that history. Ideologies do not float untransformed through history but are dialectically constituted within it. What may be identified as a traditional Confucian ethic of personal relations is itself the product of a complicated dialectic between state and popular ideologies through several thousand years of history. The postrevolutionary state defines itself against this ethic even while partaking of it, to the extent that a Confucian ideal of the responsibilities of the state to ensure a just society is part of its own self-image. Although the relationship of the socialist state toward what it now dismisses as "peasant egalitarianism" has been complex and uneven, its own self-image is too bound up with the idea of economic equity to abandon it completely lest it be appropriated by the popular domain. And lest one fall prey to the temptation to dismiss this egalitarian sentiment to some essential notion of a peasant moral economy, one must reconsider the efficacy of the socialist state in inscribing the past with a mythic history to justify its present. Finally, given the very real accomplishments of Chinese socialism, it would seem incredible that those who are not participating in the present prosperity should fail to note that what is making that prosperity happen for some is to a certain extent based on an agricultural and rural industrial infrastructure that was built up under collective management at the expense of communal privation and collective labor! This is becoming more apparent as ten years of reform have produced a deterioration of this rural infrastructure due to the lack of collective accumulation of capital.[36]

Finally, one should not underestimate the force of popular enthusiasm for a folk conception of the socialist utopia, even when that conception may seem, at first glance, unsophisticated and naive. In a recent story by the peasant writer Gao Xiaosheng, his protagonist may have envisioned the achievement of socialism in very material terms: "To Li Shunda, building socialism meant to build an upstairs and a downstairs with electric lights and a telephone."[37] But implicit in that conception was the universal achievement of that ideal and not just its realization for a few.

Notes

1. Andrew Watson, "Agriculture Looks for 'Shoes That Fit': The Production Responsibility System and Its Implications," *World Development* 2, 8 (1983): 712.

2. Anita Chan, Richard Madsen, and Jonathan Unger, *Chen Village: The Recent History of a Peasant Community in Mao's China* (Berkeley: University of California Press, 1984), for an account of some of the negative results of contracting everything out. I have perhaps overstated the present degree of decentralization. See also Andrew Watson, "New Structure in the Organization of Chinese Agriculture: A Variable Model," *Pacific Affairs*, 57, 4 (Winter 1984–85): 621–45, which describes how the collective organization continues to function and how this functioning may vary according to local circumstances.

3. A major source of information has been letters to the editor that have appeared in Chinese newspapers in the post-Mao period. These letters often report problems and complaints that newly prosperous peasants encounter. A series of such letters appeared in the *People's Daily* under the slogan "How to treat newly prosperous peasants?" over a period of several months in 1984.

4. For instance, the first ten months of 1984 showed a dramatic increase in the number of civil cases involving threats to the legitimate rights and interests of specialized households (JPRS-CPS, March 4, 1985, p. 35).

5. Kaut's study of contractual relations among Tagalogs is remarkably similar to parallel processes in Chinese society. The limits of reciprocity in Tagalog society are expressed by the term *pahingi*, which apparently means "to ask for something which is needed from someone who has the obligation and ability to grant it." See Charles

Kaut, "Utang no loob: A System of Contractual Obligation Among Tagalogs," *Southwestern Journal of Anthropology* 17 (1961): 261. My thanks to Aram Yengoyan for this reference.

6. Chandra Jayawerdana, "Ideology and Conflict in Lower Class Communities," *Comparative Studies in Society and History* 10 (1968): 413–46.

7. See Eric Wolf, "Types of Latin American Peasantry: A Preliminary Discussion," *American Anthropologist* 57, 3 (1955): 454–71, for the classic definition of such communities in Latin America. Some the superficial similarities with the Chinese village of the 1960s and 1970s include integration into the larger society channeled through an organized communal structure, communal land ownership, state demands on production imposed on the level of collective ownership, restricted consumption, and a cult of poverty. One could stretch a point to say further that the family in these Latin American communities as the "unit for the restriction of consumption and the increase of unpaid performance of work" parallels the work team in the Chinese village, especially for the period when moral incentives were emphasized at the expense of material rewards to increase production. Parrish and Whyte have also noted some aspects of this resemblance. See William L. Parrish and Martin K. Whyte, *Village and Family in Contemporary China* (Chicago: University of Chicago Press, 1978), p. 303.

8. A study of Ying county in Shanxi province revealed that 43 percent of the households primarily engaged in specialized economic activities were cadres or former cadres. Forty-two percent were educated youth and demobilized soldiers. This suggests that those individuals with experience in economic management and contacts outside the village are the ones most likely to prosper under the new policies. *People's Daily*, January 5, 1984.

9. See Sidney L. Greenblatt, ed., *The People of Taihang: An Anthology of Family Histories* (White Plains, N.Y.: International Arts and Sciences Press, 1976), Introduction, for a discussion of how this history was invoked as a warning of the reversibility of class struggle.

10. See Richard C. Kraus, *Class Conflict in Chinese Socialism* (New York: Columbia University Press, 1981), for a detailed discussion of class as caste in contemporary China.

11. In fact, in many areas the policy to encourage diversification worked too well, and positive incentives for households specializing in grain production had to be reinstated to counter the market incentives for abandoning grain agriculture in favor of more lucrative sidelines.

12. I deal with it more fully in two other papers: "Magical Practice, Birth Policy, and Women's Health in Post-Mao China" and "The Moral Transformation of the Countryside." See also Ann Anagnost, "Hegemony and the Improvisation of Resistance: Political Culture and Popular Practice in Contemporary China," Ph.D. dissertation, University of Michigan, 1985.

13. See Michael Taussig, *The Devil and Commodity Fetishism in Latin America* (Chapel Hill: University of North Carolina Press, 1980).

14. A chapter from my dissertation "The Uses of the Past: Representations of Class and Market Relations in a Local History," discusses how this history has been written, rewritten, and performed in the years since Liberation.

15. *Chinese Peasant Gazette*, February 1, 1981, p. 5.

16. Economic prosperity has been accompanied by a veritable explosion in housebuilding. A new house is a visible marker of household prosperity that figures prominently, among other things, in assessing the desirability of the household by prospective daughters-in-law.

17. *Chinese Peasant Gazette*, February 1, 1981, p. 5.

18. Ibid., January 4, 1981, p. 5.

19. See *People's Daily*, April 15, 1984, for sabotage; March 24, 1984, for failure to repay small loans; January 25, 1984, for theft; and *China Daily*, January 22, 1985, p. 6, also for petty theft. Prosperous peasants also become the victims of more overtly criminal elements. See *Sichuan Daily*, February 2, 1985, for the case of a specialized household who became the victim of a protection racket. He received a letter from "The Fourteen Heavenly Heroes" ordering him to pay 5,000 yuan or risk bringing harm to his entire family.

20. One cartoon, for example, lampoons the myriad claims on the wealth of the newly prosperous, in this case a "specialized household." A chicken farmer is confronted with a steady stream of visitors, all bearing claims on his generosity under the guise of congratulations. The first carries a congratulatory banner in one hand and an empty chicken cage in the other. Presumably he doesn't intend to leave empty-handed. The others each bear in turn an account book which records the payment of "special" surcharges, a briefcase to receive *guanxi* contributions (gifts to bureaucrats to insure their continued goodwill), a book to record contributions given to the collective as a demonstration of the proper ideological attitude, and finally a placard announcing special "stipends" to friends and kin. The use of animal representation evokes the popular saying "The weasel visits the hen." The implied ending is, of course, "Up to no good intentions."

21. *People's Daily*, January 25, 1984.

22. Perhaps one can define the essence of the potlatch here as "returning with interest gifts received in such a way that the creditor becomes the debtor." See Marcel Mauss, *The Gift: Forms and Functions of Exchange in Archaic Societies* (New York: Norton, 1967), p. 35. The term is used metaphorically here. In this context, the competitive display of generosity takes the form of individual contributions to the collectivity, rather than the classic sense of shaming one's guest through a display of generosity. By putting the community in one's debt, so to speak, a household can not only attempt to defuse immediate feelings of envy and resentment, but it may also be intended to accrue "credit" against the possibility of a future policy reversal. At the same time, it garners for the giver a significant store of symbolic capital.

23. In addition to money, specialized households are encouraged to share their tools, production expertise, and marketing skills.

24. *Chinese Peasant Gazette*, October 3, 1982. With local party branches increasingly urged to recruit prosperous peasants into the party, one wonders if this sort of generous behavior is not obligatory for party membership. For instance, an Anhui peasant, after becoming a 10,000-yuan household, set up the rest of his village in a sideline enterprise that qualified him for party membership. *People's Daily*, April 18, 1984.

25. The problem of "false models" must be frequent enough judging from the number of editorials that appear on this topic. See, for example, "Model Must Be

Worthy of the Title," *China Daily*, February 20, 1986, and "Philosophy of Balance Misused," ibid., March 1, 1986. This problem is of course related to a much larger one, that of misreporting to higher authorities. See "Strictly Guard Against Being Prone to Boasting and Exaggeration," *China Daily Report*, December 5, 1984, p. K6.

26. William Hinton, *Shenfan* (New York: Random House, 1983).

27. Gu Hua, the author of *Pagoda Ridge*, says that he based his story on real events that he heard about when he was in the Wuling Mountains in southern Hunan in 1977. A team leader had been arrested that year and sentenced to nine years imprisonment: one year for each of the nine years he had "followed the capitalist road." See Gu Hua, "Pagoda Ridge," *Chinese Literature* (Summer 1984): 161–254.

28. The incentive to hide wealth continues to operate for some households who feel that public perception of their increasing prosperity may prove to be a potential source of danger. See *Zhongguo nongmin bao*, November 11, 1982, for the story of a Hubei peasant who had been labeled a *baofa hu* in an earlier campaign. He buried some valuables on the household's private plot and reported to the local authorities that he had been robbed. This was in response to public discussion that had condemned his taking on several "apprentices" in his duck-raising business as "capitalist exploitation of labor."

29. It would be interesting to pose here the possibility of popular categories that may be used in opposition to those that occur in official discourse. One example might be the epithet *nengren* (able person), which opposes the negative connotations of *baofa hu* with a more positive appreciation for the skillful use of *ji* (stratagem), used to subvert or work the official structure for one's own ends. The stories of *baofa hu* that appear in the press not uncommonly refer to the fact that the wile of these individuals was first widely admired before its meaning was rewritten by official voices.

30. This thesis is developed in considerably more detail in my unpublished paper, "Magical Practice, Birth Policy, and Women's Health in Post-Mao China."

31. This discussion owes much to John Thompson's helpful Introduction to Claude Lefort, *The Political Forms of Modern Society: Bureaucracy, Democracy, Totalitarianism* (Cambridge: MIT Press, 1986), p. 79.

32. Ibid., p. 6.

33. Ibid., p. 7.

34. *Wall Street Journal*, January 19, 1988, p. 24.

35. Watson, "Agriculture Looks for 'Shoes that Fit.' "

36. Since the institution of the reforms, rural irrigation works have increasingly deteriorated to the extent that the state is initiating a controversial compulsory labor program for their maintenance. *Wall Street Journal*, January 19, 1988, p. 24.

37. Gao Xiaosheng, "Lin Shuda Builds a House," in *The New Realism: Writings from China After the Cultural Revolution*, ed. Lee Yee (New York: Hippocrene Books, 1983).

12

HEGEMONY AND PRODUCTIVITY: WORKERS IN POST-MAO CHINA

Lisa Rofel

The economic reforms the party-state in China has introduced into urban industries have one essential goal: raising workers' productivity. No longer portrayed as the bearers of a revolutionary consciousness, workers, under the current ideological regime, are loudly and publicly blamed for the ills to which industrial production is said to have befallen during the Cultural Revolution—and implicitly during the entire Maoist era.[1] The Cultural Revolution, one often hears, inculcated a lazy work ethic in workers. This laziness is metonymically captured in the four-character idiom *chi daquo fan*, "eating out of one big pot." State bureaucrats and factory managers now hope to instill in workers a disciplined[2] approach to work through the institution of new, hierarchical wage and bonus systems, with differential rewards and punishments. Through their negative characterization of workers, managers and state cadres justify forcing them to submit to these pressures for higher productivity.

This essay addresses current social relations of production in China's urban industry by examining this issue of productivity. My concern is not primarily with production statistics, which, while they have their use, fail to enlighten us about the social process through which workers have experienced these changes. Indeed, statistics taken by themselves tend to obscure the dimension of human agency and gloss over the issues that provoke the greatest intensity of feeling. To paraphrase the English historian E. P. Thompson, behind these seemingly objective statistics lies a complex structure of human relationships, a structure that legitimates certain types of conflicts and inhibits others.[3]

My discussion of workers and productivity therefore begins with the assumption that "productivity" stands for something more than simply a concept self-evidently tied to measurement and quantification. More significantly, it represents a discourse on the values that the state and factory managers currently attach to what they measure: specifically, values attached to age hierarchies, the division between mental and manual labor, and gendered work relations. Attempts to increase productivity have both refracted and given rise to a constellation of cultural meanings and practices diametrically opposed to those of earlier socialist work relations in China.[4] Moreover, this discourse, at once a social and ideological process, is one in which workers challenge and sometimes resist the domination of reform. Workers' contestation of production pressures stems not from mere laziness, as state cadres and factory managers would have it, but from their experience of past practices, the memory of which serves to raise serious questions about the state's current fixation with productivity.[5] Some workers continue to claim the importance of other aspects of their lives currently dismissed as hindrances to "efficiency," and in so doing, they implicitly call into question whether "productivity" should be the exclusive goal of production.

In addressing workers' productivity, this essay speaks to two additional theoretical questions: the concept of socialism and the issue of state ideology. First, the problem of how one represents the nature of socialism is inherent in the narrow focus on workers' productivity and the reintroduction of hierarchical wage systems, for these goals were criticized in the Maoist era as signifiers of the social inequality and inhumanity in socialism's theoretical opposite, capitalism. Arif Dirlik and Maurice Meisner cogently argue in the introduction to this volume that Western scholars often highlight the contradiction in the Chinese party-state's theoretical stance, yet they rarely attend to the dichotomies within our own representation of socialism. These representations veer from socialism as the ideal solution to the human alienation of capitalist societies or, in the anticommunist rhetoric, to the hell we might end up in if we fall out of capitalist heaven.

Western Marxist scholars have long been critical of socialist governments,[6] but only recently have such scholars produced ethnographic and sociological studies of what have come to be known as "actually existing socialist societies."[7] These studies offer important insights. Yet they still leave us without a method for comprehending socialism and capitalism as discursive categories that people also use in meaningful and consequential ways. What does one conclude, for example, about a situation in China where the state encourages factory managers to adopt so-called capitalist methods to pursue profits but, when they do so, accuses them of not having the proper socialist spirit? Capitalism and socialism clearly exist not simply as objective social systems but as discursive categories always ideologically construed, in countries that pride themselves on being socialist as well as in

Western democracies.[8] The specific content of these categories is worked out not simply on an abstract level but in the context of everyday life with its mundane problems and contradictions. Thus the meanings of socialism and capitalism in urban industry in China are not instituted from above by the state, but are taking on new shapes as workers and managers struggle over the new reforms. There is not space within this essay to address more than the specific context of Chinese industry, but ultimately any examination of China should juxtapose these meanings against our interpretations.

The second theoretical issue upon which this essay touches is the concept of "state ideology." Much of the literature on contemporary China equates the economic reforms with dominant state policy and ideology, so that social transformations become a natural effect of the state's intentions.[9] The implicit assumption is that ideology is something the state has that it then passes down to the rest of the people. If we examine social relationships in local factories, however, we begin to realize that ordinary managers' and workers' interpretations of the reforms are as much a part of these reforms as any government pronouncements about them. This situation is not merely self-serving mystification by the state, with either false consciousness or cynical rejection on the part of the rest of the people. Rather, in this essay I treat ideology as a process of hegemony; that is, an ongoing process of the creation of meanings and values that has to do with lived experience, the practical consciousness of everyday life and what we might call ordinary common sense. As Raymond Williams has argued of this Gramscian concept, hegemony is a process tied to unequal power relations such that dominant discourses shape people's interpretations and practices, but they never determine them.[10]

In the following discussion, then, I address these issues by focusing on efforts to raise workers' productivity. The local site is the silk industry of Hangzhou, a center of light industry, where I engaged in fieldwork for twenty months from 1984 through 1986.[11] While in agreement with the caveat about claims to knowledge of Chinese society by virtue of having been there, I still believe that an intensive ethnographic approach, which involves working closely with people over a long period, is more likely to produce a complex body of information than does observation from a distance. Most importantly, this method allowed me to learn of the way ordinary people think about the transformations in their lives resulting from economic reform. It is on this basis that I present the following analysis.

Eating Out of One Big Pot

The state's determination to put an end to "eating out of one big pot" is a fundamental repudiation of Cultural Revolution ideology and politics. In the Hangzhou silk industry, challenges to hierarchical divisions of labor during that time (especially from 1965 to 1973) took several forms. Many, though not all, managers in the silk industry were "sent down" to work at menial jobs within the factory. Additionally, wages were frozen, and workers who started jobs in the factories were paid the same wage, regardless of their assigned job task. Finally, bonuses were nonexistent, for material rewards were considered to be a hindrance to the development of a socialist work ethic. Serious political battles broke out in the factories over these issues, which led to massive disruptions in factory life.

During the Cultural Revolution, workers were said to have learned a lazy work ethic; they learned that going to work meant they could "eat out of one big pot." The idiom refers to a joint household that shares both its food and its living quarters.[12] Within the family, it is a metaphor that implies that every member is entitled to share out of the family food and money pot, without a close calculation of how much each individual has contributed. When used to refer to factory workers, "eating out of one big pot" means that no matter how much or how little workers produced, they all ate the same "food"; that is, they received the same wages. Those who continued to work hard were not given their just desserts. Therefore, so the current critique goes, workers learned to slack off.

Many workers were active during that period. They actively challenged managerial authority through speak bitterness sessions where they humiliated managers, sometimes beating them as well. At other times, due to structural constraints in the flow of raw materials, workers did not engage in consistent production. While it is obvious that workers did not remain fixed to their production positions, what makes "eating out of one big pot" an ideological characterization is its imputation to workers of a natural disposition toward laziness. This negative interpretation of workers' identity is above all a renunciation and inversion of Cultural Revolution class relations, in which workers held the dominant political voice in many factories, if only for a short period. It is equally a rejection of the collectivist ideal of the Maoist era, in which workers were not ranked or measured individually.

The Position-Wage System

The new wage and bonus system, introduced into the Hangzhou silk industry in the spring of 1985, is known as the "position-wage system" (*gangwei gongzi zhi*). Designed to raise workers' productivity through differential rewards and punishments, this new system applies to workers but not to cadres and is based not on seniority, as with the old system, but on job position or category. Jobs are divided into five main categories: (1) weaving, (2) warp preparation, (3) weft preparation and inspection, (4) transport, and (5) miscellaneous—sweeping, machine cleaning. Weavers are in the top category and receive the highest wages, with the other categories following at a distance of five yuan from one another. Workers just entering the factory were put on this new wage scale. They did not start at the wages set for each category, however, for it will take them six and a half years to reach these wages. As for workers already at the factory, older workers above the scale will keep their original wages until retirement; those not yet receiving top wages will gradually be given raises.[13]

Bonuses for workers in the silk industry are based on piecework. After workers fulfill a set quota, which represents their basic wages, they earn the rest of their income through the bonus. Quotas are set such that workers must exceed them to make a living wage—that is, the wages for each category include the bonus. The problematic nature of the bonus portion of the wage is reflected by the fact that most workers in the silk factory say that their bonus gets deducted if they fail to reach the maximum amount rather than that they made an extra amount. The wage then actually has two components: one fixed and one variable. They label the latter portion the bonus.

The position-wage system is said to be the answer to ridding factories of the phenomenon of "eating out of one big pot." As such, it is cast as a way to liberate industry from the constraining political categories of the Cultural Revolution and thereby allow work to return to its so-called natural rhythms. Silk Corporation cadres and factory managers explain and justify the new system in the context of a wider discussion on individualism and individual responsibility now current in China. Those individuals who are willing to work hard, so the ideology goes, will get ahead. They thus present it as judging workers on an individual basis, blind to any attributes other than their productivity. However, one can see hegemony in process in this new system—hegemony as I have defined it earlier as a lived process of the production of meanings and values, tied to unequal power relations—because, if one examines the situation more closely, one discovers that the very notions of "hard work" and "productivity" are not neutral but are based on changing interpretations of age, status, and gender.

Contested Discourses

Yang Zhuren,[14] a party cadre at a state-run silk weaving factory and someone with whom I had numerous conversations, explained to me the dominant interpretation of age in relation to productivity informing the *gangwei* system:

> The previous system wasn't appropriate. With textile workers, when they are old, the quality of their work is not good. They say of textile workers, "They mature early, they contribute early, they deteriorate early." When someone has

> just entered the factory, after a few years, around twenty years old is when they produce the highest quality. But they were getting the lowest wages. It was not fair.

This representation of youths as the most productive workers stands in radical opposition to the former notion that older workers, as *shifu*, or masters in their trade, should be rewarded for their knowledge and experience. In one sense, this reverence for youth reflects a more general notion prevalent in China today: that people are their most creative and can offer their greatest contributions to the advancement of society in the early years of their career.[15] There is much talk now in China of the need to "juvenize" (*qingnianhua*), to encourage older people, especially cadres who occupy leadership positions but do nothing, to step aside for more capable people stuck in junior positions. This discursive elaboration of the positive qualities of youth represents a fundamental challenge to the kind of seniority still prevalent in the party and most workplaces. Furthermore, emphasis on the greater capacity of youths draws on an implicit assumption about a direct relationship between biology and productivity. This idea has much credibility in the present social and political milieu in which science has replaced Marxism as the source to which people turn for answers to current dilemmas.

The new position-wage system rewards youths relative to elders in that those who entered the factory only a few years ago receive the same wages as those who have worked in the factory for twenty or thirty years. Additionally, in the future, older workers will not receive wage increases after they have reached the top of the scale. This system, based on changing interpretations of productivity, does not simply reward individual workers who work harder as compared with their fellow workers on a one-to-one basis, as implied in the policy to end "eating out of one big pot." It rewards a category of workers—youths—based on the hegemonic representation of youths as possessing a greater potential capacity to produce. That youths do not always produce more became clear when I asked one assistant director of a collective silk-weaving factory which types of workers had their pay docked most frequently. She promptly replied, "Mostly it is the 'naughty' boys. After work they go out and play. They play late, so they have no energy to work the next day." But the fact that youths' actual work performance does not always reflect the current belief in their capacity has in no way diminished that belief as it becomes part of the position-wage system.

The very definition of "productive" in relation to age is thus going through a fundamental transformation as the new position-wage system gets put into place. But this transition is far from a straightforward process of imposing a dominant ideology onto the factories. Managers and workers in the local silk factories, through the experience of their everyday work lives, are interpreting and contesting the meaning of the new reforms. Managers in upper-level positions in the factory tend to agree with the view expressed above by the party cadre that youths are more productive. But lower-level managers, such as workshop supervisors, have mixed sentiments. On the one hand, they too want to find the best way to raise productivity, which may mean greater incentives to youths. On the other hand, they argue with the managers above them on behalf of older workers in their shops who complain to them that their wage increases are too low in comparison with those given to younger workers. The older workers, angered that the new system no longer recognizes seniority and thus interrupts their expected life trajectory, feel that they should be rewarded for the many years of hard work they did in their own youth.

One older worker, Yu Shifu, explained the inequalities as she saw them: she had begun work in the silk factory at the age of fourteen, in the early 1950s, when the factories were first formed. She had fought to become a weaver and had worked hard ever since, for thirty years. In the past, older workers could transfer to less strenuous jobs without losing any wages in their last few years before retirement. She had looked forward to the job transfer to which she felt she was entitled, for she had given the factory a lot over the years, and factory management should "look after" (*zhaogu*) her. But with the new wage system, transfer to another job category means a cut in pay. This worker was upset about the changes. These new changes, she said, *xin butong* (literally, won't go through my heart; my heart won't accept them). These arguments and discussions in the factories force one to rethink the relationship between ideology and the state in China: that ideology is not something that party cadres have and pass on to the workers. The hegemonic interpretations informing the new wage system are taking shape through the lived experience of workers, cadres, and managers that leads them continuously to interpret and contest the reforms.

In addition to the cultural category of age, the new wage and bonus system is equally infused with changing interpretations of the status of various job categories. This is especially evident in the current attempts to reinstitute weaving as a job task of higher value than prep or inspection work. Some managers now claim that the skill level and labor intensity of weaving are greater than those of these other tasks. Historically, weaving was considered a highly skilled job. But now the entire textile industry is seen as one of low skill in comparison with the more highly technological industries that have been introduced since 1978. The silk industry does not have the ring of modernization to it, and in a country that wants to look modern as fast as possible, these older industries lack the flash of computers and nuclear power plants. The silk industry does, however, bring in a substantial amount of foreign currency from its export of silk. Forty percent of the production is for export.

Despite this shift in notions of skill within the broader context of industrialization, managers can justify the identification of weaving as a skilled job in the silk factories and assign it to the highest wage category because weaving takes more time to learn than prep or inspection work; it is associated with more complicated machinery; and more discrete tasks are involved in weaving than in the other jobs.

Weaving occupies the highest wage category not only because of the skill level it is now said to have relative to prep and inspection work but also because it is considered the most productive job. But its productivity is not determined by measuring and comparing the value of labor added onto the silk cloth at each stage of the production process. Rather, weaving receives higher pay because the work is said to be more "bitter" (*ku*) than the other jobs. Bitterness and suffering were once considered positive socialist epithets. Now, however, their heroic glory has faded, and few people take it as a matter of pride that they do this kind of work. In this sense, the notion of productivity is defined by the idea of bitter work.

The "bitterness" of weaving, as I learned during the time I spent at one silk-weaving factory, is due to the fact that almost all mistakes found in the finished cloth are blamed on the weaver. The weaver is not necessarily always at fault, as both managers and workers readily admit, but it is too difficult to trace the mistake to any other source. In the weaving shop, an argument ensued one day between a weaver and a prep shift leader over a mistake in a piece of cloth still in the weaver's loom. The weaver insisted the mistake must have been the result of poor thread preparation, but because he was unable to convince the prep shift leader, he had to take the loss. More than any other workers in the silk factories, weavers regularly have their pay docked for falling short of the new, more stringent quality standards. Weavers thus find themselves more burdened with responsibility for the finished cloth. In this sense, their work is more bitter. Productivity is thus additionally defined in terms of accountability for mistakes.

Under the new wage system, workers are rewarded differentially but again according to category of worker and not merely individual effort. A particular prep worker, for example, could conceivably work harder, in terms of actual job performance, than a particular weaver, even though the latter's task is considered more bitter than the former's. The new wage system is about inducing workers to work harder but is based on categories constructed from changing interpretations of, in this case, status. "Skill" and "productivity" are not transparent economic categories that are self-evident and analyzable without taking into account the ways in which they are discursively construed.

Managers and some workers agree with these changes, but other workers contest the new status relations reflected in the position-wage system. At one state-run factory, I happened to walk out of the factory reception office one afternoon at the moment when the dining hall workers—about ten of them—marched into the Labor and Wages Office. I, along with several others, stood outside the window of that office and listened as these workers proceeded to berate the head of that section. Their actions amazed me, because they recalled the Cultural Revolution and therefore, I thought, would be politically dangerous. The factory director then squeezed his way into the room and they turned to berate him. Again, this contradicted everything I had read about hierarchy and the power of the party in China. But the dining hall workers were quite angry about the new wage and bonus system just introduced into the factory. They were angry that, with this new system, they would now receive lower wages than other workers and their jobs would be of lower status because they were fixed at the low end of the pay scale. The managers responded that if they wanted higher pay they could go be weavers. The dining hall workers insisted their job deserves recognition for the hard work involved. After several hours of heated discussion, the argument finally wound down. The dining hall workers, only temporarily mollified, left the office, dispirited and dissatisfied with the results.

The dining hall workers' resistance to the dominant interpretations of the wage and bonus system stands as directly oppositional practice. Other workers have accepted the new cultural representation of themselves as in need of raising their productivity, but they do not always act on it in the way the state intended. In the weaving shop of the factory I worked in, there was a thirty-one-year-old unmarried man named Sun who did the lowest paying and lightest job in the shop—sweeping up the garbage. He complained that his wages were scarcely enough to support him—he ate them all every month. But he had no interest in learning to be a weaver to earn higher pay. He lived with his retired parents, who gave him money for the requisite fashionable clothes and cigarettes de rigeur among young unmarried male workers. Quite by accident one day, I came across him selling the latest clothes from Hong Kong on the free market. Free markets have been opened since 1978, and unemployed youths are encouraged to establish what are known as "individual enterprises" in these free markets. However, workers with jobs in state-run factories are not permitted to set up individual enterprises. But this worker had struck an agreement with his shop supervisors that if he showed up for work every day they would overlook his en-

trepreneurial activities. His sideline enterprise net him three times his wages in the factory, but he did it not only for the money; he liked to use his brains, he told me, and "because it lets me lead a life better than the common worker. I can eat things they can't afford to eat, and I can go places they can't go. I want to be like that." Young male workers like Sun have been inculcated with the state's praise for high productivity, but they have deployed these meanings in unintended ways. Their high productivity, that is, does not always go to the state. Anthony Giddens has emphasized the importance of unintended consequences of praxis for the social reproduction of relations of domination.[16] But these unintended consequences of state policy cannot be accounted for in an analytical model that equates state ideology with the social practice of the economic reforms.

The status notions informing the new wage categories among workers in the silk industry also inform the division of labor between managers and workers, a division that has become increasingly salient under the current reforms. Here, too, these changing interpretations are tied to larger social processes in which "social position" as a concept has once again been given positive value in China, and the social hierarchy of the Cultural Revolution has been overturned and replaced by one where intellectuals now have the most prestige. In the current milieu, where intellectual work is much more highly valued than the "mere" execution of ideas, the division between mental and manual labor has grown even greater. Yang Zhuren insisted that the differential compensation for managers and workers is based on the fact that the value of their labor is not the same. The value, or productivity, of mental labor is, however, difficult to measure. The assistant director of a collective factory—a woman I often sought out because I admired her sense of purpose about her work—told me that cadres are paid according to the "heaviness" of their responsibility. When I asked her to spell out the details of how they measured that heaviness, she replied, "For example, if the director of the factory gets 100 yuan, . . . then the section head gets 80 yuan." The degree of responsibility is thus decided by the job title. But no exact correlation between job title and degree of productivity can be drawn.

Prior to 1986, the differences in wages and bonuses between managers and workers were not marked, still a holdover from Cultural Revolution practices. Yet the highest reward in an office job lies not in the wages, but in the job itself. Every worker hopes to be promoted to a desk job, where he or she no longer has to stand up all day; where everyone works only the day shift, instead of the four-shift system for production line workers (two days on day shift, two days on evening shift, two days on overnight shift, and two days of rest); and where the work load, from a worker's point of view, is significantly lighter. From workers' viewpoints, then, a manager's responsibility might be heavier, but the work load is not. Nonetheless, in the winter of 1986 a new wage and bonus system for cadres was introduced, a revision of the grade-level system, which will create a larger gap between the incomes of managers and workers.

These cultural interpretations of status and skill underlying the *gangwei* wage system are themselves infused with particular notions of gender. This gendered interpretation of productivity can be seen through the fact that the position-wage system applies only to work increasingly considered women's work—weaving, prep work, and inspection work. Tasks such as machine repair and transport (truck driving) are considered skilled manual labor and are defined as men's work. The manager/worker divide also coincides with divisions of labor between men and women in the silk industry. Some women can be found in silk factory management, but the majority are men, and management is becoming more of a male domain under the current reforms.

To appreciate fully the gendered implications of these new reforms, a brief review of the recent history of the silk industry and its sexual division of labor is in order. Prior to Liberation and in the first few years after the 1949 Communist Revolution, silk production in Hangzhou still took place almost exclusively in household workshops. Generally speaking, men did the weaving and ran the household business, and women and children prepared the thread. In 1954 the state merged these household workshops into state-run factories. Men entered the factories with their looms and continued to do the weaving. Most of the women from these household workshops who entered the factories continued to do the prep work. A few of these women, however, struggled to become weavers. For them, it meant higher pay, a skill, and more control over their labor. One should also note that during this time, and up to the current economic reforms, a substantial number of managers rose up from the ranks of weavers.

With the 1958 Great Leap Forward campaigns to bring more women into the work force, and the division of tasks so that weaving and machine repair became separate jobs, women began to do more of the weaving in Hangzhou silk factories. Beginning in the 1960s, silk weaving and prep work were gradually deskilled and devalued, although the technology remained virtually unchanged during this time. Women increasingly predominated in silk production. Wages were lowered both absolutely and relative to the more prestigious industries men began to enter.

By the mid-1960s the silk industry was experiencing a decided feminization of its work force. This trend has continued apace, with a slight reversal in the period immediately after the Cultural Revolution. At that time, urban youths could inherit their parents' factory jobs as a way to return to the cities from what they viewed as their rural purgatories. Young men entered the silk factories again. They took up jobs as weavers, machine repairmen, and transport workers. The male weavers I spoke with during their cigarette breaks laughed at my suggestion that they might ever do prep work. They said they would be too embarrassed. Their hands are too rough and they don't have the patience, they explained.

With this brief jog through recent Chinese history, two points should be noted. One is the historical contingency of the emergence of this gendered division of labor. This is not a teleological tale of the evolution of functionally superior technological systems. Instead, I want to emphasize that the development of this gendered division of labor has depended on a number of background conditions, both within China and related to China's place in the world economic system, including the nationalization of industry, the initial closing of the borders to Western trade, the disastrous economic conditions after the Great Leap Forward, and the social effects of the Cultural Revolution. Second, the industrialization process that has shaped this gendered division of labor has not evolved according to an inner structural logic, or inner structural contradiction, but has depended on political and economic conditions in China.

Since the early 1980s, only women have entered the work force, and only women from the countryside. Virtually no urban youths desire jobs in the silk industry any longer because of the low pay and poor working conditions. As urban workers can now test into the factory of their choice, no one from Hangzhou—male or female—has shown up to work in the silk factories. To resolve this labor crisis, managers have turned to recruitment of peasant women, most of them relatives of current factory workers.

Under the economic reforms, an increasingly rigid distinction is being drawn between the production line jobs of weaving, prep, and inspection work, which have been construed as manual labor, and those jobs now more highly valued as skilled technical and mental labor—machine repair, transport, and managerial work. Concurrent with this process is a transformed sexual division of labor: the manual labor tasks are now becoming defined as women's work while the technical and mental labor is considered men's work. This sexual division of labor is taking shape through gendered interpretations of work capabilities such that women and men are said to have different capabilities uniquely suited to these divergent tasks. One cadre told me that the new wage system is for tasks considered boring, of low skill but requiring energy. Women in China are believed suited to these kinds of tasks—they are said to have the requisite patience, to be less complaining about boring work, to have nimble fingers (which, according to this ideological construction of biology, uniquely suits them to prep work). On the other hand, they are said not to be suited to machine repair. Machine repair work entails climbing up on top of the machines, and this is said to be inconvenient for women. Because gender capabilities are defined in opposition to one another, men are thought to be good at machine repair because men are said to be uniquely capable of technical tasks. A few women in the silk industry have job assignments as machine repairers, but this in no way calls into question the fundamental beliefs that adhere in the sexual division of labor. To the extent they are seen as capable, these women are thought to resemble men.[17]

Representations of the appropriate managerial qualifications are also gendered. Women are said to lack the intellectual capabilities of men and the necessary leadership qualities. They do not know how to resolve disputes or how to make the social connections so essential for getting anything done in China. Male cadres would invariably tell me that managerial work is inconvenient for women due to their family responsibilities. Given the sexual division of labor of child care and housework in China, their claim has some validity, but only if that division remains unchallenged. With telling omission, they do not raise this objection for women doing production work on the shift system.

These gendered interpretations of women's physical and intellectual capabilities serve what Foucault has called a regime of bio-power in which women's bodies are culturally inscribed in a way that makes them objects to be manipulated and controlled.[18] Through these gendered representations of women, factory management can attempt to subject women to the microtechnologies of factory work discipline to raise their productivity.

Many women workers, through their daily practical experience of living in a world structured by gender, accept these reciprocally confirming yet still hegemonically construed representations of their gendered selves as fundamentally tied to family responsibilities and to biology. That is, the objective structure of the gendered division of labor becomes part of their lived subjective experience. This subjective experience can, however, be applied to originally unintended purposes—in this case, resistance to the new pressures for higher productivity. Women take off of work more often than men for family reasons—to prolong a maternity leave, care for a sick child, or breastfeed a newborn. Young mothers look forward to the extra hour they can take each day to breastfeed their babies for the first year after birth. Xiao Tang, a shift leader in a weft prep shop, told me, after her return from a supposed visit with her newborn, that she does not breastfeed, but that she likes to visit her mother during that hour. In these quotidian strategies to lessen the burden of their silk work, women themselves reproduce aspects of the larger culture. This resistance thus paradoxically reinforces the sense that women are less productive than men.[19]

Wage differentials, as I have emphasized, are justified under the reforms because they are said to reflect individual differences in productivity. When one thinks of productivity, one assumes it has to do with something measurable, like piecework. And the bonuses do reward piecework. But, more importantly, the position wage system reflects an enshrinement of a distinction between mental and technical labor versus manual labor. Weaving is no longer the category for gender distinctions or for struggles over control of one's labor. Now the divide stands between management and production workers—management categories are about men and production categories are about women. Women workers now contrast themselves with management, not weavers, when they raise issues of working conditions or better jobs. These reforms represent a critical reshaping of the classification of work that more or less elides with gender. The productivity of women's labor is now going to be evaluated on a different, and lower, scale than men's because women's work has become equated with manual labor. Since the jobs that men do are defined as the more productive ones, men inevitably come to be seen as more productive than women. These representations of men and women will continue to appear as commonsense truths as long as this gendered division of labor prevails.

Conclusion

The economic reforms in the silk industry, as exemplified by the new wage and bonus system, are thus not a simple, straightforward policy to reward individual workers who work harder. The criticism of workers for shirking their responsibilities and living off the labor of others is an ideological representation entailed in a rejection of the Cultural Revolution. But the new wage policy is much more complex than a mere attempt to solve even that issue taken as a problem prima facie. It signifies a fundamental shift now in process in notions about the nature of work and productivity. This new hegemony is far from a coherent, articulated system of meaning. "Productivity," at present, stands as a trope for a range of interactive concepts: bitterness, responsibility, skill, and status, some of which are at times contradictory. The notions of "hard work" and "productivity" are further based on beliefs about categories of people: "youths," "managers," "men," and workers in jobs considered "bitter" and essential to the production process. These kinds of people are now said to be more productive by definition. The whole notion of productivity as tied to the division of labor under this new system is thus not a neutral concept. It is infused with beliefs about age, status, and gender.

This brings us back to the two issues I raised in the beginning of this essay. What can the case of the economic reforms in the silk industry tell us about the relationship between socialism and capitalism, on the one hand, and between social practice and state ideology, on the other? To take up the issue of socialism and capitalism first, I am suggesting that "socialism" and "capitalism" are representational constructs always up for grabs as people in socialist societies struggle over their meaning. I am not denying that socialist societies or capitalist societies exist, nor that they have observable differences in their organizations of production. What I do want to stress is that capitalism and socialism exist primarily as politically resonant signifiers, not as objective structures. To paraphase Laclau and Mouffe, "socialist societies" or "socialist relations of production" are not abstract entities but the "[loci] of a multiplicity of practices and discourse."[20] In the current period of economic reform in China, workers and managers strategically deploy these categories in their arguments about the labor process.[21] If these arguments were analyzed using objectivist models, they would have to be dismissed as rhetoric in the pejorative sense, which would take us back to the outdated understandings of ideology as mystification. It is necessary to recognize that these interpretive struggles over meaning are simultaneously struggles over "material" needs.[22] Socialist societies are always ideologically construed, not in the abstract, but in the course of quotidian practices. As party cadre Yang once mused, "It's not clear what is reasonable. These questions of political economy are a matter of controversy. A socialist economy can use capitalist methods. Some say this will make ours a capitalist system. The country's leaders say we can't change into a capitalist system. But if we don't watch out, we will."

Recognition of the importance of situated interpretations is equally critical for understanding the relationship between everyday practices and state ideology. One could hardly deny the power of the party in China, nor the all-pervasive presence of the state in people's lives. But, as is so obvious in this case, the ideology informing the new wage policy is not a static or absolute set of ideas imposed by the state onto workers in the silk factories. Power does shape the discourse about the new wage and bonus system. But that power is not emanating from one direction only. As Anthony Giddens has pointed out, subordinate actors' very involvement in social relationships gives them a certain power.[23] Workers in China, as a dominated group, nonetheless display great creativity in challenging and transforming the dominant interpretations of the economic reforms, and the final configuration of those reforms will be an outcome of these struggles. One must recognize, in other words, that ideology is always modified by culturally meaningful practice. Pierre Bourdieu has made this point by emphasizing that ideologies are inscribed with a history of power struggles for the legitimation of particular visions of the social world.[24] Thus ideological, or symbolic, struggles constitute an ongoing process in which these visions become articulated through the practical consciousness of social actors as they go about their quotidian activities. Dominant discourses shape but never determine ordinary people's interpretations. The state's dominant discourse is continuously modified and transformed as workers resist those representations outright, or accept them but deploy them in ways that lead to unintended consequences, or use them from within as strategies of resistance that yet reproduce the hegemony. "Even" in socialist societies ordinary people actively create meaning and hence their social worlds. My fortunate arrival in China at a time when the new wage system was just introduced led me to recognize that workers in the silk factories are never passive recipients of state policy. Certainly the dining hall workers' angry explosion should remind us of that.

Notes

I would like to thank the workers, managers, and state bureaucrats of the Hangzhou silk industry who patiently taught me about their world; the CSCPRC for research funds without which I never would have been able to enter that world; and the people who read and commented on earlier drafts of this essay—Arif Dirlik, Akhil Gupta, Emily Honig, Susan Mann, G. William Skinner, Jonathan Unger, and Sylvia Yanagisako.

1. Penelope B. Prime, in chapter 7 of this volume, questions the predominant view that the Cultural Revolution was an utter economic disaster. She argues that substantial economic growth occurred during the Cultural Revolution, although attendant problems followed upon this Maoist model of growth.

2. I use the term "discipline" here in both its Weberian and Foucauldian senses. I take it to mean both that work, or production activity, becomes the goal of human efforts instead of the reverse through self-conscious norms and rules, and that workers imperceptibly internalize and habituate themselves to routines of work through microtechniques directed at the movements of the body (e.g., spatial relations) and through hierarchical rankings (e.g., by "skill" or production quotas fulfilled). See Max Weber, *The Protestant Ethic and the Spirit of Capitalism* (New York: Charles Scribner's Sons, 1958 [1905]), and Michel Foucault, *Discipline and Punish* (New York: Vintage, 1979 [1975]).

3. E. P. Thompson, *The Making of the English Working Class* (New York: Vintage, 1966), p. 205.

4. Even the appearance of the term "productivity" signals a rejection of the Maoist political order.

5. One might think of this fixation in terms of the Marxist notion of fetishism. See Karl Marx, *Capital* (New York: International Publishers, 1967 [1867]), 1:71–84. See also Michael T. Taussig, *The Devil and Commodity Fetishism in South America* (Chapel Hill: University of North Carolina Press, 1980), for a slightly different usage of the concept.

6. E. P. Thompson, "Outside the Whale," in his *The Poverty of Theory and Other Essays* (New York: Monthly Review Press, 1978 [1963]); Perry Anderson, *Arguments Within English Marxism* (London: Verso, 1980).

7. Rudolf Bahro, *The Alternative in Eastern Europe* (London: Verso, 1978); Michael Burawoy, *The Politics of Production* (London: Verso, 1985).

8. An elaboration of this point can be found in Ernesto Laclau and Chantal Mouffe, *Hegemony and Socialist Strategy* (London: Verso, 1985).

9. This is especially true of works in the discipline of political science. See, for ex-

ample, Stuart R. Schram, "Decentralization in a Unitary State: Theory and Practice, 1940–1984," in *The Scope of State Power in China*, ed. S. R. Schram (London: University of London, 1985), pp. 81–127; Harro Von Senger, "Recent Developments in the Relations Between State and Party Norms in the People's Republic of China," in ibid., pp. 171–207; and Tang Tsou, "Marxism, the Leninist Party, the Masses, and the Citizens in the Rebuilding of the Chinese State," in *Foundations and Limits of State Power in China*, ed. S. R. Schram (London: University of London, 1987).

10. Raymond Williams, *Marxism and Literature* (Oxford: Oxford University Press, 1977). Williams' and my own treatment of hegemony are based on Antonio Gramsci, *Selections from the Prison Notebooks* (New York: International Publishers, 1971). There is now a growing literature on the concept of hegemony. See Perry Anderson, "The Antinomies of Antonio Gramsci," *New Left Review* 100 (1977): 5–78; James Brow, "In Pursuit of Hegemony: Representations of Authority and Justice in a Sri Lankan Village," *American Ethnologist* 15, 2 (1988): 311–27; Chantal Mouffe, ed., *Gramsci and Marxist Theory* (London: Routledge and Kegan Paul, 1979); and Kathleen Weiler, *Women Teaching for Change: Gender Class and Power* (South Hadley, Mass.: Bergin and Garvey, 1988).

11. While there, I conducted formal interviews with over one hundred managers, workers, and government bureaucrats. I further carried out a participant-observation project in one medium-sized state-run silk weaving factory, in which I had the opportunity to engage in casual conservations with workers, office staff, and managers. I was then able to form friendships that carried over outside the bounds of the factory walls.

12. Margery Wolf, in *The House of Lim* (Englewood Cliffs: Prentice Hall, 1968), writes "If the guest hall can be considered the symbol of the larger family, the stove is the symbol of the living family. Members of a family are defined as those who share a cooking stove; the colloquial term for the act of family division is literally 'the dividing of the stove.' This identification of stove and family is so important that those who cannot afford to add a room to house the stove of a newly created family unit build a second stove in the same kitchen" (p. 28).

13. For a more detailed discussion of the position-wage system, see my dissertation, " 'Eating out of One Big Pot': Hegemony and Resistance in a Chinese Factory," Stanford University, 1989.

14. I have given pseudonyms to all my informants for obvious reasons of protection. *Zhuren* means the head of an office. These hierarchical titles of address, in a telling reflection of current concerns, have replaced the ubiquitous "comrade."

15. This preoccupation with the positive qualities of youth recalls the May Fourth Movement—a period, not coincidentally, that inspired many of the older party leaders. Chow Tse-tsung, *The May Fourth Movement* (Stanford: Stanford University Press, 1967).

16. Anthony Giddens, *Central Problems in Social Theory* (Berkeley: University of California Press, 1979), p. 59.

17. As Aihwa Ong has recently noted about women workers in Malaysian factories, "These ideologies operate to fix women workers in subordinate positions in systems of domination." "The Production of Possession: Spirits and the Multinational Corporation in Malaysia," *American Ethnologist* 15, 1 (1988): 35.

18. Michel Foucault, *The History of Sexuality*, vol. 1 (New York: Random House, 1980 [1976]).

19. This approach to housework as a strategy of resistance has implications for leading us out of the impasse in feminist arguments about whether housework is socially necessary labor and provides a "material" basis of women's oppression; whether the family is the locus of women's oppression or provides support for working class families; and in which ways the "reproductive" sphere of the family is related to the productive sphere of work from the point of view of female actors.

20. Laclau and Mouffe, *Hegemony and Socialist Strategy*, p. 102.

21. I have not taken up here the relations between factory managers and state bureaucrats, but they, too, accuse one another of improper interpretations of capitalist practices and socialist goals as they vie for control over factory resources.

22. I am suggesting that we consider "needs" as historical products tied to changing social divisions of labor. For a more thorough discussion of this issue, see Agnes Heller, *The Theory of Need in Marx* (London: Allison and Busby, 1976).

23. Anthony Giddens, "Power, the Dialectic of Control and Class Structuration," in *Social Class and the Division of Labour*, ed. Anthony Giddens and Gavin Mackenzie (Cambridge: Cambridge University Press, 1982), pp. 29–45.

24. Pierre Bourdieu, "The Social Space and the Genesis of Groups," *Theory and Society* 14, 6 (1985): 723–44.

13

CHICKEN LITTLE IN CHINA: SOME REFLECTIONS ON WOMEN

Marilyn Young

There were three of them, all in their late twenties, all Han Chinese, and all in Beijing for a two-year course of study before a mandatory return to middle school jobs in a remote province. XX was clearly their leader. Tight jeans, red shirt, a wide, ready, terribly eager smile, a strutting walk that was positively startling in the Beijing context. "Beijing is paradise," XX said. "And Beijing compared to America must be like my home is to Beijing." Her friends nodded rather depressed agreement. "At home I would be stoned in the street for dressing like this." "I was jeered at for less," one of her quieter friends broke in. What did they think of Jiang Qing? "She was great," XX burst out. "Maggie Thatcher too! They make men afraid." There was a silence then, as the three women took in the somewhat stunned expression of their American friend's face. "Of course Jiang Qing was also very bad." XX added. "Very bad," her friends chimed in.

The title of this essay draws upon two tales, one Western, the other Chinese. In both the sky is understood as something solid; in both it is subject to falling down. In the Western story an overexcited and misinformed chicken alarms the barnyard with a rumor that the sky is about to crash down on everyone's head. The Chinese tale is more static: once upon a time women were said to hold up half the sky. I want to explore the nature of the Chinese story, a favorite during the Cultural Revolution, and think about it in relation to the period after the Cultural Revolution when, looking around at women and then up at the sky, one might begin to wonder if Chicken Little had a point after all.

The starting place for any discussion of women and Chinese socialism is the premise of the revolution itself and the promise held out to women: that the liberation of women would be an integral part of the proletarian revolution. And that has indeed been the case. Initially, the revolution in power, no more imaginative than its Soviet avatar, relied upon the mobilization of women into "social production," that is, wage labor, as a necessary, and it was hoped sufficient, first step. But, as Phyllis Andors has persuasively argued, state policy toward women in China is an intimate variable of the overall revolutionary process.[1] The mobilization of women into as well as out of the labor force followed not only, nor perhaps even primarily, the vagaries of the labor market but more centrally the debate within the leadership over the direction, speed, shape, and duration of the revolution itself. At times women were the named subject of particular policy endeavors (efforts to socialize women's work during the Great Leap Forward, for example, or the periodic encouragement to women to retire to the household in a becoming socialist manner); sometimes they were explicitly unnamed (as in the Cultural Revolution, which, among other things, declared that it was not about a "sex" revolution). Always, of course, the effect of policy was gender specific, whether or not it was framed with gender in mind.

Women, in China as elsewhere, comprise a double or even triple category of analysis. There is gender, of course, but also class and race or ethnicity. Women embody social contradictions. They are workers, or the wives of workers, middling or ruling class (by marriage or kinship rather than in their own persons), members of racial or ethnic minorities. No single line of analysis will cover their case. Frequently, when writers talk about "workers" they mean, really, male workers—and women workers become invisible. Or, from another analytic perspective, when "women" are discussed their membership in a particular social class is forgotten.

In a country that defines itself as a dictatorship of the proletariat, the contradiction of women's doubled identity (and often consequent invisibility) makes their relationship to the state of vital importance. Uniting with the men of their class almost always means the disappearance of those concerns that are specific to their gender. Uniting with women of other classes on the basis of gender ignores real class divisions and is, or was, ideologically suspect. Unable, then, to marshal sufficient social force to act on their own behalf, without independent power or leverage, women are placed in the position of depending on what Judith Stacey has called the "public patriarchy"—the state and the party—to a greater extent than other groups in the society. In a *Women in China* forum conducted several years ago, an older woman doctor asserted that women could achieve many things if they were actively supported by the state. "You see," she explained, perhaps adapting one of Mao's most familiar quotations, "state support is essential for women, just as water is indispensable for fish."[2] Thus in China, the withdrawal or modification of strong central government support for women has a major impact on their welfare. And in launching a massive central government campaign, such as the Cultural Revolution, the inherently contradictory position of women, as well as the contradictions that inhere in women, are revealed in high relief.

Kay Ann Johnson, in *Women, the Family and Peasant Revolution in China*, succinctly summarizes the interpretive framework within which policy on women was set during the Cultural Revolution.[3] First, the barrier to full equality between women and men was located in the superstructure—bourgeois ideology and/or remnant feudal ideas. Second, the slogan "politics in command" meant, with respect to women, a conscious, ongoing effort to expand their public political roles as well as economic ones. Yet finally, since class was the primary analytic category for understanding all social problems, the ideological attack on inequality left structural issues untouched.

In a largely unchanged rural setting, what this could mean in practice was an unplanned consonance between traditional "feudal" mores with respect to women and leftist denunciations of "bourgeois" individualism and personal freedom. Not that it need always mean that. In at least one South China village, young people intent on marrying within the village in defiance of traditional exogamous practice successfully accused disapproving elders of "feudal attitudes" and got their way.[4] But on the whole, Johnson argues, the emphasis on class made things worse for women. It meant a tendency to deny considerations of gender and to repudiate manifestations of feminism, which anyway were always high on the enemy list of classic Marxist-Leninism. Thus, with perfect consistency, the Women's Federation was abolished in 1966 on the logical ground that, since class struggle was what it was all about, a separate organization of women made little sense.

Yet precisely because of its insistence on gender neutrality, the Cultural Revolution pushed women into the public realm as no movement since the Great Leap Forward has done. As Johnson writes, "the Cultural Revolution . . . witnessed the most vigorous affirmative action efforts since 1949 to recruit larger numbers of women into political organizations."[5] At the same time, the firm refusal to acknowledge structural constraints on the position of women meant that public responsibilities, as well as work in the factory or on the collective farm, were simply added onto domestic burdens. A woman was expected to put her revolutionary work first and then tend to her husband and children. No one in China could ever have remarked, as did the late female Nicaraguan ambassador to the United Nations, "The truth is, with a revolution and kids, you don't have much time for a husband."[6]

What gender neutrality meant in fact was the requirement that women work harder than ever before. The standard for achievement remained resolutely male. The Iron Girls, whose production in heavy agricultural labor rivaled that of men, are a case in point. Enormously appealing in their energy and effort, they had a simple claim to equality: they could work as hard or harder than men (and even then only rarely for equal workpoints). Therein lay their honor; and, from a feminist standpoint, therein lay their failure.

The proletarian woman, Mao told Malraux in 1965, man to man, was yet to be born.[7] Meanwhile her prototype during the Cultural Revolution was finally, under the banners, a remarkably familiar figure: the uncomplaining working mother, ready to retire or join the work force as needed. Indeed, the Cultural Revolution, for all its heady rhetoric, in this regard worked out to a logical conclusion one tendency in Marxist approaches to women, an approach that Marxism shares with liberal ideologies. Both liberals and Marxists reject all notions of biological determinism; both embrace a concept of universal humanity. For both as well the universal human is male—a class conscious revolutionary for the one; an autonomous individual for the other, but in neither case a woman.

Liberals and Chinese Marxists share another characteristic—a conviction born of their common belief in human agency, that social change can be the product of the transformation of "attitudes." If, then, the definition of the problem facing women is that they are *seen* as women, the solution seems fairly evident. At the level of material reality, of course, they will continue to bear and rear children and be responsible for their usual chores. At the ideological level, however, this implicit aspect of their identity can be put aside. In the public realm they are to be *seen* as men. Standing in the way, however, are "feudal attitudes" that restrict women's movements and participation in the world of work and politics and "bourgeois attitudes" that lead women selfishly to focus on their own small family responsibilities. With sufficient effort, both attitudes can be overcome and the path cleared for the new woman, a kind of socialist androgyne: for public purposes a man, at home a loving wife and mother; genderless in public, chaste wives and selfless mothers in private. Moreover, in China this division is consonant with much more ancient culture constructs, in which gender is firmly tied to role rather than to biological sex. A woman active in the public realm must be sexually invisible. Indeed, the most effective way to delegitimize a woman exercising political power is to insist upon her sex—as Jiang Qing was to discover.

Some of the misunderstanding that arises between Chinese and Western feminists is a result of cultural misreading. Tani Barlow, watching a play in which an uppity wife is brought into a properly submissive relationship with her husband—part of a Woman's Day celebration in 1981—was astonished when her Chinese hosts said the play had nothing to do with male-female antagonism but was rather a conflict over rank.[8] The 1962 movie *Li Shuang-*

shuang and the 1982 movie *The In-Laws* have radically different representations of women.[9] In the earlier movie, Li Shuangshuang is a leading force in the Great Leap Forward in her village, hampered at every turn by her small-minded husband. The 1982 movie heroine, by contrast, turns out to be a dutiful daughter-in-law. To any Western audience the movies are about women and the changes in representation since the 1960s. Yet Chinese discussions focus instead on the issues of production in one case and intergenerational conflict in the other. Moreover, an analysis of how the camera works in both films reveals, once more in direct contrast to Western cinematography, that the audience is in effect blocked from taking a gender-identified point of view. As Chris Berry explains: "the place of the viewing subject [i.e., audience] only becomes gender-identified . . . at negative points in the text, points of transgression, failure and collapse." One cannot be surprised then, Berry writes, "if a discourse of sexual differences concerned with the individual interests of one gender versus the other is absent from discussion of the films as a discourse of individual interests, for in this example it is to the very negative assertion of individual interests that sexual difference is attached."[10] Here Chinese socialism and Chinese culture are braided together, collectivism reinforced by feudalism, an anti-individualist class perspective by an older vision of fixed social estates.

Nevertheless, there remains a profound and instructive difference between *Li Shuangshuang* and *The In-laws*. The former may indeed be understood by Chinese audiences as being about production, but the clear message of the movie is that production, a central national goal, is sabotaged by Li Shuangshuang's backward husband. The message of *The In-laws* is that private familial harmony is sabotaged by a selfish daughter-in-law. Both movies reject bourgeois individualism, but what they reject it for makes a considerable difference, and in that difference lies the history of the last two decades, including the history of women as such.

The Cultural Revolution, in its effort to salvage the vision of revolutionary possibility Mao had earlier vested in the Great Leap Forward, encouraged policies of radical mobilization and mass participation that, as Phyllis Andors has written with respect to the Great Leap, created "a more favorable atmosphere and generated forces in which all kinds of inequality—including that of women—could be effectively challenged."[11] Moreover, the 1973 campaign to criticize Lin Biao and Confucius, which the Chinese would now date as falling within the period of the Cultural Revolution, was explicitly focused on women's issues, publicizing the efforts of rural women to gain equal workpoints, stimulating research into the ideological origins of women's subordination, publishing hagiographies of women rebels, and linking anyone who opposed the equality of women to such villains as Liu Shaoqi, Lin Biao, and, of course, Confucius himself.

Revolutionary committees, at that time the governing bodies in factories, schools, and government agencies, were instructed to "pay greater attention" to the role of women and to make sure that in "organs of political power at all levels and in mass organizations, there should be a certain number of women representatives and in actual work their opinions should be listened to seriously and with respect."[12] Women, the campaign trumpeted, held up half the sky and could certainly do whatever men did. And yet, even in the most favorable assessment of its impact, the campaign's focus on ideology left structural and cultural problems untouched. The conflict between gender and class was never effectively confronted.

I want now to shift the focus of analysis. Instead of thinking about Chinese women in this period in terms of various categories relating to revolutionary processes, I want to place them in a different, comparative context. If the experience of mass mobilization is taken as central to the period, then it might be illuminating to look at the Chinese experience in light of the mobilization of women in other times and places.

In both the United States and Great Britain (and very differently in Japan and Germany), the years of the Second World War required a shift in gender ideology and practice in order to mobilize women into the work force for the war effort.[13] Although in both countries efforts were made to retain prewar gender roles in the face of changing practice, the actual experience of women during the war profoundly disturbed the status quo. Women were more mobile than they had been, often moving to places where jobs in war industries were available; they did jobs previously defined, and jealously maintained, as male. Many women found themselves independent, economically and socially, in ways they had not anticipated and for which they had no political language. There was no feminist movement as such during the war. But national exigencies transformed the lives of women in ways a later feminist movement could and would raise to consciousness.

While the war thus brought women everywhere unprecedented mobility, they were not everywhere mobilized in the same way. In the West they were mobilized on the basis of gender and patriotism; in China, on the basis of class and revolution. Nonetheless, the fact of mobilization itself may be more significant than this difference. For Chinese women, the experience of the Cultural Revolution could have a particularly powerful effect because of the peculiar fluidity of their ideological situation. The early promises of liberation through incorporation into socially productive labor had posited an explicitly antifeudal conception of women's roles. For most women this was, at best, only fitfully possible. However, during the Cultural Revolution, state-sponsored insistence on the participation of women in the public realm inevitably unsettled the status quo of gender relations or, more basically perhaps, the given hierarchy of power and authority, and encouraged women to take action against it. The hierarchy at issue was, in addition to its other features, generational. Perhaps one way to understand the reports of the quite stunning ferocity of female middle school students against figures of authority (including beating people to death) is as a rebellion against the weight of prior social repression, as well as a means to extirpate old stereotypes of feminine behavior. Criticized as bourgeois for having worn a dress, Li Xiaochang went to school the next day in trousers, then joined a Red Guard organization and participated in a range of violent activities which she describes with considerable vigor (and some chagrin) today: "We caught the members of street gangs too, like the 'Nine Dragons and a Phoenix.' They sounded frightening, but when we caught them, we beat them until they begged us 'Red Guard ladies' for mercy."[14]

In these actions, as in their participation in the exchange of revolutionary experiences or the movement to "go down to the countryside," young women were physically sprung loose from a home, school, or work environment that, until then, they may not have consciously felt to be oppressive. Listening to one Chinese friend recount a series of Cultural Revolution horror stories, I was surprised to find her smiling broadly as she remembered being left entirely on her own when she was thirteen or fourteen, her parents and elder siblings having been scattered around the country. "That must have been awful," I said sympathetically. "Oh no," she insisted. "You don't understand. I was free, I could do what I wanted. It was wonderful."

Many other women, none of whom intended to praise what they all agreed had been largely a personal and national disaster, talked enthusiastically about specific aspects of their time in the countryside. "Because I did the work better than anyone, better even than any of the men, I was made team leader," a woman whose life had, in almost every respect, been thoroughly devastated by the Cultural Revolution told me. "And that meant I sat," she gestured at her kitchen table, "there, in the seat of authority, of the most respected person, where no women had ever sat before." Another recalled riding horses in Inner Mongolia. "I rode at night," she said proudly. "All the boys were frightened to do that, but I loved it. And fast, I rode very fast." Which is not to deny that many young women found separation from their families terrifying, nor that an unknown number of urban female students suffered varieties of sexual abuse in the countryside—from peasants or from their male comrades. Thus Li Xiaochang remembers what it was like to learn to ride a horse really well. "I began to appreciate the great outdoors. Riding slowly across the great grasslands was beautiful. If now I have a sense of wonder, or of powerful, indefinable nostalgia, if I have an understanding for melancholy and quietness, it all goes back to those days." But later, in that same place, where the herdsmen who taught her to ride had also become her friends, she was raped. "The whole family was there and they helped him." Her urban-educated male comrades charged her with seduction and invited her to do a self-criticism. "There was no question of bringing a case against the boy," she concludes. "They were national minorities and this was their custom."[15] Yet for some there was sexual pleasure as well as danger, the possibility of experimentation that both the material and the ideological conditions at home precluded.

It is worth noting the frequency with which female figures in current literary and film treatments of the Cultural Revolution are depicted as especially venal, or authoritarian, or brutal. "Marxist Grannies" are figures of fun, but the antiheroine of Liu Binyan's *People or Monsters* is far more threatening.[16] A play popular in Beijing in 1985 featured a truly loathsome girl Red Guard leader who seemed to be the only Red Guard in her neighborhood. Her voice was shrill, she had the most sympathetic characters in the play beaten and arrested—an altogether evil child who, in the last act of the play, grows up to be, in the context of the current reforms, a corrupt, quarrelsome, and self-seeking woman. These examples are, of course, contemporary reconstructions intended for current consumption. But they may also contain a measure of truth. Perhaps the behavior of women in power should be understood as a reaction against long-established constraints on women. Given the possibility of some portion of power, they seized it, exercised it with maximum force, even relished it, not as power to do something, but, in a manner hardly peculiar to women, as power over others.

Finally, whatever else might be said of the Iron Girls or their epigones in hundreds of feature magazine articles on women pilots, high tension wire workers, and boat crews, women in nontraditional jobs broke standard gender stereotypes. They were tokens, to be sure, but a token signs a promise; eventually it becomes a sign of the breach of the promise.

What happened after the Cultural Revolution and after the war in the United States and Great Britain was both analogous and, of equal interest, very different—a difference correlated in part to the difference in the mobilizing ideologies themselves and the societies in which they occurred. Women in the West were eased out of the work force into the home as consumers, as the stipulated bearers of harmony and stability, as essential reproducers, literally and figuratively, of the cold war social order. Some though hardly all women put by their wartime experience and welcomed a return to "normalcy." The ideology of gender roles remained essentially hegemonic and difficult to resist.

In China, normalization required a direct attack on Cultural Revolution ideology. Women were not fired, though there has been considerable pressure to persuade, or even force, them to take lengthy maternity leaves and earlier retirement.[17] Neither in the West nor in China was this a matter of conscious conspiracy, and certainly women were complicitous in it. But it is necessary to discriminate between what was self-generated, by women themselves, and what was externally imposed. Neither in China nor in the West do women fully possess the power of self-definition.

After the fall of the Gang of Four in China, among the early expressions of rejecting the past, was a movement by women to define for themselves what it meant to be a woman with needs and goals different from those of men. Freed of an imposed asceticism, women sometimes could find no better expression of pleasure in their difference than in astonishing numbers to get their hair permed; in the newspapers there was an explosion of fashions, cosmetics, beauty tips.

At a more political level, in the 1980 local election campaign in Beijing, a woman candidate opened her campaign with a big-character poster on the subject of "Oriental beauty." She was attacked for such a nonpolitical choice and, in response to posters criticizing her, wrote one called "Women are human beings too." The text is a tangle of contradictions which, however, clearly reflects the legacy of recent Chinese cultural instructions to women. "Women," it argues, "are human beings too. Why should their specific attributes, their interests, their development as a sex, and many other aspects of their womanhood not be important questions?" Women must be allowed to develop their own personalities, their point of view, and "widen and reinforce the overall understanding of things." Through struggle, women will "acquire the right to be human beings and the right to take up responsibilities and the honors that flow from them."[18] Here two things are going on simultaneously: an appeal to women's special attributes and point of view while the definition of the normative human being remains male. The double bind is familiar, a consequence of the fact that women's identity *is* doubled in any modern or modernizing society. We are dealing here with what can only be called the dialectic of female identity, within which different terms are stressed depending on the larger social situation. Ironically, the Cultural Revolution delivered women into the modern era by wrenching them free of feudal models, proposing instead their dispersion and dissolution into society at large. But women cannot be made to disappear in this way. In modern society their identity is of necessity both individual and generic. The feminist argument is compelling: the secret of modern equality is the suppressed inequality of women. Women's special attributes are exactly what make them unfit to be human in a male sense. Responsible for children, they can no more fulfill the goals of the four modernizations equally with men than they could those of the preceding revolutionary period.

Of necessity, then, post-Cultural Revolution reform and restoration has had to make the subject of women's place central. There are two simultaneous aspects to the ongoing construction of female gender roles. First, the explicit repudiation of the past. Iron Girls brigades are the subject of comic clapper talks, critical discussions in the press, snide comments. In a style familiar to women elsewhere, the idea that one can somehow lose one's gender by behaving inappropriately is regularly deployed. Iron Girls were unwomanly, unmarriageable, unattractive, in short, "false boys." At a recent symposium attended by sociologists, legal scholars, literary critics, and philosophers in Beijing, it was pointed out that "young men want women to have a pretty face, a nice figure, be good at housework, and have a gentle disposition."[19] The higher a woman's educational attainments, the harder it is for her to find a suitable mate. Women with "strong career interests" are not considered desirable wives—a strong echo of the traditional notion that a woman without talent is virtuous. Indeed, unmarried women over the age of twenty-eight constitute a social problem that causes much worry. Sometimes the women are blamed for being "too picky." But on other occasions men themselves are criticized for ignoring the value of an older woman. Several men who married women three years older than themselves wrote of their satisfaction in a popular youth magazine—such women were socially experienced, capable housewives, and wonderfully supportive of their husband's work (one young man marveled gratefully that he had written twenty articles since his marriage). While the Beijing forum was critical of many current attitudes, the men who participated (described by the reporter as being the "more voluble" participants) were uniform in their denunciation of "iron women" and "fake boys." "A woman who becomes masculine is a mutant. Capable women should be different from men. They have their own special charm, for example exquisiteness and depth of emotions, and well-developed imagistic thinking. Women's own latent abilities should be called forth."[20]

In thus rejecting the approach set forth by the Cultural Revolution, which attacked the notion that biology was destiny but only by holding out to women the promise that they too could be like men, the participants in the Beijing forum embraced a different but no less unequal view of women. Here biology *is* destiny—but a pleasant one. Women and men are complementary, gender polarity is to be honored, and women are, as they had been all along, instrumental to the realization of Chinese development—whether Maoist revolutionary or Deng Xiaoping reformist.

In dramatic writings about the "ten years of turmoil," women in political roles are universally depicted in the most negative way. Perhaps it is easier to focus anger on the women who carried out policy than to attack directly the men who actually made it. Perhaps, as in prerevolutionary China, woman characters are again the vehicles through which male writers express social criticism. But it matters that abuse of power is most easily denounced when it has been feminized. Evil itself has been feminized, and the message to women is clear: there is something in the natural order of things that does not love a woman exercising public power.[21]

The slogans of the past, as they relate to women, are emphatically rejected. That women can do what men can do, I was told by Women's Federation cadres in two different cities, is a "reactionary" idea that ignores their actual physical weakness compared to men. A popular play in Shanghai referred to the part of the sky that women held up as "less weighty" than the half sustained by men. The sexually undifferentiated style of dress and manner urged on women during the Cultural Revolution has been overwhelmingly rejected, and women's magazines feature careful diagrams of instruction on how to sit down, stand up, and walk in an appropriately female fashion. And if your body is insufficiently feminine to meet current needs, you can reform it, even revolutionize it. The inside back cover of a recent issue of *Zhonguo funu* (Women of China) is entirely devoted to an advertisement by the Silver Star Plastic and Color Printing Factory of Jiangmen City, Guangdong, which, in the patriotic pursuit of "eliminating the flaws in female development," has invented and is currently marketing a "Rapid Healthful Beauty Bust Enhancer." Consisting of a rubber cup and a small length of hose, this wondrous mechanism will stimulate the "secretions of the pituitary glands in the chest, expand the spongeability of the breasts," and allow "flat breasts to become full and protruding in a short period of time." Testimonials from satisfied users claim that the device will also "promote blood circulation in the breasts, prevent breast cancer, guard against neurasthenia, make both breasts a uniform size," and, especially important in a country that considers them a major defect, "cause freckles on the face to disappear naturally." A satisfied user, Kuang XX, claimed it cured her insomnia as well.[22]

There is a small industry of essay writers generating lists of female as opposed to male characteristics. In one typical article the author asserts that "the thinking of male classmates is comparatively broad and quick. They have wide-ranging interests, a strong ability to get to work, and they like to think things out for themselves; but sometimes they are not careful or thorough enough. Female classmates often have stronger memory and language ability, are more diligent and meticulous. But they have one-track minds, do not think dynamically enough, have a rather narrow range of activity, and easily become interested in trivial matters. Their moods fluctuate easily, they are shy, and they don't dare to boldly raise questions." Another account notes that the "nervous system of females is not as stable as that of males. . . . Women are highly sensitive, so much so that the slightest misfortune can make a woman cry. Men, in contrast, only shed tears on extremely tragic occasions." Moreover, women can quickly stop crying, but "a crying man finds it difficult to calm down." The same is true of other emotions. "Women's laughter for the most part is like a light breeze; it sweeps past and is gone. The laughter of men is not often heard, but is very infectious." In a version of the dialectic that would have made Mao Zedong weep long (or laugh infectiously), the writer concludes that the two sexes "must form two aspects of equal value that unite into a whole. Conversely, without differences, combination would be an unsuitable goal."[23] (Mao always did insist that "one breaks down into two" rather than two combining into one.) A 1985 *Life Handbook for the Contemporary Woman* has a convenient checklist of characteristics reminiscent of the tests one used to take at the back of magazines. If you're a girl you love to talk, are very refined, understand other people's feelings, are devout, pay attention to your appearance, are neat, clean, quiet, need security, love art and literature, and easily express "gentle feelings." If you're a boy, on the other hand, you are aggressive, independent, not influenced by others, dominating, not troubled by trivia, vigorous, risk taking, decisive, not dependent on others (which is apparently different from being independent), and pay little attention to your appearance.[24]

All these messages are contradictory, reflecting an ongoing, inconclusive debate. Women should learn the arts of adornment but refrain from their undue exercise; women should be filial toward parents and in-laws but modern, independent, antifeudal; women should certainly follow the dictates of state population policy, and are of course the primary child-rearer, but they must learn, from professional experts, how to avoid spoiling the single child; women should fully participate in the drive to realize the four modernizations, but they might just want to take three, four or even ten years maternity leave as well. Romantic love is an acceptable socialist notion, but women are responsible for controlling their own and male sexual behavior, and sex itself should be indulged in only after marriage and strictly within its confines. Struggling to understand how it is possible, under a social system "that guarantees equal rights for both sexes legally, economically, politically, and educationally," that women nevertheless fall behind, one author sorts through both objective and subjective causes. The objective causes are that the "weaknesses of women ideologically and educationally, shaped in the course of centuries, give many the reason to persist in considering them inferior." Not surprisingly, this objective situation has a decidedly negative subjective impact, giving young women an "inferiority complex" and leading them to be dependent on others. A final subjective factor is that girls are "near-sighted and complacent." Confined to a smaller circle of friends than boys, "girls are apt to discuss clothes and make-up and other such immediate concerns rather than bigger social issues."[25]

Gender roles and family organization, Foucault has taught us, are not objects of social policy but the necessary instrument through which the policy is expressed and enforced. In China today, a release of individual energy, deemed necessary to fuel the four modernizations, must nevertheless be constrained so that it remains amenable to centralized control. A stable nuclear family, maintained by women who are at the same time as available for paid labor as the developing economy requires, has proven historically the most efficient form of social and personal organization to achieve such a controlled empowerment of individuals—with one requirement: that nuclear families be induced to restrict the number of their children. But given China's population problems, the restriction needs to be drastic: preferably to one child per family. For families to be satisfied with one child, the status of women must become more nearly equal to that of men—else the preference for high status sons continues; couples whose first child is a girl will be radically dissatisfied. At this time, however, conditions of unemployment and underemployment make it impossible to hold out to women the old promise of socialist liberation—that their equality will devolve from their integration into the paid work force and the socialization of household chores and child rearing.

One possible and tempting solution, as I have suggested above, is to revive a gender ideology that stresses the "natural" differences between women and men, limits the notion of socialized housework to improved domestic technology, and condemns "iron women." Thus "modern" ideas about women in China are once again conveniently consonant with traditional views, and the new in turn reinforces the old. "Socialist spiritual civilization" is invoked to control such unwanted results of the open door as prostitution and pornography. The contents of that civilization are rarely spelled out in any detail. Sometimes, with respect to women, socialist spirituality sounds remarkably like traditional Confucian morality: both subordinate the interests of the individual to that of the family. And the family is, in both, the province of the male head of household. The current Confucian revival—the renaissance in Confucian studies, the refurbishing of the sage's birthplace, the feature articles on his descendants and praise for their unbroken filial piety despite the ravages of revolution—is more broadly an effort to revitalize a cultural heritage that is uniquely Chinese in the face of the erosive, even corrosive impact of the West. The special problems women incur from this revival focus a general question: the nature of the relationship between a "feudal" ideology that assigns women a set of inherited roles and one that aims to be both socialist and modernizing.

"Women in China," a Chinese friend told me, "cannot do what women in the West can do. After all, if peasant women started to act like women in the West, the world would turn upside down." My friend's vision of how Western women act was vague at the edges, but at its heart she correctly perceived a striving for autonomy, which is a goal that calls into question the premises of both liberal and socialist revolutions. For, despite the promise to women held out by virtually all modernizing strategies, their actual role has been to stabilize the world; to be the still point around which the axis of revolution can rotate more freely.

Given Mao Zedong's passion for contradictions, it is a pity he does not seem to have reflected more on the subject of women. What he did say indicates that his ideas were more complicated than current official Chinese formulations. Liberating women, he argued, was not like manufacturing washing machines. By this he seems to have meant two things—that genuine liberation was not simply a matter of the development of the forces of production, and that the production of devices that cut back on women's household labor would not by themselves guarantee that liberation. Moreover, in philosophic moods, Mao was wont to speculate on the ultimate disappearance of the family altogether—in a thousand years, perhaps, as part of the ongoing evolution of human society. The cosmic, permanent, absolutely indeterminate dialectic upon which Mao insisted, a universe in which equilibrium was of necessity a sometime thing, has been stilled, frozen. Class struggle has been abolished by the fiat of definition. But the social and gender divisions that mark reality in China no less than in the United States cannot be defined out of existence.

Notes

1. See Phyllis Andors, *The Unfinished Liberation of Chinese Women, 1949–1980.* Bloomington: Indiana University Press, 1983.

2. *Women in China* (April 1983): 10.

3. Kay Ann Johnson, *Women, the Family and Peasant Revolution in China* (Chicago: University of Chicago Press, 1983), esp. ch. 12.

4. Anita Chan et al. *Chen Village. The Recent History of a Peasant Community in Mao's China* (Berkeley: University of California Press, 1984), p. 190.

5. Johnson, *Women, the Family and Peasant Revolution*, p. 182.

6. Nora Astorga, quoted in the *New York Times Magazine*, September 28, 1986.

7. Mao was reflecting on the meaning of revolution: "It isn't simply a question of replacing the Tsar with Khrushchev, one bourgeoisie with another, even if it's called communist. It's the same as with women. Of course it was necessary to give them legal equality to begin with. But from there on, everything still remains to be done. The thought, culture, and customs which brought China to where we found her must disappear, and the thought, culture, and customs of proletarian China, which does not yet exist either, must appear. The Chinese woman doesn't exist yet either, among the masses; but she is beginning to want to exist. And then, to liberate women is not to manufacture washing machines." As quoted in Andre Malraux, *Anti-Memoirs* (New York: Holt, Rinehart and Winston, 1968), pp. 373–74.

8. Tani Barlow and Donald M. Lowe, *Teaching China's Lost Generation: Foreign Experts in the People's Republic of China* (San Francisco: China Books and Periodicals, 1987), p. 95.

9. See Chris Berry, "Sexual Difference and the Viewing Subject in *Li Shuangshuang* and *The In-Laws*," in *Perspectives on Chinese Cinema*, ed. Chris Berry (Ithaca: China-Japan Program, Cornell University, 1985).

10. Ibid., p. 42.

11. Andors, *Unfinished Liberation*, p. 99.

12. Ibid., p. 125. For Andors' final summation of the campaign, see p. 149. See also Elisabeth Croll, "The Movement to Criticize Confucius and Lin Piao," *Signs: Journal of Women in Culture and Society* 2, 3 (Spring 1977): 721–26.

13. See, for comparison, Leila J. Rupp, *Mobilizing Women for War: German and American Propaganda, 1939–1945* (Princeton: Princeton University Press, 1978), and Margaret Higonet et al., eds., *Behind the Lines: Gender and the Two World Wars* (New Haven: Yale University Press, 1987).

14. "Diploma," in Zhang Xinxin and Sang Ye, *Chinese Lives: An Oral History of Contemporary China*, ed. W. J. E. Jenner and Delia Davin (New York: Pantheon, 1987), p. 56.

15. Ibid., p. 57.

16. Liu Binyan, *People or Monsters? And Other Stories and Reportage from China After Mao*, ed. Perry Link (Bloomington: Indiana University Press, 1983). One Chinese friend, who otherwise found the model operas of the period stunningly boring, remarked approvingly that none featured "couples." Kay Ann Johnson would probably interpret this as a feature of the traditionalist-Maoist coalition against romantic love, but it could also be understood as a focus on female agency.

17. The one-child family has had little impact on the ruminations of Chinese men on such matters. Arguing for an extended leave, one journalist noted that since women "are the ones who bear children, and because they are, on the whole, more diligent, patient, and hard-working, they are the natural candidates for taking charge at home, even if that means they have to do more housework. Conversely, it would be no 'liberation' if they have to work and take care of the home at the same time. Three years of leave would alleviate their physical and mental burdens. This is the way to true 'liberation.'" Xing Hua, "A System of Employment by Stages Should Be Instituted Among Chinese Women," in *Chinese Women (1)*, ed Stanley Rosen, special issue of *Chinese Sociology and Anthropology* 20, 1 (Fall 1987): 83. See also Elisabeth Croll et al., *China's One-Child Policy* (London: Macmillan, 1985).

18. Anita Rand, "To Be a Feminist in Beijing," in *Wild Lilies, Poisonous Weeds: Dissident Voices from People's China*, ed. Gregor Benton (London: Pluto Press, 1982), pp. 195ff.

19. Emily Honig and Gail Hershatter, *Personal Voices: Chinese Women in the 1980s* (Stanford: Stanford University Press, 1988), pp. 25–26.

20. Ibid. My quotation was drawn from the original manuscript of *Personal Voices*. See note 38, p. 345, for full citation on the symposium.

21. I am reminded of the marathon German film answer to *Holocaust*, Reitz's *Heimat*. Here the most evil man in the village, the only member of the SS, is a suspiciously effeminate individual who is accused by village women of being a "shirker" and avoiding combat. As Erick Rentschler puts it in "The Discourse on Bitburg," *New German Critique* 36 (Fall 1985), *Heimat* illustrated the way "forgetfulness can lie in remembering."

22. Honig and Hershatter, *Personal Voices*, pp. 68–69.
23. Ibid.
24. Ibid., pp. 35–36.
25. Zhang Xiping, "Cultivation of New Women," in *Chinese Sociology and Anthropology* 20, 1 (Fall 1987): 48, 49.

14

FEMINIST HUMANISM: SOCIALISM AND NEOFEMINISM IN THE WRITINGS OF ZHANG JIE

Roxann Prazniak

The relationship between socialist and feminist thought, sometimes regarded as an "unhappy marriage," has been the subject of much discussion among both Marxists and feminists.[1] The development of socialism in China and the questions it raises concerning the future of women there provide an occasion for reflecting on issues central to this discussion as well as to the problems of the Chinese revolutionary experience. I am particularly interested here in pursuing two basic questions: How do Chinese women who are consciously concerned with the realization of women's emancipation within a socialist framework conceive of the emancipation process today? What is the relationship of their outlook to the international feminist discourse?

The discussion below is based for the most part on the writings of Zhang Jie, an author of the post-Mao era, who addresses in her fiction the relationship between women's problems and socialism. In contrast to much recent Western scholarship on Chinese women, Zhang expresses a critical but optimistic view of prospects for both women and socialism in China. The perspective provided by Zhang's contribution to the contemporary Chinese discourse on socialist/feminist goals reveals the limitations of feminist concepts as they have been shaped by Euro-American experiences, and points to ways in which those concepts can be expanded by including voices from the Chinese experience.

Zhang's is but one of recent voices in an ongoing Chinese discourse on gender oppression. Sustained interest in the problems of women first appeared in China in the late nineteenth century to the accompaniment of national discussions on social and political dilemmas resulting from encounters with foreign industrial capitalism. From the beginning socialists, especially anarchists, were most attentive to the links among political change, social reform, and the release of women from their subjugation within the status quo. With the founding of the Chinese Communist Party in 1921, Marxist theory and practice provided the vehicles for addressing the conditions of both rural and urban women. As in many parts of the world, the interaction between Marxist and feminist issues in China from the 1920s to the present has produced numerous conflicts over daily priorities as well as theoretical assumptions.

Scholars outside of China (prominent among them Phyllis Andors, Margery Wolf, Judith Stacey, and Elisabeth Croll) have acknowledged the strides Chinese women have made as a consequence of the Communist revolution but have argued nevertheless that Chinese women today live under a socialist variant of patriarchy in which they are subordinate within the family and manipulated to suit state policies on economic development.[2] Margery Wolf concludes from her interviews with Chinese women from many walks of life that women under the present socialist government of China, in acquiescing once again to postpone their demands in favor of national interest, have subjected their consciousness to a state that offers them little hope of liberation. Similarly, Judith Stacey convincingly argues that patriarchy has proven compatible with socialism, and that the resulting contradictions, if they are to be resolved at all, cannot be addressed by socialist practice and theory alone. Although a Chinese woman such as Zhang Jie might agree that these are accurate assessments of the actual conditions of women, these conclusions misleadingly suggest that women in China have no significant consciousness of their situation. Reflecting on these analyses, Suzanne Pepper queries, "is there anyone besides foreign feminist scholars left to care that the liberation of Chinese women is still 'unfinished' or their 'revolution postponed'?" Pepper leaves open the possibility that there may be unrecognized manifestations of concern within China, but she does not ask why we, as outside observers, might be missing some of these signs, and instead goes on to draw the apparently unavoidable conclusion that with regard to prospects for the improvement of women's living and working conditions in China, "For the time being . . . there is no sign of forward movement from any direction."[3] No sign of movement, that is, from the state or from women themselves. Speaking to an audience of like-minded American and Western European feminists who have grown suspicious of the claims of socialism when it comes to women's problems, these authors give the collective impression that there are few opportunities for improving women's status in socialist China and no significant women's consciousness that might push for change. It is the willingness to hear the voices of women consciously struggling with socialism that is lacking in the Euro-American literature on China.

The difficult but engaged and in some ways triumphant struggles of the women who inhabit Zhang Jie's fiction contrast sharply with the impression of a generally demoralized state created by Western authors' assessments of women's progress toward emancipation in China today. This apparent contradiction is due, I think, to the inability of a narrow Western feminist perspective to comprehend the problems of women in a developing socialist society. Feminists from other socialist countries may speak more directly and with less distortion to the situation Zhang describes in China. Rada Ivekovic, a Yugoslav feminist, has used the term "neofeminist" to describe the struggle for feminist goals in a society in which many of the political and economic issues relevant to women have been legally addressed by state socialism but where many of the social, sexual, and psychological dimensions of women's emancipation remain essentially unexplored within formal societywide channels.[4] The neofeminist perspective, Slavenka Drakulic-Ilic makes clear in her "'Six Mortal Sins' of Yugoslav Feminism," signifies that "The women's movement does not mean a separation from socialist forces. On the contrary, it means contribution to socialist transformation of society, from a specifically woman's perspective."[5] Women in socialist societies have found the idea to be relevant: in 1980, two years after the first neofeminist conference in Belgrade, Polish feminists founded a Neofeminist Association.[6]

Zhang Jie's views are more in the socialist neofeminist than in the Euro-American feminist vein. Zhang herself actively rejects the term feminist as she knows it from the Western European and U.S. contexts in which it is embedded in liberal legal and political individualism. She also makes it clear that she is concerned with existential problems that are not limited to women alone.[7] The insights and strategies Zhang (as a socialist and Third World woman) proffers may of necessity differ in some respects from those of women in societies shaped by the Western European historical experience, but they are not therefore inferior or irrelevant. On the contrary, in providing an alternative perspective on the problems of women, these experiences remind us of the necessity of resisting the singular perspective of any one socially restricted approach to the problems of women that, if unchecked, may undercut the universalism essential to feminism as a liberating idea.

The discussion below does not dwell upon the failures of Chinese socialism for women, though there have been many failures as well as successes, or on the inability of Chinese women to conceptualize the final outcome of female emancipation, which is a task in process and hence no more apparent to Chinese women than to anyone else. It seeks instead to bring a way of thought expressed by one socially conscious Chinese woman into the ongoing discussion of the problems of gender oppression in China and the world—into a dialogue that makes room for all women and men, as authentic participants within a global discourse on human emancipation. Zhang Jie's work expands the discussion of social relations under patriarchy and explores the relationship between the state and social change. Her characters remind us that all women engaged in struggle are motivated in part by the fictive possibilities that animate any forward-looking consciousness.

Zhang in the Chinese Literary Context

Zhang Jie was born in 1937, came of age during the early years of the post-1949 Chinese revolution, and was a mature adult at the time of the Cultural Revolution. A member of the post-Mao generation of writers in China, she first published after 1979 in such journals as *Beijing wenxue* (Beijing literature), *Shouhuo* (Harvest), and *Shanghai wenyi* (Shanghai literature and art). In 1986 some of her short stories and her novella *Fangzhou* (The ark) were translated into English in a volume titled *Love Must Not Be Forgotten*. An earlier novel, *Chenzhong de chibang* (Leaden wings), was translated in 1987.[8] Zhang's writings are part of the discourse on Chinese socialism that took shape in the years from 1979 to 1983 when questions of alienation in a socialist society and the significance of humanism for socialism were more widely discussed than before or since.

Compared with her peers among the writers of the post-Mao era, Zhang at first glance appears considerably less radical in her direct political challenges to the status quo.[9] She retains a strong sense of social responsibility, does not condemn the Cultural Revolution wholesale, and does not seek to reveal intrinsic weaknesses in Marxist thought. In fact, Zhang's approach is at once both highly subversive and constructive, pursuing a humanist critique of past and present policies that is sympathetic to socialism but firmly rejects the selfish exercise of power over others, whether the wielders of that power are male or female. Unlike many younger women authors, Zhang Xinxin for example, Zhang Jie is unwilling to endorse individualistic solutions at the expense of social consciousness. Unlike many of her peers, such as Bai Hua in the story/film "Bitter Love," Zhang does not dwell on the shortcomings of Maoist politics.[10] Zhang, as will become clear through the life histories of her characters, sees the unintended positive as well as negative consequences of adversity experienced during the Cultural Revolution. Finally, unlike Li Ping, who in his story "When Sunset Clouds Disappear" struggles with the relationship between the limitations of a materialist point of view and the religious vision of a Chan Buddhist monk,[11] Zhang Jie assumes the importance of a transcendent, spiritual element in life and finds no contradiction between this and what she considers to be the original intent of Marxist thought, namely the creation of a compassionate, fair society built on the fulfillment of human potential. Zhang Jie's audience includes holders of power within the Chinese political system, but unlike many of her peers she is also addressing women as a group. In *The Ark* in particular, she raises issues that do not leave uncontested any pattern of domination and that speak directly to what women can do in their own lives to contribute to more humane social relations.

It is significant that Zhang's main character in her novella, *The Ark*, is a woman who is engaged in an attempt to recover the "forgotten meaning of Marxism" (p. 158).[12] Zhang's critique of socialism in China has not led her to disillusionment with Marxism. Instead she chooses to explore experiences that are not easily packaged by existing Marxist approaches. She emphasizes socially conscious, self-reflective experience as a corrective to theoretical blindspots that hinder understanding of and action toward social change. "Life is complex," Zhang writes, "and each person must discover those personal, intangible answers herself. If one does everything according to convention and custom only, they will forever carry around with them the heavy, restricting burden of such an encyclopedia" (pp. 141–42).

Zhang attributes her optimism in part to her place in the generational makeup of Chinese society. In *The Ark* she writes of a woman of her own age group (those in their thirties during the Cultural Revolution): "She possessed neither the unshakeable optimism of previous generations, nor the blind pessimism of the younger generation. Her generation was the most confident, the most clear-minded and the most able to face up to reality" (p. 172). Zhang, like many of her generation, retains socialism as an ideal and envisions women's emancipation within that larger social context. Her views, often highly critical of the corruption and inefficiency of the socialist status quo in China, have their source in a humanism informed by compassionate individuality, historical perspective, and social responsibility.

While Zhang's views may not represent a general social consciousness, just as the interpretations of women's conditions in any society vary widely, the audience that her work commands, and the controversy it has generated, provides compelling evidence of a significant concern with questions of gender relations.

Socialism and Neofeminism in Zhang's Fiction

The world Zhang creates through her characters is one shaped by socialist political principles but flawed by human behavior and attitudes that perpetuate patterns of domination and subservience. Her characters, male and female alike, live with positive reference points for overcoming gender oppression in the legal, economic, and political spheres. There are also, however, cultural and psychological norms that have yet to be transformed. The transformation process is both personal and social. For the most part, Zhang's characters (both male and female, young and old) as well as her settings are drawn primarily from urban, intellectual environments. The characters reveal the ways in which Chinese women have been able to work with socialism to improve their lot as well as the problems they have been unable to overcome. Her writings explore the possibilities of women working with socialism to realize their goals.

The novella, *The Ark*, Zhang Jie's most fully developed commentary on issues concerning educated, urban women in China today, is the centerpiece of the discussion that follows, supplemented with themes from other stories that expand on ideas in *The Ark*. *The Ark* itself, I would suggest, is a neofeminist allegory about three women struggling together to understand themselves as creative social beings, often in opposition to the demands of social convention and contemporary political ideology. Three powerful and vulnerable women inhabit this novella. Cao Jinghua, a former school teacher and current member of the Chinese Communist Party, struggles with a debilitating back problem and writes theoretical pieces on the "forgotten meaning of Marxism." She is a childless divorcee who married at a young age out of necessity. Her one pregnancy ended in abortion, which contributed to her husband's hostility and eventually to her divorce. Liang Qian is a dedicated film director. She and her estranged husband have been unable to get a divorce because it would damage her father's influential official standing, as well as destroy her husband's hopes of gaining anything through his wife's family connections. Liang Qian has one sixteen-year-old son from whom she feels largely estranged. Liu Quan, the third main character, works in the office of an export company. In college she studied English, and she is trying to obtain a position as translator at the Foreign Affairs Bureau. She is divorced and has one small son.

The three women are old schoolmates who meet once again in their early forties only to discover that their lives have encountered similar problems. Sharing an apartment along with Mantou, a cat of seemingly considerable compassion, and Mengmeng, Liu Quan's son who visits once a week, the three women support each other and wonder together how their lives have "gone wrong." They share a conviction that they are better off despite all of the difficulties and self-doubts, and that like the ark of biblical lore, their tiny apartment afloat in a sea of disappointment carries lives that are part of a movement toward a new future—in this case, a future in which the problems faced by women will be truly appreciated and addressed in the constitution of a society in which the proverb that begins the story, "You are particularly unfortunate, because you were born a woman," will no longer be true.

Women and Socialist Achievements

Among other things, state socialism in China has guaranteed women legal, economic, and political equality. All three main characters in *The Ark* take this for granted. Formal state policies are an empowering reminder that equal treatment, free of gender bias, is ostensibly the norm. To take but one example, equal pay for equal work is a legal fact (if not always a reality) in China. Whereas in the United States women earn 50 percent of what men earn, in China the figure is 70 percent. The legal side of equitable treatment has been achieved in China and other socialist countries and is an important reference point for further social change. This is no small accomplishment and one that women in the United States have been seeking to achieve since 1787. As Joan Hoff-Wilson has pointed out, "Because women were left out of the 1787 Constitution and the Bill of Rights, it has taken them almost two hundred years to approximate equality under the law with men."[13] China has gone far in this respect within a short period.

A feature of the society in which Zhang's characters have grown to maturity is that they have not been excluded from political activity, for better and worse. Although it is still true that women hold very few higher party and government positions, they were included in political campaigns of the past that drew women as well as men into local struggles based on a "mass line" approach. Men controlled the major decision-making circles, but movements such as the Cultural Revolution were far from exclusively men's affairs. As Marilyn Young points out in her essay in this volume, state promotion of male-female equality and women's active political participation during the Cultural Revolution "inevitably unsettled the status quo of gender relations" and "encouraged women to take action against it [the state]."

Zhang and the characters she portrays belonged to the generation of women in their late twenties and thirties who had bitter and yet self-strengthening experiences during the Cultural Revolution. Liang Qian was in prison for a reason that is not made known to the reader, and Jinghua lived in a forest area where she learned to work with a plane and make furniture. The experience exacerbated her back condition but strengthened her arms. Whenever she encounters difficulties now, her one source of solace is to plane a piece of wood or create a small item of furniture, a skill she values highly. Women have been the beneficiaries as well as the victims of past political activity. They clearly have a place for themselves in the public sphere which has been reinforced by socialist ethics.

The legacy of socialist theory and practice shapes the historical perspective that Zhang's characters bring to their lives. At the same time, Zhang reflects on the limitations of historical understanding. History is grounded in material and social reality for Zhang, but she also suggests dimensions beyond historical comprehension. In personal narratives especially, history is important as a source of illumination and encouragement in present difficulties, but it also has significant limits. Zhang brings the historical materialism of the public realm into the private sphere, and in so doing she broadens her notion of history to include the intersubjective and even the transhistorical. She suggests that history is more than what humans perceive in social relations. She retains a socialist faith in historical progress and at the same time senses that many of the problems she explores are beyond history, beyond what we can know through the material investigation of life, lodged perhaps somewhere in the emotional aspects of life shaped by human biology, psychology, or spirituality.

In "Love Must Not Be Forgotten," a daughter finds guidance and meaning for her life as she reflects across generations and thinks of her mother's divorce and unrequited love.[14] Like a true historian, she gathers her sources—she recalls conversations with her mother and reads passages from the latter's diary. The purpose of the daughter's inquiry into her mother's experience is to try to gain some perspective and insight into her own decision to marry or not. In the story "Emerald," Linger returns to her former workplace after twenty years of absence and confronts her current situation in the context of remembrances from the past and emotional traces that carry into the present.[15] Women's consciousness evolves in Zhang's narratives, within this dialectic between past and present, as well as between personal and public realms.

In addition, history has its own dynamics, which are not always open to human comprehension or susceptible to human intervention but may provide some comfort in the abstract. Jinghua in a moment of despair over her political situation finds comfort in the idea that, "Ultimately, history would be the fairest judge of all" (p. 146). Earlier, she wonders, "If it were really true that the world developed in cycles, then wasn't a return to the matriarchal society inevitable?" (p. 114). But there is also a sense of helplessness: "It seemed as if all three of them were separated from men by some unbridgeable chasm. Was it because men were historically more advanced than women—or women more advanced than men—so that they could no longer find any basis for communication? Well, if this was the case, then neither men nor women could really be blamed. No one could help or change the historical circumstances which had gone into creating these distorted positions" (p. 154).

Social responsibility as a source of personal fortification against life's major and minor traumas is another contribution of socialist ethics to the struggles of Zhang's characters. Liang Qian as a child during the Korean War collected newspapers and rubbish to sell, turning over the money she earned to her teacher to help support the front line. During the "Four Pests" campaign, she had spent her midday rest period "squatting in the lavatory with a fly swatter" (p. 144). These childhood experiences, while seemingly trivial, had instilled in her a sense of social responsibility that fortified her to cope with her many disillusionments with life. Liu Quan's efforts to enter the Foreign Affairs Bureau as a translator, for example, had several levels of meaning for her. "She was searching for something, not just struggling to break free. Every illusion she ever had, had been extinguished by bitter experience. What remained were her authentic feelings of social responsibility and conscience: she must justify the 56 yuan she earned each month" (p. 145). This sense of responsibility sometimes seems overwrought, but it is deeply connected to other values and experiences. Liu Quan notes at another point that, "When no one bore responsibility, there was no way you could fight" (p. 168). A sense of social responsibility and the effort to establish this as a social norm is, Zhang seems to be saying, a vital ingredient in the making of a humane society. Perhaps Zhang lets her characters assume too much responsibility for their conditions. Nonetheless, Jinghua goes on writing despite the difficulties and criticisms that come her way because in the end, "if no one had any sense of social responsibility, what would the world be like?" (p. 146).

The importance of a social orientation also means that commitment to the group is a kind of life raft. "The friendship between [*sic*] the three of them was one area of their lives that was clean and untarnished. They knew how hard such friendships, those that had been cemented through struggle and hardship, were to come by in this vast world. And, indeed, the bond had taken work and, at times, cost each of them dearly. Experience had taught them the risks as well as the value of friendship, and now that they were entering middle age and had lost their youthful vigor, it turned out to be the only solid element in their lives" (p. 171). Zhang does not advocate that women live separately from men, but there is a strong suggestion that at this historical moment there is a need and purpose for such communities among women and that women should not scorn but welcome this alternative as the best that can exist under certain circumstances. It is very important in the lives of Zhang's characters that women not struggle alone. Liang Qian tells Jinghua, "I want you to write, write, write. . . . I want you to make a contribution toward revolutionary theory, or if you can't do that, I want you to support those who can, and not let them struggle on alone" (p. 158). The entire history of socialism in China has drawn attention to the problems of women as a distinct social group and to the need for solidarity among people who struggle. While the state has not fully honored the implications of this experience in the present, the importance of the message resurfaces in the consciousness of Zhang's fiction.

Women's Problems with Socialism

Zhang is clear that the legal and economic achievements of women under socialism are insufficient for full emancipation. She explicitly takes issue with the party's position that women are not oppressed under socialism—that the need for female emancipation is an issue for capitalist, not socialist, societies. Zhang writes, "True liberation was more than gaining improvement of economic and political status; it was also necessary that women develop confidence and strength in order to realize their full value and potential" (p. 156). Liang Qian, after having her film picked apart for its "ideological errors" (a working class man snores too loudly, thus insulting the working class, and an actress has too high a bust line, which the studio leader worries might lead to pornographic films), attacks the false "socialist" righteousness of her critics and proclaims, "Women's liberation is not only a matter of economic and political rights, but includes the recognition by women themselves, as well as by all of society, that we have our own value and significance. Women are people, not merely objects of sex, wives, and mothers. But there are many people, women among them, who think that their sole purpose in life is to satisfy the desires of men. This is a form of slavery, an attitude of self-depreciation left over from the ideas of the past" (p. 191).

This attitude of "self-depreciation" and its social foundations is clearly one of the major problems for women that socialism has made it difficult to confront because of the state's ideological claim that socialism has eliminated all significant sources of oppression. To the extent that there is official recognition of this problem, the steps to remedy the situation, which would inevitably challenge male control of and support for the party/state, are avoided. Therefore, social groups that seriously address women's problems remain informal and highly vulnerable, and topics that are most heartfelt to women are slow to be articulated by women themselves, and even slower in gaining a hearing from the powers that be.

Zhang's discussion of the relationship of people to state or workplace authority centers around the problem of corruption. For Zhang, the issue becomes one of good people being willing to stand up for what is right. I think there is a major leap of faith here in her analysis. "Well," says Liang Qian, "I believe that although there really are few evil people, their powers are considerable, and this forces good people into defensive positions. But if anything is going to change we must break their backs, stop them from ruining people's lives" (p. 173). How does one guided by empathy and social responsibility, and sensitive to uncertainties and frailties, approach those who are intent upon operating according to codes of domination and personal aggrandizement? Zhang's views are in marked contrast to someone like Liu Binyan, who in *People or Monsters?* makes it clear that individuals at best only make a temporary or small impact on a system that must be structurally changed if sources of corruption are to be eliminated.[16] In *The Ark*, Zhang writes of "complacent well-endowed officials" as the source of problems, and she comments, "No wonder our efficiency is so poor. You've got to spend 70 percent of your time buttering up the leaders and that only leaves you 30 percent to get on with your job" (p. 189). But in the end, she seems convinced that if people just did not butter up to such leaders, the situation would greatly improve. The possibility of this kind of response from below having a significant impact on state policies is tenuous, but it is Zhang's vision. Zhang's main character in *The Ark* wants only to "work steadily according to the party spirit . . . and her high Communist ideals" (p. 147), but will the party seriously hear her thoughts and take into account her observations? Can the political networks that set policy and allocate resources be addressed at the level of culture and consciousness? She can only persist and hope.

The failure of socialism to integrate a well-developed subjective dimension into its social analysis presents clear difficulties for Zhang, for whom intersubjective realities are essential to political understanding. Zhang draws on Buddhist and psychological insights to illuminate this aspect of consciousness. She talks about the interior life in terms of compassion, inner peace, personal will, and the fundamental interconnectedness of all life. She appears convinced that this is entirely compatible with socialist goals, and she hopes through her work to develop exactly this neglected realm of the human spirit. Buddhism is in the air in Zhang's stories even if it is not explored in formal religious terms. "Liu Quan felt overwhelmed by a sudden sense of dreariness. Taking off her apron, she flopped limply onto the sofa, right on top of Mantou who had been purring quietly to herself, as if reciting the Buddhist scriptures" (p. 192). This lifetime is thought of in terms of future and past lives, if not practically at least in terms of an effort to gain perspective. There is patience, mercy, and a search for the joyful in the present integration of immanence and transcendence. Zhang's exploration of consciousness in relationship to social change also draws heavily on subjective sources of behavior. "Overattention like that could only produce a timid child" (p. 122). "He was simply a stubborn person and would make Mengmeng into someone as emotionally inadequate as himself" (p. 190). "She rarely knew how to act in such situations so she fell back on her instinct to serve him" (p. 194). In the end, it is Zhang's focus on the social and historical that prevents this introspection from losing its activist impulse.

In spite of Zhang's socialist education, she seems to think that class analysis offers little in understanding social forces. Gender and generation, good and bad people are for her the categories of analysis. Zhang has set out to create a literature that advocates, "human dignity . . . sympathy . . . and the beauty of human nature."[17] In so doing she attempts to speak to a common humanity, but she dangerously risks overlooking the different material needs and psychic experiences of women of different classes. Her emphasis is on the subjective in the dialectic between public and private spheres. One suspects that by examining her own intellectual, urban experience as a woman Zhang hopes to delve into the essential core of women's problems across class and cultural boundaries, if this is indeed possible. In a story titled "Who Knows How to Live," a young woman who sells tickets on a bus line in Beijing appears as the heroine who holds her own against a young man who hassles her intentionally about his ticket, hoping to fluster her and weaken her so as to "conquer" her. The young woman comes across almost Buddha-like. The young man's friend, a factory worker who reads poetry, admires her strength and reflects that "personal will and determination are completely dependent on one's attainment of inner peace. It wasn't the ticket-seller who was frail, but Wu Huan . . . and maybe even himself."[18] It turns out that this same young woman who sells tickets is a poet of special talents who writes in her spare time away from work. Is this an image of the socialist woman who combines intellectual and manual labor? Or is this a confusion of realities that imposes upper middle class values and distorts the concerns of working women? Most likely, Zhang intends to convey the idea that certain sources of human strength are universal, that class analysis can obscure these more essential, common aspects of human experience.

In the history of its own development the Communist movement in China has underlined the importance of small group associations for effective political change, yet at the same time the party and state today create barriers to the formation of effective social groupings that might nurture individuals and develop a dialogue that could contribute to a further discussion of social problems and ultimately to social transformation itself. Both as a writer and as a woman, Zhang Jie has spoken vehemently on the problems of creating social spaces that have some autonomy as sources of support for individuals engaged in nonconventional thinking or lifestyles. At a writers conference in Anhui in July 1980, Zhang spoke of "artistic democracy" and the need for the freedom to say "no" to restrictive and excessive government regulations and interference.[19] Zhang was rumored to have been hosting a literary salon in Beijing, for which she was criticized. Why should writers need separate space? It would only focus too much attention on their own concerns and not enough on society. Zhang and others argued that writers needed to be free to talk to each other in order to create literature with both social relevance and high artistic quality.

A similar kind of alternative social space is created with much difficulty in *The Ark*. The apartment shared by the three women, who themselves form a community based on common circumstances and attitudes, provides a space that is unavailable to them in any other corner of society—a space in which to cultivate an alternative consciousness and generate support for overcoming the personal and societal bounds that confine them. The small group itself becomes confining and detrimental to human growth only when it adopts the patterns of hierarchy and dominance borrowed from the society at large. Unlike activist Chinese women who at many times in the past have focused their attention on enlarging women's control of formal networks, such as the party-sponsored Women's Federation, Zhang emphasizes informal small groups and is aware of how precious and difficult to sustain these groups are in present-day China. I doubt if she would oppose greater membership control of formal women's organizations, but this is not her primary concern. She does not argue, as did Deng Yingzhao so convincingly in the early 1950s, that socialism that does not allow for independent women's political organization is a socialism that has failed. Ultimately, Zhang's conviction is that women themselves, once politically empowered, may act as obstacles to their own emancipation unless they delve into the kind of socially oriented introspection in which her *Ark* heroines engage. Zhang's female characters in *Leaden Wings*, her novel on industrialization, exemplify the domineering patriarchal behavior of which women are capable. Likewise, she has also explored the possibility in her fiction of males displaying a nonhierarchical consciousness when relieved of the social pressures that discourage it (see below).

Because the state does not facilitate small group discussion or encourage its integration into policy formation, many subjects most pertinent to women and the possibility of alternative social arrangements are not fully explored. Marriage and divorce are two such subjects. The weight of presocialist social norms and party dictates for family life combine, in Zhang's view, to create unnecessary burdens for women's lives. She suggests that women might do better not to marry at all unless their match is based on love. If women divorce, she argues, they should not bear a stigma for so doing. On the subject of marriage, Zhang writes in *The Ark*, "As people get older they become clearer about some things, and one realization is about how difficult marriage is. They begin to see marriage as a tragedy or, if not a tragedy, a lottery in which only a few meet fortune" (p. 140). Zhang is not arguing against marriage, but she does see it as only one variety of love for others that should not overshadow alternative considerations. In particular, she does not think that one should marry without love and thus pervert one's life and sense of self just to appear to be happily married. As the daughter in her story "Love Must Not Be Forgotten" puts it, "Even waiting in vain is better than a loveless marriage. To live single is not such a fearful disaster. I believe it may be a sign of a step forward in culture, education, and the quality of life."[20] Zhang suggests that women must mature beyond motherhood and wifedom as part of their essential journey to self-awareness—not necessarily by abandoning the roles of mother and wife but by choosing them under conditions that support their self-confidence and awareness as full social beings. This is part of the dialectic between self-realization and social transformation that Zhang stresses.

The stigma of divorce arises as a major burden for women in Zhang's world. Liu Quan's father did not approve of her marriage, but when she decided to get divorced, it was an even bigger family embarrassment. Zhang writes, "So ultimately it seemed as though the ancient customs, handed down over thousands of years, dictated that she should stick to her husband, for better or for worse. Although her father had studied in England, returning with all the regalia of his Western education, his thinking was still bound up by these traditions. . . . In this respect, at least, we have not yet conquered Confucius" (p. 141). In the experience of Zhang's characters, divorced women found it even more difficult than usual to find housing, and during political campaigns they were especially vulnerable as targets. At one point Jinghua despairs that this attitude toward single women even extends to single cats. "Could single cats really evoke the same disapproval as single women?" (p. 122). Finally, Zhang notes that despite the high personal cost, divorce among women in their forties in China has become a visible social phenomenon, and she is critical of the party for dismissing this as a product of "bourgeois ideology" instead of seriously looking into the causes (p. 117).

Women and Socialist Transformation

The effort to broaden and humanize Marxist thought by focusing on the individual and the small group as the primary locus of emancipatory social activity is at the heart of Zhang's vision of future social progress. She combines the Buddhist notion of compassion which works through individual consciousness with the Marxist emphasis on social relations as the ultimate arena of human fulfillment. Historical vision, a sense of place in the human narrative, is itself liberated by human empathy and compassion which can best be nurtured in the nonhierarchical small group setting. This is perhaps Zhang's most radical insight into the relationship between female emancipation and the claims of historical materialism. Grounded in social and material reality, the potential for liberation in human history can be realized only through compassion for the human condition, not as an abstraction but as a lived daily effort here and now.

In Zhang Jie's thinking, women do not have a monopoly on compassion, but they are somewhat privileged for this task by both their nature and their social experience. Women such as Qian Xiuying in *The Ark* who manipulate femininity to gain their security in relationship to men betray this female potential (pp. 164–65). Grace and Bamboo in *Leaden Wings* are as manipulative and domineering as their male associates. While recognizing the ability of women to behave "like men," Zhang is most concerned with identifying the creative feminine potential and drawing it out into social usefulness. She sees female maturity as a process achieved through personal and public struggle. "Liang Qian stared out into the twilight, moved by a feeling of peace. Her mind wandered back through the past, and into the future where further troubles and bitterness might await them, and through it all they would become even more mature" (p. 157). Men have a different self-image, Zhang suggests. They see themselves as more constant. Because of men's socialization, and perhaps something in their nature, change comes to them with even greater difficulty. In *The Ark* Zhang comments in passing that "Women, unlike men, must always find some object for their affections, as if loving were their sole purpose in life. Without love their lives would lose all joy. And if they have no husband or child to dote on, even a cat may become the object of their affection, or for that matter a piece of furniture or cooking in their kitchen" (pp. 140–41). Potentially it is through struggle as full human beings to express this love, which may also be directed toward one's work or other public activity, that women may liberate themselves and transform social relations in the process.[21]

Zhang's discussion of love, which runs through so many of her stories, reflects the many faceted, contextual ways in which she thinks about love experiences. Her emphasis on romantic love, expressed most vividly in her story "Love Must Not Be Forgotten," is part of a return to subjectivity shared by many authors in China today, but not always handled with the social consciousness that Zhang brings to bear. The experience of unrequited love arises for some of her characters out of lives that are confined and share a sense of limited options rather than the boundless possibilities suggested by Faustian romanticism. It is perhaps a common initial response to political circumstances that have often crushed the human spirit while attempting to enrich it.

Zhang's definition of love is, however, much broader than that expressed through romantic male-female attachments. Love, for Zhang, also has a social meaning beyond personal relationships. Male-female love is unique, but one should not pursue it at all costs or dwell upon it to the loss of other possibilities. Zheng Linger in "Emerald," who reflects upon a love in her past, decides that "Once in a lifetime someone may fall passionately in love, but that need not prove the deepest, most enduring passion of his or her life."[22] It is in a final passage of this story that Linger tries to think of what she might say to a young bride on her honeymoon who has just lost her beloved husband in a drowning accident. The young bride is beside herself with grief and has fallen asleep. Linger paused. "She must wait until the young woman woke up. And she would tell her that, as well as her dead husband, there were many other things in this world worth loving; she would tell the bride that her love had already been reciprocated, that she had already experienced the most profound love, the kind that is reciprocated, and that even one day of that love can be enough. So many people lived their whole lives without ever experiencing it."[23]

In several stories Zhang suggests that the path to greater humaneness is not so different whether taken by male or female traveler. Compassion and self-awareness set in a social/historical context are central to the process which at root is gender independent. On the other hand, social experience has given rise to significant differences in male and female patterns of behavior. From Zhang's perspective, men are more isolated in their struggles. In general they are less motivated to undertake the initially painful introspection and development of consciousness that would alleviate gender oppression. Zhang suggests that men, except at the point of death or when severely debilitated physically, make no concentrated, sustained effort to develop an understanding of gender relations and other social arrangements that debilitate them emotionally and in spirit. Their recognition of the problem and the inclination to act remain diffuse and elusive. They are blocked from this course of inquiry by their own association with socially legitimized political power and their either presumed or real ability to manipulate others accordingly. This is, of course, also a statement on the "normal" daily conditions that bring some women to seek their own greater self-social awareness as a means of overcoming social death and debilitation in which their lives are more thoroughly embedded.

In *The Ark*, which conveys a sense of the everyday quality of typical male-female relations, most of the male characters are either abusive or timidly helpful in their interactions with women. Liang Qian's estranged husband, Bai Fushan, shows up at the apartment, which he treats as his own because technically it belongs to his wife. He is oblivious to the commanding and insulting way he speaks to Liang Qian and her two roommates. Typically, he comes to see if Liang Qian has changed her mind about getting her father to pull some strings so that he can go abroad. Manager Wei, Liu Quan's boss, is more overt in his harassment. He tires to block Liu Quan's transfer to the Foreign Affairs Bureau, so that he can keep her under his control. There are abusive sexual overtones to much of his behavior. On one occasion, Liu Quan had been unable to avoid going on a business trip to Hunan province with Wei. On a bus ride Wei had made a point of pressing himself against her. "It had been summer; so their clothes had been thin. In desperation Liu Quan had pushed toward the man on the other side of her; almost pressing her head into his chin, so close she could smell the odor of cigarette smoke coming from his nose and mouth. Luckily, the man must have realized Liu Quan's plight, for he quickly made space for her and put his bag between her and Manager Wei. Liu Quan had given the man a hasty, pitiful look of gratitude" (p. 140). The next year, Lao Dong, who recognized Wei's insulting behavior, got Liu Quan out of another business trip with him by telling Wei that she was busy with other work. With an expressionless face, "as blank as a carved Buddha," Lao Dong would also stage telephone calls to help Liu Quan get out of difficult situations with Wei (p. 139). Only one male character, Lao An, emerges as a fully self-aware supporter of women in their plight. He says of himself, "I was born in the old society, when women suffered the most terrible oppression. So now I have particular respect for women" (p. 151). This old comrade speaks eloquently on Jinghua's behalf when she is accused of "liberalism" for her political views which challenge party dogma. He recalls the revolutionary days when party members worked underground in Nationalist-controlled areas. People met in small groups, and no ideas were excluded from discussion, even those that could be considered the most reactionary (p. 150). As with the incident in which Liang Qian listens to criticism of her film, Zhang here draws out the connections between women's problems and political issues of general concern.

Only in some of Zhang's female characters does one find individuals who attempt to make compassion the foundation of their social relations in the course of the trials and tribulations of everyday life. The three women of *The Ark* encourage and assist one another with the patience of the Buddhist goddess of mercy. Their inner circle protects and strengthens them. It is the one place where they can vent all of their true feelings. Liang Qian rushes home in a heavy rainstorm especially to invite Jinghua to the preview of her film, only to find Jinghua collapsed on a rain-soaked floor after her back gave out while unloading a cart of coal. Jinghua will not be able to attend the preview, and Liu Quan will also miss it on her account, yet Jinghua knows how important the preview is to Liang Qian. "How can I help worrying? I know that this film is your baby"—a baby more significant to her in many ways than the son she bore many years ago but in whom she no longer finds any traces of herself. Both Jinghua's physical pain and Liang Qian's disappointment are transcended by their concern for each other and their efforts at mutual support and encouragement. Liang Qian is peaceful and content to care for Jinghua, but this is not a feigned show of concern. "She did not want to give Jinghua any false words of comfort or encouragement; they were no longer children and the truth was that the time would inevitably come when Jinghua would be paralyzed and unable to get out of bed. Jinghua herself knew this better than any of them, though it was never spoken" (p. 157). Liang Qian tells Jinghua not to go on with her woodworking, which only irritates her condition. She tells Jinghua she must take care of herself so that she can go on writing.

In another incident, when Liu Quan takes a group of foreign visitors out to lunch, Manager Wei, hoping to block Liu Quan's transfer to the Foreign Affairs Bureau, starts rumors that she had sex with the foreigners. Liang

Qian tells Liu Quan that she must fight back. At first, "She felt infuriated by Liu Quan's passive, compliant attitude. Why did she have to look for justification, as if she had done something wrong? What had happened to her self-confidence?" (p. 174). Liang Qian's ability to be compassionate instead of judgmental, and Liu Quan's openness to Liang Qian's suggestions, come from the common understanding that underneath their differences, Liang Qian was as weak as the rest of them—little girls who could be made to cry when treated meanly, and women who had to make the most of their lives. Jinghua confides that after Lao An spoke on Jinghua's behalf during the criticisms of her writing, rumors started that he had done so because of a "special relationship" between them. At one point Jinghua offers to go with Liu Quan to make a telephone call to start to straighten things out. "Liu Quan needed support, even if only from someone as weak as herself " (p. 179). In the end, when Liu Quan still feels embarrassed and demoralized about the rumors she has since countered by talking to a sympathetic male coworker and bringing charges against Manager Wei, Jinghua points out, "You shouldn't get so upset. . . . Those who should really feel upset are people like Manager Wei. Morally, you are the real winner, and not only morally either" (p. 199).

Throughout *The Ark* this kind of compassion is the norm; it is the language in which the three women communicate with one another. It is the cornerstone of their approach to life and draws sustenance from their own weaknesses and candor. Linger in "Emerald" and the young woman ticket-seller in "Who Knows How to Live" share this same quality as they confront the challenges of their daily lives. The compassionate approach to life for each of these characters is in conflict with the social patterns of domination around them, but it is also a source of personal integrity which they hope in the long run will help transform social relations. If in the end it has little impact on society, it is still their way of living which is truest to their hearts.

The potential for compassion and love is not restricted to women, but Zhang seems to feel that it is more difficult for men to realize. Only through life-threatening crises do men establish contact with this potential they share with women. In her stories "Under the Hawthorn" and "The Unfinished Record," Zhang explores, through two male characters, the sources of human compassion and the factors that aid or hinder their emergence as constructive social forces. Suffering, whether in its physical, emotional, or intellectual aspects, must ultimately be understood, Zhang suggests, as part of the formation of social relations that are created and recreated on a daily basis. The possibility of interrupting the reproduction of patterns of suffering, of which gender oppression is one variety, is inherent and limited at any one moment, but a step forward can always be taken. Zhang places great and perhaps too much emphasis on what the individual can achieve in this way, but it is the essential starting point for all further change as she sees it.

Wu Cangyun is an elderly patient in a sanatorium where he spends much of his time sitting alone under a hawthorn tree watching other patients receive visitors. He finds it difficult to talk with people because they always have stories to tell, and he can never think of anything to say. He has lived his life, and things have happened, but they have no particular significance to him that he can communicate with any purpose to his fellow patients. He has never grasped his life or authentically attempted to make choices that would will its course. "Like the old hawthorn, Wu Cangyun's history was obscure, dim. He had lived a narrow, almost invisible life, one which became devoid of meaning, leaving him no comfort, desire, or will."[24] When he learns one morning that his best friend Juru, who has been suffering from cancer, has committed suicide, he is struck with deep grief and profound disbelief. Wu is convinced that "a man who lives his life as quietly as a shadow does not do something so conspicuous. There was no question in his mind, these were lies, more lies about good men, about his loyal friend Juru" (p. 94). Wu cannot accept that a person who has shown so little will in life has willed the end of his life. Wu insists that it was the cancer that caused his friend to put his head in the noose, not the fully conscious will of Juru himself. Distraught over this development, Wu retires to his place beneath the hawthorn tree. A young child, also a patient at the sanatorium, joins him on his bench. In the child's distress over her medical treatment, which has changed her appearance so that she looks more like a boy with uncut hair than a girl, Wu finds himself puzzling over what he can do to help the child feel better. In his empathy for her, he finds his will, the same will he realizes that Juru finally discovered at the end of his life. Wu is moved to make up a story unburdened by what has happened before or what is absolutely true or not true. In so doing he begins to counter the institutional effects of treatment by medical personnel who have not shown sufficient concern for the trauma the young girl has experienced. Wu not only helps the girl, but "without even being aware of it, Wu Cangyun had found at last, within his compassion, the beginnings of his story" (p. 99).

In "An Unfinished Record," it is an aged historian who has lost the connection between emotion or compassion and the potential of daily social realities. Consequently, he has also lost a sense of possibilities that are within his power to will, whether they succeed or not. The historian has devoted his life to the study of Ming history and has overlooked all of the creative complexity of his own present life. His one romantic attachment has been relegated securely to his past and is as carefully enshrined and removed from the present as the documents he studies. At the end of his life he begins to see that he has mistakenly felt that all of his emotions belonged to the past. The present too had possibilities which he had never explored and which now he would never know in this lifetime. As he packs up his small apartment before checking into a hospital where he will undergo an operation and live his final days, waiting for his terminal illness to overcome him, he realizes that he leaves behind and unfinished more than just his historical work. Not only has he not completed correcting the proofs of an article on the Red Turban Army of peasant rebels, but he also has never acted to overcome his own indifference to making his life more comfortable, more fulfilled in terms of his own simple desires and emotions. The old historian now realizes it is too late for anything to be done. "I used to think that all my emotions belonged in the past, to history, but I know that I yearn for the future just like everyone else. Even as life draws to a close. . . ."[25]

Conclusion: Chinese Women and Socialist Development

Kumari Jayawardena, in *Feminism and Nationalism in the Third World*, points out that "those who want to keep the women of our countries in a position of subordination find it convenient to dismiss feminism as a foreign ideology. It should, therefore, be stressed that feminism, like socialism, has no particular ethnic identity."[26] Feminism is international because the experience of female subordination is universal. As Haleh Afshar and others argue in *Women, State and Ideology*, the pattern of state efforts to control women as a group vary depending upon whether one looks at China or Israel or Iran, but the formation of ideologies and policies that deliberately exclude or constrain women's role is a common feature in each of these states.[27] Slavenka Drakulic-Ilic has written with simple clarity on the local and universal aspects of women's subjugation: "It is not possible to look at women's problems separated from their local social, economical, cultural, and political background; it is also impossible to look at them separated from the international situation, especially considering feminism's international character (and how central it has been to all workers' movements at their inception, too)."[28] This is not to say, of course, that feminism, like any other concept, cannot be narrowly applied and misused.

One might say, in light of the discussion above, that feminism does indeed have a "local" identity, that while it is a global phenomenon, it finds particular expression in different contexts (like any other social ideology) according to vernacular social and political circumstances.[29] The concern of feminists should not be to capture the terrain of "feminism" for their own locally inspired or determined version of women's problems and their solutions, but rather to enrich feminist consciousness by drawing upon the consciousness of women as it unfolds in response to different situations of social, political, and cultural oppression. Feminists are as vulnerable as anyone else to cultural parochialism; if feminism is to attain its aspirations as a liberating idea, it must strive for a cultural pluralism that can provide a critique not only of gender oppression but of all cultures of oppression. Others may need our insight into oppression. We need theirs!

Zhang Jie recognizes the international dimension of women's problems and the existence of women's sensibilities across national boundaries, but she has not developed this theme. She traveled to the United States in 1982, but her attention has remained firmly fixed on China's domestic situation in relative isolation from its world context. Nevertheless, in one passage of *The Ark* her main character, Jinghua, reflects briefly on the international aspect of women's condition. "She remembered a foreign film she'd seen the previous year, *A Strange Woman*. There was nothing especially strange about her—what she wanted from men seemed perfectly justified, but it was said that the film had met with considerable criticism. The things that woman sought were exactly those things which Jinghua and most other thinking women looked for. No matter what race, nationality, or language, these seemed not to matter—the problem was one of universal dimensions" (p. 155). One would hope that the party's current emphasis on developing "studies on women in a Chinese way"[30] would not cut off the Chinese discourse from its international setting. For Zhang's part, I suspect that familiarity with the connections between feminism and the antinuclear and environmental movements around the world as well as connections between women's problems and socialist development outside of China would develop in powerful ways her intuition that the problems of women do indeed have a universal dimension and major consequences for social reformation.

Juxtaposing the Chinese experience and the international discourse of feminism raises some important issues. In the perspective to which Zhang Jie gives voice, perhaps the most noteworthy feature is her persistent focus on the links between women's issues and sensibilities and larger sociopolitical problems. Zhang's exploration of this relationship between personal and public gives primary importance to the role of consciousness in transforming social relations. In Zhang's vision, women, given the opportunity, can and will behave as oppressively as men unless they actively seek to develop their feminine attributes of empathy and nurturing—attributes that also reside within the male, but in socially and possibly biologically more restricted form. Zhang here affirms with absolute certainty a point often overlooked by liberal feminists, namely, that the entry of women into positions of power within the status quo in itself does not promote emancipatory activity. By refusing to step into a narrow definition of feminism, Zhang has sketched out a feminine sensibility that is in many respects beyond socially constructed notions of gender but whose initiators for this historical moment are primarily women. Zhang's emphasis on introspection in a social and historical context is a valuable corrective to the overly individualistic and apolitical or narrowly political tendencies that characterize many of the more visible varieties of feminism in Western Europe and the United States. Similarly, the elements of Buddhism in Zhang's thinking, which emphasize the importance of consciousness, integration instead of division, and empathy for instead of control over others, challenge many of the conflict-oriented structures of thought so central to the Western monotheistic traditions. In the final analysis, it is the capacity for mutually empowering cooperation based on a sensibility for the interconnectedness of all environmental phenomena (social as well as natural) that is at the heart of feminism, whether it is labeled feminism or not.

Within the People's Republic of China today, the successes and shortcomings of Chinese socialism for women are being widely discussed for the purpose of defining the roles women will play in the development of China in the post-Mao era. As in most of the world, women's problems in China are closely linked to general problems of development. Zhang Jie is keenly aware of the interrelatedness of both issues. The problems of development and the need to reassess national economic policies have provided room for greater discussion of women's issues in China as well as in other socialist countries in the last decade. The Belgrade Neofeminist Conference in 1978 emerged to the accompaniment of new political discussion in Yugoslavia concerning the reality of social and economic "stratification" in their socialist and therefore "classless" society. If classes have not disappeared under socialism, perhaps women's oppression has also not disappeared with the establishment of socialism. The Neofeminist Association in Poland emerged alongside the founding of Solidarity, which posed its own challenges of reform to the Polish socialist state but did not address many issues of special relevance to family life and women.[31] The recent discussion of women's problems in China has itself accompanied the reforms of Deng Xiaoping. The government's efforts in this area became visible when the All-China Federation of Women, a party-sponsored organization, called a National Symposium on Theoretical Studies on Women in Beijing in 1984.[32]

The discourse in China today and among feminists in other socialist countries clearly suggests that socialism and feminism as liberating ideals are still very much under discussion as meaningful concepts for addressing the social ills that riddle the contemporary world. Those with feminist concerns in Western Europe and the United States have much to learn from and major contributions to make to this international discourse, and both are best done with an empathetic ear to the voices of those women in socialist and developing countries who have achieved certain rights and continue to struggle for fuller emancipation. Yes, there are many besides foreign feminists left to care that the liberation of Chinese women is far from complete. This is not to minimize the difficulties of small group and activist formations under state socialism, but neither should one overlook the potential of the will to humaneness even under the most mystified and oppressive of circumstances, whatever their particular political manifestation may be.

Notes

I would like to thank Elizabeth Meese, Alice Parker, Gabrijela Vidan, and Myriam Diaz-Diocraetz, organizers of the 1988 Dubrovnik Conference on "Writing and Language: The Politics and Poetics of Feminist Critical Practice and Theory," for including me in the second international meeting of this symposium. Many conversations with other participants from a variety of intellectual and political backgrounds contributed significantly to my thinking about problems of development and socialism in relationship to Zhang Jie's fiction. I thank Hampden-Syndey College for generously funding my travel to this conference. Finally, I want to thank Arif Dirlik for his helpful suggestions and advice on editing made during the crucial last stages of writing this essay.

1. For some of this discussion see Lydia Sargent, ed., *Women and Revolution* (Boston: South End Press, 1981).

2. Among the recent literature on women in contemporary China is Phyllis Andors, *The Unfinished Liberation of Chinese Women, 1949–1980* (Bloomington: Wheatshef Books, Sussex/Indiana University Press, 1983); Elisabeth Croll, *The Politics of Marriage in Contemporary China* (Cambridge: Cambridge University Press, 1981); Kay Ann Johnson, *Women, the Family and Peasant Revolution in China* (Chicago: University of Chicago Press, 1983); Judith Stacey, *Patriarchy and Socialist Revolution in China* (Berkeley: University of California Press, 1983); Margery Wolf, *Revolution Postponed: Women in Contemporary China* (Stanford: Stanford University Press, 1985).

3. Suzanne Pepper, "Liberation and Understanding: New Books on the Uncertain Status of Women in the Chinese Revolution," *China Quarterly* (December 1986): 712, 713.

4. Rada Ivekovic, "Yugoslav Neofeminism," in *Sisterhood Is Global*, ed. Robin Morgan (New York: Anchor Books, 1984), p. 735.

5. Slavenka Drakulic-Ilic, "'Six Mortal Sins' of Yugoslav Feminism," in ibid., p. 738.

6. Anna Titkow, "Let's Pull Down the Bastilles Before They Are Built," in ibid., p. 565.

7. Feminism as a term has been incorporated into the Chinese language with clear negative connotations. The term itself is not widely used and is confined primarily to intellectual circles. In general it is associated with a narrow reading of Western feminism which emphasizes an emotional antimale outlook. While some Chinese dictionaries translate feminism as *nannu pingdengjuyi* (ideology of equality between men and women), the most commonly used term in conversation is *nuquanjuyi* (woman power ideology). The latter term implies power of women over men and is associated in the Chinese context with figures such as the Empress Dowager Cixi or Jiang Qing, a

leader of the "Gang of Four" during the now much denounced Cultural Revolution.

8. *Fangzhou* (The ark) originally appeared in *Shouhuo* (Harvest) 2 (1982): 4–59. It was also included in translation in the volume of Zhang's fiction entitled *Love Must Not Be Forgotten* (Beijing: Panda Books, 1986). The short story "Ai shi buneng wangji de" (Love must not be forgotten), which is also included in the translated volume of the same title, first appeared in *Beijing wenyi* (Beijing literature and arts) 11 (1979): 19–27. Zhang's earlier novel, *Chenzhong de chibang* (Leaden wings), was published in *Shiyue* in 1981 and translated in 1987 by Gladys Yang for Virgo Press in London.

9. For discussions of Zhang Jie in the context of contemporary Chinese literature, see Michael S. Duke, *Blooming and Contending: Chinese Literature in the Post-Mao Era* (Bloomington: Indiana University Press, 1985); Kam Louie, "Love Stories: The Meaning of Love and Marriage in China," in *After Mao: Chinese Literature and Society, 1978–1981*, ed. Jeffrey C. Kinkley (Cambridge: Harvard University Press, 1985), pp. 63–87; and Leo Ou-fan Lee, "The Politics of Technique: Perspective of Literary Dissidence in Contemporary Chinese Fiction," in ibid., pp. 159–90.

10. Duke, *Blooming and Contending*, p. 137.

11. Ibid., p. 202.

12. Page numbers for *The Ark* refer to the English translation in *Love Must Not Be Forgotten*.

13. Joan Hoff-Wilson, "The Unfinished Revolution: Changing Legal Status of U.S. Women," *Signs* (August 1987): 7.

14. Zhang Jie, "Love Must Not Be Forgotten," pp. 1–13.

15. Zhang Jie, "Emerald," in *Love Must Not Be Forgotten*, pp. 15–62.

16. Liu Binyan, *People or Monsters?*, ed. Perry Link (Bloomington: Indiana University Press, 1983).

17. Duke, *Blooming and Contending*, p. 50.

18. Zhang Jie, "Who Knows How To Live?" in *Love Must Not Be Forgotten*, p. 110.

19. Duke, *Blooming and Contending*, pp. 38–39.

20. "Love Must Not Be Forgotten," p. 13.

21. A few words may be in order here concerning possible antecedents for Zhang's thinking in the history of Chinese radicalism. Zhang's stress on love, her tendency to gloss over issues of class in favor of gender and generation, and her stress on small groups (informal and voluntary associations) against state activity are explainable in terms of the frustration with a state-directed socialism that would seem to characterize the psyches of Chinese intellectuals today. It is noteworthy, however, that these themes are reminiscent of pre-Marxist radicalism in China around the time of the May Fourth Movement (1919), especially anarchist radicalism. So are the references to Buddhism, which had a special appeal for the anarchists. Whether or not Zhang is aware of this, or consciously seeks to revive an earlier Chinese radical outlook, is not possible to tell; her references to old comrades who yearn for a lost radical vision are at best suggestive. Nevertheless, the suggestions may be worth keeping in mind for their revival of themes in Chinese radicalism that have a long, powerful legacy—regardless of whether they reveal a tendency on the part of Chinese intellectuals to respond similarly across time to similar frustrations, or the continuing vitality of memories that have been suppressed officially for six decades now. For this legacy, see Arif Dirlik, *The Origins of*

Chinese Communism (New York: Oxford University Press, 1989), and Edward Krebs, "Liu Sifu and Chinese Anarchism 1905–1915," Ph.D. dissertation, University of Washington, 1975.

22. "Emerald," p. 53.

23. Ibid., p. 62.

24. Zhang Jie, "Under The Hawthorn," in *Love Must Not Be Forgotten*, p. 92.

25. Zhang Jie, "An Unfinished Record," in ibid., p. 90.

26. Kumari Jayawardena, *Feminism and Nationalism in the Third World* (London: Zed Books, 1986), p. ix.

27. Haleh Afshar, *Women, State and Ideology: Studies from Africa and Asia* (Albany: State University of New York Press, 1987), pp. 1–9.

28. Drakulic-Ilic, "'Six Mortal Sins,'" p. 737.

29. For these concepts, I am indebted to Ivan Illich. For an example, see *Shadow Work* (London: Marion Boyars, 1981).

30. "Development of Women's Studies—The Chinese Way," in *Chinese Women (1)*, ed. Stanley Rosen, special issue of *Chinese Sociology and Anthropology* 20, 1 (Fall 1987): 18–25.

31. Titkow, "Pull Down the Bastilles," p. 564.

32. "Development of Women's Studies," p. 18.

15

THE LAMENT OF ASTROPHYSICIST FANG LIZHI: CHINA'S INTELLECTUALS IN A GLOBAL CONTEXT

Richard C. Kraus

The relationship between American and Third World intellectuals is never easy but is often full of stress, awkwardness, and embarrassment, as our links to China show in stark terms. For many years there was only minimal intellectual contact between our nations, as our governments sneered at each other with hostile rhetoric. Two decades ago, American intellectuals learned to cope with charges of cultural imperialism. Many attempted to understand a militantly anti-imperialist point of view, to address Chinese grievances in their research, and to avoid condescension in discussing modern Chinese history, society, and politics. Many sought earnestly, if sometimes inappropriately, to learn from China. Others sought arrangements whereby they might share research materials with Chinese scholars.

Today, with closer commercial and strategic ties, intellectual links have become much stronger. Our universities bustle with Chinese graduate students, Chinese academics meet their American counterparts at international conferences, while many American intellectuals have visited China as tourists, foreign experts, or teachers and researchers. Earlier debates now often have a quaint air. China's intellectuals are less likely to condemn us for cultural imperialism than they are to embarrass us with their enthusiasm for Western ways. Americans find it emotionally easier to deal with Chinese respect than hostility, but the new relationship carries political problems of its own. What stance should American intellectuals take toward our Chinese admirers? Scholarly responsibility, political intervention, and our respect for the "other" whom we study as specialists are all involved.

The case of Fang Lizhi, the astrophysicist who was dismissed from the Communist Party in January 1987, raises these issues directly. Fang Lizhi is a hero to many intellectuals in China for his outspoken demands for political reform. In the party's judgment, Fang advocated bourgeois liberalization in the fall of 1986; he was also accused of stirring up student unrest. Many foreign scholars expressed their concern after Fang's dismissal from the party. Merle Goldman, a leading expert on the politics of Chinese intellectuals, argued that "We in academe must refuse to accept without protest the persecution of our colleagues in China, much as we do when our colleagues in other Communist countries are persecuted."[1]

I have two purposes in this essay. One is to examine two of Fang's controversial speeches, to convey some sense of what he represents in China today. I find that Fang is less an advocate for democracy than a spokesman for a group of intellectuals who are resentful that they do not have greater privileges in China today. My second goal is to discuss the obligations of Western China specialists toward China's intellectuals, which I believe to be more limited than does Goldman. American intellectuals should certainly oppose the mistreatment of fellow humans anywhere, but should they demand special rights for intellectuals as intellectuals? My tone is consciously polemical, not because I feel satisfied with my own thinking on this complex subject, but because I feel strongly that we need some discussion of our own role and interests in the mental links that bind the United States to China.

Fang Lizhi's Political Activism

In December 1986, Chinese university students in Shanghai, Beijing, Hefei, and other cities organized public demonstrations. Under the vague slogan of "democracy," the students pressed for faster reform in the political system, as well as for improvements in the conditions under which they live and study. The parading students were nonviolent, but their unauthorized activism shocked many Chinese. The Communist Party's initial response was restrained; but when semester examinations and the month-long Spring Festival holiday brought the demonstrations to an end, the political reaction was sterner.

Party leaders were embarrassed by the apparent breakdown in public order, and by the obvious expression of discontent from an important social group. In sharp response, Hu Yaobang lost his post as party secretary-general, and the party initiated a campaign of discipline by expelling from its ranks three prominent intellectuals. One was Wang Ruowang, a Shanghai writer who openly expressed his contempt for party rules.[2] A second was Liu Binyan, whose investigative reports in *People's Daily* delighted readers with their exposure of corruption and high-handed behavior by big-shot officials.[3] The third to be expelled was Fang Lizhi, vice-president of the Chinese University of Science and Technology in Hefei, Anhui. Fang was accused of inflaming the students through his speeches on university campuses, where he regularly demanded political reforms. Fang lost his academic position, although he was quickly given another in Beijing. He was not compelled to make a self-criticism.

Fang Lizhi is a product of China's 1950s' education system. Born in 1936, he became a student activist after entering the physics department at Beijing University in 1952. His outspoken personality led him to collision with the authorities during the Hundred Flowers Movement; he was labeled a rightist and dismissed from the Communist Party in 1957. His party membership was restored in 1979, when tens of thousands of former rightists were rehabilitated as Deng Xiaoping consolidated his power.[4] As vice-president of the Chinese University of Science and Technology, Fang was a prominent academic bureaucrat during a period of rapid expansion in technical education.

Fang made speeches at universities and research institutes all over China in 1985 and 1986. Already a political celebrity, he was attacked in May 1986, after he published a critique of Engels' "Dialectics of Nature." Some party leaders wanted to expel Fang from the party again for his disrespect; others demanded his self-criticism. Some intellectuals publicly defended Fang, including Xu Liangying, head of the History Research Institute of the Academy of Social Sciences, who threatened to organize a letter of protest if Fang were not left alone.[5] Emboldened by his surviving this crisis, Fang continued his public political activity. By November 1986, unofficial copies of Fang's speeches were apparently available to members of his audience; as Fang spoke, he referred casually to remarks made on other campuses.

Fang's speeches have been regarded variously as a model of bourgeois liberal thought (in the eyes of his Communist Party critics) or as "a most precious resource" (in the words of one of his many student supporters). Early Western discussion of the causes and aftermath of the student demonstrations paid little attention to what Fang actually said. Instead, Fang has been treated as a simple victim of a nasty Communist Party. But this is too naive, and it seems to assume that China's party leaders find special delight in persecuting intellectuals.

I will examine two speeches Fang gave in Shanghai in November, only a few weeks before the demonstrations began on December 5. One was at Jiaotong University on November 15, the other at Tongji University on November 18. Both speeches were recorded; Fang's supporters sent copies to the United States, where they were printed in *Zhongguo zhi chun* (Chinese spring). Their motive was partly to spread Fang's message, but also to protect Fang against quotation out of context by Communist critics in China.[6]

Fang is an important voice for the Chinese intelligentsia (but not its only voice), and he expresses this group's hurts and demands with simple eloquence. Fang is a man of obvious self-confidence; he postures before his audience, bragging about his past bravery, almost daring the party to silence him, turning him into a modern-day Tan Sitong.[7] He mocks the cult of the Long March, a myth obnoxious to many intellectuals, who have tired of nearly forty years of glorifying peasant rebels. He boasts of publicly criticizing such leftist leaders as Hu Qiaomu, dares to mock openly the quality of national leadership: "China today must not only bring forth technology, it is even more important to bring forth a prime minister" (pp. 25, 14, 28, 15). The speeches were clearly bracing to his audiences of elite students, who reveled in Fang's refreshing bluntness and daring.

Reading Fang is confusing. He is brave, but he also oversimplifies many complex issues about China and the West. I will consider three slogans that recur in his talks: democracy, the responsibility of intellectuals, and wholesale Westernization.

Fang on Democracy

The students' noisiest demand was for "democracy," a popular slogan, but one that could be used to demand anything from better campus housing to an end to one-party rule. "Democracy" is a word almost impossible to understand out of context; Chiang Kai-shek used it, as did Stalin and Franklin Roosevelt.

Fang's conception of democracy is strikingly Western and liberal:

> Democracy's basic meaning first recognizes the rights that come from each individual, and are later combined to create a society. The implication is that these rights are not given from above, but are each person's from birth. (p. 15)

Party leaders who charge Fang with bourgeois liberalism find their strongest evidence here. Fang resembles neither Chinese Marxists nor the Confucian tradition, where humanity is defined in terms of social relations and obligations to others. Fang's explicit reference to rights rather resembles the social contract theory that accompanied the growth of capitalism in European political theory. C. B. Macpherson describes this "conception of the individual as essentially the proprietor of his own person or capacities, owing nothing to society for them. The individual was seen neither as a moral whole, nor as a part of a larger social whole, but as an owner of himself."[8]

Fang repeatedly strikes out against China's traditional veneration of officialdom. He regards the ability to criticize political leaders as a mark of democracy, and he refers to his own 1985 public criticism of Beijing Deputy Mayor Zhang Baifa as evidence of his own credentials as a fighter for democracy (pp. 14, 28).

Fang is cautious about linking democratic reform too closely to the career of any individual politician, preferring to see democracy in institutional rather than personal terms. In Fang's view, Chinese have too long regarded proper moral leadership as the key to political well-being. Fang is indifferent, for instance, to the question of Deng Xiaoping's retirement, which he regards as a question of personnel, rather than an issue involving the whole political system (p. 19).

In many respects Fang's stance is similar to that of liberal reformers in Europe in the nineteenth century, who pressed for democratic reforms against authoritarian states. Fang insists that democracy cannot be bestowed upon a people from on high, but must be won by the people themselves.

> Democracy is ultimately a right that is properly ours; it is not something that anyone else can give you. Since it is a proper right, then it can only be truly obtained through your own struggle.

Fang quickly adds that this fight assumes many forms, such as changing public opinion and holding meetings, and that "extraordinary fierce" (but unspecified) methods may not be necessary (p. 15).

Like many early fighters for liberal democracy in the West, Fang argues for a gradualist strategy. He says that if one speaks merely 6 percent more boldly each year, there will be a complete turnaround in a decade. He himself has moved from criticizing the Municipal Committee in 1986 to taking on the Political Bureau in 1987 (p. 14).

Fang is not just a dreamy critic of China's politics. He has given serious thought to the means to democratize the Communist Party. He acknowledges that one-party democracy is possible, pointing to Sweden and Japan as nations generally regarded as democratic, but which have had decades of rule by the same political party (p. 32). China's hope is for the Chinese Communist Party to change by absorbing new members, especially university students. Students should join the party and change its face (pp. 20–21). Fang's appeal here is in keeping with recent party efforts to increase student recruitment; 9 percent of university students are party members.[9]

But in the end, Fang is afraid of democratic institutions because intellectuals would be consistently outvoted by China's great mass of peasants. Fang asserts that China's peasants are not ready for democracy:

> You can go travel in the villages and look around; I feel those uneducated peasants, living under traditional influence, have a psychological consciousness that is very deficient. It is very difficult to instill a democratic consciousness in them; they still demand an honest and upright official; without an official they are uncomfortable. (p. 20)

Here Fang's situation differs sharply from that of nineteenth-century

Western advocates of liberal democracy.[10] In the West, the universal franchise was only an ideal, as women, slaves, and the poor were excluded from the circle of those with political rights. Liberal intellectuals in the West could advocate democracy, meaning political rights for the "responsible" middle class, knowing that the great unwashed masses would continue to be excluded, and unable to threaten their interests. But China has had a mass popular revolution, and whatever one may think of the quality of political rights in the People's Republic, it is now politically impossible to introduce an electoral system that would disenfranchise the great majority of the population.

There is a contradiction inherent in Fang's position. His dilemma is how to press for "democratic" political reforms that will aid the intelligentsia, while avoiding other "democratic" political reforms that might lead to actual political power by the peasant majority.

Fang on the Political Responsibility of Chinese Intellectuals

Although Fang's remarks about democracy often resemble bourgeois liberalism, his comments about intellectuals seem more like the beliefs of an old-fashioned mandarin. Fang's Confucian pain over the separation of intellectuals from political power resonates anxiously, often angrily, throughout his speeches.

Fang's most consistent message to the student elite is their obligation as intellectuals to serve China. Intellectuals are an "independent stratum occupying a leading place." "History has bestowed on you a leading place but have you risen to claim it?" "Naturally we want to bring into play our historical duty and social duty, but this is still difficult under Chinese conditions." "Since we say that intellectuals are the leading force, responsibility for China thus falls on our shoulders" (pp. 13, 15). In Fang's eyes, intellectuals are an embattled elite, selflessly dragging China into the modern world against the feudal instincts of the majority.

Fang links a very Confucian conception of moral responsibility to some notions from Western pop sociology. He is convinced that the color of people's collars is the key to understanding social class, adopting a long-discredited idea that workers (with their blue collars) are becoming less important in the work force, supplanted by better educated, higher status, and better paid white collar workers of the service and information society. There is now ample evidence in the United States that the much-vaunted growth in the information and service economy creates more jobs for fast-food workers than it does for aeronautical engineers, and that this whole vulgar theory has a strong whiff of capitalist ideology.[11]

Fang correctly states that China's peasants are declining as part of a "process of historical development," and that many of them "are migrating to the cities and becoming workers. Today in the developed nations, blue collar workers are already beginning to decline; there are already more white collar workers, who control technology and knowledge." "[A]s society develops, workers (meaning blue collar workers) will decline because the things they represent are not advanced" (pp. 12, 13).

Perhaps Fang absorbed this thesis from Alvin Toffler, whose *Future Shock* has been widely read in Chinese translation.[12] Many intellectuals find it appealing, because it purports to demonstrate their growing importance. Many Chinese accept Toffler uncritically as a serious Western social scientist, much as they mistake Herman Wouk, Irving Stone, and Eric Segal for serious novelists.

For Fang, it is clear that the Communist Party must respect a law of history by which intellectuals will surely rise to a position of natural leadership.

> At present the party-building principle is that established by Lenin fifty years ago, emphasizing the working class; at that time the peasantry was backward, and the working class was advanced. But if you wish to establish an advanced political party now, whom should you cultivate? This kind of party-building principle ought not be the same as before, but must be revised anew, and ought to take intellectuals as the most advanced section. As we develop party members in the course of party work we must in the first place develop intellectuals, not industrial workers. (p. 13)

After Mao's death, the party declared that intellectuals were to be considered as part of the working class, abandoning the former classification of most intellectuals as "bourgeois." This change shielded intellectuals from political criticism for occupying a social position antagonistic to workers.[13] Fang's speeches go one step further: from claiming membership in the working class, Fang claims that intellectuals are the legitimate leaders of the working class.

> Marx classified people into different groups according to the means of production they owned. In my view, this was tenable in the last century and the beginning of this. However, in modern society, the development of science and technology, knowledge and information, including high-tech and soft science, have become an important force propelling society forward, and are bound to involve a change in the concept of who leads in the political and economic fields. Intellectuals, who own and create information and knowledge, are the most dynamic component of the productive forces, this is what determines their social status.[14]

But according to Fang, this new leading class, like Marx's proletariat, has the interests of all humanity in its collective heart. When asked what characteristics the advanced class should have "now, in the age of soft science," Fang responded:

> Generally speaking, people, who have internalized the elements of civilization and possess knowledge, have hearts which are relatively noble, their mode of thought is invariably scientific and they therefore have a high sense of social responsibility or even self-sacrifice. They also have grievances and may be discontent. Their point of departure is not their personal interest, but social progress.[15]

Fang argues that scientists are full of virtue by the nature of their work.

> Since physicians pursue the unity, harmony and perfection of nature, how can they logically tolerate unreason, discordance and evil? Physicists' methods of pursuing truth make them extremely sensitive while their courage in seeking it enables them to accomplish something.[16]

Fang illustrates this proposition with curious evidence from the postwar technical history. Because "major social problems are often unclear to those without a scientific background,"

> Almost invariably it was natural scientists who were the first to become conscious of the emergence of each social crisis. For instance, in the 1960s, they called the government's attention to environmental pollution; in the 1970s, they pointed out the potential energy crisis, in the 1980s disarmament of course.[17]

Americans are perhaps more jaded than most Chinese, who have not been subjected to decades of trust-the-scientist advertising about "better living through chemistry," "the friendly atom," and "progress is our most important product." The role played by scientists in providing the tools for despoiling the environment, for exhausting energy supplies, and in creating modern weapons of mass destruction seems self-evident.

Fang was quick to tell the students things they like to hear, such as his opposition to their political study, or any form of party supervision over the work of intellectuals. He bragged that the party congress at his university did not meet for sixteen years (pp. 21–23). At one point Fang won applause for criticizing the tiresome cliché of education officials: "You should study hard, and cherish this excellent opportunity which the party has given you."

> Where did the state come from and how did it give an opportunity to you? You ought to know that education is a right of each of our citizens; everyone should receive education, and it is not an opportunity that anyone gives you.

> Thus the above way of speaking is a kind of feudal viewpoint, as if everything is granted from above; in fact it is not so. (pp. 15–16)

This is an easy shot, assured of easy cheers from students who are fed up with sanctimonious speeches from university officials. But Fang ignores the great political fact of Chinese education; access to universities is conditioned by the accident of birth; although most Chinese are peasants, few of their children were among the Shanghai students in Fang's audience. If education in China is a right, why is that right not enjoyed more equally?

Just as Fang redefines intellectuals to be the vanguard of the proletariat, so he appropriates the word "youth" to refer to students. Fang forgets the fierce competition in China to enter this elite group. In 1982 there were 4.4 million college graduates among China's billion people. In 1984 0.6 percent of Chinese were college graduates, while nearly a quarter of the population was illiterate.[18]

Fang believes that intellectuals receive more respect in the West than in China. Certainly Western intellectuals have not had to endure the abuse and humiliation of the Cultural Revolution, but neither have they enjoyed the respect that literati have received from Confucian tradition. Fang simplifies a complex issue by telling his story of the pope and the president of Italy respectfully listening to scientists at his Rome conference as they talked about Halley's Comet.

Fang shows an added misunderstanding of Western intellectuals when he says that they hold their Chinese counterparts in "contempt" for suffering ill-treatment during the Cultural Revolution.

> When I travel abroad I often tell foreign friends of the extreme tragedy of intellectuals during the period of the Cultural Revolution, when the universities were closed, and we had no rights at all. Of course they express sympathy, but I can also discern that they in fact have some contempt for China's intellectuals; to put it into words, why did you not display any of your own resolve, where was the consciousness of the intellectuals? Why did you not show your disapproval, and oppose the methods of the Cultural Revolution? (p. 16)

Western intellectuals have shown a variety of attitudes toward the fate of their Chinese counterparts during the Cultural Revolution, ranging from revulsion at the entire movement to relief not to have suffered its excesses to guilt for being elitist within Western society. But I have never encountered a single instance of such contempt. I think this feeling can only be understood by situating Fang in historical context, where Chinese intellectuals have long felt both a duty and a right to moral and political leadership. Western intellectuals, more accustomed to being ignored, are unlikely to scorn Fang for weakness against Mao.

It is important that Fang is an astronomer, rather than a professor of history or literature. His science reflects the glamour of modernization and adds credibility to his words in a nation whose people are eager to get on with the business of catching up with the West. Scientists are popularly regarded as a new breed of personally disciplined and boldly objective Chinese intellectual. Fang criticizes literary intellectuals for not daring to make use of the freedoms they have been granted, and he criticizes social scientists for their weakness for quoting the words of political leaders as they explain social problems (pp. 21, 17).

Fang is a familiar figure from Western science: the scientist who feels that social problems are important, and that social scientists have mucked it up, and should turn social issues over to clear-thinking physicists and engineers. This perspective is often true. At its most responsible, this tradition gives rise to Carl Sagan's leadership on the question of nuclear war. But there is also the figure of William Shockley, ready to move on from his Nobel Prize to plain talk to Americans about the need for eugenics and the racial superiority of whites, or the Strangelove figure of Edward Teller.

Fang demands that officials leave his science alone: "What does my teaching physics have to do with your class struggle?" (p. 17). "If you understand cosmology, we welcome your opinion, but if you do not understand it, then please stand to the side" (p. 28). But, as will be seen below, Fang does not apply this rule to himself.

Fang on Wholesale Westernization

The party has for some time criticized those who allegedly advocate "wholesale Westernization," but I had always imagined this to be a red herring, a party exaggeration of Westernizing inclinations into a position that no Chinese intellectual could actually hold. But Fang Lizhi is no straw figure, and he openly and proudly advocates "whole Westernization," revealing along the way a large dose of hatred of Chinese culture.

> Today our Chinese economy is no good, nor are our culture, education, and science any good. We need modernization in each aspect; people's consciousness about these aspects is already high. Our so-called spiritual civilization and culture is no good, our level of so-called virtue is no good and our politics are also no good. . . . I myself appreciate the standpoint of wholesale Westernization. (enthusiastic applause) My understanding is that we must open up completely and in all aspects. What is the meaning of this? This is to say our culture is not backward in one aspect, but in all aspects. (enthusiastic, prolonged applause) This is not my opinion, but is common knowledge.[19] (p. 24)

It is not just China's size, poverty, and population that cause problems.

Fang maintains that socialism has had no successes in any nation since World War II. "I myself feel that these decades since Liberation, this period in which we have practiced socialism, calmly speaking, this period is a complete failure" (p. 24). Or more comprehensively, "I say that the socialist movement from Marx, Lenin, Stalin, and Mao Zedong is a complete failure" (p. 25).

In Fang's analysis, China is still a feudal society; in this context, capitalism will be more progressive and revolutionary in its changes than socialism (pp. 22, 28–29). Fang is in the end a May Fourth figure, arguing for Mr. Science and Mr. Democracy, like Hu Shi, seventy years ago.

The trouble with Fang's "wholesale Westernization" is that it rests upon a bizarre set of simplifications about the West. Fang has traveled extensively, visiting some twenty nations, which gives his comments great authority among Chinese students. If only the West were as good as Fang imagines it to be! Here are six examples of Fang's fantasies of Western life.

1. Fang has a charmingly romantic notion of America as land of opportunity, almost like the myths of Horatio Alger. He explained in Shanghai that 30 percent of Americans attended college and 50 percent community college:

> Everyone is a university student. The youth of the West and of China are different; the West is a free society, and opportunities for young people are relatively great, and people who have tempered themselves are relatively many. Because opportunities are many and the competitive nature strong, you only have to go do something; there are none who cannot find opportunities. Therefore their students first temper their own independent, creative ability; you only need to have ability, then you can do anything. (p. 29)

This sounds like nothing so much as Ronald Reagan's games with help-wanted advertisements, by which our former president proved the lack of get-up-and-go among the American poor. When asked about beggars in Western nations, Fang dismissed them quite sharply: "Some of them are illegal immigrants, not local workers, the government cannot easily drive them away, out of common humanity."[20]

2. "Many people lack a practical understanding" of the United States, Western Europe, and capitalism, proclaims Fang to the adoring students of Shanghai. He explains that Lenin's theory of imperialism is disproved by the antitrust laws of the United States.

> Everybody says that imperialism is monopoly capitalism; America is definitely imperialist, but it has "antitrust" laws; for example, if your company is too big, it surely will be broken up. Thus the slogan of calling imperialism monopoly capitalism is incorrect. I feel that the kind of person who spreads this kind of

> propaganda lacks true knowledge, and only searches for a Marxist-Leninist concept to use.

After assuring the students that American corporations are not allowed to become "too big," Fang continues to boast that physicists, unlike propagandists, are precise in their definitions and measurements (p. 29).

3. Fang also idealizes New England town meetings, which he extends to the whole of America:

> When American city governments hold meetings, citizens may freely participate. According to the rules, if no citizens take part, that meeting is void (applause). This is an excellent system. (p. 22)

Ah, it is an excellent system, but where is it practiced? The Beijing Communist Party Committee does not welcome outsiders to its meetings, so one can easily understand Fang's enthusiasm for open meetings. But Fang does not report to his student audience that a major problem in local politics in the United States is compelling public boards and commissions to obey open meeting laws.

4. Fang lived for several months in New Jersey, while he was associated with the Princeton Institute for Advanced Study. There he had his first exposure to junk mail put out by state legislators as they seek to impress their constituents.

> A New Jersey legislator sent me a lot of materials, describing his activities and votes, and telling the citizens his political accomplishments. Even though I was a temporary resident, this legislator sent me many materials. American legislators must allow the citizens to evaluate their accomplishments within a certain period, and so must report to the citizens. We say that the bourgeoisie has false democracy, but we ought to do better than they! What are our people's representatives like? I have forgotten who was elected to serve as my representative in Anhui, and I do not know what the people's representatives do, or what they say; whose democracy is true and whose is false is very clear in the end.[21] (pp. 22, 26)

One does not have to prefer Anhui legislators to those of New Jersey to feel saddened by Fang's naiveté. Fang accepts these packets of distortions as truths and is unaware that many Americans regard their legislators' mailings at government expense as a corrupt (if legal) abuse of power, granting incumbent politicians an unfair advantage over their colleagues.

5. Fang thinks the pope champions intellectual freedom, unlike his predecessors who persecuted Galileo. Western religion has changed since those days, "but because Chinese rarely receive the influence of religious feelings and atmosphere, they cannot understand this." Fang has not en-

countered the Reverend Falwell, and has not noticed the millions of Americans who dream of saving heathen souls, including his own. Fang's pope is a jolly fellow interested in science, who has little in common with superstitious old ladies burning candles in church (p. 18). Neither does Fang's pope oppress women or support right-wing governments.

6. Fang admires the Princeton Theological Seminary for training specialists in American religion who are less hypocritical than China's political propagandists.

> The lips of the propagandists preach some things, but in their own hearts they do not believe them; when they are through speaking from the platform they come down and become different people; therefore we should think of raising the efficiency of our propaganda; best would be to send some people to study for doctorates in theology. (p. 30)

Fang has mistaken ideas about how voluntary religion is in the United States. Worship according to the "faith of your choice," but worship, nonetheless, is essential for careers that nourish upon the social contacts of religion to maintain business ties and social responsibility. Religion is also compulsory for our politicians, who are required to swear oaths of fealty upon bibles.

Fang's views of Western life are probably less bizarre than many of our notions about China. Yet Fang is full of confidence as he articulates his misunderstandings before naive student audiences.[22] The Communist Party must bear some responsibility for Fang's profound ignorance of the West, but so must Fang, who claims to speak as a responsible scientist. But what sort of scholar makes public political analyses based upon one hour in an airport? Fang spent that long in transit in Taibei; because he didn't see any soldiers, he is certain that the Guomindang is changing (p. 29).

China's Intellectuals and Deng's Reforms

Fang's speeches reveal an iconoclastic, self-confident, and angry man, pressing hard for political change in China. Fang uses the popular slogan of democracy, by which he does not mean popular rule, but greater political power for the intelligentsia. Fang's speeches are significant not for his contradictory notion of democracy, but for his public demands that China's intellectuals reclaim their traditional position of moral and political leadership.

Fang's disdain for peasants, and his zeal for intellectuals to displace workers in the Communist Party evoke anger from many partisans of peasants and workers. In addition, career bureaucrats regard Fang's speeches as a direct threat to the powers they have accumulated since Liberation. It is easy to understand why Fang was dismissed from the Communist Party.

Fang lost both his party membership and his position as vice-president of the Chinese University of Science and Technology. But he was given a new job in his academic speciality at the Beijing Observatory. Fang was also permitted to travel to Italy in June 1987 (but was not permitted to accept an invitation to visit the United States). Fang's wife, Li Shuxian, a physics professor at Beijing University, was elected to the people's congress by the citizens of Beijing's Haidian District, the city's university quarter.[23] Fang abandoned his plans to convene a meeting to commemorate the twentieth anniversary of the 1957 Antirightist campaign, a political occasion the party is not yet ready to tolerate.[24] The Chinese government has taken pains to show that Fang is not suffering, reporting that he wrote or edited five books and a dozen papers since his purge, that he received a promotion, has a housekeeper, and that his son studies in the United States.[25]

The relationship between intellectuals and Chinese society has been problematic since the 1911 Revolution. The old imperial system relied upon and honored scholars as has no other state. In or out office, the literati used their learning as a source of moral authority that conveyed the right to give counsel on state policies. The various regimes of the early twentieth century paid intellectuals empty honor, at best, while the peasant-based Communist revolution has had continuing conflicts with the intellectuals, culminating in the Cultural Revolution of 1966–1976.

During that low point for China's intellectuals, thousands were sent to work in the countryside, under conditions that were often harsh. But from around 1973, working and living conditions have steadily improved, with marked changes after Mao's death in 1976 and after the 1979 declaration that intellectuals were to be counted as members of the working class. As Deng Xiaoping has consolidated his power, he has appealed to intellectuals, including former rightists, by offering higher social status and new housing. His cultural policies have also been markedly looser than Mao's, although every few years he has struck out at a few intellectuals for going "too far" for the party's left. The campaign against Bai Hua was one of these moments, as was the abortive drive against "spiritual pollution."

Given China's past record for harshly treating disgraced public figures, the purge of Fang Lizhi, Wang Ruowang, and Liu Binyan seems relatively gentle; it may be a sign of China's new ability to fight domestic political battles in more conventional ways than the People's Republic has hitherto known. It is also a sign that intellectuals have gained a position of strength that they have not previously enjoyed, keeping the 1987 purge from turning into a new antirightist campaign.

One widely read analysis of the 1987 purge was entitled "China: Intellectuals at Bay?"[26] Instead of viewing the intellectuals on the defensive, many in China may well think that they have been on the attack, their influence, self-confidence, and demands growing faster than the rewards they have received from Chinese society.

Fang personifies not democracy, but intellectuals' resentment over an insufficiency of privilege in China today. As Deng Xiaoping consolidated his power, intellectuals participated in a curious alliance with supporters of market reforms in the economy. After the 1978 Third Plenum, Deng loosened central control over Chinese society, offering intellectuals greater tolerance for cultural diversity, and offering entrepreneurs and peasants greater individual material incentives. A fundamental contradiction in Deng's reform program has been between the interests of those who want looser controls over the economy and those who want looser controls over culture.

For all his Western enthusiasms, Fang is not an advocate of unlimited capitalism. His audience of intellectuals is in fact anxious about its economic fate under Deng's reforms. Intellectuals have enjoyed higher prestige under Deng, and a clear improvement in economic condition, but there is still much to cause unhappiness.[27] In 1984, income for scientific researchers was 1,070 renminbi; personnel in education, health, and social welfare earned 946 renminbi.[28] Many intellectuals' families have subsidies in other living expenses. It it quite common for intellectual husbands and wives both to work, which may double the family income. Despite constant grumbling about the supposed economic advantages enjoyed by peasants under the reforms, urban intellectuals enjoy obviously higher incomes. In 1984 peasant family income was 355 renminbi.

The real complaints of the intellectuals are not against reform and improvements in the peasantry's wretched lot, but against the rapidly rising incomes of urban entrepreneurs. Figures are difficult to obtain, but even lowly entrepreneurs as taxi drivers can make 2,500 or 3,000 renminbi, while speculators can do much better. The number of urban entrepreneurs increased from 150,000 in 1978 to 3,390,000 in 1984. This causes resentment somewhat akin to that often felt by American professors toward the incomes enjoyed by such skilled workers as plumbers, but the growth in the entrepreneurial economy is seen as fueling an inflation that intellectuals, tied to their bureaucratic salaries, are ill-equipped to withstand. A 10 percent pay raise for school teachers in the fall of 1987 is a response to intellectual discontent. The reintroduction of rationing for pork and sugar in China's major cities at the same time may not please enthusiasts for market reform, but is popular with intellectuals, whose fixed incomes were insufficient to buy meat for their families.

Fang has little to say about economics, although it is on the minds of his questioners. He agrees that the work of intellectuals is undervalued, and that the reforms have left intellectuals' incomes lagging behind their contemporaries: "their creations are not rewarded according to their labor; I feel that today the lives of young intellectuals are very bitter, yet their demands are extraordinarily modest" (pp. 30, 17).

The elitism of the intellectuals' discontent isolates them from China's workers, in contrast to political movements such as Poland's Solidarity or the recent turmoil in South Korea, where both workers and students attacked an authoritarian government.[29] Chinese student strikers are as likely to direct that ire against workers as the government. In 1987 students at Beijing's Central Finance and Banking College struggled over physical facilities with the Beijing Tobacco Works, which had been assigned part of the campus during the Cultural Revolution.[30] Indeed, among several episodes that sparked the students of Shanghai to demonstrate in December 1986 was a misunderstanding at a concert by the old American rock group, Jan and Dean. When a Jiaotong University student responded to a call for dancing, the police confused him for a worker and roughed him up in order to maintain order in aisles. Shanghai's university students were outraged that the police had not deferred to the person's status as a young intellectual.[31]

Despite the different interests of intellectuals and those in the commercial sector, the 1987 crackdown on intellectuals was followed by campaigns against illegal peddlers and corrupt advertising executives. It is not a political advantage for intellectuals when their interests are publicly associated with those of speculators, peddlers, and the looser elements of the Chinese economy.

The Internationalism of the Intellectuals

Marxists long ago discovered that workers cannot easily make alliances that cross national boundaries. The revolutionary ideal of "proletarian internationalism" was shattered by the eruption of national chauvinism across Europe in World War I. The subsequent development of global capitalist production has pitted workers of one nation against others in competition for jobs. Chinese rhetoric of proletarian internationalism reached its greatest intensity when China pursued self-reliance, only to fade softly away once China became an eager participant in the world economy. The economic policies of the Cultural Revolution minimized the competition of Chinese laborers with their counterparts in other nations, while now Chinese workers must sell their labor internationally, in rivalry with Koreans, Thais, Malaysians, and Mexicans.

Labor organizers know that the easy mobility of capital allows owners an easier time making international alliances than workers, although capitalism's internal conflicts nonetheless have often coincided with bitter national rivalries.

We intellectuals, in contrast, can relate most easily to our counterparts in other nations. Most of us have a shared interest in the unfettered expression of ideas, even if we are sometimes less enthusiastic about spreading the ideas of other groups. More importantly, there are few material interests that separate intellectuals of one nation from another. We are a relatively international species. We may not actually own the means of communication, but we do effectively control our internal memoranda we call journals of opinion and scholarship. We have a hard time understanding the interests of other groups, and we sometimes wax sentimental about solidarity with our fellow intellectuals in other lands, imagining ourselves to be in their positions without knowing much about what they in fact think, say, and write.

But what do we, as intellectuals, owe our counterparts? Are we all brother/sister intellectuals together, always vigilant for our corporate interests vis-à-vis governments of any stripe?

Many, perhaps most, American intellectuals would agree that we have an obligation to protest the murder or physical mistreatment of intellectuals at home or abroad, and that torture, beatings, and imprisonment for crimes of conscience are always abhorrent. But Fang Lizhi has not been tortured, imprisoned, or even left without a desirable job. Are we obligated to aid Fang and our other Third World cousins when their demands for greater privileges are rejected? Is it our right to tell foreign political parties whom they should and should not have as members?

Why are China's intellectuals our responsibility, but not others whose lives are damaged by the social turbulence of a developing society? Why not women, who suffer systematic discrimination, or peasant youth, victimized by the accidental geography of their birth, or why not the new class of migrant agricultural laborers? Apart from intellectuals, the only groups that seem to have any Western patrons are Christians, as in the old days, and Tibetans. But why not other victims of Han domination, such as the Yi or the Moslems of Xinjiang and Yunnan? Where do we stop, and why do we selectively favor our fellow professionals, the Chinese intellectuals? Our obligation as intellectuals surely is to oppose the ill-treatment of all humans, not just our professional counterparts.

The American press presents Fang as defender of academic free speech, as if his position in China were simple. We do not easily learn that Fang is also an opponent of political rights for peasants and a poorly informed worshiper of the West. Similarly, when student demonstrators threw copies of *Beijing ribao* into a bonfire, book-burners were transformed into protesters for pluralist democracy.

Fang's enthusiasm for the West appeals to intellectuals, grateful at last to have a sympathetic hearing in the Third World. His appeal is similar to that of novelist and essayist V. S. Naipaul, whose eloquent and entertaining critiques of Third World shortcomings place the responsibility on the dark-hued "other," allowing Western readers to avoid guilt about their comforts. If only all Third World intellectuals were so respectful to us as Fang Lizhi. But just as we do not understand peasants and workers, we flatter ourselves that we can readily comprehend Third World intellectuals, whose interests, perspectives, and problems are not our own. From my brief review of Fang Lizhi's speeches, it is apparent that he has some mandarin values rather different from those of most American intellectuals.

Americans have two competing models for trying to deal with Chinese intellectuals.

One is a "save-the dissident" model, heavily influenced by our traditional anticommunism. However blandly our mass media treat China these days as the "good" Communist state, the horrors of Communism remain an issue for many liberal intellectuals in the United States, some of whom have never given up the hope that a "third road" between Communist authoritarianism and right-wing brutality will somehow emerge, if only we press hard enough. Fang Lizhi is the latest candidate for this honor.

But enthusiasts for right-wing brutality have also joined Fang's case. Senator Jesse Helms has hypocritically championed Fang's case in a pair of Senate resolutions, in which Helms attacked Chinese criticism of Fang, Liu Binyan, Zhou Houze (former head of the Communist Party Propaganda Department), and Su Shaozhi (former head of the Institute of Marxism-Leninism-Mao Zedong Thought). The right's fondness for Fang has nothing to do with his human rights, and everything to do with embarrassing China's government. It happened as the United States Information Agency provoked China into an international incident by including a portrait of General Douglas MacArthur in an exhibition of American paintings scheduled to travel around China. Chinese know MacArthur as the man who wanted to drop atom bombs on Manchuria during the Korean War. When the Chinese declined to accept the offensive portrait, Charles Z. Wick, producer of the film "Snow White Meets the Three Stooges" and head of the United States Information Agency, canceled the show, muttering darkly that "there is absolutely no way that we can yield to censorship. We are the architects and advocates of the free flow of information and expression."[32]

But the save-the-dissident model has not made much headway as a framework for explaining figures such as Fang. Perry Link has suggested four reasons for Western disinterest in Chinese dissidents, in contrast to Soviet counterparts. First, Chinese intellectuals are simply less dissident, which certainly seems true of Fang Lizhi, who wants to remake the Communist Party, not overthrow it. Second, the Russian literary tradition is closer to our own, and thus we can understand more easily the issues of Soviet cultural politics, especially its romantic, individualistic aspects. Third, the cold war makes the United States particularly eager to unmask the dark side of the Soviet Union, while our relations with China are more ambiguous. Fourth, there are no Jews in China, which means that strong Zionist pressures to secure the right of emigration for Chinese dissidents do not arise.[33] One should add that Americans have a hard time pronouncing or remembering Chinese names, further diminishing public interest in China's dissidents.

Our second pattern for understanding Chinese intellectuals is a missionary model, which borrows from past American approaches to China, rather than contemporary attitudes toward the Soviet Union. In the protracted effort to Christianize China, missionaries cultivated Chinese believers, whom they would assist materially as well as spiritually. Often the protection included gunboats and punitive expeditions, methods not currently available to today's proselytizers for liberation, who are so far reduced to sending petitions demanding better treatment for *our* Chinese.[34]

Amnesty International's criticisms of China avoid singling out one social group for special treatment; indeed, the new report on torture deals with mistreatment of ordinary working class criminals, not intellectuals.[35] But other protests directed at China are much more clearly aimed at protecting a special class of Western-oriented intellectuals. Goldman and Wagner conclude their analysis: "Protests from the West may not be of much help to those now under attack. Still they might prevent the current campaign from turning into a second antirightist movement."[36] News that the Ford Foundation is opening a human rights office in China raises questions of how class-neutral it can be, when there are apt to be more claims for intervention on behalf of intellectuals favorable to the United States than for common criminals who are abused in prison. In the past, foreign protection of Chinese Christians often backfired in the course of xenophobic movements. One hopes that such violence and resentment are things of the past, but even the appearance of protection runs the danger of eliciting resentment from social groups that do not enjoy our favor.

There have been other Chinese intellectuals in recent years who have been just as inaccurate about the West as Fang, only from a leftist point of view. In the purge of the "Gang of Four," many were jailed, sometimes by kangaroo courts, or were dismissed from the Communist Party. Because they were anti-imperialist, they elicited little support from American scholars, no matter how much their rights may have been trampled (their own respect for the rights of others is of course a separate question). What is the principle by which one group of Chinese intellectuals warrants support and another does not?

Chinese will surely fantasize about the West, just as Westerners have imagined China to be just as spiritual, or wise, or revolutionary as they have needed it to be for their own purposes. Thinking about the West in China must be confusing, following decades of relentlessly hostile propaganda suddenly turned to favorable comment, as the Chinese government sought to reverse the thrust of public opinion. In this context, one can easily appreciate Chinese intellectuals' skepticism toward official Chinese discussions of Western social problems. But the West does have serious social problems, and China's intellectuals, especially the most ardent friends of the West, need to know about them. Perhaps we have an obligation to help them be better informed, although they will certainly form their own judgments. Misunderstanding seems likely only to increase the alienation of China's intellectuals from the society in which they must live, and which they hope to help make a better place for all.

We intellectuals in all nations are skilled at concealing our own political interests in concepts of the greatest apparent universality, making it difficult to recognize our true common interest.[37] Instead of leaping to the defense of groups that we think we understand, American intellectuals might ask about how to overcome our insensitivity toward members of other classes, even in our own land, much less in a developing, Third World society. And if we are determined to protect our fellow intellectuals, why are we so interested in China, whose problems are at least of its own making, instead of nations to whose disorders Americans have more actively contributed, such as Nicaragua, El Salvador, Zaire, Angola, Indonesia, Israel, or Chile?

Notes

I thank Cynthia Brokaw, Mary S. Erbaugh, Joe Esherick, Michael Fishlan, Esther Jacobson, Angela Jung, Wendy Larson, and David Milton for their comments on a draft of this essay.

1. Merle Goldman, "Intellectuals in China: Outwardly Relaxed, Inwardly Tense," *The Chronicle of Higher Education* (June 24, 1987): 80.

2. See Kyna Rubin, "Keeper of the Flame: Wang Ruowang as Moral Critic of the State," in *China's Intellectuals and the State: In Search of a New Relationship*, ed. Merle Goldman, with Timothy Cheek and Carol Lee Hamrin (Cambridge: Harvard University Council on East Asian Studies, 1987), pp. 233–50.

3. See Liu's articles in Perry Link, ed., *People or Monsters? and Other Stories and Reportage from China after Mao* (Bloomington: Indiana University Press, 1983). Liu especially enjoyed publicizing the misdeeds of leftists, rarely writing about the corruption associated with Deng Xiaoping's economic reforms. This preference no doubt earned him hostility among critics of reform.

4. "Fang Lizhi he Wen Hui, Ming Lei de duihua" (Conversation of Fang Lizhi with Wen Hui, Ming Lei), *Zhengming* 117 (July 1987): 17–36. See also Orville Schell, "China's Andrei Sakharov," *The Atlantic* 26, 5 (May 1988): 36–37.

5. See Luo Bing, "Beidaihe huiyi neiqing" (Inside the Beidaihe Conference), *Zhengming* 107 (September 1966): 9.

6. The Jiaotong University speech is reprinted as "Zhishi fenzi he Zhongguo shehui" (Intellectuals and Chinese society), and the Tongzhi University speech as "Zhongguo xuyao quanfangwei de xiandaihua" (China needs modernization in all directions), *Zhongguo zhi chun* (Chinese spring) 45 (March 1987): 11–33. Unless otherwise indicated, all quotations from Fang come from these two speeches. For the sake of accuracy, I have translated these literally, rather than gracefully.

7. Tan, executed for his role in the Qing dynasty's 1898 reforms, has long been regarded as a martyr by intellectuals in China.

8. C. B. Macpherson, *The Political Philosophy of Possessive Individualism* (London: Oxford University Press, 1962).

9. "Quarterly Chronicle and Documentation," *China Quarterly* 98:399.

10. The classic discussions are in T. H. Marshall, *Class, Citizenship, and Social Development* (Garden City: Doubleday, 1964), ch. 4, "Citizenship and Social Class," and Reinhard Bendix, *Nation-Building and Citizenship* (Berkeley: University of California Press, 1977), ch. 3, "Transformations of Western European Societies since the Eighteenth Century."

11. See Reeve Vanneman and Lynn Weber Cannon, *The American Perception of Class* (Philadelphia: Temple University Press, 1987). Wright and Martin find that the percentage of workers in the United States dropped from 54.3 percent in 1960 to 50.5 percent in 1980. But this is hardly a wholesale embourgeoisement. Their explanation for this unexpected result is that capitalism today is global, so that proletarianization is taking place on a worldwide scale, making it inappropriate to analyze classes simply on a material basis. See Erik Olin Wright and Bill Martin, "The Transformation of the American Class Structure, 1960–1980," *American Journal of Sociology* 93, 1 (July 1987): 1–29.

12. Alvin Toffler, *Future Shock* (New York: Random House, 1970).

13. See Richard Curt Kraus, *Class Conflict in Chinese Socialism* (New York: Columbia University Press, 1981), pp. 170–77.

14. "Intellectuals and Intellectual Ideology," *Beijing Review* 29, 50 (December 15, 1986): 16–17 (originally in *Guangming ribao*).

15. Ibid.

16. Ibid.

17. Ibid.

18. Guojia Tongjiju, ed., *Zhongguo tongji nianjian* (China Statistical Yearbook) (Beijing: Zhonguo Tongji Chubanshe, 1985), p. 191. Orleans argues that this figure should be halved, rendering college graduate status even more elite. See Leo A. Orleans, "Graduates of Chinese Universities: Adjusting the Total," *China Quarterly* 111 (September 1987): 444–49.

19. Fang later denied using the phrase "wholesale Westernization." See Schell, "China's Andrei Sakharov," p. 42.

20. "Fang Lizhi he Wen Hui, Ming Lei de duihua," pp. 22–23.

21. Curiously, Fang had been a district people's representative from Hefei. See ibid., p. 26.

22. Other examples: Sweden has abolished its proletariat; Japan's postwar econo-

my was comparable to China's in many respects; some Western governments give money to support universities but exercise no control over higher education. Consider also this gem of political analysis: "In the American continent, it is the politically unified United States which is developed, while the disunited South Americans are undeveloped; the key is that the United States practices democratic politics, while South America is still under a feudal political system" (p. 23). Which does Fang believe leads to prosperity—democracy or central governments—or does he mistake one for the other?

23. Edward A. Gargan, "China Needs Democracy, Dissident Says," *New York Times*, June 28, 1987.

24. Merle Goldman and Rudolf Wagner, "China: Intellectuals at Bay," *New York Review of Books* 34, 5 (March 26, 1987): 17–20.

25. Li Chun and Liu Yusheng, "Fang Lizhi's Academic Achievements," *Beijing Review* 31, 18 (May 2–8, 1988): 27–28.

26. Ibid.

27. The following discussion is based upon *China Statistical Yearbook* (1985), pp. 946, 556, 570, 325, 645–55.

28. In 1987, 3.71 renminbi equaled U.S. $1.00.

29. Fang's spirit is similar to the elitist Czech intellectuals who supported the Dubcek reform government in 1968. See Ernest Gellner, "The Pluralist Anti-Levellers of Prague," *Archive europeenes de sociology* 12, 2 (1971): 312–25.

30. Zhao Zonglu, "Students Protest Factory on Campus," *Beijing Review* 30, 28 (July 13, 1987): 9.

31. Personal communication, Elizabeth Perry, March 21, 1988. Similarly, Beijing University students demonstrated for special protection against hooligans after a murder near the campus in June 1988.

32. Irvin Molotsky, "U.S. Cancels Exhibit of Portraits in China," *New York Times*, July 16, 1987.

33. Perry Link, "Intellectuals and Cultural Policy After Mao," in *Modernizing China: Post-Mao Reform and Development*, ed. A. Doak Barnett and Ralph N. Clough (Boulder: Westview Press, 1986), p. 97.

34. Fox Butterfield, "160 U.S. Scholars in Appeal to China," *New York Times*, February 24, 1987.

35. *China: Torture and Ill-Treatment of Prisoners* (New York: Amnesty International, 1987).

36. Goldman and Wagner, "China," p. 20.

37. "The answer to Mannheim's reverence for the intelligentsia as 'free-floating' is to be found not in the reactionary postulate of its 'rootedness in Being' but in the reminder that the very intelligentsia that pretends to float freely is fundamentally rooted in the very being that must be changed and which it merely pretends to criticize." Theodor W. Adorno, *Prisms* (Cambridge: MIT Press, 1981), p. 48.

16

BETWEEN PRAXIS AND ESSENCE: THE SEARCH FOR CULTURAL EXPRESSION IN THE CHINESE REVOLUTION

Ted Huters

> The next day the cadres declared that the atmosphere of our gathering had been unhealthy. They criticized us sharply. Why had Lao Shi sung of suffering, for freedom, when we were suffering only for our crimes, they asked. I was attacked even more strongly; in my soul, they said, I was still opposed to the Party's policies. If I wanted a tomorrow that was different from today, then apparently I was dissatisfied with the current situation. Their accusation stung me, for I had sung with all my heart, my voice filled with hope, only to be told that it was forbidden to imagine a better future.[1]

The cadres' attack on Yue Daiyun's "utopianism" reflects one of the primary dilemmas underlying Chinese Marxist cultural policy: how to make people content with social formations that all parties regard as less than ideal even as the constantly stressed ideal is evolution toward the utopia of pure communism. More than this, however, one gets the distinct impression that it was the artistic expression of Yue's social longing that elicited the particular strength of the party's rebuke. In this respect, the episode can be taken as an emblem of the party's relationship to the arts. On the one hand, the voluntarism the Communists required to mobilize their vision of social and political construction was dependent to a significant extent upon authentically moving cultural forms, while, on the other hand, the constant propensity of those forms to assume a voice beyond the party's control confronted the party with its most severe challenge to control over the manner in which both present and future were to be perceived. Literature was at the very center of this contention, both because of its ability to combine discursive analysis with emotional appeal and, equally important, because of the particular intensity of its long historical relationship with ideological expression in China.

The prominent role literature has played in contemporary China is a constant theme in the Chinese press, particularly in times of political activism. As a *Wenyi bao* editorial noted during one such period (1958): "Today the foremost task of the whole population is to establish socialism, and at the same time to prepare the conditions for the transition to communism. The literary and art workers should become the vanguard of our era."[2] Western scholars have often noted this propensity to give literature pride of place in the revolutionary process and have adduced a variety of factors to explain it—some point to continuities with a Confucian tradition of didactic literature, others to the need for avenues of communication in a society of sophisticated politics and primitive technology. The coincidence that many prominent Communists have literary backgrounds has also been noticed, as has the need for literature as an avenue of indirect discourse in a society where direct statement of political concerns has most often been hazardous. Finally the influence of various foreign models is often noted, principally Soviet ideas brought in by the victorious revolutionaries in the 1940s. It is undeniable that all these factors have contributed mightily to the political status of literature, but it is the contention of this paper that very specific factors in China's intellectual and literary history prepared the ground for the extraordinary coincidence of literary and overt political values that has been such a prominent feature of modern Chinese history.

At first glance, the theoretical basis on which the edifice of post-1949 Communist control of literature stands is remarkably slim. As Bonnie McDougall has noted, the problem with Mao Zedong's only major statement on literature and culture, the 1942 "Talks at the Yan'an Forum on Literature and Art," is that, whatever its applicability to the difficult wartime circumstances to which it was addressed, it was so much a product of its particular times as to be "limited and overly simple for general use."[3] The ad hoc and unsystematic nature of his remarks, however, stands in marked contrast to their widespread practical application in China and the variety of interpretations advanced about them in the rest of the world. There is something almost Confucian about the way in which what seem at face value to be little more than *obiter dicta* on the question of the nature of literary art have been assumed to have absolute indicative value regarding the attitude of Mao and the party toward literature, an assumption shared by Communist and anti-Communist alike. Responsibility for this inflation of the "Talks" must ultimately be laid at the door of Mao and the party cultural apparatus, for they assiduously cultivated the ideology of the universal applicability of the "Talks" for thirty-five years after their promulgation.

Exploration of both the short- and long-term background to Mao's pronouncements, however, reveals the choices available to a revolutionary regime in particular and to new forms of Chinese cultural expression in general to have been sharply overdetermined by a number of factors traceable to the radical transformation of Chinese notions of culture and literature that began so abruptly soon after the Japanese victory of 1895. Careful examination of some of the resulting structural limitations to modern Chinese literary discourse reveals much not only about the reasons for the thinness of the "Talks" themselves, but why they were so depended upon for guidance in the years after they were delivered.

Simply put, the defeat by Japan and the failure of the palace reform of 1898 forced Chinese intellectuals to look at their tradition in a new light to try to determine why they had come to such a desperate political impasse. The almost immediate upshot of the introspection of the post-1895 years was a sense of being caught between wishing to discard those features of traditional practice that Chinese thinkers saw as inhibiting the transformation of an obsolete political structure while at the same time finding some way to maintain a sense of national identity. If this does not seem to us to be a very complex task, the Neo-Confucian sense of organic links between theory and practice made it an intensely problematic enterprise in China. Since baby and bath-water were, as it were, seen as two sides of the same entity, the question became not so much how to avoid throwing out one while preserving the other, but whether this could be done at all.

As Laurence Schneider has pointed out, the transformation of culture in general and literature in particular into an ideology of "national essence" made it possible to begin to attempt to separate indigenous cultural entities from the traditional political system out of which they had originally sprung. Language and literature came to be seen more as symbols of a historically enduring national polity than as signifiers of particular moral points of view within that polity.[4] Vital to this new sense of literature was the example of Western literature's success in representing the distinct nation-state. Taken as equally important, however, was the idea that the Western novel had been markedly successful in reaching a mass audience and thereby playing a key role both in building the strength of the West and in Japan's successful emulation of Western modernization.

This confluence of "national essence" ideas with imported and more democratic notions of literature created a heady mixture that facilitated the rise of the utopian spirit alluded to by Thomas Metzger in his provocative work *Escape from Predicament*. The critic Tao Zengyou, for instance, in 1906–1907 contributed a characteristic series of articles with titles like "Lun wenxue zhi shili ji qi guanxi" (On the power and significance of literature) to the fiction magazines that flourished in eastern Chinese cities during the first decade of this century. His prose is rich enough that a small sample will suffice to show the melange of ideas that coalesced into a concept of literature offering writer, reader, and nation alike the promise of a tool powerful enough to control their respective fates:

> I have heard that to establish a country on this globe requires a particular spirit . . . . And for it to be strong for eternity, it requires natural endowment for strength. . . . Ah! What is this particular spirit? What is this natural endowment? It is literature!
>
> "When letters receive their proper treatment, the world will know a wave of reform." Countrymen! Countrymen! Do you not know that this literature is superior to other branches of learning? That it truly possesses the greatest of power? That it should enjoy the most beautiful of names? That it contains limitless significance? And that it also should alone occupy the highest position in the world?[5]

Even the most cursory examination of such writings reveals that utilitarian concerns of a very traditional nature were continually breaking through the thin skin of utopian theorizing about a new, presumptively transcendent role for literature. Another article by Tao from the same period, in which the critic talked of fiction in precisely the same effulgent terms, demonstrates this point even more forcefully.

> Oh! There is a great monster at the heart of the twentieth century. It walks without legs, flies without wings, sounds without speaking; it stimulates the mind, surprises the eye, opens one's mental horizons and increases the intelligence; it can by turns be solemn, facetious, lyrical, acrimonious, angry, hortatory, satirical or mocking. . . . It has immense strength and attraction as well as unimaginable force; in the realm of literature it casts a particular brilliance and indicates a special quality. What is this thing? It is the novel (*xiaoshuo*). Since the appearance of the noun "novel," it is only this novel that has heightened the trend to restiveness both East and West as well as enabling [us] to grasp the advantages and disadvantages of past and present. It is also only the novel that has influenced the common tendency in the world toward the good and transformed the general direction of the movement for nationalism. The novel! It is truly the most noble vehicle in world literature.[6]

The euphoria so clearly present in Tao's writing makes it difficult to gauge precisely where (or even if) he draws the line between fiction and other literature or, even more to the point, how (or even whether) he makes any demarcation between higher and lower forms of literature. Turning to the work of the young classicist Liu Shipei (1884–1919), however, one can see that such distinctions were never far below the surface in the new thought about literature:

> Speaking of writing in terms of the general theory of evolution, China upon coming into the modern age must reach the stage of allowing the common lan-

> guage to enter literature (*wen*). . . . Uniting speech and writing will lead to an increase in literacy and using the vernacular to promote books and periodicals will allow those who are even slightly literate to place [these publications] in their homes, thereby aiding in the awakening of the people. This is indeed a pressing task in today's China.

At first glance this would seem to be simply a more guarded version of Tao's enthusiasm. But Liu goes on to put the whole complex of ideas into much sharper perspective when he adds: "How can we, however, then rush to discard the ancient language? Contemporary writing should thus be divided into two schools: One devoted to the common language and used to enlighten the mass of people, and one using the ancient language and used to *preserve the national learning*."[7] In other words, traditional writing was to become privileged as a sort of purified essence of the tradition, while the basis for sanctioning the vernacular was nothing more than simply as a one-way conduit from Confucian elite to mass audience. That vernacular fiction had traditionally been held in somewhat less regard among Chinese men of learning than is day-time television among American intellectuals made this mixture of enthusiasm, disdain, and condescension the only ground on which its acceptance could be contemplated by the learned establishment.

Much of the discussion of *xiaoshuo* in this period is couched in terms similar to those used by Liu Shipei in his discussion of the vernacular. In these pronouncements the novel is seen as preeminently a device for providing the lower orders with the notions of moral rectitude necessary for a new age of increased mass participation in the Chinese polity. The following passage from an anonymously written essay entitled "Lun xiaoshuo zhi jiaoyu" (On the educative value of fiction) illustrates this point. After reciting the standard litany of charges against the bad influence of the old novels, the text explains how this influence can be transformed:

> [We should] begin to have beneficial things told to the masses, but still not change people's habits of listening to story-telling. For what has been told up until now is all baseless talk, but if that can be changed to that which is useful to life and what people need to know, then not only will it penetrate the streets and tea-houses, but will be [tantamount] to establishing countless schools there. Will there be any who do not hear and then come to exhort one another [to the good]?[8]

The didactic element of this declaration is as old as the Confucian tradition itself. The sense that the pedagogical effort is ultimately directed at an entirely different group from the elite readers of the document itself, however, is a radical departure from past apologies for writing which, hortatory though they often were, were still directed at a group of peers. Concomitant to this is the clear implication that literature for the masses can never be of the same high quality as that of the elite, newly charged as it was with a central role in national self-preservation.

Placing traditional *belles lettres* off in a new and sacrosanct area where it was to be virtually synonymous with national identity, however, put the emerging concept of "pure literature" into a parlous state. Instead of creating a situation in which literature was subjectively glorified in the minds of its creators even as its actual influence in society declined, as Raymond Williams suggests happened as the result of a superficially similar "purification" of the idea of literature in the West,[9] the Chinese transformation was to cause successive generations of Chinese thinkers to demand ever more from literature and to treat it as a key indicator of the social situation. And with the initial cleavage within writing so firmly set at the beginning as being between high and low rather than between utility and nonutility, it was almost impossible to maintain any clear demarcation of literature as an entity meant to transcend political practice. Since links between expression and praxis had always dominated notions of writing and representation in China, privileging literature simply caused most people to ask it to provide the ultimate solution to the increasingly serious crisis China found itself in in the new century.

The New Culture Movement of the late 1910s and early 1920s represents the logical expansion of the concerns of ten years earlier. As lapses of communication between rulers and ruled had long been identified as one of the crucial practical disorders of the traditional polity, the move to use the vernacular for all purposes—not simply as a conduit from elite to masses—after 1917 represented a significant move in the direction of the utopian promise of a renewed and truly inclusive national community. As Zhou Zuoren wrote in the early days of the May Fourth Movement:

> Commoner [*pingmin*] literature cannot simply be thought of as popular literature. Commoner literature in the vernacular is assuredly more popular than classical prose, but popularization is not its only goal. This is because commoner literature is not strictly meant to be read by commoners, but instead is a literature that studies the life of the commoners—of the people. Its goal is not in fact to depress the mentality and taste of the human race to the level of the commoner but instead to raise the level of the commoners' lives to an appropriate position.[10]

While Zhou clearly has a unified literary language as his goal, the purpose and audience he has in mind for it resists clear resolution. For one thing, he never allows himself to come out flatly for popularization, but hedges ever more emphatically until he comes close to denying that he wants any popularization at all. This is made dramatically explicit in the sentences that follow when he says: "the words of leaders and of people of foresight are never understood by all the people. So commoner literature does not need to be comprehended by every 'hayseed and rube' [*tianfu ye-lao*]." For another, the passage wavers between suggesting that "commoner literature" is designed for an implied elite to "study" the ordinary people or for the ordinary people eventually to read and learn from.

Moving the totality of discourse into the vernacular would seem to have rendered distinctions of intrinsic merit on the basis of linguistic level much more difficult to make, at least in the short run. Leveling the language, however, also made it even more difficult, if not impossible, for future theorists to distinguish between what was merely for utility and what was in harmony with essential ideas about the nation and the culture. The potential conflict between the promise of a radical democratization of literary discourse and the continuing need for a high culture that would serve as a means of national self-definition very soon became an actual one. The resulting debates about what the new literature was to be, the medium to be used, and, eventually, even the nature of the vernacular itself illustrate how serious this tension was to become.

Most of the young critics who took the literary stage by storm in the years after 1917 clearly specified that the new, more democratic literature could not be modeled on anything already existing in China. The classical writing of the elite was too obscure and directly representative of the ideology of the discredited imperial bureaucracy while traditional popular literature was at once too crude and representative of the obverse of the imperial ideology: it encapsulated the vile customs and degraded culture forced upon the populace by the depravities of the evil empire.

By default, then, the Chinese critics turned to the highly developed critical discourse of the West, settling quite soon upon nineteenth-century realism as the most useful mode to serve the disparate needs of simultaneously exposing the old, formulating some sense of what was to replace it, reaching the masses, and satisfying the conflicting desires of the writers themselves in their self-assigned roles as keepers of the flame of culture. Perhaps the root cause of all the strife to follow was the extraordinary degree of overdetermination of the concepts of culture in general and of literature, as cultural praxis, in particular. Statement of the things literature could not be gives perhaps the most vivid sense of the problems involved: it could not be part of the tradition, yet it could not simply ape the imperialist West; it could not be too obscure for popular consumption, yet it could not pander to vulgar tastes; and beyond this, it had to satisfy a traditional desire for universality by meeting the entirely new criteria of a recently discovered "world literature" even as it had to continue to meet particularly Chinese tastes, and it needed to embody culture even as it played the major part in dismantling the culture that was already there.

Attacks on the new literature from opposite sides of the political spectrum demonstrated the extent to which these ideas came into conflict. In the early 1920s Western-trained professors of literature called the new writing vulgar because it was composed in the language of "water carriers and carters," while ten years later Qu Qiubai focused on the ostensible elitism of the transformed vernacular and the profundity of its debt to Europeanized syntax and vocabulary. Both attacks had in common, however, the idea that there was something distinctly un-Chinese about the new literary enterprise. While the attack from the right raised significant questions about how it would be simply to dispense with a long cultural legacy, in the long run its attempts both to maintain the classical language and to transplant Irving Babbit's aesthetics to China doomed it to irrelevancy. Qu's challenge, however, was more enduring, providing as it did the foundation of an extended left-wing critique that culminated with the "Yan'an Talks" of 1942.

While Qu himself attained as limpid a vernacular style as has existed in Chinese before or since, he not only obdurately insists that a successful *baihua* has yet to be created but locates all possibility for future success in its creation in a utopian sphere formed only after a true proletariat has come together and created a common language representing a pooling of features from their respective dialects. The empirically minded Mao Dun's practical demonstration that this was not the way things were actually developing serves to point out the essentialist elements of Qu's theory—it is a kind of mirror-image of Zhang Binglin's "national essence" idea that all the Chinese dialects could be traced back to one *ur*-language. Qu's investment of utopian ideas in language and literature combined with his clear desire to blame earlier literary development for a variety of political failures (in this case, the party's failure to mobilize the masses during and after the 1927 revolution) is characteristic of modern Chinese literary discourse in general.

The thorny point of Qu's critique, however, lies in its impeachment of the European origins of May Fourth neo-elitism. His use of the term "new classical" (*xin wenyan*) to describe the new vernacular arising from the May Fourth Literary reform represents the most telling indictment, equating as it does the new literary language with the thoroughly discredited writing of the traditional culture. Unsustainable as his argument is linguistically, however, there is a sense in which it strikes upon an important truth: the view of the literary language of the late Qing as the essential vehicle of all cultural value had been taken over by the earnest young reformers of the 1920s. Their resort to Western models was also obvious to all concerned—it was, after all, vital to the task of proving that Chinese was now both equal to and part of a broadly defined world culture—but it constituted a serious difficulty for that vast majority of Chinese intellectuals who felt that cultural value somehow had also to come uniquely from within.

If Chinese literature in its moment of democratization had, because of its resort to vulgar language, ceased to offer the transcendent answers it needed to offer and thus paradoxically turned in a mood of self-negation to the foreign as a last resort, the foreign could by definition simply not offer the required sense of indigenous cultural authenticity. Qu thus felt obliged to reject the May Fourth literature on nationalistic grounds. But neither could he simply accept native forms—their presumptive incapacity to accommodate the new culture in the process of formation made this impossible. As he wrote in his famous essay, "The Question of Popular Literature and Art," "[T]he new literary revolution must not only continue to clear out the remnants of the classical language and overthrow the *so-called* vernacular of the new classical, but it must also *firmly oppose the vernacular used in traditional fiction*, because, in fact, it is dead language."[11] All that Qu can do, then, is to express the plaintive desire that "the goal of the new literary revolution is to create the laboring masses' own literary language."[12] The a priori unsuitability of the alternatives—classical or the old vernacular—left literally nothing to replace them with, except the promise of some new, necessarily unprecedented popular culture, situated in a utopian future.

For all the future significance of Qu's argument, its momentary centrality to Chinese critical discourse was supplanted in its turn by other equally pressing issues concerned with the creation of a revolutionary literature. Qu's concerns were only resurrected as the focus of literary concern by a short statement by Mao uttered in October 1938, when the new exigencies of the war against Japan forced a reexamination of the question of the relationship between the uneducated majority and literary expression. As part of the speech entitled "The Role of the Chinese Communist Party in the National War," the words that came to be applied so assiduously to literature were originally part of a broader effort to incorporate Chinese reality into the Marxist theory then in the process of formulation at Yan'an. They thus presage the "Talks" of three and a half years later as a text applied globally to situations that the author did not initially have in mind. The remarks are as follows:

> Foreign stereotypes must be abolished, there must be less singing of empty, abstract tunes, and dogmatism must be laid to rest; they must be replaced by the fresh, lively Chinese style and spirit which the common people of China love. To separate internationalist content from National Form is the practice of those who do not understand the first thing about internationalism. We, on the contrary, must link the two closely.[13]

These few words sparked a debate about the relationship of literature to popular form that carried on through 1939 and 1940 and constitutes the most important intellectual backdrop to Mao's formulations at the Yan'an Forum of May 1942. Raymond Wylie has demonstrated the debt Mao's pronouncement owes to certain ideas advanced by Chen Boda in the spring of 1938. Chen's ideas go far beyond Qu Qiubai's in advocating compromise with tradition: "Regarding the popularization movement, I consider that the use of traditional forms to introduce new contents will be especially effective" and "If we are to transform our traditional national culture and morality into a new national culture and morality in a living, vital, intelligent, and scientific way [we must allow] new contents in traditional forms." Chen does not, however, completely abandon the prevailing wish for completely new forms that originated with May Fourth: "This is not to deny our need for new forms. What we are saying is that new contents in our culture will give birth to new forms, but new contents in our culture may emerge in any form, however old."[14] His emphasis on acceptance of traditional form, even if not for the long term, nevertheless represents a significant diminution of the utopian implications never far from the surface in Qu's writing.

In the ensuing debate over this issue, the critic Xiang Linbing (Zhao Jibiao) gave sophisticated dialectical expression to the ideas concerning continuity versus new cultural departures outlined by Chen and Mao. He made a distinction between "popular forms" (*minjian xingshi*) and "national forms" (*minzu xingshi*), with the former being those that already existed. National forms, on the other hand, were those entities that were to come into being in the future "out of the womb of the old through a process of self-negation of the old" that would in turn "give rise to the independent existence of the new."[15] Xiang argues that since literature is to be used for national mobilization, popular forms must be used, since they are what the masses are accustomed to and are thus the only avenue through which they can participate in aesthetic life and the war effort of which that life is a vital symbolic part. If this is not done,

> If the new [May Fourth] forms are taken as the central source of national form and popular forms are dismantled and fused with the literary forms, then, because the oral quality has been removed, the possibility of direct popular appreciation will have been sacrificed. If one thus adduces a theory of external causation to literary popularization one starts from putting the masses in the passive position of simply receiving instruction. (p. 428)

Of all the critics engaged in the debate, Xiang is unique in being so affirmative about the possibilities of popular initiative. His conspicuous silence concerning artistic quality, however, is another, more telling, characteristic of his work. All the other participants are obsessed with the question of literary merit, which no doubt accounts for the almost unanimous hostility to Xiang's article among the writers who took part. The statements of Zhou Yang—the chief official in charge of party policy toward the arts—are particularly revealing about why this was so. Zhou devotes the major portion of a long essay on issue of "old forms" published in February 1940 to an intelligent explanation of the strength and limitations of May Fourth literature and literary language. He points out the necessary transformation of letters in China following growth of a bourgeois sector of society in the first three decades of the century and stresses that European influence was an integral part of this transformation, one not dominated by Europeanization, but one that was able to absorb the influence in such a way that it "became an organic part of the flesh and blood of the Chinese nation."[16] The problem lay not in the straw-man of Europeanization, then, but in a more general inability of Chinese writers to grasp the complex reality around them, a problem that Zhou seems to deduce from a perception of deficiencies in the literary quality of post-1917 literature. This problem has become particularly acute with the advent of the war, which has brought about the need to do justice both to a more complex environment—the countryside, where old ways continue to dominate—and the needs of the new, rural audience.

Since Zhou, along with almost all his contemporaries, sees content as determining form, he admits the difficulty of conveying new ideas with traditional forms, although he never brings himself to recognize the extent of the logical contradiction involved. As he prepares himself to admit the true agenda behind his advocacy of old forms, the almost total lack of concord between his notions of aesthetic quality and of political necessity make it obvious why he cannot allow himself fully to countenance the difficulties in reconciling the contradictions:

> Utilizing old forms, however, is not purely a type of artistic exploration or experiment, but is rather a matter of the demands of the objective situation—the needs of the war—to create an artistic weapon of mass propaganda and education. The great need for old forms lies in this. Asking of old forms the sort of high artistic quality they cannot possess arises from the sort of malicious attitude associated with the gentry. To think that just because old forms can secure the applause of the masses they are of the highest artistic quality is also unnecessary—it smacks of a discounted optimism and self-intoxication. This is because the barrier between the masses and art has been created by several thousand years of social history; it is the result of the long separation between mental and physical labor. (p. 423)

To satisfy both sides of the argument, Zhou concludes his essay for calling for two types of literature—one using old forms and meant for the masses, and another, "new literature," to meet the needs of the intellectuals and students (but that should still "not abandon the effort to win over the masses").

It is impossible not to see in Zhou's ideas the old distinction between a literature to embody cultural value on the one hand and one of diminished stature designed simply to inculcate elite values in the uneducated. What seems most remarkable is that for all Zhou's rhetorical devotion to the cause of the people, he does not seem to entertain even for an instant the idea that their modes of expression could have any real artistic value. It is noteworthy that nowhere in the passage does he blame imbedded reactionary ideas on this artistic barrenness—it is simply a matter of the historical situation of the populace. The contrast with Xiang Linbing, who at least allows the inference that the people might be something other than passive receptors of cultural light shed from above, is instructive. Moreover, what is even more noteworthy in regard to the national forms debate as a whole is that every writer participating in the discussion either explicitly or implicitly agrees with Zhou Yang on the question of the artistic merit of popular forms. They blame this deficiency on one factor or another, and few are as forthright as Zhou Yang in their certainty about the absolute impermeability of the gap between "popular" and "aesthetic," but they all agree on the central point.[17] In light of Chinese literary policy in subsequent years, it is often difficult to keep in mind that this was a discussion carried on exclusively on the left. Zhou was, in other words, charged with implementing a policy that he quite literally only half believed in.

Had Mao in 1942 himself come out in straightforward advocacy of popular forms as a way of bridging this unhealthy chasm between aesthetic belief and political expediency, his excoriation of the left-wing literary scene would have been instantly comprehensible. But there is no evidence from the published proceedings of the Yan'an Forum that he felt much differently about the artistic merit of popular culture than the people he was criticizing. He seems rather to hark back to Qu Qiubai in his disdain for contemporary Chinese literature and the most commonly mentioned alternatives. Mao does admit that having models from the past marks "the difference between being civilized or vulgar, crude or refined, advanced or elementary, fast or slow; therefore, we certainly may not reject the ancients and foreigners as models, which means I'm afraid, that we must even use feudal and bourgeois things." His true lack of enthusiasm for this course of action comes through, however, when he adds: "But they are only models and not substitutes; they can't be substitutes. Indiscriminate plagiarization, imitation, or substitution in literature and art of dead people or foreigners is an extremely sterile and harmful literary and artistic dogmatism."[18] While Mao talks continually about learning from the people, the tone of his utterances suggests that aesthetics is not one of the categories in which the people are to be taken as the greatest authority. Indeed, when he discusses what he means by popular forms, he can only mention the peoples' "budding literature and art (wall newspapers, murals, folk songs, folk tales, popular speech, and so on)" (p. 66). His failure to mention such more established (and no doubt more genuinely popular) genres as local opera and storytelling suggests he is following the difficult road of Qu Qiubai in a radical dissatisfaction with all forms of literature that currently exist.

On artistic merit, however, Mao has this to say:

> Literature and art for a wider audience and literature and art to raise standards are both processed forms, so what is the difference between them? There is a difference of degree. Literature and art for a wide audience indicates that the processing has been relatively limited and crude, and therefore relatively easy for the broad masses at the present time to accept readily, while literature and art to raise standards indicates that the processing had been relatively extensive and skillful, and hence, relatively difficult for them. (pp. 70–71)

Since, like everyone else, he sees the need to produce art for a wide audience in this time of troubles, Mao comes down firmly on the side of pure utility. This is, after all, only to be expected, but his apparent agreement with the taxonomy of letters reached by consensus in the preceding years would indicate that he is quite willing to sacrifice what they all agree to be the entire aesthetic side of writing in pursuit of political mobilization (although he does admit at one point that more educated readers need better literature, he will not allow such literature to be created in the midst of the current struggle) (p. 727).

Were the "Talks" confined to these observations and recommendations for creating a new mass literature based on them, they would not be in drastic disagreement with the loose consensus reached two years previously. Mao adds to the mix, however, generous helpings of abuse for writers, generally accusing them of not being clear about the primacy of meeting the needs of the audience. Since the one thing that writers agreed upon—other than the lack of quality of popular literature—was the importance (and the difficulty) of meeting the needs of this audience, the acerbity of Mao's attack suggests that other issues are being addressed beneath the surface. The passages toward the end of the "Talks" where he addresses the issue of writing in the "Lu Xun style" and the question of "literature of exposure" provide important clues to Mao's real concern. Mao's vehement denial of the validity of these two modes of writing in the transformed situation in Yan'an and concurrent injunctions to the writers to place more emphasis on class analysis and to choose the forms that would best serve the revolutionary classes (i.e., the Communist Party) suggest that he was in fact contending with the writers over the issue of who is to be licensed to interpret the present and suggest the shape of the future.

In practical terms, this adds up to a drastic disagreement with the writers over the proper mode of expression. The focus of almost all post-May Fourth writers, especially in the national forms debate, on the sanctity of realism can best be understood by recalling Fredric Jameson's discussion of the term in *The Political Unconscious*:

> As any number of "definitions" of realism assert, and as the totemic ancestor of the novel, Don Quixote, emblematically demonstrates, that processing operation variously called narrative mimesis or realistic representation has as its historic function the systematic undermining and demystification, the secular "decoding," of those preexisting inherited traditional or sacred narrative paradigms which are its initial givens. In this sense, the novel plays a significant role in what can be called a properly bourgeois cultural revolution—that immense process of transformation whereby populations whose life habits were formed by other, now archaic modes of production are effectively reprogrammed for life and work in the new world of market capitalism. The "objective" function of the novel is thereby also implied: to its subjective and critical, analytical, corrosive mission must now be added the task of producing as though for the first time that very life world, that very "referent"—the newly quantifiable space of extension and market equivalence, the new rhythms of measurable time, the new secular and "disenchanted" object world of the commodity system, with its post-traditional daily life.[19]

Some comments made by the writer Ye Yiqun in 1940 show a remarkable similarity—on a rather more basic level—to Jameson's notions, with one significant exception:

> I think that national forms are a question of what lively forms can be used to express the realities occurring in China. Only new forms can express the complex realities of Chinese society and these new forms are none other than those that the new literature has been pursuing experimentally for all these years. The new literature has fought to abolish foreign stereotypes and has been opposed to dogmatism. One cannot find a single example over the three-year period of the war of "pouring new wine into old bottles" to successfully depict Chinese reality.... Chinese literary forms are constantly moving forward.[20]

> But the Chinese people are alive and progressing; they are not stagnant. Things they would not have done in the past they are doing today. For example, three years ago to [tell of] a peasant hurling a grenade at a tank would probably have been taken as a joke, but today it is a fact. From this one can draw a truth: in the process of selection of literary forms, one should take the Chinese masses' real lives as the standard. Whatever can most completely and satisfactorily represent these lives is the best form.[21]

The same emphasis on the destruction of old literary forms is evident in Ye's subtext, as is the stress on new forms of realism giving expression to new modes of life. The obvious difference is that Ye and the other writers do not see themselves as the vanguard of the "bourgeois cultural revolution." While Mao clearly does see the writers as such, formal considerations are not uppermost in his mind. His grounds, as argued above, principally consist of a concern that the writers are insufficiently concerned with their audience and are writing in a critical mode inappropriate to the new situation. The reams of paper devoted to the debate over "national forms," as well as the cavalier attitude Mao demonstrated in the "Talks" to the national forms already in existence, should be enough to convince one that Mao's real concern lay with the question of critical attitude.

This worry on Mao's part reflected a fundamental irony of the literary scene after 1942. With the left having insisted upon literature becoming overwhelmingly a discourse in opposition to the prevailing social structure, the party bore considerable responsibility for having created a corps of writers determined to root out social injustice. With the party now suddenly in power, however, what was it to do with this group of highly censorious writers that it had helped to create? The writers understandably insisted upon continuing to take seriously their role as guardians of the shape of a culture that all sides agreed was a consciously politicized formation—their painfully acquired identity required it. Ironically, Mao takes their insistence even more seriously than they do, which accounts for the vehemence with which he tries to take that role away from the writers (and from literature in general) and give it to the party.

Ultimately, however, the way in which Mao attempted to remove literature from its position as the cultural nexus only brought to the foreground the reasons it had been there in the first place. Literature's view of itself as complementary but slightly predicatory to politics was confirmed by Mao's very act of challenge to those qualities. If literature before Yan'an had never been able to merge its two contradictory roles of being transcendent cultural essence and practical messenger to the people, Mao's attempt to reduce it to a position as simple transmitter and to remove from it the high aspirations it had for itself allowed those aspirations to be put in the only place where they could still realistically be held—the utopian realm of the potential. With his arrogation of final cultural authority for the party, on the other hand, Mao sought the virtually unrealizable complete unity between theory and practice that literature had reached toward but never grasped. When the inevitable failure of this goal became obvious, the literature that Mao had so unceremoniously removed from its position as being in advance of policy returned with representations of spectral images of how political ideas could have been accomplished. In essence, the "Yan'an Talks" strictures guaranteed the perpetual recurrence of the ambitious "Panglossian optimism" of literary May Fourth whenever controls were lifted.

In the years after 1949, however, with enforcement of this literary policy in the hands of Zhou Yang, the obverse of this utopianism was a certain built-in cynicism in regard to the literary works produced under the aegis of the party. This is evident in the summary Zhou wrote in 1946 of the import of the work of Zhao Shuli, one of the new rural writers to emerge with the ostensible valorization of popular forms. Zhou writes that Zhao's "success is no accident but is due to the fact that he has put into practice the directives on literature and art given by Mao Zedong. Zhao Shuli deliberately calls his works 'popular stories,' *although they are not, of course, popular stories in the ordinary sense of the word, but real works of art*, in which artistry and popular appeal blend."[22] The gap between aesthetics and utility remains, in other words, with a vengeance, and it is perceived in the same way as ever: "high" art is contrasted with "popular," the one the domain of aesthetics and the other the province of transmitting messages.

It is thus no wonder that within a few years after 1949 a report on the literary situation in Shanghai should find a pervasive stagnation, the result of a stalemate between different views of what literature should be. In the words of Lars Ragvald, the report noted that

> nothing much was done that deserved the name of literature and art. In particular there was little application . . . to local conditions and little writing of good works in the different units. Most cadres were, if at all interested, inclined towards expensive reproductions of famous literary models. Others demanded such a close relationship to the ongoing [political] drives that no difference could be found between the speeches of the production leaders and plays that were staged to stimulate production. The fact that these very statements frequently reappeared during the *mingfang* [Hundred Flowers] in the provinces in May and June 1957 gives credence to the assumption that this might have been the common state of affairs in most localities.[23]

One finds, in other words, the characteristic division between aesthetics and utility continued, with aesthetics now safely lodged in canonized work insulated from practical concern. Utilitarian work, thoroughly cowed by the campaigns launched against writings that exposed the defects of socialist society, stuck as close to the current line as possible. The use of foreign models had in the interim undergone a complete turnabout. Whereas in the May Fourth period, theories of European realism had bolstered the aesthetic position of the new writing, after 1949 heavy reliance upon Soviet models of the Stalin era provided cosmopolitan support for the bureaucrats in charge of the utilitarian line. While use of these foreign models may have reassured Chinese intellectuals that they were members of a wider world of discourse, it also served as another layer of mystification concerning the underlying nature of the literary issues involved.

Utopian hopes for literature had not faded, however, a fact to which the very existence of the Shanghai report gives testimony. Neither critical writers nor the party could be happy with the poor quality of literature produced by the literary policies pursued after 1949; both sides continued to harbor grand views of the potential of literature that made the compromises involved with the creation of literary work in the 1950s seem morally reprehensible. At the same time, the clarity and urgency of these visions fostered a mentality that could only see some sort of intellectual or moral perversity behind any obstacles that stood in the way. The propensity for the most relentless sort of struggle over ethical absolutes was therefore built into the literary debates to follow. With the stakes defined as high as they were, the more dangerous game of linking up with whichever faction in the party leadership offered the best terms in the struggle against the enemy was ultimately to become an irresistible temptation.

Much of the force of the convictions each side held had to do with the fact that both writers and spokesmen for the party shared an idealized and essentialist notion of aesthetics, in keeping with the long-standing wish in the Chinese intellectual community that literature fill a transcendent role in national discourse. As had been the case so many times since 1895, however, aesthetics and utility proved to be immensely difficult to separate in practice. In fact, what the key constituents making up aesthetic value were to be ironically became the locus of fierce political struggle of the most utilitarian and realpolitik sort.

The critical writers, when encouraged to speak during periods of relaxation such as the Hundred Flowers campaign, blamed the domination of party dogmatism for their inability to achieve realism. The definition given by Qin Zhaoyang, one of the principal dissidents of the Hundred Flowers period, of what makes literature appealing demonstrates, however, the extent to which his notion of realism conflates the artistic and the political:

> All distinguished progressive literary works have a strong concern with ideological thought and politics. It is obvious that, inescapably, literature has greatly served politics. The reason these literary works possess such great persuasive power is that the authors have been faithful to objective reality and have achieved high artistic quality as well. This is linked with the positive aspects of the author's world view. These literary works were not produced merely to fulfill a certain duty; they have a long-range social significance and are artistic works of great realistic achievement.[24]

By way of contrast, Qin points out the defects of work that is not faithful to reality: "Although propaganda work is necessary and has its unique, important value, it cannot substitute for literary and artistic work. So-called literary and artistic work which are similar to propaganda material will disgust people. . . . The loss will be invisible. Literature will fail in its original purpose, which is to serve politics" (p. 132). While it may be true that Qin's notions of how to write will be more productive than those of the people he is writing against, it is noteworthy how the political subtext emerges at the forefront whenever the aesthetic qualities of realism come up for discussion. The question of whether the party or the writers will control the process of giving shape to reality seems never to be very far from Qin's consciousness. There can be little doubt that the tenacity of the concept of realism owes much to the idea that the writer who commands realism thereby gains privileged insight into (and control over) popular perception of the way society is constituted and its prospects for the future.

In rebutting the view of literature advanced by Qin, Yao Wenyuan, eventually to emerge as the major spokesman for the far left of the literary spectrum, was prevented by the centrality of realism to literary discourse from denying that the concept lay at the heart of the aesthetic canon, and that a certain "skill" was required to achieve it. Almost as soon as he sets the idea forth, however, he seeks to supplant the aesthetic definition of skill with a strictly political one:

> Skill, however, is not the essential factor in literary creation . . . the writer's convictions are another decisive factor. The portrayal of life, and the acquiring of experience in observing and giving expression to the realities of life, are invariably related to the author's attitude toward life itself. . . . The ideological factor is intrinsically related to the factor of skill and serves to govern the exercising of the latter. Consequently, a shift in one's ideology will often result in a revision of one's creative method.[25]

The political commitment underlying his notion of aesthetics, however, comes through most clearly when he pronounces toward the end of the essay that "There has never been an instance of a reactionary writer producing an immortal character" (p. 160). Politics here emerges in its most undisguised form. If Qin Zhaoyang at least paid lip service to the idea of keeping aesthetics distinct in some theoretical measure from the demands of politics, Yao here attempts to show the utter impossibility of such a position and the ultimate contingency of art on politics.

During the activist days of the "Great Leap Forward" in 1958, this propensity to put politics in command reached a new high point. Among other things, there was a widespread movement to sponsor amateur "folk" poetry, most of which relied unabashedly (and/or unconsciously) on traditional classical forms. Given the determination of the left not to differentiate aesthetics and utility as well as the peculiar history of popular forms in modern Chinese literature, it is not surprising that the radicals were by now incapable of making any real distinction as to what was "folk" and what was "classical." In the ensuing burst of enthusiasm, those who sought to make clearer discriminations were under severe pressure to conform. As Ragvald notes of the critic and poet He Qifang:

> He represented those few who openly dared to defend the May Fourth tradition against the onslaught of classical form and political pragmatism. He, to be sure, was prepared to admit the great usefulness of folk song style at the moment but thought that it would not prevail. Many of his "co-debaters" and critics, as he shows in his [articles on the subject], confused usefulness with the desirable and likely trend.[26]

The profound merging of the language of aesthetic and political evaluation on both sides that marked literary debate in the years to follow, however, made it easy, if not inevitable, for each party in this continuing debate to blame the other for the failure of a new and satisfactory literature to come into being. The writers saw restrictions on subject matter, form, and tone as debilitating, entirely unnecessary impediments, while the Maoist left saw the failure to create bright encomia to the new society as evidence that writers were willfully resisting the call to help in the construction of the new Marxist dispensation. As frustration with the failure of either line to prevail decisively grew, moreover, the situation became more highly charged, with the polarity becoming most acute in periods of factional strife at the top levels of the party. In such times, each side moved to take advantage of their resources in such a way as to deal the other side as severe a setback as possible. The perception of the Great Leap Forward as a catastrophe, for instance, moved those of a critical disposition who had survived the various purges before 1958 to a dissenting position against Mao veiled only by the thinnest pretext of historical allusion: the dramas and Beijing operas performed and published with the connivance of party officials critical of Mao marked the final acceptance by "liberal" critics of their inability to separate the political and aesthetic strands of their concerns as well as the recognition that factional infighting was an essential part of their struggle.[27]

The initiative launched by the left in the Cultural Revolution represents for its part a messianic effort to resolve the impasse between the "two lines" and to assure optimal conditions for the art of socialist utopianism. The rapid collapse of resistance to the Maoist line in 1966 brought a sense to the surviving literary discourse (now dominated in spirit by Yao Wenyuan) of a millennial triumph: with the final defeat of their enemies the Maoist vision of the world was without further impediment and could achieve its aesthetic and political apotheosis. The language of the initial pronouncements of the movement reflects this utopian mood:

> On the 25th anniversary of the publication of Chairman Mao's *Talks at the*

> *Yenan Forum on Literature and Art*, while the great victories of more than a year of the proletarian cultural revolution are being acclaimed, the brand-new opera *On The Docks*, born and matured in the intense class struggle, is presented for the vast audience of workers, peasants and soldiers. We warmly congratulate its sources and ardently wish for more and more images of heroes armed with Mao Tse-tung's thought to occupy the Peking opera stage.[28]

It is not coincidental that the early polemical writings of the Cultural Revolution are full of denunciations of Soviet revisionism and American imperialism—the left in its shining moment was now inspired to discard all foreign theoretical props and project a vision of a purely Chinese utopia. This, combined with drastic attempts to diminish the role of professional writers in favor of amateurs from the ranks of the "workers, peasants, and soldiers" betokened the culmination of the trend toward iconoclasm with respect to the entire modern literary tradition since May Fourth.[29]

Neither is it an accident that both the expository and literary prose (in the model Beijing operas in particular) produced during the period move to the same rhythmic cadences marked off by formulaic expressions. The impact of this form of writing was surely to urge that all movement-inspired prose share a ritualistic sense of the power of words to move both mountains and foolish old men. In an important sense the Cultural Revolution marks the ultimate step in the fusion of aesthetics and politics: it signals the aestheticization of politics as much as the politicization of aesthetics. Was this, then, the "fresh, lively Chinese style and spirit which the common people of China love" that Mao demanded in 1938, the "national essence" that had proved so elusive from the time of the late Qing? Initially there seems to have been some belief that this was indeed the case. There seems wide agreement, for instance, that the model operas were, at least in the beginning, quite popular.[30]

The euphoria that initially attended the capture of discourse by the Maoist left was, however, inevitably short-lived. The reality that the new language had struggled so mightily to create soon began to elude the capacities of a prose that aspired at once to describe and to control. As the events that transpired so rapidly after the death of Mao demonstrate, society proved resistant to the force of literary language to give it direction. That this language and what it allowed itself to represent were both exceedingly shrill and limited to a narrow range of permissible modes of behavior and plot motif was part of the problem, but the series of reckless political events that the left engaged in during the years after 1969 demonstrated more than anything else that the left's political practice continually exceeded the bounds theoretically set for it by its own discourse. The apparently dismal responses to the campaign against Deng Xiaoping in mid-1976 was emblematic of the exhaustion of the utopian language of the Chinese left.

This is not to say that politics and literature have been cleanly separated by events following 1976. The various campaigns launched by party conservatives (the same people who had sponsored the anti-Mao literary movement of the early 1960s) since 1981 show how tenacious the idea of unity between utility and aesthetics remains. Writers themselves seem at times to be as reluctant as anyone else to give the notion up. The young writer Zhang Xinxin, for instance, when asked a question during a speech in New York about how freedom of the press would affect China, responded to the effect that such a move would make Chinese literature superfluous. The utopian hopes that literature once embodied seem, however, largely to have died with the Cultural Revolution. Comparing the Chinese literary scene of the late 1980s—which would appear to center around the question "How do we win the Nobel Prize?"—to the desperate pursuit of human perfectibility that dominated the early stages of the Cultural Revolution vividly illustrates the extent to which ideology has lost its power to impel action.

Notes

1. Yue Daiyun and Carolyn Wakeman, *To the Storm: The Odyssey of Revolutionary Chinese Woman* (Berkeley: University of California Press, 1985), pp. 92–93.

2. Lars Ragvald, "Yao Wenyuan as a Literary Critic and Theorist: The Emergence of Chinese Zhdanovism," Ph.D. diss., University of Stockholm, 1978, p. 133.

3. Bonnie S. McDougall, Introduction to *Mao Zedong's "Talks at the Yan'an Conference on Literature and Art": A Translation of the 1943 Text with Commentary*, Michigan Papers in Chinese Studies no. 39 (Ann Arbor: University of Michigan Center for Chinese Studies, 1980), pp. 41–48.

4. Laurence A. Schneider, "National Essence and the New Intelligentsia," in *The Limits of Change: Essays on Conservative Alternatives in Republican China*, ed. Charlotte Furth (Cambridge: Harvard University Press, 1976), esp. pp. 57–60.

5. Tao Zengyou, "Zhongguo zhi wenxue gaiguan," in *Zhongguo jindai wenlun xuan*, ed. Luo Genze and Guo Shaoyu (Beijing: Renmin wenxue, 1962), 1:241.

6. Tao Zengyou, "Lun xiaoshuo zhi shili ji qi yingxiang," in ibid., 1:251.

7. Liu Shipei, "Lun wen zaji," in *Liu shenshu xiansheng yishu*, ed. Nan Peilan and Cheng Yufu (N.p., 1934–1936), 20:1b. Emphasis added.

8. Anon., "Lun xiaoshuo zhi jiaoyu," in *Zhongguo jindai wenlun xuan*, ed. Luo Genze and Guo Shaoyu, 1:263.

9. Raymond Williams, *Culture and Society, 1780–1950* (New York: Harper and Row, 1966), esp. pp. 30–48.

10. Zhou Zuoren, "Pingmin de wenxue," in *Zhongguo xin wenxue daxi* (Hong Kong reprint: Xianggang wenxue yanjiu she, n.d.), 1:236–39.

11. Qu Qiubai, "Dazhong wenyi de wenti," in *Qu Qiubai wenji* 2:889, trans. in *Revolutionary Literature in China: An Anthology*, ed. John Berninghausen and Ted Huters (White Plains, N.Y.: M. E. Sharpe, 1977), p. 49. Emphasis in original.

12. Ibid., 2:907–908.

13. Mao Tse-tung [Mao Zedong], "The Role of the Chinese Communist Party in the National War," in *Selected Works of Mao Tse-tung* (Beijing: Foreign Languages Press, 1967), 2:209–10.

14. Raymond Wylie, *The Emergence of Maoism: Mao Tse-tung, Ch'en Po-ta, and the Search for Chinese Theory, 1935–1945* (Stanford: Stanford University Press, 1980), p. 79.

15. Xiang Linbing, "Lun 'Minzu xingshi' de zhongxin yuanquan," in *Wenxue yundong shiliao xuan* (Shanghai: Shanghai jiaoyu, 1979), 4:425.

16. Zhou Yang, "Dui jiu xingshi liyong zai wenxueshang de yige kanfa," in ibid., 4:418.

17. For the considerable unanimity on this issue, see the two roundtable discussions collected in ibid., 4:452–88. For a competent analysis of the various viewpoints, see Márián Gálik, "Main Issues in the Discussion on 'National Forms' in Modern Chinese Literature," *Asian and African Studies* 10 (1974): 97–105.

18. Mao Zedong in *Mao Zedong's "Talks,"* ed. McDougall, p. 69.

19. Fredric Jameson, *The Political Unconscious: Narrative as a Socially Symbolic Art* (Ithaca: Cornell University Press, 1981), p. 152.

20. Ye Yiqun, "Minzu xingshi zuotan biji," in *Shiliao xuan*, 4:475.

21. Ye Yiqun, "Wenyi de minzu xingshi wenti zuotanhui," in ibid., 4:467.

22. Zhou Yang, "Zhao Shuli and His Stories," in *Rhymes of Li Youcai and Other Stories* (Beijing: Foreign Languages Press, 1980), p. 185. Emphasis added.

23. Ragvald, "Yao Wenyuan," pp. 173–74 n. 39.

24. Ho Chih [He Zhi] [Ch'in Chao-yang (Qin Zhaoyang)], "The Broad Road of Realism—A Reassessment of Realism," in *Literature of the Hundred Flowers*, vol. 1: *Criticism and Polemics*, ed. Nieh Hualing (New York: Columbia University Press, 1981), p. 130.

25. Yao Wenyuan, "Is Realism Forever Changeless?" in ibid., 1:158–59.

26. Ragvald, "Yao Wenyuan," p. 202 n. 94.

27. For details on the use of drama as a political weapon by critical intellectuals in the period after 1958, see Rudolf Wagner's book forthcoming from University of California Press.

28. Hsieh Wen-ping [Xie Wenbing], "A Fierce Struggle for Control of the Peking State Opera—The Production and Staging of *On the Docks*, a Peking Opera on a Revolutionary Contemporary Theme," in *On the Revolution of Peking Opera*, by Chiang Ching [Jiang Qing] (Beijing: Foreign Languages Press, 1968), p. 33.

29. For a description of the anti-foreign and anti-May Fourth sentiments of the early period of the Cultural Revolution, see Merle Goldman, *China's Intellectuals: Advise and Dissent* (Cambridge: Harvard University Press, 1981), pp. 125–27.

30. See, for instance, ibid., p. 181.

Part IV
Conclusions

17

THE DERADICALIZATION OF CHINESE SOCIALISM

Maurice Meisner

In the early years of the century, and some years prior to the Russian Bolshevik Revolution, Robert Michels (who has the somewhat dubious distinction of being known as one of the founders of the modern discipline of political science) made a cynical prediction. "The socialists might conquer, but not socialism, which would perish in the moment of its adherents' triumph," he prophesied.[1]

Nearly a century after the time Michels wrote, and with all the historical experience with which our century has blessed us, or plagued us, it would be difficult indeed to deny the apparent fulfillment of Michels' prophecy. The twentieth century has been, among many other things, a century of socialist revolutions. Marxian socialist parties have come to power in many countries since 1917 and today are the ruling parties in lands inhabited by one-third of the world's population—lands which the leaders of these parties proclaim to be socialist and which are also conventionally called socialist from afar, perhaps simply out of habit and for want of any better term in our limited historical lexicon. Yet there are relatively few these days, beyond the leaders of Marxist-Leninist parties in power (whose claims to moral and political legitimacy rest on their alleged socialist credentials and accomplishments), who are inclined to regard these countries as socialist in any meaningful sense of that term—and certainly not in terms of that vital vision of the good society that the word "socialism" inspired for generations before our own. The history of the twentieth century thus appears as confirmation of Michels' depressing prediction. Socialists have frequently triumphed, but these political victories, dramatic and far-reaching as they sometimes have been, have yet to yield a genuinely socialist society. Not unless, of course, one is inclined to apply the label "socialist" to all societies where the means of production are under state ownership or control—a distorted definition of socialism that has little to do with (indeed, is the antithesis of) the vision of society that the term was originally intended to convey and what it traditionally has meant.[2]

Does this mean that socialism, or at least genuine socialism, is historically impossible? Is it a "utopian" dream in the usual sense of the term "utopian," which is to say, something impossible in principle? Is capitalism, or some version of it, the final destination of history, the necessary, desirable, and eternal socioeconomic order, as its proponents claim? Or has twentieth-century history produced new types of social formations that are neither capitalist nor socialist, and for which we have yet to invent a name, much less understand their inner workings and future historical directions?

These are rather cosmic historical questions, for which I lack answers. But what I would like to do is to raise again the matter of the alleged historical impossibility of socialism, and reflect a bit on what aspects of the postrevolutionary Chinese historical experience, and especially the more recent post-Mao experience, reveal about the prospects for socialism, if not in the world as a whole, then at least in China.

Before considering what contemporary Chinese history might or might not tell us about the prospects for socialism, it might be useful to review the major theories that have been advanced over the years to tell us that socialism is a historical impossibility to begin with. These theories, which do not necessarily maintain that socialism is socially undesirable in principle, do suggest that the realization of socialism is historically precluded in principle. Such arguments have been advocated for a long time, and they have profoundly influenced the ways in which scholars and others treat the strivings for socialist goals by socialists both in and out of power—and the standards that have been employed to evaluate socialist movements in China and elsewhere. Of these arguments, all of which of course tend to be highly deterministic, one can—for the sake of convenience and brevity—identify three main types, all of which have innumerable variants.

Political Determinism

One general argument, and perhaps the most influential, was set forth by Robert Michels himself. Michels' prediction that "the socialists might conquer, but not socialism" was not simply an expression of political cynicism. It was derived from his observation of the behavior of Marxian Social Democratic political parties in Western Europe in the pre–World War I era and based on a rather elaborate analysis that found its primary expression in what he called "the iron law of oligarchy." In accordance with that "law," he argued that "the majority of human beings, in a condition of eternal tutelage, are predestined by tragic necessity to submit to the dominion of a small minority" and thus "must be content to constitute the pedestal of an oligarchy." Michels took it as a matter of historical inevitability that oligarchy is "a preordained form of the common life of great social aggregates." It is interesting to note (although difficult to grant the proposition) that Michels maintained that this "iron law of oligarchy" was not in conflict with Marx's conception of history but rather an extension or "completion" of Marx. Michels accepted, indeed championed, the doctrine of class struggle, for example, but argued that "class struggles invariably culminate in the creation of new oligarchies which undergo fusion with the old." History, for Michels, thus appeared as "a tragicomedy in which the masses are content to devote all their energies to effecting a change of masters."[3] This, of course, is hardly a Marxist vision of history or of the role of the masses in the making of history, despite Michels' claim that he was enriching and "completing" the materialist conception of history.

However that may be, Michels derived his politically deterministic assumption on the impossibility of socialism not only from the views of his intellectual predecessors (especially Mosca and Pareto), but also from the actual histories of the powerful socialist parties of the advanced capitalist countries in the early years of the century, particularly the German Marxian Social-Democratic Party. He saw, quite accurately, in those Marxist parties a willingness to accommodate themselves to the existing order of things, party leaders who thirsted for power within established parliamentary systems, and especially a strong tendency for the party organization to become an end in itself rather than a means to serve socialist ends. The revolutionary party, Michels observed of Marxist parties in the advanced capitalist countries of Western Europe, inevitably becomes "a finely conservative party which . . . continues to employ revolutionary terminology, but which in actual practice fulfills no other function than that of a constitutional opposition." It is transformed into simply "a rival of the bourgeois parties for the conquest of power." "Thus, from a means organization becomes an end," he concluded.[4]

Michels wrote before Lenin's scheme of party organization had become a politically noticeable phenomenon, and certainly long before the Leninist concept of the vanguard party had historically revealed its consequences and implications. Had Michels been aware of Leninism, as was to be the case with those who later pursued his analysis in various ways, it no doubt would have served to reinforce his argument.

However that may be, or might have been, Michels presented the essential elements of the major politically deterministic explanation for the failure of socialism in the twentieth century. Simply put, socialism is doomed to fail by virtue of "the iron law of oligarchy." This does not preclude political victories for socialist parties, but such victories are political triumphs for the leaders of these parties, and certainly not a victory for the masses of their followers, much less for socialism. There have been innumerable versions and variants of this argument over the years, but they convey essentially the same message Michels' analysis was designed to convey, that is, that socialism is a historical impossibility, inevitably precluded by the very political means socialists must employ to gain political power. In most of the arguments, the Leninist concept of party organization is of course presented as the principal example of how the political means of socialism inevitably subvert socialist ends.

Economic Determinism

If "the iron of oligarchy," or some variant of it, is at the core of most politically deterministic arguments that deny that socialism is historically possible, there are an equally great number of economically deterministic theories that arrive at the same conclusion. These theories take as their point of departure the great irony of the history of Marxism in the modern world, namely, that Marxist-led socialist revolutions have been successful not in the advanced capitalist countries where Marx assumed they would first take place, but rather, beginning with the Russian Bolshevik Revolution, in economically underdeveloped countries lacking the Marxian-defined social and material prerequisites for socialism. Ironically, although Karl Marx obviously did not argue that socialism was historically impossible (indeed he proclaimed it historically necessary if not necessarily historically inevitable), he nevertheless was among the intellectual godfathers of these economic deterministic theories that deny the possibility of realizing the socialist vision that he held. Marxism, after all, is a theory that rests on the central proposition that socialism presupposes capitalism, that only modern capitalism produces the necessary material and social preconditions for socialism, namely, large-scale industry and the modern proletariat, the essential social agent of the socialist future. What distinguished Marxism from other nineteenth-century socialist theories was precisely its acceptance of capitalism as a necessary and progressive stage in historical development. Marx's critique of other socialist doctrines he pejoratively labeled "utopian" rested, in large measure, on the failure of the authors of those doctrines to take into account the historically progressive nature of capitalism. The "utopian socialists," Marx and Engels charged, recognized neither large-scale industry as the essential material foundation for the future socialist society nor the modern proletariat as the social agent destined to bring about that future, thus condemning themselves to historical irrelevance.[5]

Original Marxist theory, in contrast, presented itself not simply as a critique of capitalism but also as a doctrine that championed the historical necessity of capitalism, even if not its social desirability.

Marx not only assumed that socialism presupposed a fully developed capitalist system, he also warned against the futility and social dangers of "premature" attempts to carry out socialist revolutions—in historical situations where, as he put it, "the material conditions are not yet created which make necessary the abolition of the bourgeois mode of production." People, he warned, "do not build themselves a new world out of the fruits of the earth, as vulgar superstition believes, but out of the historical accomplishments of their declining civilizations. They must, in the course of their development, begin by themselves producing the material conditions of a new society, and no effort of mind or will can free them from this destiny."[6] For Marx, a genuine socialist reorganization of society could be accomplished only on the basis of the highly developed productive forces and technologies created by modern capitalism—for only conditions of economic abundance would allow people to free themselves from the tyranny of the division of labor, permit the shortening of the working day, and thereby permit the leisure time for the emergence of new "all-round" people who would freely and creatively develop their true human potentialities, one of the defining features of socialism and communism, as traditionally understood. Without that material foundation, whose creation Marx assumed was the historical task of capitalism, a socialist revolution would yield not socialism but only what he termed a "crude social leveling," and that in turn would eventually result in the growth of new social inequalities and the reemergence of what Marx called all "the old muck" of the past. It was thus that Marx insisted that "the successive phases of [a society's] normal development" could not be avoided either by "bold leaps" or by "legal enactment."[7]

There are, of course, significant places in Marx's writings where he was seemingly less rigid on the necessity for all societies to follow "the successive phases of normal development," most notably when he considered the Russian Populist argument that socialism could (and indeed should) be achieved by bypassing the capitalist stage of development. The interest of the late Marx in the peculiarities of Russian economic history, and his other research into a variety of precapitalist socioeconomic formations, are fascinating and controversial areas of inquiry.[8] It is not my purpose here to join the controversy—save to note that in my own reading Marx seriously entertained the Russian Populist view only to the extent that the possibility of Russia's "skipping over" the capitalist stage of development occurred in an international revolutionary context, with the working classes of the advanced capitalist countries taking the revolutionary lead. Marx, after all, always conceived of the socialist revolution as an international revolutionary process, both in content and in spirit, not a national revolutionary event. However that may be, it seems clear that the message of Marx's writings as a whole, and certainly the logic of his theory of history, was that socialism could only be built on the material, social, and cultural foundations laid by capitalism. As he put it in one of his more deterministic pronouncements, in the preface to the first German edition of *Capital*: "The laws of social development are now pushing their way with iron necessity, and the underdeveloped countries have to pass through the same phases of economic development which the developed ones have already completed; the country that is more developed industrially only shows, to the less developed, the image of its own future."[9]

Marx and Engels, of course, were not out to deny the historical possibility of socialism. Indeed, precisely the opposite was their purpose—to proclaim that socialism was historically necessary and (depending on how one understands the word) inevitable—although their warnings about the historically retrogressive dangers of forcing a socialist reorganization of society in situations that were not yet materially and socially ripe for the task have a certain contemporary historical relevance, and especially a contemporary Chinese relevance. But what needs to be noted here is the profound influence of the more deterministic strands in nineteenth-century Marxism on the various versions of modernization theory that have dominated the historical and social sciences in the Western countries since the end of World War II. Modernization theorists have been attracted, directly or indirectly, to the developmental aspects of original Marxism (especially Marx's analysis of the triumphant emergence of capitalism out of feudal society), the universalist and Europocentric features of Marxism, and the implications of these aspects of Marxism for the modernization of economically backward lands.[10] Needless to say, they have not followed Marx beyond the development of capitalism, to the point where Marxism becomes a liberating *telos* prophetically pointing toward the forthcoming world proletarian revolution. What modernization theorists have done is to seize on the more deterministic strands in Marxism, ignoring Marxism's socialist and social content, to perversely arrive at economically deterministic conceptual schemes that treat socialism as both undesirable and impossible—or, at best, as a "dysfunctional" intrusion in "the modernization process." Modernization itself is usually treated in cosmic terms, as an all-pervading, impersonal and universal process. Inexorably propelled by the impersonal historic forces of modern technology and industrialism, virtually all aspects of political, social, and even intellectual and cultural life are molded by those economic forces, "functions" of the "modernization process." The process itself is unusually conceived as leading to a more or less homogeneous global end, with the advanced capitalist states of the West as they exist at present implicitly accepted as the final historical destination at which the rest of the world eventually will arrive. Traditionally, the United States has been the model of models, although it can be anticipated that Japan might soon be offered as a more attractive substitute.[11]

One of the more interesting variants of modernization theory, which typically precludes socialism as a historical possibility, is Adam Ulam's explanation of why Marxism found intellectual and political roots in the economically backward countries of the non-Western world.[12] Ulam attributes the appeals of Marxism, to intellectuals and masses alike in economically underdeveloped lands, to Marxist theory's appropriateness to the social psychology that accompanies the transition form preindustrial to industrial society. Marxism, having originated in similar historical circumstances in early and mid-nineteenth-century Europe, is thus "the natural ideology" for twentieth-century societies striving for industrialization. Such contemporary societies are thus simply repeating the economic transformation that took place in the Western countries more than a century ago, albeit now under Marxist and socialist banners. However, Marxism, according to Ulam, is not really about socialism but rather about industrialism, whatever the conscious intentions of its original authors or contemporary adherents. As Ulam writes: "The birth pains of modern industrial society, which Marx often mistook for the death throes of capitalism, are being enacted before our eyes" (p. 6).

Thus what we are witnessing at present, according to Ulam, is not the building of socialism, or even the economic preconditions for socialism, but essentially a repetition in the non-Western countries of an earlier Western transformation to modern industrial society. In this universal process, albeit one separated by gaps in time and space, Marxism serves not as a socialist theory but as an ideology of modernization. The contemporary regimes engaged in this universal process pose as socialist but are, in essence, capitalist. Ulam therefore counsels that one should not be distracted

> by the revolutionary phraseology of Marxism into believing that from the economic point of view the stage of socialism represents a drastic break with capitalism. Quite the contrary: socialism, once it assumes power, has as its mission the fullest development of the productive resources of society . . . the [socialist] state will in no wise proceed differently from the capitalist: i.e., it will take the worker's surplus labor in the form of surplus value and will sink it in further investment. . . . What, then, is socialism? It is simply capitalism without the capitalists. . . . Except for the abolition of private property in the means of production (its rationalization), socialism continues and intensifies all the main characteristics of capitalism. (p. 45)

For Ulam the course of history is clear, and it will be determined largely by economic forces. The most important "harbinger of the future," he declares, is "the pace of economic development and social adjustment to industrialism" (p. 286). "Social adjustment to industrialism," as Ulam understands it, of course means the demise of socialism and all forms of revolutionary utopianism and the universal emergence of socioeconomic orders that resemble the advanced Western capitalist countries. Socialism itself is characterized by Ulam, as if to fortify his ethnocentric credentials, as but "a kind of rearguard action which withdrawing radicalism conducted against the triumphant march of industrialism and liberalism."[13] And Ulam condemns most of socialist thought in general as "but a critique of the values and traditions of the West."[14] Socialism, an eminently Western doctrine, is here purged from the Western tradition. This is not only ethnocentric but historically nonsensical. However that may be, Ulam's argument is marked by an economic determinism that denies socialism as a real historical possibility and by a Western-based ethnocentrism, both characteristic features of most versions of modernization theory.

Historical Determinism

Socialism, or at least a genuinely socialist society, also has been consigned to the realm of the impossible by a variety of theories that deal with the life-cycles of revolutions and the presumably inevitable phases through which they all must pass. Perhaps the best-known of these schemes is to be found in Crane Brinton's comparative study of revolutions, *The Anatomy of Revolution*, which has been enormously influential in Western thinking about the fate of revolutions since its original publication in the 1930s. Brinton identifies one phase that he calls "the universality of the Thermidorean reaction." The Thermidorean reaction is defined as the point in the revolutionary life-cycle, after the old regime has been overthrown, when there is "a convalescence from the fever of revolution" and a partial return to prerevolutionary "normalcy." That time comes, in the classic case of the French Revolution, with the fall of Robespierre on July 27, 1794 (the 9th of Thermidor of the Year II under the revolutionary French calendar); in 1657 during the English Revolution, when Cromwell became Lord Protector, and more fully three years later with the restoration of the Stuarts; in the case of the American Revolution (perhaps a poor case for comparative historical purposes), in the decade of the 1780s, when there was a general relaxation of war discipline, a renewed scramble for wealth and pleasure, a general moral letdown, and a partial return to prerevolutionary styles of life; and in Soviet Russia with the rise of Stalin, the tyrant who imposed order, dampened revolutionary ideals and hopes in practice if not in rhetoric, and betrayed the original ideals and goals of the revolution.[15]

The "Thermidorean reaction," as Brinton uses the term, is not a counterrevolution or a restoration of the old regime, but rather a conservative reaction against revolutionary radicalism that marks the death of the original revolutionary spirit—and, in the case of a socialist revolution, signals the termination of any real striving for socialist goals. In Brinton's scheme, "Thermidor" is a natural, probably desirable, and certainly historically inevitable phase in the revolutionary life-cycle. "The phenomenon of reaction and restoration seems almost inevitably a part of the process of revolution," he concludes (p. 236).

The notion that revolutions necessarily die as a consequence of their very success has been around for a long time. It has found a more or less theoretical formulation in recent years in Robert Tucker's concept of "deradicalization," a notion similar in many respects to what is conveyed by the term "Thermidor." Tucker, however, is concerned specifically with Marxist movements rather than with revolutions in general, and he also applies the concept of "deradicalization" to Marxist political parties that do not achieve power (but do achieve a measure of political success within existing bourgeois parliamentary systems) as well as to successful Marxist-led revolutions.[16] His analysis seems particularly relevant for understanding some of the changes that have taken place in post-Mao China over the past decade, especially ideological changes and changes in the relationship between theory and practice.

Tucker begins with the assumption that "worldly success fosters deradicalization" (p. 187) and the accompanying assumption that this process is historically inevitable, even if not necessarily desirable. Deradicalization "must be the eventual fate of all radical movements," he declares (p. 180). Tucker's concept of deradicalization does not involve any elaborate theoretical structure. What he means by the term can be simply summed up in the phrase "coming to terms with the existing order" on the part of a once revolutionary movement. "In the stage of deradicalization," he writes, "the movement loses its revolutionary other-worldliness, the alienation from existing conditions arising out of its commitment to a future perfect order, and makes an accommodation to the world as it stands" (p. 186). Among the typical signs and symptoms of deradicalization are a decline of revolutionary utopianism, the fading of the Marxist vision of a future perfect communist order, and the loss of an activist faith in the possibility of attaining that vision. There is, instead, a stress on immediate short-term objectives to be attained through nonradical means; a marked deemphasis on class struggle (or what Tucker calls a preference for "a well-behaved class struggle"); and a growing gap between revolutionary theory and reformist practice. "Not the end of ideology but rather the growth of a stable discrepancy between ideological symbols and political deeds is the true mark of deradicalizing change in once-radical movements," Tucker writes (p. 214). And he prophetically observes, in an essay first published in 1967, that Mao Zedong's "fear of the coming deradicalization of Chinese Communism is well founded" (p. 213).

In rereading and reconsidering these various theories that prophesize the inevitable death of socialism, at least reconsidering them from the perspective of the post-Mao Chinese historical experience, I must confess that I find some measure of truth in most of them—even though I find none wholly convincing or politically congenial. While I am not a partisan of "the iron law of oligarchy," for example, it does seem to have been the case that the organizational means of socialism have proven stronger and more lasting than the socialist ends they were originally intended to serve, a problem exacerbated by the elitist and bureaucratic implications of the Leninist scheme of party organization. The fact that socialist-oriented revolutions have taken place in economically underdeveloped lands lacking the Marxian-defined social and material preconditions for socialism has created enormous problems and dilemmas for victorious socialist revolutionaries. One need not be a proponent of any version of modernization theory to know that the first and foremost task confronting newly born socialist regimes under such circumstances has perforce been modern economic development—and it requires no special powers of historical insight to recognize that the means and ends of socialism have become hopelessly confused in the process of attempting to construct socialist institutions while simultaneously building their necessary economic foundations. One need not take the "Thermidorean reaction" or "deradicalization" (or whatever one wishes to call it) as some inevitable and cosmic law of history to know that this has been a very real and pervasive phenomenon in the history of revolutions, which perhaps might best be understood as a reflection of conservative social interests among those who have (or develop) a stake in the existing order of things. When revolutionaries become rulers, a profound social and ideological as well as political transformation takes place—and one need not reduce history to a cyclical process of the "circulation of elites" to understand this.

Maoism and Deradicalization

All of these (and other) problems, which long have been anticipated in many of the antisocialist theoretical schemes briefly discussed above, have abundantly manifested themselves in the history of postrevolutionary China—and not only in the post-Mao era. Deradicalizing tendencies were quite apparent throughout the history of the Maoist regime. Indeed, it might well be said that the deradicalization of the Chinese Communist revolution began with the very establishment of the Communist state in 1949. All states, beyond being repressive mechanisms and expressions of alienated social power, tend to become conservative forces that function to preserve the social status quo. And this was no less the case with the post-1949 Chinese Communist party-state apparatus than it has been with other states in other historical times and situations. The new Communist state soon came to incorporate a multitude of new bureaucratic and social interests thrown up by the revolution, subordinating all other interests and long-term goals to the preservation of the sociopolitical order that had been fashioned by the mid-1950s—a process politically and ideologically symbolized by the Eighth Party Congress of 1956. The Chinese Communist state presided over familiar processes that transformed one-time revolutionaries into newly privileged rulers, whereby revolutionary organizations became conservative bureaucratic apparatuses, and new socioeconomic inequalities emerged and were institutionalized to replace old ones. The state soon took up its customary conservative role as the political protector and ideological sanctifier of these processes. The concept of a "revolutionary state," at least over an extended period of time, is a contradiction in terms. Indeed, the notion of the state as the agency of the socialist transformation of society is a Leninist and Stalinist invention that is quite incongruous with original Marxist theoretical perspectives.

Mao Zedong came to recognize (in his own fashion and his own terminology) these deradicalizing tendencies that were proceeding under the auspices of the state he led; he expressed his concern about them in increasingly strident terms; and he attempted to combat them by such means as he could devise, albeit means that sometimes assumed archaic forms. As is well known, Mao was increasingly concerned over the years with the decline of revolutionary and ascetic values among his once-revolutionary cadres and their turn to bureaucratic careerism. He was concerned with the social implications of modern industrialism. Although by no means the Luddite the popular press now portrays him to have been, he nonetheless feared the social consequences of the very process of rapid industrialization he so ardently promoted. And he was above all concerned with the postrevolutionary party-state apparatus as the site and source of a new ruling and exploiting elite, which he eventually condemned as a functional bourgeoisie, albeit one whose power and privileges were based on the holding of political power rather than property. It was because of his concerns with these and similar phenomena, and his various (even if failed) attempts to combat them, that Mao came to occupy a unique place in the histories of postrevolutionary societies, even though not much is said about that these days when it is more fashionable to simply dismiss him as China's Stalin.

The Maoist era in the history of the People's Republic did not result in the creation of a socialist society, nor even one that was necessarily moving in a socialist direction. But it was an era notable for its resistance to the processes of deradicalization that would have completely precluded the possibility of a socialist future or even any serious striving for socialism. Maoism did keep socialist goals and values alive as meaningful guides to social and political action, however one may choose to judge the wisdom and results of those actions. Maoism did offer powerful resistance to the bureaucratic institutionalization of the postrevolutionary order. And here Mao himself was in a most ambiguous position, being both the principal creator of the Chinese Communist bureaucracy and its principal critic. He was, as Richard Kraus so aptly characterized the ambiguity, both "the chief cadre and the leading rebel."[17] Nevertheless, despite the ambiguity, or perhaps because of it, Mao did manage to keep the new political structures produced by the revolution from becoming solidified into a permanent and routinized bureaucratic machine. He was not the Stalin of the Chinese revolution. And Maoism was distinguished by its attempt, ultimately unsuccessful, to reconcile the means of modern economic development with the ends of socialism, a historically unique effort to keep the socialist values and institutions of the revolution from being overwhelmed by the imperatives of modern industrialism. In short, Mao kept "the pot boiling," as Benjamin Schwartz once put it.

The Maoist era was a period of both great successes and spectacular failures, and both in abundant measure. How one weighs these successes and failures, and the judgment of the Mao period one eventually arrives at, depends in large measure on what standards of judgment and criteria one chooses to employ. My own assessment of the Mao era has been offered elsewhere,[18] and I won't burden the reader with a repetition of it here—save to note that in my unconventional view, Mao ironically was more successful as a modernizer than as a builder of socialism. However that may be, Maoism was unsuccessful in the end in realizing its own aims. That failure was apparent well before Mao's death in 1976. The abortive Cultural Revolution revealed a regime that had exhausted its once great creative energies, incapable of dealing effectively with China's increasingly grave economic and political problems in the early 1970s. The last years of the Mao period were dreary and demoralizing ones at best. The failures of Maoism at the end opened the way for the forces of deradicalization, hitherto largely held in check, to be given full rein. The post-Mao regime has not only accepted but actively promoted deradicalizing tendencies.

Deradicalization in Post-Mao China

The deradicalization of Chinese communism that has taken place over the past decade is, in its general outlines, well known, and it has been duly celebrated in both Western scholarly and journalist circles, most of whose practitioners regard socialism as undesirable as well as historically impossible. This is not a view shared by the political and ideological leaders of post-Mao China, who insist that the People's Republic remains essentially socialist, albeit at a "primary stage" of socialism, and that the policies being pursued at present are laying the necessary material preconditions for a fully developed socialist society that will flower at some time in the distant future. There is much to be said for the view that it is impossible and foolhardy to attempt to build socialism amidst conditions of extreme material scarcity, and that therefore the development of a high level of productive forces is the first and essential task to be undertaken for the eventual realization of a genuine socialist society. Certainly Marx and Lenin said a good deal to this effect. But even if economic modernization is perforce a long-term process, and even if social change must proceed gradually and slowly in accordance with the development of the productive forces, as the present leaders of the People's Republic emphasize, one nevertheless would expect that their social and economic policies would be broadly consistent with the transition from the "primary stage" of socialism to "developed socialism," however slowly and gradually that process is conceived and proceeds. That, however, clearly has not been the case, at least not up until now. The social tendencies that have resulted from the post-Mao deradicalization of Chinese economic, social, and political life—otherwise known as "reforms"—are simply incongruous with any conception of socialism, much less with a society that is officially described as proceeding from lower to higher stages of socialism, albeit in a gradual evolutionary fashion.

This incongruity is apparent in virtually all aspects of contemporary Chinese life. For example, whereas socialism, by any definition, assumes progressive reductions in socioeconomic inequalities, the policies of the past decade have generated increasing inequality, and at a very rapid rate. These inequalities have naturally and inevitably flowed from an increasing reliance on market forces, from the decollectivization of agriculture and the return to individual family farming, from the encouragement of private entrepreneurship in cities and countryside alike, from wider wage differentials in industrial and other enterprises, and from the partial privatization of even such basic social services as medical care and education. While these inequalities might be seen and justified as temporary phenomena, as the necessary and immediate price of economic progress in a situation where the rapid development of the productive forces is the overriding priority, their future disappearance can by no means be guaranteed, and they certainly do not rest easily with the official argument that social (and socialist) progress follows naturally in the wake of economic development.

That the growth of new socioeconomic inequalities is not likely to be a transient phenomenon—that they are not intended as temporary expedients—is suggested by the strenuous efforts that the regime has expended in ideologically justifying the phenomenon, first, by invoking a flexible interpretation of the socialist principle of "payment according to work," and second, by denouncing (in absolutist terms) the heresy of "egalitarianism," allegedly the pernicious ideological legacy of an old peasant small-producer economy—much in the same fashion Stalin once condemned egalitarianism as something "worthy only of a primitive sect of ascetic monks." In place of egalitarian strivings, traditionally identified with socialist aspirations, the regime presents the entrepreneur who heeded the official injunction to "get rich" as the new hero of a new age. The social values conveyed by the new model are hardly in accord with socialist ideals and are not likely to prove conducive to any future process of socialist transition.

No less antithetical to socialism, either as the practice of the present or as an ideal for the future, is the post-Mao regime's emphasis on the virtues of orderly careerism and professional expertise, and its promotion of an elite of technocrats and intellectuals. Reinforcing the already sharp distinction between mental and manual labor rarely has been seen as a way to construct socialism, or even its preconditions, save of course for the dubious exception of Stalin.[19] In the case of China, the social conservatism reflected in the effort to institutionalize the position and privileges of urban elites is ideologically rationalized by Deng Xiaoping's old formula that intellectuals "are part of the working class."[20] And just as Deng prizes professionalism and specialization in economic life, so he has attempted to bring these alleged virtues to political life through the rationalization and routinization of bureaucratic rule. What is meant by "political reform," it is now clear, is not "socialist democracy," as promised in 1978, but rather the more mundane goal of making the bureaucracy "better educated, professionally more competent, and younger," as Deng put it.[21] Insofar as efforts to professionalize the bureaucracy are successful, they will serve to make bureaucrats a more distinct social group, more fully conscious of their status and interests. Solidifying the already enormous distinction between rulers and ruled in Chinese society may please disciples of Weber, but it hardly augurs well for any future movement in a socialist direction.

Rather than extending this dreary list of post-Mao incongruities with socialist ideals and principles (one can of course easily compose a long Maoist list of incongruities as well), let me turn, in conclusion, to a brief discussion of how the general process of deradicalization has expressed itself in aspects of post-Maoist Chinese Marxist ideology, especially as manifested in the treatment of the socialist goal itself.

The present leaders of the People's Republic still proclaim socialism and communism as ultimate goals, and there is no need to question the sincerity of the proclamations. However, the realization of these goals has been entrusted to the workings of impersonal historical forces which, we are told, are governed by "objective economic laws." Such "objective laws," derived from a deterministic reading of original Marxist texts, leave little place for human will and consciousness in the making of history in general or in the construction of socialism in particular. Rather, the achievement of socialist goals, or of a "developed" socialist society, is conceived as a gradual evolutionary process that proceeds through various "stages" of development, with each stage essentially determined by the level of the developing forces of production. This scheme, according to its authors, does not deny that China is at present a socialist country. Indeed, it is insisted that China is firmly and forever socialist, but still in what is called "the primary stage" of socialism, formerly termed "undeveloped socialism."[22] The "primary stage" of socialism is rather ill-defined, save for the fact that it is characterized by conditions of economic backwardness, thereby permitting the term "primary stage of socialism" to be applied to whatever the existing situation may be and, at the same time, conveniently sanctioning whatever policies the regime wishes to pursue at any given moment.

By making the socialist future the product of the workings of "objective" economic and historical "laws," post-Mao Chinese Marxism postpones the emergence of a "real" or "genuine" socialist society to a very distant and unpredictable time in the future. For objective socioeconomic laws, especially when they are conceived as analogous to the laws of nature, perform their work slowly and yield their results in a gradual and evolutionary fashion. Moreover, such laws can only be obeyed and cannot be altered or hastened along by human intervention, which, as the Mao period presumably demonstrated, can only bring economic failures and political evils. Moreover, since true socialism presupposes very high levels of economic development, and since modernization is perforce a lengthy historical process, the arrival of the good society cannot be anticipated in the foreseeable future.

The difficult and long-term nature of the task is reinforced by the enormous emphasis contemporary Chinese Marxists place on the burdens of the Chinese past. The present is burdened not only by a heritage of economic backwardness but also by China's long history of feudalism. Even if feudal institutions no longer exist, the pernicious influences of the ideology that historically accompanied them persists into the present, making both the tasks of modernization and socialism all the more difficult and lengthy.

That "true" or "genuine" socialism resides far in the future, well beyond the lifetimes of those who might at present be contemplating the prospect, has been repeatedly emphasized. Deng Xiaoping recently remarked that it will not be before at least the middle of the next century that it will be possible to say that "we are really building socialism."[23] Deng is a relative optimist on the matter. Other leaders and theoreticians have suggested several centuries might be required, observing that as capitalism developed over a period of three or four centuries, the development of socialism might span an equally lengthy historical era.

By placing socialism (or, as Deng would have it, even the "building of socialism") at so distant a point in the future, indeed at a future time that is historically and humanly unimaginable, contemporary Chinese Marxist theory serves the function of severing any meaningful relationship between the practice of the present and the socialist goals of the future. This, of course, allows for great flexibility in the social and economic policies pursued in the here and now. As socialism (not to speak of communism) is safely ritualized at so remote a time in an unimaginable future, and since its eventual advent ultimately will result more or less automatically from a lengthy historical process of economic development, all that can be effectively done in the present is to turn all energies to the task of developing China's productive forces—not to the building of socialism but to constructing its rudimentary economic foundations. And as the present is no longer tied to, or governed by, the socialist goals and values of the distant future, the economic tasks of the present can be carried out by whatever means are most convenient or seen as most economically efficacious, not excluding capitalist means and methods (for which there are a variety of additional ideological rationalizations).[24] Indeed, anything (carried out by whatever means) that contributes to economic growth is automatically labeled "socialist" or contributing to that eventual end. Thus, modernization, however performed, is ipso facto "socialist modernization." And private entrepreneurs, especially those who have succeeded in "getting rich," are hailed as "socialist entrepreneurs."

Even socialism itself tends to be defined in strictly economic terms and evaluated according to purely economic criteria. And here means and ends become not only confused but often reversed. The aim of socialism, it has been repeatedly said, is "to liberate the productive forces," which of course is what Marxists traditionally have regarded as one of the functions of capitalism.[25] And Deng Xiaoping once remarked that "the purpose of socialism is to make the country rich and strong,"[26] thus not only reversing the means and ends of socialism but confusing it with nationalism as well. But such is the level of theory attained by China's "paramount leader," whose "thoughts" recently have been praised (in terms once reserved only for Mao Zedong) by his disciple, Zhao Ziyang, as "a great development of Marxism in China."[27]

Many of the features of post-Mao Chinese Communist theory and practice, it must be acknowledged, are anticipated in the deterministic and antisocialist theories discussed earlier, theories which all (in one fashion or another) predict the inevitability of the "deradicalization" of revolutions and revolutionary movements. For example, the economic determinism that pervades post-Mao Chinese Marxist thought (and its conception of socialism) has less in common with Marxism than it does with Western modernization theory, where social change—and all other change—is seen as but a "function" of an all-embracing and impersonal process of economic and technological development. In contemporary Chinese Marxism, the human agent of socialism has been virtually eliminated, and, as in most versions of modernization theory, everything automatically flows from the level of economic development. Marx, by contrast, never assumed that socialism was simply the product of economic and technological progress, or even of changes in social relationships. No less important, and indeed essential, was the socialist transformation of human beings through what Marx termed "revolutionizing practice." "The new society," he wrote, "presupposes the emergence of new men." Such "new men" with socialist values and the conscious determination to build a socialist society (and indeed the whole Marxist notion of praxis) are largely ignored in the current Chinese version of Marxism. And it seems most unlikely that a populace schooled in the "four modernizations," as currently practiced, will yield the human agents necessary for the building of socialism, however ripe the economic situation eventually may become.

An economist doctrine that teaches that the development of the productive forces is the panacea for the solution of all other problems, not excluding the problem of building socialism, and therefore counsels that all human energies be devoted to the single-minded pursuit of economic work, reduces Marxism to little more than an ideology of modernization. And thus the history of the People's Republic in the post-Mao era lends powerful support for Adam Ulam's theory about the essentially nonsocialist nature and function of Marxism in the modern world.

It might be observed, in passing, that the economic determinism that so dominates current official Chinese Marxist theory conveys not an optimistic faith in the inevitability of socialism but rather admonitions about the difficulties involved in attaining it.

If, as Robert Tucker has written, "an accommodation to the world as it stands" is a major symptom of deradicalization, then it must be acknowledged that post-Mao China has proceeded far along the path. The regime of Deng Xiaoping has not only accommodated China to the world capitalist market but accommodated itself to China's existing social structure, even while attempting to rationalize and "modernize" it. Since current Chinese Marxist theory assumes that social development is the reflection and product of economic development—and since China is economically impoverished—it is an ideology that conveys the message that little social change, certainly not in a socialist direction, can be anticipated in the foreseeable future. Deng's conservative social policies (which logically accompany an evolutionary conception of socialism that will span a century or longer) would certainly be applauded by Adam Ulam as a desired "social adjustment to industrialism."

But perhaps the most telling symptom of the deradicalization of Chinese communism in the post-Mao era is the decline of revolutionary utopianism and the ritualization of socialist and communist goals, a striking reflection of the phenomenon described by Tucker as a revolutionary movement's loss of its "alienation from existing conditions arising out of its commitment to a future perfect order." In contemporary Chinese Marxist ideology, that perfect order, and even that not-so-perfect "developed" socialism, has been lodged in a future so distant that it has no meaningful relation to the present, thus severing any links between the ultimate goals that are still ritualistically proclaimed and the social and political practice of the present. Nor are there any interim goals set forth in the ideology, save for the prospect of a gradually improving material standard of life, thus precluding that sense of activism that is so essential to preserving the radical mentality. Few of the many versions of Marxism that have been formulated in this century are so profoundly anti-utopian as the present official version of Chinese Marxist theory—and it serves to dampen all hopes that anything socialist can be achieved, or even be striven for, in the here and now. The question that Arif Dirlik posed some years ago—whether "socialism can survive the extinction of the socialist vision"[28] assumes increasing relevance as the post-Mao years wear on.

Finally, to return to Robert Michels and the transformation of organization from a means to an end, where this essay began, one sees as a further sign of the deradicalization of Chinese communism the triumph of the political means of revolution over the socialist revolutionary ends the former were originally intended to serve. Socialism has not fared well in China in recent years, but what survives (and thrives very well) as the lasting product of the Chinese revolution is the organization conceived as the bearer of Chinese socialism, which now assumes the form of the Leninist party-state, and which is the object of national celebration and patriotic worship. That state, as I have argued elsewhere,[29] paradoxically stands as a barrier to both socialism and capitalism in China.

Notes

This chapter was originally presented as a paper at the Montgomery Symposium of the University of Nebraska, Lincoln, in March 1988. I am deeply grateful to Professor Peter Cheng for having so skillfully organized the symposium and to Arif Dirlik for his always stimulating comments and criticisms.

1. Robert Michels, *Political Parties* (New York: Dover, 1959), p. 391.

2. A distinguishing feature of socialism, properly understood, is not state property but rather what Marx termed the "property of the associated producers." Political power, insofar as it still exists, is exercised as "the self-government of the producers," permitting the immediate producers to control the conditions and products of their labor.

3. Michels, *Political Parties*, pp. 377–92.

4. Ibid., pp. 373–74.

5. For the original Marxist critique of utopian socialism, see part 3 of the *Manifesto*, in *Selected Works*, by Marx and Engels (Moscow, 1950), 1:51–60; and F. Engels, "Socialism: Utopian and Scientific," in ibid., 2:86–142. For a discussion of the Marxian critique, see Maurice Meisner, *Marxism, Maoism and Utopianism* (Madison: University of Wisconsin Press, 1982), pp. 6–13.

6. "Die moralisierende Kritik und die kristisierende Moral," in *Selected Writings in Sociology and Social Philosophy*, by Karl Marx (London: Watts, 1956), p. 240.

7. Karl Marx, Preface to the first German edition of *Capital* (Chicago: Kerr, 1906), p. 14.

8. The most persuasive argument that Marx, in the last decade of his life, significantly changed his views on the revolutionary potential of precapitalist societies is presented by Teodor Shanin, *Late Marx and the Russian Road* (New York: Monthly Review Press, 1983). For a fascinating study of the intellectual interaction between Marx and the Russian Populists, see A. Walicki, *The Controversy Over Capitalism* (Oxford: Clarendon Press, 1969).

9. Marx, Preface to *Capital*. Engels summarized the original Marxist view on the economic preconditions for socialism in 1875 in responding to Russian Populist arguments on the possibility of bypassing capitalism—and in doing so raised (as had Marx) the spectre that attempts to force the pace of history might prove historically regressive: "Only at a certain level of the development of the productive forces of society, an even very high level for our modern conditions, does it become possible to raise production to such an extent that the abolition of class distinctions can be real progress, can be lasting without bringing about stagnation or even decline in the mode of production. But these productive forces have reached this level of development only in the hands of the bourgeoisie. The bourgeoisie, therefore, in this respect is just as necessary a precondition of the socialist revolution as the proletariat itself. Hence a man who will say that this revolution can be more easily carried out in a country that has no proletariat but has no bourgeoisie either only proves that he has still to learn the ABCs of socialism." ("On Social Relations in Russia," in *Selected Works*, Marx and Engels, 2:46–47.) However unorthodox Lenin proved to be in other areas of Marxist theory and practice, he always held to the original Marxist belief that socialism presupposes capitalism. He appeared on the Russian revolutionary scene as an advocate of the progressiveness of capitalism, proclaiming (in his polemics with the Narodniks) that "no historical peculiarities of our country will free it from the action of universal social laws."

10. The influence of Marxism on contemporary Western modernization theory is perceptively discussed in Robert C. Tucker's essay "Marxism and Modernization," in

The Marxian Revolutionary Idea (New York: Norton, 1969), ch. 4.

11. For an incisive critique of the antirevolutionary biases present in most versions of modernization theory, see James Peck, "Revolution versus Modernization and Revisionism," in *China's Uninterrupted Revolution*, ed. Victor Nee and James Peck (New York: Pantheon, 1973), pp. 57–217.

12. Adam B. Ulam, *The Unfinished Revolution: An Essay on the Sources of Influence of Marxism and Communism* (New York: Random House, 1960).

13. Ulam, "Socialism and Utopia," *Daedalus* 94, 2:392.

14. Ibid., p. 399.

15. Crane Brinton, *The Anatomy of Revolution* (New York: Vintage, 1965), esp. pp. 205–36.

16. Robert C. Tucker, "The Deradicalization of Marxist Movements," in *The Marxian Revolutionary Idea*, ch. 6.

17. Richard Curt Kraus, *Class Conflict in Chinese Socialism* (New York: Columbia University Press, 1981), p. 181.

18. In chapter 22 of my *Mao's China and After* (New York: Free Press, 1986).

19. One of the hallmarks of the Stalinist regime in the Soviet Union was of course the creation of a privileged intelligentsia. Thus the journalist Liu Binyan, lionized in the Western press as a great democrat, finds Stalin preferable to Mao because "Stalin, unlike Mao, valued the utility of intellectuals." Liu Binyan, "China's Stake in Glasnost," *New York Times*, June 19, 1988.

20. Deng set forth at the Eighth Congress in 1956 the proposition that "intellectuals are part of the proletariat" and the difference between them and manual laborers is "only a matter of division of labor within the same class." This was established as an orthodoxy in the post-Mao era. See Deng's "Report" in *Eighth National Congress of the Communist Party of China: Documents* (Beijing, 1956), 1:213.

21. Deng Xiaoping, speech to Politburo on August 15, 1980, text in *Issues and Studies* (March 1981).

22. The concept of "undeveloped socialism" was set forth by Su Shaozhi and others in 1979. See Su Shaozhi, "On the Principal Contradiction Facing Our Society Today," *Xueshu yuekan* (June 1979). It was replaced by the term "primary stage of socialism," with essentially the same meaning, apparently to convey more forcefully the view that China is indeed socialist, albeit in an early phase of development.

23. Deng Xiaoping, *Fundamental Issues in Present-Day China* (Beijing, 1987), pp. 176–78.

24. Most notably, the enormous emphasis in post-Mao Chinese Communist ideology, derived from original Marxism (and to a lesser extent from Lenin), on the historically progressive character of capitalism—especially in lands where "feudal remnants" have yet to be fully uprooted by a full-fledged bourgeois-democratic revolution.

25. The pervasiveness of economic criteria for evaluating virtually everything was reiterated recently by Zhao Ziyang: "The extent to which the productive forces are freed should be the major criterion for judging whether something is progressive or retrogressive; practice is thus the sole criterion for testing truth." Speech of May 13, 1987, published in *Renmin ribao*, July 10, 1987, translated in *Beijing Review* 29 (July 20, 1987): 34–35. "Practice," as has been the case since 1978, is economic practice, pure and simple, and has little in common with the Marxist conception of revolu-

tionary practice or praxis.

26. Remarks made to a visiting Rumanian delegation in November 1980, *New York Times*, December 30, 1980, p. 1.

27. Zhao speech of May 13, 1987.

28. Arif Dirlik, "Socialism Without Revolution: The Case of Contemporary China," *Pacific Affairs* 54, 4 (Winter 1981–82): 632.

29. *Mao's China and After*, ch. 23, esp. pp. 482–85.

18

POSTSOCIALISM? REFLECTIONS ON "SOCIALISM WITH CHINESE CHARACTERISTICS"

Arif Dirlik

In the discussion below, I consider the interpretive possibilities of a conceptualization of Chinese socialism that is primarily deconstructive in intention, although it may also provide an occasion for a new reading of its meaning and, by implication, of the meaning of socialism in our day. My immediate goal is to find a way out of the conceptual prison into which Chinese socialism is forced by ideological efforts to constrict it between received notions of capitalism and socialism. Chinese society today is the subject of radical transformation, which is expressed at the level of ideology by an intense struggle between two discourses that seek to appropriate its future for two alternative visions of history. These discourses, I will argue, are both irredeemably ideological (or, viewed from an alternative perspective, utopian). Chinese socialism justifies itself in terms of a historical vision that has no apparent relevance to the present. This renders it vulnerable to negation at the hands of a discourse, embedded in the history of capitalism, that strives to colonize the future for its own historical vision. In the process, both discourses impose upon the insistently ambiguous evidence of contemporary Chinese socialism interpretive readings that may be sustained only by ignoring evidence contrary to their historical presumptions. Stated bluntly, any representation of China's present historical path as capitalist is not just descriptive but also prescriptive; in other words, such representation is intended to shape the reality that it innocently pretends to describe. The counterinsistence that China is a socialist society headed for communism covers up under theoretical conventions a social situation that distorts socialism out of recognizable form. In his illuminating study, *Class Conflict in Chinese Socialism*, Richard Kraus observed that class analysis "is an aspect of the class conflict it is intended to comprehend."[1] Much the same may be said of the question of socialism in China which, in the affirmation or the negation of the relevance to China's future of a socialist vision, is part of an ongoing struggle over the future of socialism in Chinese society—and, by extension, globally—in which the major casualty is the concept of socialism itself. The conceptualization I offer here is necessitated by a recognition that to represent present-day Chinese socialism in terms of one or the other of these categories is inevitably to become party to ideological activity that suppresses the most fundamental problems presented to existing ideas of socialism and capitalism by the momentous changes in Chinese society.

It is the concept of socialism that is of necessity the point of departure for this discussion, since it is from ambiguities in its meaning that these problems arise. In its current usage, the concept bears two primary meanings. First, it is used to depict the present condition of socialist states, what Rudolf Bahro has called "actually existing socialism."[2] Second, it is used also to describe the future state of these societies, what in theory they strive to become in order to achieve the ultimate goal of communism (this distinction corresponds to what Bill Brugger and others have described as "system" and "process").[3] The question of meaning arises out of the gap between these two usages, between system and process, reality and vision. So long as the future appears as an immanent condition for the present, so that a striving to achieve communism guides present policy, the two meanings of socialism are easily collapsed together. It is when the future and the present are separated, when the future, though it is still conceived as an ultimate goal, ceases to play a direct part in the formulation of present policy, that the question of meaning appears in its most undisguised form. Under circumstances where the present has ceased to derive its inspiration from a conviction in the immanent relevance of the socialist vision, but instead resigns itself to the continued hegemony of contemporary circumstances that are at odds with its vision, can socialism remain socialism for long, or must it be recaptured inevitably by the forces emanating from its irreducible global context, which is dominated by capitalism?

This is the point of departure for the discursive struggle over Chinese socialism today, where the affirmation of faithfulness to a future socialist vision on the part of the socialist regime in China seeks to fend off its negation by the claims to the future of a powerful ideology of capitalism that derives its plausibility from overwhelming evidence of historical success that the regime concedes in its deeds, if not always verbally. It is precisely because of the seriousness of this discursive struggle, with all the uncertainty it implies for the future, that we must not hasten to accept the claims of either discourse, to affirm or to negate the claims of Chinese socialism, either to take it at its word or to deny validity to its self-image.

It is this condition of ideological contradiction and uncertainty that I describe here by the term "postsocialism," which allows taking Chinese socialism seriously without sweeping under the rug the problems created by its articulation to capitalism, or forcing an inevitably ideological choice between its own self-image (socialism) or an image of it that denies validity to its self-image (the discourse of capitalism). The term is intentionally residual, since the historical situation that it is intended to capture conceptually is highly ambiguous in its characteristics.

By postsocialism I refer to the condition of socialism in a historical situation where: (a) socialism has lost its coherence as a metatheory of politics because of the attenuation of the socialist vision in its historical unfolding; partly because of a perceived need on the part of socialist states to articulate "actually existing socialism" to the demands of a capitalist world order, but also because of the vernacularization of socialism in its absorption into different national contexts; (b) the articulation of socialism to capitalism is conditioned by the structure of "actually existing socialism" in any particular context which is the historical premise of all such articulation; and (c) this premise stands guard over the process of articulation to ensure that it does not result in the restoration of capitalism. Postsocialism is of necessity also postcapitalist, not in the classical Marxist sense of socialism as a phase in historical development that is anterior to capitalism, but in the sense of a socialism that represents a response to the experience of capitalism and an attempt to overcome the deficiencies of capitalist development. Its own deficiencies and efforts to correct them by resorting to capitalist methods of development are conditioned by this awareness of the deficiencies of capitalism in history. Hence postsocialism seeks to avoid a return to capitalism, no matter how much it may draw upon the latter to improve the performance of "actually existing socialism." For this reason, and also to legitimize the structure of "actually existing socialism," it strives to keep alive a vague vision of future socialism as the common goal of humankind while denying to it any immanent role in the determination of present social policy.

I would like to illustrate this thesis below through a brief examination of the contradictions in contemporary Chinese socialism, and the ideological interpretations to which they have been subjected. At the heart of official socialism in contemporary China lies a contradiction that gives it its ideological shape and animates its motions. Official description of what Chinese socialism is, or should be, is encompassed within the phrase "socialism with Chinese characteristics" (*you Zhongguo tesidi shehui zhuyi*), which has assumed the status of orthodoxy since it was presented to the Twelfth Congress of the Communist Party of China in 1982 by Deng Xiaoping, the unofficial guiding light of Chinese socialism.[4] The urgent declaration of a Chinese claim to a Chinese socialism that is implicit in the phrase, however, has been accompanied since then by an equally powerful urge to represent this Chinese socialism as a phase in a universal metahistorical vision of which the end is communism. At the Thirteenth Party Congress held in October 1987, Party Secretary Zhao Ziyang described the current stage of Chinese socialism as "the initial stage of socialism" (*shehui zhuyi chuji jieduan*), in the transitional stage of socialism that in this metahistorical vision lies between capitalism and the final, communist, stage of history.[5]

The Marxist view of history that informs this conception of history presupposes that societies in their progress in history follow paths that are conditioned by the inner logic of their historical constitution. There is no account in this representation of how a "socialism with Chinese characteristics" will link up with the historical progress of other societies with their individual characteristics to end up with a conclusion to history that is universal in its characteristics (unless the process is intermediated, as I suggest below, by a "universal" capitalism that may transform the globe in its own self-image, which was the original Marxist idea). The representation satisfies a double need for legitimacy in Chinese socialism: socialism must have a Chinese coloring and meet the needs of Chinese society if it is to be legitimate within a Chinese context, but this socialism, if it is to remain socialism, must reserve a place for itself in a history that is not just Chinese. The resolution thus achieved of these conflicting demands for legitimacy at the level of representation requires suppression of a fundamental contradiction between Chinese socialism and its global capitalist context, between particularity and universality in socialism, and, ultimately, between Chinese socialism as a historical project and its metahistorical presuppositions.

The contradiction, if recognized, suggests that the socialism of "socialism with Chinese characteristics" may be so much ideological whitewash to cover up a national appropriation of socialism to which socialist commitment may be a theoretically necessary (for legitimation purposes) but practically marginal consideration. Indeed, Chinese socialism, always strongly nationalistic in its orientation, appears more transparently than ever today as a disposable instrument in "the search for wealth and power." On occasion, it is even possible to encounter representations of the goal of socialism in terms of the traditionalistic phrase in which an incipient reformist nationalism in the nineteenth century cloaked its goals: "a wealthy nation and a strong military."[6] To make matters worse, if "socialism with Chinese characteristics" has a substantial content—in other words, a social and political agenda—that content has appeared so far as a broadly conceived program to articulate socialism to the demands of a capitalist world order so as to achieve rapid economic development. As the phraseology of the goals of

Chinese socialism recalls nineteenth-century reformism, so do some of the policies that have been proposed to achieve those goals; a case in point is the recent proposal by Zhao Ziyang to make all of coastal China into a special foreign trade zone—an eventuality the fear of which was one of the basic motivating forces underlying the socialist revolution in China.[7]

A revolutionary socialism, long conceived by China's socialists as a prerequisite to the achievement of national autonomy and development, appears today as an obstacle to that goal; and the regime has devoted considerable effort over the last decade to dismantling the social relationships and the political organization of socialism which go back in their origins not just to the Cultural Revolution, as is commonly portrayed, but to the early period of the People's Republic in the 1950s, and even earlier to the period of the revolution before 1949 when Chinese socialism acquired an identity of its own. Around the turn of the century, the Chinese who first began to advocate a socialist resolution of China's problems did so with the conviction that socialism offered the best means to China's survival in a world where the days of capitalism seemed to be numbered.[8] The attitude toward socialism that prevails today is the opposite: that China will be doomed to backwardness and decrepitude unless socialism is amended by the proven methods of capitalist development. National concerns, which during a century of revolution found their expression in a socialist vision of the world, seem today to be possible of fulfillment only in the extensive incorporation of China into a world order of which capitalism is the organizing principle. When Chinese in our day speak in defense of this shift in attitude that Chinese socialism is different from socialism elsewhere, they seem to overlook conveniently that China does not exist in a political or economic vacuum, that this difference does not imply that Chinese (or anyone else for that matter) are free to define socialism or to choose the future as they please, but that every choice implies a corresponding relationship to a global capitalism. It is impossible to establish a Chinese socialism, in other words, without at the same time opting for a certain relationship to capitalism. What is at issue here is not a Chinese prerogative to define a Chinese socialism, which I for one am not prepared to challenge, but the implications of any such definition for the metahistorical vision of socialism that Chinese socialism continues to profess as its ideological premise, and which serves as the legitimation for this socialism in the first place. The contradiction, at the very least, creates a "legitimation crisis" for socialism—in China and elsewhere.

It is this crisis that fuels the discursive conflict over Chinese socialism. The question is: does the compromise with capitalism, justified by recourse to a nationalized socialism, leave socialism untouched as a long-term goal, or does it imply an inevitable restoration of capitalism, with socialism consigned to historical memory? The question of the future of Chinese society is not to be resolved at the level of ideology. The capitalist world order into which China seeks admission to realize its national goals demands as the price of admission the reshaping of Chinese society in its own image. China, on the other hand, seeks to admit capitalism into its socialism only on condition that capitalism serve, rather than subvert, national autonomy and a national self-image grounded in the history of the socialist revolution. The outcome in actuality will depend on the form taken by the interaction between the two social and economic systems. But ideology does play a key role in the conceptualization of the relationship, if only by defining its limits; it is important, therefore, to understand the implications of the relationship for the ideology itself.

Chinese defenders of the new policies have claimed that "Westerners . . . mistake socialism with Chinese characteristics for capitalism and unbridled free enterprise."[9] "Mistake" is a misnomer here, I would like to suggest, because what is at issue is a discursive appropriation of "socialism with Chinese characteristics" for a vision of history grounded in the history of capitalism. The tendency to read into the attenuation of Chinese socialism the inevitability of a capitalist restoration is based on a non sequitur: that any compromise of a strict socialism must point to a necessary assimilation of Chinese socialism to capitalism. Such an assumption may be justified only by an ideology of capitalism which, in its projection of its own hypostatized self-image indefinitely upon a history that is yet to be lived out (and is, therefore, unknowable), forecloses the possibility of any significant alternatives to its vision of the future.

Let me illustrate this with an anecdote. In 1980, the *Charlotte Observer* published a series of articles on China on the theme of "China: The Challenge of the Eighties," sponsored jointly by the North Carolina branch of the National China Council and the North Carolina Humanities Committee. I was asked to contribute a piece to the series discussing the implications for Marxism of changes in post-Mao China. It was the shortest piece that I have ever written, but the writing took the longest of anything I have written. Part of the reason was the adjustment it took on my part to write in a style appropriate to a newspaper. But much of the time was taken by a running dispute with the editor of the editorial page, who clearly did not like what I had to say about Marxism and showed great creativity in inventing a seemingly endless series of excuses (including the ignorance of the readership of the paper of such words as revolution, colonialism, and imperialism) to deflect the basic thrust of the article, which was favorable to Marxism and argued that, given the historical experience of the Chinese revolution, the abandonment of Marxism might have debilitating consequences for Chinese society by compromising China's economic and, therefore, political autonomy. When we were at last able to agree on a final version, I submitted the article under the rather neutral descriptive title of "Marxism and the Chinese Revolution." When the article appeared in the paper, it was under a heading that was quite contrary to both my intention and its content: "Will Progress Doom Marxism?" He had had the last word, I suppose, by telling the readers through the title how to read and interpret the article. But the vengeance did not stop there. When the series was completed, the articles were compiled in a little booklet for distribution to high schools in North Carolina. Possibly because the editors assumed that North Carolina students would not be familiar with the verb "doom," but more likely, as I prefer to view it, because they were desirous of "dooming" Marxism, the title of the piece indicated an escalation in the level of violence; it was now changed to read: "Will Progress Kill Marxism?"[10]

The episode is revealing, I think, not as an exhibit of ideological hostility, about which there is little that is novel or interesting, but for the agenda embedded in the simple title, "Will Progress Doom Marxism?" or "Will Progress Kill Marxism?" Noteworthy is the opposition that the title sets up between progress and Marxism, and its suppression of the ideological content of the word "progress." By establishing rhetorically that Marxism may be inconsistent with progress, the question suggests that Marxism has so far owed its staying power in Chinese society to backwardness. Moreover, the reader knows as well as the editor that "progress" here refers to a specific kind of progress: that associated with capitalism. Rather than state this explicitly, the phraseology represents "progress" as an abstract universal. In an explicit phrasing, the question should read: "Will Capitalism Doom Marxism?" in which case the opposition should appear as a conflict or competition between Marxist and capitalist ideas of progress. The tacit location of capitalism within an abstract idea of progress universalizes the claims of capitalist ideas of progress while underlining further the parochialism of Marxism and its alleged status as a feature of backwardness. One must also suppose that this abstraction somehow softens the murderous intent implicit in the verb "kill"; "progress" might get away with killing Marxism—for capitalism to "kill" Marxism, on the other hand, might have proven too shocking even for an eighth grader!

Not everyone may share in the bluntly expressed desire of the *Charlotte Observer* to do away with Marxism; but the ideological negation of Chinese Marxism (embedded in a tacit and sometimes explicit affirmation of the appropriateness to China of capitalism) has been commonplace over the last few years in the nation's leading public media, as well as in academic evaluations of Chinese socialism. It shows through rewards bestowed upon Chinese leaders who advocate compromise with capitalism and, therefore (the conclusion follows automatically), promise the imminent demise of Marxism: Deng Xiaoping has been named man-of-the-year more than once in leading periodicals for his supposed contributions to this end.[11] It shows in academic conferences in attitudes that range from the denial of historical legitimacy to socialism (of which a striking illustration is a recent tendency to view the Chinese socialist revolution as a "historical aberration" which has not only been responsible for perpetuating China's backwardness but also for the moral subversion of the Chinese people) to the denial of functionality to socialism in a world of "progress" (that socialism is a passing phase of human history since it seems to impede the kind of progress that is necessary to national survival and the improvement of life). It shows in the reduction of socialism into a proxy for some deeper urge in Chinese history, more often than not rooted in a cultural legacy that is held to be contrary to everything that socialism stands for. Socialism appears in this perspective as an intruder upon a vast historical landscape, at best an expression in disguise for some longing, more often than not for national wealth and power, that haunts that landscape. In a new preface to a recent reprinting of his *Chinese Communism and the Rise of Mao* (first published in 1951), the first scholarly study to argue cogently that Chinese communism was communism of a new kind, motivated by particularly Chinese concerns, Benjamin Schwartz observes that the book has been criticized for stating the obvious, namely, that Chinese communism was but an expression of Chinese nationalism. He defends the book on the grounds that when it was first published (in the days of McCarthyite anxieties about global communist conspiracies), this was not a generally accepted view.[12] In our day, this view is indeed the generally accepted one: that Chinese socialism has been but a disguise for, or instrument of, the national quest for wealth and power to which socialism as an ideology in its own right has been largely irrelevant; which denies to socialism even a limited impact on the definition of national goals. Where such impact is recognized, it is portrayed in negative terms: that taking socialism too seriously has undermined China's national goals. These goals, it seems, may be fulfilled only if China rejoins the capitalist stream of history from which it has been held apart by a century of socialist revolution that now appears as a historical aberration, or at best as an account of national self-delusion.[13] Any signs of the persistence of socialist qualms about joining this stream of history is readily attributed not to general Chinese qualms about capitalism—which are, after all, as old as the history of the Chinese revolution and one of its basic motive forces—but to the continuing hold on power of aging revolutionaries (now dubbed "conservatives") who cannot seem to part with their illusions about socialism.

While the ideological premises of this discourse may be readily evident, it does not follow that we may ignore the questions it raises, as is suggested by Chinese defenders of official socialism. Such premises are no longer restricted to "Western" critics of Chinese socialism or apologists for capitalism, but are very much an integral part of Chinese speculation over the future of Chinese socialism. Indeed, it is quite "un-Marxist," I would suggest, to claim that socialist consciousness is immune to significant changes in socialist existence, that the changing relationship between socialism and capitalism may have no significant implication for either socialist consciousness or the Chinese conception of socialism.

The socialist regime in China today insists that the compromise with capitalism represents nothing but an innovation within socialism, at most a temporary detour that is intended to consolidate socialism and carry it to a higher plane of achievement. It has good theoretical justification for its policies. Socialism appears in the Marxist conception as a postcapitalist transitional phase on the historical path to communism, and presupposes an advanced economic (and cultural) basis established during the capitalist stage of development. China, for historical reasons, never fulfilled this premise of socialism, but instead bypassed capitalism to establish socialism upon a backward economic foundation. The discrepancy ("contradiction") between advanced social forms and a backward economic basis is responsible from this perspective for the deep problems that Chinese socialism has encountered, which are also likely to obstruct permanently the transition to communism if they are not resolved. Chinese society must backtrack, as it were, to fulfill the necessary economic preconditions for socialism so as to be able to move forward once again toward communism. Historically, Chinese society at present is placed in the initial phase of socialism—the so-called undeveloped socialism. Under the circumstances, the compromise with capitalism represents not a departure from socialism but a necessary step to put China back on a historical path that will lead, through advanced socialism, to the ultimate goal of communism.[14]

There is no more reason not to take seriously the ideological intention underlying this theoretical defense of current policies of the socialist regime than there is to deny the ideological seriousness of the views I have just discussed. While the fact that this is a defense of an official socialism may cast some doubt upon it (which may be confirmed by the willingness of the leaders of Chinese socialism on occasion to go beyond the requisites of "undeveloped socialism" in their flirtation with capitalism), as a theoretical formulation it reflects the views of China's most distinguished Marxist theoreticians such as Su Shaozhi.[15] And although it is clearly a formulation that provides theoretical legitimation for compromises with capitalism, for reasons that should be apparent from the above discussion, there is no reason to read it as a disguise to cover up an insidious intention to restore capitalism in China.

The question is: is this formulation of the state of contemporary Chinese socialism any less ideological (or utopian) than the capitalist vision to which it is opposed? I think not, because the explanation of this retreat from socialist relations that had advanced beyond the means of the forces of production to sustain them, however sound theoretically, offers no account of how a socialism, having moved backward, will move forward again; how the socialist system as it exists will return to the process of socialist development, having consolidated itself further with the aid of capitalism; or the ways in which "actually existing socialism" contains within it the promise of the Communist society that it aspires to create. Indeed, the formulation utilizes theory to suppress these fundamental questions, which suggests that faith in an eventual return to socialist development toward communism can be sustained only by a hopelessly utopian vision of the future. This is a problem for all socialist societies of the present; in the case of China the problem may be even more severe because of the negative image impressed upon all suggestion of utopianism by the experience of the Cultural Revolution, which represented a historically unique attempt to bridge the gap between the present and the future of socialism. Theory may suggest that with the development of the forces of production the gap will close of itself. Historical experience provides little reason to justify privileging theory over practice, which would suggest that such advance, especially with the aid of capitalist methods of development, is more likely to create social relations and a structure of power with a corresponding ideology that is likely to render the vision more remote than ever.[16]

Chinese society today provides ample evidence of the likelihood of this latter possibility, and so does this very formulation itself, which radically limits the status of socialism as a motive force of historical development. I can think of no better way of arguing this point than by "reading" the justification for "socialism with Chinese characteristics" (the Chinese version of "undeveloped socialism") in the theoretical formulation above within the context of a specifically Chinese adaptation of a Marxist metahistorical design in the course of the socialist revolution in China. The contemporary formulation of the problems of socialism invokes in the listener a strong sense of déjà vu. Viewed from the perspective of a specifically Chinese discourse on socialism, this formulation represents the most recent articulation of a nonrevolutionary socialist alternative that is as old as the history of socialism in China.

I noted above that in its understanding of the social relations appropriate to the present stage of China's economic development, "socialism with Chinese characteristics" has moved past the Cultural Revolution and the collectivization of the 1950s to the earliest days of the People's Republic of China. We need to recall that the victory of the Communist Party in 1949 was viewed by the party not as the victory of communism, or even of socialism, but as a victory of "New Democracy" or the "Democratic Dictatorship of the People." The idea of New Democracy was first enunciated by Mao Zedong in early 1940 as a specifically Chinese route to socialism (and generally as an idea that might be applicable to societies placed similarly to China within the capitalist world system).[16] The considerations that it drew upon were as old as the history of socialism in China. Its primary concern was to integrate national considerations into a Marxist "scheme" of historical development. According to the idea of New Democracy, countries such as China which were placed in a semicolonial status in the world system of necessity followed different paths to socialism than either advanced capitalist societies or societies, such as the Soviet Union, that did not experience colonial oppression and exploitation. Before moving on to socialism, such societies had to go through a phase of development that was neither capitalist (because it was under the direction of the Communist Party) nor socialist (because it represented an alliance of all the progressive classes, including the bourgeoisie, in a struggle for national economic, political, and cultural development). Both in economic organization and in politics, the New Democratic phase of development would be a mixture of socialism and capitalist forms, with its development toward socialism rather than toward capitalism guaranteed by the guardianship of the Communist Party. With the incorporation of this idea, the familiar Marxist "scheme" of historical development represented in the consecutive stages of feudal–capitalist–socialist–communist societies was rephrased into the stages of feudal–semicolonial semicapitalist (or semifeudal)–New Democratic–socialist–communist social formations.

The idea of New Democracy represented an ingenious effort to find an equivalent to capitalist development that would not only answer the demands of socialism, but respond to national needs for autonomous development as well. What is of interest here is its conception of socialism. While the idea of New Democracy reaffirmed socialism as the goal of historical development, it rendered socialism for the time being into a guardian over a process of development that drew its economic dynamism from capitalism, which would be allowed to exist until China had fulfilled the economic conditions for socialism. This policing role assigned to socialism becomes even more evident if we remember that the idea of New Democracy drew directly on the social and political vision of Sun Yat-sen who, as the first political leader in China to introduce a socialist agenda into a national political program in 1905, deserves to be remembered not only as the father of Chinese nationalism, but as the father of Chinese socialism as well. Sun had very early on rejected capitalism as a viable development option for China and proposed socialism as the preferable path of development. Sun's idea of socialism, which I think has been a persistent one in the history of socialist thought in China, was a limited one: he was a confirmed believer in the value of competition as a motive force of development, but since he observed from the European experience that unbridled competition created class division and conflict, he believed that socialism was necessary to keep in check the undesirable consequences of capitalism. His conception of socialism, in other words, did not require the repudiation of capitalism, only its control. He meant by socialism state policies that would be designed to guarantee such control.[17]

Although Mao's idea of socialism in his conception of New Democracy was not restricted to Sun's conception of socialism, the latter was very much part of the New Democratic phase of the revolution as he conceived it. Indeed, it is possible to suggest that New Democracy contained two contradictory ideas of socialism: as a future vision and as a guard against capitalism in a national situation that necessitated capitalist methods for national development (as well as a prerequisite to an imagined socialist future).

In the conception of Chinese Marxists today, "socialism with Chinese characteristics" represents a return to a developmental phase that is directly adjacent to New Democracy. "Socialism with Chinese characteristics" differs from New Democracy because it follows upon the abolition of private property and the socialization of the means of production which was completed by 1956 (although the tendencies toward reprivatization in the economy obviously make for serious strains in the boundary between New Democracy and the transition to socialism). But as an "initial phase" of socialism, it is also endowed in Chinese socialist thinking with many of the characteristics of New Democracy, for example, in the need to combine a market economy with a socialist economy, the stress on the need for economic development before further moves are made toward socialism, and most importantly in its class policies which recall the united front premises of New Democracy. These economic and social realities are expressed at the level of ideology in the new status assigned to socialism in historical development. The perspective provided by New Democracy confirms that "socialism with Chinese characteristics" does not envisage a return to or a restoration of capitalism; since it is New Democracy, and not capitalism, that sets the boundary to its retreat from socialism. On the other hand, the very move back in history pushes farther into the future the lofty goal of socialism, which may persist as an ideal but becomes ever more blurred in its features. The contradiction within the idea of New Democracy was from the beginning a contradiction between future vision and present reality ("utopia" and "actual conditions," as Mao put it in his essay). The difference between the early 1950s and the present with regard to policy is a difference in the interpretation and resolution of this contradiction. Mao (and the rest of the party in the 1950s), when forced to confront the contradictions presented by

New Democratic policy, erred on the side of "utopia" against the dangers of the dissolution of the vision into "actual conditions," and pushed on to socialism. The resolution at present is in the opposite direction. The role socialism occupies in "socialism with Chinese characteristics" is not that of immanent vision, pushing society further along the road to socialism, but of ideological guardian, to check the possibility of a slide into capitalism. The prominent illustration of this role is the insistence since 1982 on the infusion in Chinese consciousness of the values of a "socialist spiritual civilization" which, contrary to official claims for it as a key to realizing socialism, is most striking as a means to controlling through the medium of ideology the disruptive tendencies that have been created by the introduction of capitalist practices and values into the existing socialist structure.[18] This policing role assigned to socialism may be subversive of its status as an ideal and even as a system—since it appears in this role as a regressive element in a process that derives its dynamism from other sources, mainly capitalism. But it is nevertheless a role that needs to be taken very seriously not only because it is essential to the preservation of the socialist system, but also because the system in the eyes of many Chinese is essential to guarding national autonomy against the possibility of national dissolution into the capitalist world system.

By way of conclusion, I will explain briefly why I think "postsocialism" is more appropriate as a concept for describing the characteristics of this historical situation than other alternatives that are currently available. My use of "postsocialism" is inspired by an analogous term that has acquired currency in recent years in cultural studies: postmodernism. J. F. Lyotard has described as the prominent feature of postmodernism an "incredulity toward metanarratives."[19] I would suggest by analogy that the characteristic of socialism at present is a loss of faith in it as a social and political metatheory with a coherent present and a certain future.

It may seem odd that I should describe as postsocialist a society that even in the eyes of Chinese socialists does not yet qualify for socialism. This is not the issue, however. The "socialism" in my use of postsocialism here does not refer to the social situation of the future envisioned in the classical texts of socialism—Marxist, anarchist, or otherwise; while this vision as political myth has served as a significant inspiration for revolutionary social change, it has also come to serve as an ideological disguise to suppress fundamental problems that have become apparent in the historical unfolding of socialism: to legitimize societies that may justifiably claim inspiration in the socialist vision but whose very structures in some ways represent betrayals of that vision and obstacles to its realization. The term socialism refers here to socialism as a historical phenomenon; the emergence of a socialist movement that offered an alternative to capitalist development and the state structures that have issued from this movement where it succeeded. It corresponds to recent descriptions of such societies by others as "noncapitalist development" (Rudolf Bahro) or "postrevolutionary society" (Paul Sweezy).[20] Why I prefer the term "postsocialist" over these alternatives should become clear from the multifaceted suggestiveness of the term, including the challenge implicit in it to the sufficiency of "socialism" as a social vision.

Postsocialism refers, in the first place, to a historical situation where socialism, having emerged as a political idea and class-based political movement inspired by the idea, offered an alternative to capitalism; a choice, in other words, between capitalist and socialist methods of development. The Chinese who discovered socialism around the turn of the century were attracted to it because they felt that if offered an alternative to the capitalist development that had ravaged European society. While they felt that "pure socialism" (communism or the socialist vision) had already been proven to be impossible, and some compromise was necessary with capitalism, socialism provided the most desirable path for China's development.[21] In a sense, one could suggest that Chinese socialism was "postsocialist" from its origins.

With the establishment of socialist states, this alternative was delineated more sharply, and so was the problematic of the gap between socialist vision and socialist reality; since once socialism was established in power, immediate tasks imposed by social "reality" took priority over the pursuit of the vision that inspired socialist revolutionary movements. While socialists have been able to postpone recognition of this problem by shifting hopes from one socialist experiment to another, it has become apparent over the years that the socialist vision in reality has given rise to structures of power that are not only inconsistent with idealistic anticipations, but have utilized the promise of ultimate socialism to legitimize political systems that themselves would have to undergo revolutionary transformation in order to move once again toward the socialist promise. While it is necessary to recognize that these systems are not socialist in terms of an ideal conceptualization of socialism (which makes possible a *socialist* critique of "actually existing socialism"), it is also necessary to go beyond formalistic evaluations to recognize that these systems are historical products of the pursuit of socialism and that they point to fundamental problems within the concept of socialism as a political concept; it is possible, in other words, that however noble the socialist vision of society, in practice—given the actual conditions of the world—it may issue only in the structures of power represented by "actually existing socialism" in its various manifestations, which share fundamental structural characteristics. I do not wish here to participate in an antisocialist criticism of these systems, which overlooks not only much that they have accomplished for their constituencies but also that the capitalist alternative itself suffers from deep problems; I wish merely to point out that they have fallen short of their ideological claims, and that this may not be accidental but a very product of the conceptualization of socialism historically: it may be that there is a fundamental contradiction between the economic presuppositions of socialism (a planned economy, abolition of markets, emphasis on use value over exchange value) and its social and political aspirations (equality, democracy, community). Some of the essays in this volume have shown how the Cultural Revolution in China, for all its claims to communist commitment, ended up with consequences contradictory to its intentions for structural reasons. On the other hand, contemporary Chinese socialism, following a long tradition in Chinese socialism, pursues a way out of these problems by articulating socialism to the capitalist world order. To attribute these problems to the peculiarities of China or of Chinese socialism would be to overlook that "actually existing socialisms" in our day all have run into similar difficulties, although the severity of the problem may differ from case to case.

This historical tendency, that socialist states must look outside socialism in order to salvage or to sustain it, is the second characteristic of what I describe as postsocialism. I suggest that Mao Zedong, in repudiating the Soviet experience and in his uncompromising insistence on the nationalization of socialism, was every bit as "postsocialist" as Deng Xiaoping is for looking to capitalism for remedies to the problems of socialism. Both Mao and Deng, it is worth remembering, insisted on nationalizing socialism ("Chinese style socialism" for Mao), and legitimized this by arguing that Marxism needs to be adjusted to changing conditions.[22]

Third, it is the very absorption of socialism into societies such as the Chinese that from a broader historical perspective is the condition for postsocialism. The localization of socialism in its adaptation to different national contexts—what I referred to above as its vernacularization—has undermined its claims as a unitary discourse that derives its plausibility from its promise of a universal end to human history. The latter may still retain its force as a principle of legitimation, and even as a vague goal, but it is the specific historical context that in actuality gives socialism its historical shape.

The attenuation of faith in a single inexorable vision of the future is not necessarily detrimental to socialism; indeed, it creates the conditions for a more democratic conception of socialism, since it enables the imagination of the future in terms of pluralistic possibilities (this, I think, is the significance of the "Chinese" in "socialism with Chinese characteristics"). It also creates a predicament for socialism, however. The price to be paid for these possibilities may be the price that the postmodern era exacts from us all: a resignation, in the midst of apparent freedom, to the hegemony of present conditions of inequality and oppression; and the uncertainties of a history that offers no clear direction into the future. Chinese socialism, which only two decades ago boasted command of such a direction with unparalleled confidence, today finds itself in the uncharted waters of a postsocialist condition of which it is a prime example, as well as an occasion.

The contradictions within "socialism with Chinese characteristics" are products of theoretical efforts by Chinese socialists to encompass within socialism the structural ambiguities of a social situation that places an enormous, perhaps intolerable, strain on socialist ideology. The effort to articulate socialism to capitalism at the social and economic level is expressed at the level of ideology in the limitation of the ideological horizon of socialism by its very efforts to accommodate capitalism within socialism. I have argued above that the representation of this situation in terms of the conventional categories of socialism and capitalism may be sustained only by ignoring the fundamental contradiction that animates Chinese socialism today; either by dismissing the socialism of Chinese socialists, or by ignoring the implications for socialism as a metahistorical project of its assimilation to the demands of a capitalist world system. The idea of postsocialism brings this contradiction to the center of our understanding of "socialism with Chinese characteristics" as its defining feature. It allows us to recognize the seriousness of Chinese socialism without falling into the teleological utopianism that is implicit in the word "socialism," which by itself refers not only to a present state of affairs but also to a future yet to come. It is the attenuation of this future, which does not necessarily imply a return to capitalism or the abandonment of "actually existing socialism," that justifies the description of this state of affairs as postsocialist, for without an immanent vision of the future, socialist societies may make claims upon the present but not upon the future. In my use of postsocialism to describe this state of affairs I disagree implicitly with theorists such as Sweezy and Bahro, and their preference for descriptions such as "postrevolutionary society" or "noncapitalist development." The latter may salvage socialism as a political ideal by denying the socialism of "actually existing socialisms"; but in doing so, they refuse to come to terms with the historical fate of that ideal. Terms such as "market socialism," on the other hand, are purely descriptive and contain no hint as to where such a socialism may be located historically. "Postsocialism" allows including "market socialism" or "a planned commodity economy" (both Chinese usages) in the present of socialism, but also unambiguously repudiates a future teleology while underlining the significance of the past—of the socialist context.[23] Chinese society today is postsocialist because its claims to a socialist future no longer derive their force from socialism as an immanent idea. On the other hand, it is also postsocialist because socialism, as its structural context, remains as a possible option to which it can return if circumstances so demand (this is what distinguishes it from a capitalist or even a postcapitalist society where such options as collectivization, socially, and a socialist culture, ideologically, are foreclosed). Even today, the socialist regime would seem to be prepared to return to economic and social practices that it has repudiated verbally (such as collectivization) if it seems necessary to do so—which is obviously a source of constant frustration to those who wish socialism in China to disappear forever and, because of their wishful thinking, have no way of explaining why the Chinese refuse to foreclose socialist options for the future.[24] Such options retain considerable power because, at least for the older generation of Chinese, socialism is an integral component of a national self-image.

The alternative that comes closest to postsocialism is Gordon White's recent suggestion that China may be evolving toward a new mode of production, which he describes as "social capitalism."[25] White recognizes that the term may not be felicitous (although it does parallel the "social imperialism" that Chinese coined to distinguish Soviet from capitalist imperialism), but the concept is suggestive. In recognizing this "socialism" as a mode of production, it avoids the ideological notion of socialism as a transition and, therefore, a temporary compromise with reality. It recognizes the system as a serious modification of capitalism; a new mode of production does represent a break with the mode out of, or in response to, which it has evolved. And, finally, it suggests the ideological and structural limitation of this system by the capitalist world order, within which socialism as we have known it has taken shape, and which may well serve to establish the boundaries to its further development Socialism has now been incorporated into a division of labor within this world order; and it is unlikely that it may evolve further toward a socialist vision of society without changes in the world order itself.

My insistence on postsocialism, nevertheless, is motivated not by a desire to proliferate a new socialist jargon, but by an evaluation of socialism as an ideology, which calls forth considerations beyond the systemic analysis that guides White's conceptualization of the problem. Ultimately, postsocialism as a concept presupposes the perception of China (and of other socialist societies) in their relationship to the capitalist world context which has been the irreducible condition of socialism historically. Socialism has spread around the globe in the wake of capitalist transformation of the world; and the particular direction it has taken in different national contexts has been conditioned not only by specific national historical legacies but also by the history of the specific relationships to a capitalist world system in formation. Socialism in China was a response not to an internal capitalism, but to a capitalism that was introduced from the outside and appeared from the beginning as an alien force (but also, therefore, as a set of economic practices that China was free to choose from, or even reject, in accordance with national needs).[26] Hence the national element in Chinese socialism has always been prominent; it may even be suggested that there has been no autonomous socialist discourse in China, apart from or opposed to, a nationalist discourse on politics. Nationalism has enhanced the staying power of socialism, since socialism has offered the most plausible way to fend off the possibility of national dissolution into the capitalist world system. This appropriation of socialism into a national project, however, has also implied subversion of the claims of socialism as a metahistorical project. Chinese socialism, as a national liberation socialism, has played an important part in the disintegration of socialism as a unitary discourse, although it obviously may not be held responsible for a tendency of which it was as much a product as an occasion. Once Marxists had to give up hope in the possibility of a global socialist revolution (and it was nearly impossible, in historical hindsight, to entertain such a hope at the latest by the time of Lenin and the October Revolution), it was apparent that socialism could succeed only on a nation-by-nation basis within the context of a capitalist world system. This has obviously created a deep predicament for socialist societies, vulnerable by their very economic nature to recapture by capitalism; since in an authentically socialist society, the transformation of social relations must take priority over considerations of economic efficiency. China during the Cultural Revolution was to make an effort to shut off world capitalism in order to establish a firm foundation for uninterrupted progress to socialism. The disastrous failure of that attempt has made it more evident than ever that socialist societies must make an effort to incorporate themselves into the capitalist world system without abandoning a basic structure of socialism.[27] This condition, in the period of what has been described by Marxist theoreticians as "late capitalism," is the ultimate justification for the use of "postsocialism" to describe it, because the need to find some accommodation with the capitalist world order without abandoning its basic institutional structure seems to be a permanent condition of actually existing socialism unless some drastic change occurs within the world system. To call this condition "capitalism" would be fatuous because it remains to be seen what the incorporation of socialist systems into the capitalist world order will imply for capitalism itself. For socialist societies such as China, the opening to capitalism has created new possibilities; among these may be included greater openness to economic alternatives (which may be greater even than that of capitalism, which, for all its flexibility, forecloses one important option—socialism), greater possibilities for democracy than before because of the relinquishing of faith in the immediate possibility of a coercive utopianism, and richer cultural possibilities that have arisen with the recognition of global cultural diversity, which was not possible so long as progress was conceived as a unilinear movement to a uniform human destiny. On the other hand, it is also clear that within the context of a capitalist world system, the overall motions of which are shaped by a capitalism that socialism has ceased to challenge but rather seeks to accommodate, socialism can no longer claim to possess a coherent alternative to capitalism, but only a residual political identity that seeks to realize developmental goals imposed by the capitalist world system through "noncapitalist development." Postsocialism allows this situation to be described without reading into it either a capitalist or a socialist future, which, I suggested above, has less to do with the future than with a discursive struggle between present-day capitalism and "actually existing socialism" to appropriate the future.

I observed in the introduction to this discussion that the only casualty of the ideological activity to accommodate these changes may be the concept of socialism itself. It should be clear by now that the socialism to which I referred is socialism as a vision of the future, which continues to receive the homage of socialists without the power to guide the direction of socialism. This may justify predictions of the imminent demise of socialism, as some would wish, and it justifies my use of "postsocialism" to describe the present condition of socialism in China and globally. I would suggest, however, that postsocialism, rather than signaling the end of socialism, offers the possibility in the midst of a crisis in socialism of rethinking socialism in new, more creative ways. I think it is no longer possible to think of socialism as the inevitable destiny of humankind to follow upon capitalism. There may be little cause for regret in the passing of this ideological version of socialism that may serve (as it continues to do so in Chinese socialism) to counteract present uncertainty by the vision of a certain future; but there is something pernicious, as Paul Feyerabend has observed, in the notion of historical inevitability that imposes upon the present and the past the despotism of the future (much the same may be said of a vision of a future informed by the history of capitalism, which is often overlooked).[28] It is also possible to suggest that since the very origins of socialism, this ideological conception of socialism has conceived of the future not as an authentic alternative to capitalism, but primarily in terms of completing the tasks initiated by capitalism—it has, in other words, been bound by a vision of the future that is ultimately embedded in a notion of progress that was historically a product of capitalism. Freed of the commitment to such an inexorable future, socialism may be conceived in a new way: as a source for imagining future possibilities that derive their inspiration not from a congealed utopia, which postpones to the future problems that await resolution today, but from the impulses to liberation that represent present responses to problems of oppression and inequality. My use of postsocialism here is not descriptive but is intended to suggest that a radical vision of the future must move beyond what has been understood over the last century by the concept of socialism. Social and intellectual developments, partly under the impetus of socialist ideology, have revealed ever more sharply that the concept of socialism, essentially grounded in consciousness of class as the central datum of social oppression, is no longer sufficient to contain the question of social and political oppression the multidimensionality of which has impinged upon our consciousness with compelling power. To name just a few of current concern, oppression among nations, races, and genders, not to speak of state oppression of society, are not reducible to class oppression. Nor is it possible to account for such basic problems as ecological destruction, worldwide militarism, alienation rooted in a "culture of consumption," or even inequality created by a technical division of labor in terms merely of the class structure of capitalist society. Socialism as we have known it has not been able to address these questions any more effectively than capitalism; on the contrary, as the case of Chinese socialism today would indicate, the fetishism of development is so powerful that socialism has come to be judged by socialists themselves by criteria derived from capitalist development. It is an urgent task at present to reconsider the whole question of development, which requires a reconceptualization of society in terms other than prevailing ones. The question of class retains its significance, though not with the force of an earlier day, but any radical vision of the future must account for these other forms of oppression, and the social problems that are not merely products of class interests but have other sources and a life of their own.

So must we move beyond conventional ideas of socialism, without abandoning the perspective they afford, which still offers crucial critical insights into contemporary society, capitalist or otherwise. This is the ultimate purpose of my use of postsocialism to depict this state of affairs: in its open-endedness, the term may help release us from the hold of a narrowly conceived social vision and allow us to rethink socialism, in the eloquent words of Ernesto Laclau and Chantal Mouffe, in terms of the "infinite inter-textuality of emancipatory discourses in which the plurality of the social takes shape."[29] The Chinese socialist experience, in the very questions it raises about socialism, provides us with an occasion to do so.

Notes

An earlier version of this chapter was presented at the Montgomery Symposium of the University of Nebraska, Lincoln, March 3, 1988. I would like to thank the organizers, in particular Prof. Peter Cheng, for the opportunity publicly to think out the problems discussed below. I also thank Bruce Cumings, Ted Fowler, Harry Harootunian, Maurice Meisner, Masao Miyoshi, Roxann Prazniak, and Mark Selden for perceptive and constructively critical comments that helped clarify the argument. The responsibility for the argument, for better or worse, is mine alone.

1. Richard Kraus, *Class Conflict in Chinese Socialism* (New York: Columbia University Press, 1981), p. ix.

2. Rudolf Bahro, *The Alternative in Eastern Europe* (London: New Left Books, Verso edition, 1981). This corresponds to the commonplace but not exhaustive reading of socialism as a state-managed economy, in contrast to the privately managed economy of capitalism. I will not make an effort to define these terms any more precisely, since this whole essay represents a reconsideration of the ways in which we think of these terms. Since I do not agree with the restriction of socialism to state socialism, I do not consider socialist any of the socialisms to which I refer, Maoist or Dengist. But I will suggest that Maoism was revolutionary in its pursuit of a "socialist" vision, whereas Dengism represents a deradicalization of Chinese socialism that seeks above all accommodations of capitalism. My emphasis here is on relationships, not on abstractly defined concepts. A word is necessary here also on the concept of "deradicalization," which Maurice Meisner has used in describing current policies in China (see the essay above). This concept derives from the earlier Soviet experience (see Robert Tucker, *The Marxian Revolutionary Idea* [New York: Norton Library, 1969]). While I agree with the idea, my argument here is that we must understand it in the Chinese context within a Chinese discourse, which contained a deradicalized notion of socialism from its origins; so that the current deradicalization also represents a return to the past. It is the meaning of this return that I investigate, which has something to tell us, I believe, about the seemingly inevitable deradicalization of all socialist revolutions, even though the specific form the deradicalization takes depends on the particular discourse in each case. It is also clear not just from the Chinese case but from the cases of other socialist societies that the challenge to socialism has moved far past deradicalization to questions concerning its viability. That capitalism may face an equally radical challenge does not obviate the urgency of the question.

3. Bill Brugger, ed., *Chinese Marxism in Flux* (Armonk, N.Y.: M. E. Sharpe, 1987).

4. Deng Xiaoping, "Opening Speech at the Twelfth National Congress of the CPC," in *Selected Works of Deng Xiaoping* (Beijing: Foreign Languages Press, 1984), pp. 394–97.

5. Zhao Ziyang, "Yanzhe you Zhongguo tesidi shehui zhuyi daolu qianjin," (Advance along the road of socialism with Chinese characteristics), *Renmin ribao*, overseas edition, November 4, 1987.

6. Hong Xuezhi, "Fuguo qiangbing zhi dao" (The path to "wealthy nation and strong military"), in *Renzhen xuexi 'Deng Xiaoping wenxuan'* (Seriously study the *Selected Works of Deng Xiaoping*) (Hangzhou: Zhejiang renmin chubanshe, 1983), pp. 204–10.

7. See Zhao's remarks in "China Plans Export-Led Economy," *Washington Post*, January 24, 1988.

8. Arif Dirlik, "Socialism and Capitalism in Chinese Thinking: The Origins," *Studies in Comparative Communism* 21, 2 (Summer 1988): 131–52.

9. Tong Gang, "Chinese Style Socialism Misjudged," in *Policy Conflicts in Post-Mao China*, ed. John P. Burns and Stanley Rosen (Armonk: M. E. Sharpe, 1986), p. 37.

10. *Charlotte Observer* (Monday, March 24, 1980). Also see the booklet that issued from the series published by the *Observer*: *China: The Challenge of the Eighties*. It is hard to tell who was responsible for the changes described here, because the booklet names a "Charlotte author Joan Dim" as "project editor."

11. By *Time* magazine in 1984 and 1985, and *National Review* in 1985.

12. Benjamin Schwartz, *Chinese Communism and the Rise of Mao* (Cambridge: Harvard University Press, 1979), preface.

13. For an example written by a China specialist, see Anne F. Thurston, *Enemies of the People* (New York: Knopf, 1987).

14. See Zhao, "Yanzhe you Zhongguo tesidi" for this theme, which is common in much of Chinese theoretical writing. The contradiction referred to here was first formulated at the party's Eighth Congress in 1956.

15. Gordon Chang, "Interview with Su Shaozhi," *Bulletin of Concerned Asian Scholars* 20, 1 (January–March 1988): 11–35. An earlier version was published in *Monthly Review* (September 1986).

16. It makes more sense at this point to view "actually existing socialism," rather than as a transition, as a mode of production in its own right. For a discussion of this, see Paul Sweezy and Charles Bettelheim, *On the Transition to Socialism* (New York: Monthly Review Press, 1971), esp. pp. 123–35.

17. See Dirlik, "Socialism and Capitalism."

18. Arif Dirlik, "Spiritual Solutions to Material Problems: The 'Socialist Ethics and Courtesy Month' in China," *South Atlantic Quarterly*, 81, 4 (Autumn 1982): 359–75.

19. Jean-Francois Lyotard, *The Post-Modern Condition: A Report on Knowledge* (Minneapolis: University of Minnesota Press, 1985), p. xxiv.

20. Bahro, *The Alternative in Eastern Europe*. For Sweezy, see his response to Su Shaozhi, *Monthly Review* (September 1986).

21. Dirlik, "Socialism and Capitalism."

22. Mao described this as *Zhonguohua*, literally "making Chinese." The term commonly used is "sinification." I think this term is best avoided because of certain traditional associations that may distort Mao's usage. It was used traditionally in a culturalist sense, to denote *tonghua*, literally "assimilation." Mao's usage is premised upon a different conception of China than the traditional, China as a nation. Hence Marxism may be "nationalized" into different national contexts. The usage is primarily social and political, not just cultural, and it does not presuppose a Chinese civilization as the premise of "assimilation."

23. Su Shaozhi, "Interview," for one instance. "Commodity economy within a socialist context" is a variant.

24. Thus, in the face of difficulties created by privatization in agriculture, Chinese leaders have been willing to return readily to the glorification of the collective economy, as they did in the last party congress in praising the achievements of Doudian, which had refused to privatize and had been criticized earlier for its leftist conservatism. See "Bitter Harvest: Despite Recent Gains, China Is Again Facing Shortage of Grain," *Wall Street Journal*, January 19, 1988.

25. Gordon White, "The Impact of Economic Reforms on the Chinese Countryside: Towards the Politics of Social Capitalism?" *Modern China* 13, 14 (October 1987): esp. 456.

26. Dirlik, "Socialism and Capitalism."

27. The idea that China could achieve national liberation only through autonomy from the capitalist system was a basic argument for the Communist revolution. See Dirlik, "National Development and Social Revolution in Early Chinese Marxist Thought," *China Quarterly* 58 (April–June 1974): 286–309. The Chinese experience played an important part in the reconsideration of socialism from a world system perspective: that a socialist economy could not be genuinely socialist so long as it participated in the capitalist world economy. See, for example, Immanuel Wallerstein, *The Capitalist World Economy* (New York: Cambridge University Press, 1979). The argument here is similar to Wallerstein's though it does not go so far as to assert that a "socialist" economy is in essence capitalist if it participates in the world economy (pp. 68–69). Nevertheless, there is a dilemma here, currently suppressed, that returns us to the original (pre-Stalinist) Marxist idea that a socialist revolution to be socialist, must be global in scope. The obvious impossibility of this idea under present circumstances is part of the reasoning underlying the concept of postsocialism.

28. Paul Feyerabend, *Against Method* (London: New Left Books, Verso edition, 1986), Introduction.

29. Ernesto Laclau and Chantal Mouffe, *Hegemony and Socialist Strategy: Towards a Radical Democratic Politics* (London: Verso Books, 1985), p. 5.